Hindemith-Jahrbuch
Annales Hindemith
1999/XXVIII

Hindemith-Jahrbuch
Annales Hindemith
1999/XXVIII

Herausgeber
Paul-Hindemith-Institut, Frankfurt/Main

SCHOTT
Mainz · London · Madrid · New York · Paris · Tokyo · Toronto

BN 139

Einband und Typographie: Günter Stiller, Taunusstein/Ts.
Gesamtherstellung: HartDruck GmbH, 97332 Volkach
Printed in Germany
ISBN 3-7957-0139-2
ISSN 0172-956X

Inhalt

Vorwort

»Hindemith und seine Dichter« lautet das übergeordnete Thema des vorliegenden Bandes. Drei Aufsätze beleuchten – mit jeweils unterschiedlicher Schwerpunktsetzung – die Zusammenarbeit Hindemiths mit Gottfried Benn, aus der das Oratorium *Das Unaufhörliche* (1931) erwuchs. Alexander J. Fisher stellt Gemeinsamkeiten und Unterschiede der ästhetischen Positionen Benns und Hindemiths dar, Andres Briner konzentriert sich auf Aspekte der Nietsche-Rezeption der beiden Künstler. Wolfgang Rathert betrachtet *Das Unaufhörliche* vor dem Hintergrund der »konservativen Wende« in Hindemiths Kompositionsstil. Die von Gunther Nickel und Susanne Schaal edierte und kommentierte Dokumentation der Zusammenarbeit von Hindemith und Ernst Penzoldt ermöglicht es erstmals, Einblick in die Arbeit an dem gescheiterten Opernprojekt *Etienne und Luise* zu gewinnen. Unter musiksemiotischen Gesichtspunkten nähert sich Gerald Kilian der *Symphonie »Mathis der Maler«*. Zum Abschluß des Bandes spürt Gerd Sannemüller Hindemiths Verbindungen und Beziehungen zur Hansestadt Lübeck nach.

Der amerikanische Musikwissenschaftler Kim Kowalke ist für seinen Aufsatz *For those we love. Hindemith, Whitman, and an »American Requiem«*, der 1997 in *The Journal of the American Musicological Society* erschienen ist und auch im Hindemith-Jahrbuch 1998/XXVII veröffentlicht wurde, mit zwei hohen Auszeichnungen geehrt worden. Die American Society of Composers verlieh ihm 1998 den »ASCAP-Deems Taylor Award« für ausgezeichnete Berichterstattung über Musik. Die Sonneck Society for American Music ehrte ihn im März 1999 mit dem »Irving Lowens Award«, der für den besten Aufsatz zur amerikanischen Musik vergeben wird.

Susanne Schaal

Andres Briner

Marius Décombaz

Avec le décès de Marius Décombaz, la Fondation Hindemith a perdu tout à la fois son fondateur, son guide, son meilleur et plus ancien soutien.

A la disparition de Gertrude Hindemith, il a réuni tous les amis désignés dans les dispositions testamentaires de la défunte épouse du Maître. Fruit de leurs efforts, la Fondation, qu'il avait lui-même appelée de ses voeux, pouvait être inscrite officiellement, le 8 juillet 1968, au Registre du Commerce. C'est encore lui qui en a rédigé les statuts, leurs traductions en plusieurs langues et leur règlement. Chaque année, il a également été l'auteur du Rapport annuel, adressé au Département fédéral de l'Intérieur à Berne, l'autorité de surveillance des fondations.

Marius Décombaz était l'exécuteur testamentaire de Gertrude et, implicitement par conséquent, celui de Paul Hindemith. Jusqu'à ses derniers jours, il a imprimé son sens de la mesure à toutes les décisions du Conseil de Fondation. Après 1968, il obtenait en contrepartie d'un don à la Commune de Blonay quelle renonce au droit, accordé par Gertrude Hindemith dans son testament, de recevoir une part du résultat de la vente de la Villa La Chance au cas où la Fondation déciderait de s'en séparer.

Très tôt, il s'est occupé de la conservation de l'héritage artistique et scientifique de Paul Hindemith soit avant même que la succession ait été officiellement liquidée en 1973. Ce faisant, il a posé les bases juridiques de la conservation des biens et archives du Maître.

Dès sa constitution, Marius Décombaz s'attacha à donner une assise financière solide à la Fondation. Ses avis sur l'évolution de son état de fortune revêtaient la plus grande importance et il s'y est toujours montré particulièrement fidèle. Comme exécuteur testamentaire, il se sentait tenu de mettre en équilibre les idées et desseins de Paul et Gertrude Hindemith avec la situation réelle et les possibilités de la Fondation. C'est ainsi qu'en 1970 il supervisa le contrat passé avec la ville de Francfort aux termes duquel cette ville s'engageait à héberger l'Institut Paul-Hindemith. De même, il milita en faveur de l'édition des Annales dont le premier volume voyait le jour en 1971. Ce volume contenait d'ailleurs en premières pages un exposé traitant de la constitution de la Fondation Hindemith qui s'inspirait d'un rapport de Marius Décombaz. Depuis, les Annales Hindemith, tout comme l'Edition Générale, pourvoient à la conservation et à la diffusion de l'héritage du Maître. Elles sont également l'organe de communication de la Fondation.

Marius Décombaz assuma également des tâches pratiques incombant à la Fondation. C'est ainsi que, dès 1971, il soutenait moralement et financièrement «L'école Hindemith», des cours d'été organisés et dirigés par Howard et Helen Boatwright. Les concerts de clôture de ces cours comprenaient quelques oeuvres de Paul Hindemith interpretées la plupart du temps de manière inoubliable par des étudiants américains; ces concerts étaient les lointains précurseurs des activités futures du Centre musical de Lacroix.

Ce Centre musical est l'enfant spirituel de Marius Décombaz. Dans les années septante, il a soulevé la question de savoir pourquoi la Fondation préférait accorder des subventions à diverses écoles de musique sans rapport avec elle plutôt que de créer un centre d'études musicales qui lui soit propre. Poursuivant son idée, il proposait, en 1972, d'acheter la propriété de la famille Rist; dans les années suivantes et jusqu'en 1976, le grand chalet fut acquis par étapes. Des travaux d'entretien furent ensuite estimés, projetés et conduits à la perfection sous l'autorité de Marius Décombaz. C'est encore lui qui fut à l'origine de la nouvelle construction nommé Pavillon offrant des possibilités d'hébergement et de travail supplémentaires. Après une période de transition, la résidente idéale fut trouvée en la personne de Anne-Charlotte Van Cleef. Les idées fondatrices nées dans l'esprit de Marius Décombaz pour le Centre

musical de Lacroix sont encore aujourd'hui incarnées jour après jour à Blonay.
Pendant plusieurs années, les Journées Hindemith ont été des événements de première importance dans la vie culturelle de la région. En été 1974, Marius Décombaz a d'ailleurs ordonné lui-même les manifestations organisées en souvenir du compositeur à l'occasion du dixième anniversaire de sa mort. Il manifestait un grand intérêt pour les événement que représentaient ces concerts auxquels ne manquait pas d'assister avec son épouse et ses enfants.
1974 fut également l'année de l'inauguration de l'Institut à Francfort. En septembre, tous les membres du Conseil de Fondation participaient à l'événement. Marius Décombaz donnait toute son énergie à ce nouveau développement. A l'occasion d'une réunion en 1997 à Francfort, il acceptait encore les inconvénients d'un long voyage en train.
Lorsque l'accueil d'artistes l'exigeait, il n'hésitait pas à passer la nuit avec son épouse, Irène, à La Chance. Concernant cette dernière résidence de Paul et Gertrude Hindemith à Blonay, il n'hésitait pas d'évoquer, toujours franchement et respectueusement, devant ses collègues du Conseil de Fondation, la haute idée qu'il se faisait de la destination de cette maison.
Dès aujourd'hui, quelques mois seulement après son décès, la Fondation Hindemith souffre déjà de l'absence du conseil, de l'esprit et de l'intelligence de coeur, bref, de l'absence de la personnalité de Marius Décombaz. Il lui manquera encore bien d'avantage à l'avenir, lors des délibération de son Conseil. La Fondation honorera toujours la mémoire de son créateur spriritual et meilleur ami.

Traduction : François Margot

Alexander J. Fisher

Paul Hindemith, Gottfried Benn, and the Defense of the Autonomy of Art in the Late Weimar Republic[1]

For Paul Hindemith the years between 1929 and 1933 mark an important transitional period in the composer's career, a time which, on the one hand, saw a lessened emphasis on styles influenced by Expressionism and the »Neue Sachlichkeit«, and on the other hand saw an intensifying interest in the relationship of artistic production to societal concerns. Despite the well-known circumstance of Hindemith's interest in public participation in musical life – with which the admittedly simplistic term »Gebrauchsmusik« has been associated, much against the inclinations of the composer – it has been difficult to discern the nature of his relationship to the larger social and political forces which characterize the declining years of the Weimar Republic. This picture is complicated by Hindemith's association first with Bertolt Brecht in 1929 and then with the poet Gottfried Benn in the following year, two artists who by the early 1930s found themselves on opposite sides of the ideological struggle which plagued the final years of the Republic. Furthermore, to the extent that musical style can provide evidence – however elusive – of cultural and political convictions, Hindemith's juxtaposition or mixture of styles in roughly contemporaneous works, styles derived on the one hand from the »Neue Sachlichkeit« and on the other from a more lyrical approach (*Neues vom Tage* of 1928–29 and

[1] An earlier version of this article was read before the New England Chapter of the American Musicological Society in April 1996. For their comments and suggestions I am indebted to Jane Fulcher, David Neumeyer, Reinhold Brinkmann, Christoph Wolff, and Giselher Schubert.

the *Konzertmusik* works of 1930 immediately come to mind), makes generalizations about unequivocal relationships between Hindemith's politics and Hindemith's music problematic. Indeed, in a time which was characterized by artists' political polarization and an increasing brutality of public discourse, it is curious that Hindemith's political as well as aesthetic stance remains so obscure.

A closer examination of Hindemith's collaboration with Gottfried Benn in the early 1930s provides some insight into the philosophical inclinations of the composer in this atmosphere of growing incivility and intolerance[2]. Benn's embracing of the National Socialists upon their accession to power early in 1933 has, perhaps, made it more difficult to examine his significance for Hindemith's artistic development, and has resulted in a tendency to minimize his impact[3]. Nevertheless, while at first remaining unaware of Benn's proclivity for the irrational and nihilistic (a tendency far more evident in his poetry than in his prose), Hindemith saw in the Gottfried Benn of 1930 an artist unwilling to sacrifice artistic goals to the narrowly partisan political battles taking shape around him. The parallels between some aspects of the artistic philosophies of Hindemith and Benn during this time suggest that Hindemith's theatrical and quasi-theatrical works in the 1930s contain an impulse toward the recovery of artistic autonomy from the realm of cultural politics.

---

[2] Ann Clark Fehn has investigated in depth the main fruit of their association, the oratorio *Das Unaufhörliche*, in her book *Change and Permanence: Gottfried Benn's Text for Paul Hindemith's Oratorio Das Unaufhörliche*, Bern: Peter Lang, 1977, and in *Das Unaufhörliche: Gottfried Benns Text in der Vertonung von Paul Hindemith*, Hindemith-Jahrbuch 1976/V, p. 43–101. My intention in this study is not to duplicate her extensive research on the oratorio's text and its setting, but rather to explore the collaboration in a broader political context.

[3] Noted by Ian Kemp, *Hindemith*, London: Oxford University Press, 1970, p. 26–27. Kemp is correct, however, in emphasizing the consistency of Hindemith's style during this period and his willingness to reuse material from the Brecht collaboration in *Das Unaufhörliche*.

Hindemith and politics in the late 1920s

It seems unlikely, as some writers have suggested, that Hindemith was unaware of or disinterested in the political polarization and economic difficulties which plagued the declining years of the Weimar Republic[4]. The crash of the New York Stock Exchange in October 1929 only added to the difficulties engendered by Germany's faltering industrial base, the concomitant decreases in tax revenues, and the slowing of foreign investment[5]. The implications of this worsening economic situation for cultural life were significant: operatic and concert organizations were in many cases forced to shorten their seasons and hesitated to present challenging or modernistic programs (the Staatsoper am Platz der Republik in Berlin, otherwise known as the Kroll Oper, under Otto Klemperer, failed to adapt itself to changing political conditions and was forced to close in 1932[6]), government subventions for music festivals were scaled back or discontinued, publishing houses hesitated to publish larger works, and composers associated with educational institutions faced the possibility of reduced salaries or dismissal[7].

---

4 See particularly Jürgen Mainka, *Hindemith und die Weimarer Republik*, Hindemith-Jahrbuch 1988/XVII, p. 176: *Ein Verlust an Realitätsbewußtsein ist zum Ende der 20er Jahre hin bei Hindemith zweifellos feststellbar.* It is useful to remember, however, that a political victory by the National Socialists was still not inevitable in 1930, and even after they assumed power in 1933 many observers, including Hindemith, felt the regime to have few prospects of remaining in power.

5 See John Willett, *Art and Politics in the Weimar Period: The New Sobriety, 1917–1933*, New York: Pantheon Books, 1978, p. 178.

6 The Kroll Oper had, in fact, been under attack from the right at least since July 1929, when the Prussian Oberrechnungskammer had recommended its closure along with the Schiller Theater. See ibid., p. 185.

7 This picture, of course, is complicated by the declining vitality of the traditional German concert scene in the face of such challenges as film, phonographic recording, and radio, not to mention the rise of a new middle class less interested in established institutions and more inclined toward Unterhaltungsmusik and popular music imported from overseas. See Klaus-Dieter Krabiel, *Das Lehrstück von Brecht und Hindemith: Von der Geburt eines Genres aus dem Geist der »Gebrauchsmusik«*, Hindemith-Jahrbuch 1995/XXIV, p. 147–149. An example of the impact of cultural

The overt politicization of culture by 1930 was symbolized by the establishment of Alfred Rosenberg's »Kampfbund für deutsche Kultur«, an organ of the National Socialists, early in 1929, as well as by the increasing tendency in left-wing artistic circles to press art into the service of a socialist or Communist project. The Nazi-organized riots which broke out at performances of Kurt Weill's opera *Aufstieg und Fall der Stadt Mahagonny* in 1930 in Leipzig and Frankfurt were emblematic of these trends; these disturbances would be repeated upon the Nazis' rise to power three years later[8]. The increasing stridency of the Nazis also touched Hindemith personally, as his brother-in-law Hans Flesch, the director of the Berliner Rundfunk, was forced from his post and jailed over false accusations from the Nazis in 1932[9]. Artists closer to the center of the political spectrum found themselves in an increasingly tenuous position. Thomas Mann, perhaps the most prominent German literary figure of his day, lent to the Republic what seemed, superficially, to be little more than lukewarm support. In reality his writings from the late 1920s and early 1930s were a principled attempt to navigate between political extremes, remaining committed on the one hand to a rationalistic »Humanität« while not abandoning the more metaphysical aspects of Germany's artistic heritage[10]. For others the

---

politics upon musical life by the end of the decade is provided by the victory of Wilhelm Frick's National Socialists in the Thuringian legislative elections in January 1930, an event which resulted in cultural policies foreshadowing those of the later Nazi national government. Although the Nazis were only able to retain control of the state government for about a year, their tenure resulted in such measures as the »Ordinance against Negro Culture«, the dissolution of the Bauhaus, the banning of jazz in public, and the removal of Stravinsky and Hindemith from state-subsidized concert programs. See Erik Levi, *Music in the Third Reich*, New York: St. Martin's Press, 1994, p. 10–11.

[8] Ibid., p. 11.

[9] Hindemith performed at the prison at which Flesch was interned on Christmas Day, 1933. Giselher Schubert, letter to author, 12 June 1998.

[10] *The urgency with which he marshals cultural arguments in defence of Weimar has precisely to do with his concern to commend it to the deepest needs and dictates of the German cultural psyche. Mann tried to defend both reason and rationality against the*

increasing violence of the public discourse surrounding questions of cultural politics led in part to a feeling of »Weltuntergang«, or, in the case of Gottfried Benn, »Untergang des Westens«, a sentiment that colored the poet's philosophy particularly strongly in the 1930s[11]. On Hindemith's part, it is debatable that the composer shared Mann's commitment to social activism, however moderate, and it is certain that he did not partake of the sense of nihilism which Benn developed in such essays as *Können Dichter die Welt ändern?* (1930; see below); it is, however, equally misleading to suppose that Hindemith was entirely insulated from the cultural disturbances in Berlin in the late 1920s and early 1930s. For example, in 1934, during Hindemith's tenure at the Berlin Musikhochschule, a student of his reported that he had criticized the Nazis and insisted that strength of character was vital for the artist in those troubled times[12]. When considering operatic projects in the previous year, Hindemith decided to abandon the idea for an opera entitled »Etienne und Luise« (libretto by Ernst Penzoldt) in light of the changed political situation. On 10 March of that year he wrote to Ludwig and Willy Strecker:

---

swelling chorus of vitalist voices: but he also tried to give the Republic that sorely-needed cultural, spiritual, in a word, geistig validation that alone could give it the cachet of respectability. Martin Swales, *In Defence of Weimar: Thomas Mann and the Politics of Republicanism*, in *Weimar Germany: Writers and Politics*, ed. Alan Bance, Edinburgh: Scottish Academic Press, 1982, p. 9.

11 Apart from the undeniable notoriety of Nietzsche, a work achieving particularly wide resonance in the post-World War I period was Oswald Spengler's *Untergang des Abendlandes* (1918–1922), which compares the troubles plaguing modern German society with those of ancient Rome. Benn's endorsement of Spengler's work is well documented: see Alter, *Gottfried Benn: The Artist and Politics (1910–1934)*, p. 39–40; Dieter Wellershof, *Fieberkurve des deutschen Geistes. Über Gottfried Benns Verhältnis zur Zeitgeschichte*, in *Gottfried Benn*, ed. Bruno Hillebrand, Darmstadt: Wissenschaftliche Buchgesellschaft, 1979, p. 139–140; Peter Reichel, *Artistenevangelium. Zu den theoretischen Grundlagen von Werk und Wirken des späten Gottfried Benn*, in ibid., p. 325; and especially Hans Egon Holthusen, *Gottfried Benn. Leben – Werk – Widerspruch. 1886–1922*, Stuttgart: Klett-Cotta, 1986.

12 See Claudia Maurer Zenck, *Zwischen Boykott und Anpassung an den Charakter der Zeit. Über die Schwierigkeiten eines deutschen Komponisten mit dem Dritten Reich*, Hindemith-Jahrbuch 1980/IX, p. 67.

Regarding the opera, I send you herewith a letter from Penzoldt. The prospects for the next few weeks are of course bad, and I also have no idea to what extent it might be possible to bring out new operas in the autumn. To judge by what I now see happening in musical and theatrical affairs, I believe all the key jobs will shortly be occupied by rigidly national types. Next spring, by which time the first difficulties should have been got over, the prospects for an opera by Penzoldt and myself should be very good. Maybe not this particular text, though one cannot really know. Anyway, caution is called for, and I am in favour of shelving this particular subject for a while and seeking another. I have been looking around and have come on something that is innocuous and interesting and will this year and next be particularly topical. It deals with the building of the first railways.[13]

The fact that the »first difficulties« mentioned by Hindemith continued well past that spring of 1933 perhaps led him to take more seriously the idea for an opera expressive of the artist's position within the maelstrom of politics. This attitude seems to be behind an interesting passage in a letter from Willy to Ludwig Strecker dating from August 1933, by which time Hindemith had taken up the subject of *Mathis der Maler*:

He [Hindemith] *is so taken with the material* [Mathis], *with what is for him the familiar atmosphere and the magnitude of the accusations that make that time parallel with our own, and above all with the artist's lonely destiny, that he composes with an enthusiasm and personal involvement the likes of which I have never seen before*[14].

Despite the dramatic differences, then, between the total artistic personalities of Hindemith, Mann, and Benn (to cite three prominent examples), they did share a common concern with the status of art vis-à-

[13] Letter from Hindemith to Ludwig and Willy Strecker, 10 March 1933, in Paul Hindemith, *Selected Letters of Paul Hindemith*, ed. and trans. Geoffrey Skelton, New Haven, CT: Yale University Press, 1995, p. 67–68.

[14] Letter from Willy to Ludwig Strecker, 4 August 1933, qtd. in Zenck, *Zwischen Boykott und Anpassung an den Charakter der Zeit*, p. 69–70. Unless otherwise noted, all translations are mine.

vis the polarizing political culture of the period, and each expressed in their own work an impulse toward the maintenance of artistic independence from the politics of extremity.

Through his well-known one-act operas of the early 1920s (*Mörder, Hoffnung der Frauen*, *Sancta Susanna*, *Das Nusch-Nuschi*) as well as some of his later theatrical enterprises (*Neues vom Tage* in 1929), Hindemith had, in fact, contributed a great deal to the atmosphere of artistic experimentation which characterized the decade of the 1920s and fanned the flames of right-wing opposition. Yet more significant was his turn to music for amateurs (represented by the clumsy term »Gebrauchsmusik« but referred to by Hindemith as »Sing- und Spielmusik«) later in the decade, an interest which in its overt historicism and popular application led Hindemith away from the radical political tendencies and progressive teleology of much modernist composition. Hindemith's concern with the musical amateur remained central to his artistic philosophy throughout his life. *The musical layman*, Hindemith writes in his 1930 essay *Forderungen an den Laien*, *who seriously concerns himself with musical things, is as important a part of our musical life as the professional musician. He is decidedly more important than the merely pleasure-seeking listener, who in his best-known form as concert-goer is only an economic factor in musical activity today.*[15]

In a letter in the same year to the American patroness Elizabeth Sprague Coolidge Hindemith reiterates the same themes:

In recent years I have turned away from concert music and almost without exception have written music with pedagogical or social tendencies, for amateurs, for children, for radio, for mechanical instruments, etc. I hold this type of composition as being of greater importance than writing for concert purposes, because the latter is practically a technical activity for the musician and does hardly anything for the further development of music. I must therefore consider the concert as a purely commercial affair. All of

[15] Qtd. in Albrecht Dümling, *Tun ist besser als fühlen. Der pädagogische Aspekt bei Brecht und Hindemith*, Hindemith-Jahrbuch 1988/XVII, p. 82.

the music that I have composed in recent years for concert purposes was for business reasons [geschäftlichen Gründen].[16]

In this one might detect a certain distrust of culture as a capitalistic enterprise, a position which, at least superficially, might be consistent with Hindemith's decision in 1929 to collaborate with the leftist playwright Bertolt Brecht[17]. On the other hand, Hindemith's conception of Laienmusik is not explicitly a rejection of capitalism as such, but rather is suspicious of the subordination of music to non-musical ends. For Hindemith music represents, as Dieter Rexroth has pointed out, *the true task of life*, a *metaphysical activity* which has less to do with the transcendent, Romantic view of the artwork than it does with the conviction that music, and the act of *making* music, should assume a prominent status in the life of the layman[18]. This concern about fostering a wider public participation in musical life can additionally be seen as a

[16] Paul Hindemith to Elizabeth Sprague Coolidge, 8 May 1930, in Paul Hindemith, *Briefe*, ed. Dieter Rexroth, Frankfurt am Main: Fischer Taschenbuch Verlag, 1982, p. 147.

[17] It has been often overlooked that Brecht did not entirely throw his lot in with the Communist cause until 1930, quite possibly as a reaction to the brutal suppression of the riots attendant upon the May Day workers' march in Berlin that year. It seems likely that Hindemith underestimated Brecht's potential for radicalism at the time of their initial collaboration. See Willett, *Art and Politics in the Weimar Period*, p. 179.

[18] Dieter Rexroth, *Wiederklang des Dichterischen: Zu Paul Hindemiths Biografie und frühen Vertonungen literarischer Texte*, in Gottfried Benn, *Briefwechsel mit Paul Hindemith*, ed. Ann Clark Fehn, Wiesbaden: Limes Verlag, 1978, p. 172–173. Hindemith's concern with a capella music for men's chorus (see, for example, his *Über das Frühjahr* [text by Brecht] of 1929 and the three settings of Benn in 1930, *Du mußt dir alles geben*, *Fürst Kraft*, and *Vision des Mannes*) may not only be related to his interest in Laienmusik but also to the widespread and traditional cultivation of the Männerchor in German-speaking areas. An illustration of the importance of this tradition is provided by the nationwide festivals for men's choruses which took place every four years during the 1920s and early 1930s. Festivals took place in Hannover in 1924 and in Frankfurt in 1932, attracting 43,000 and 50,000 singers respectively, while a 1928 festival in Vienna attracted some 140,000 participants. See Annegret Heemann, *Männergesangvereine im 19. und frühen 20. Jahrhundert: ein Beitrag zur städtischen Musikgeschichte Münsters*, Frankfurt am Main: Peter Lang, 1992, p. 84–88. Studies of Hindemith's individual works for a capella chorus may be found in Alfred Rubeli, *Paul Hindemiths A Cappella-Werke*, Mainz: Schott, 1975.

reaction against the perceived stagnation of the traditional concert scene, which was polarized into the two extremes of an endlessly repeated canon of classic works on the one hand, and the cultivation of an inaccessible modernist aesthetic among contemporary composers on the other hand. In this light Laienmusik seems to have been well-tailored for the political center, avoiding the conservatism of the right as well as the political stridency and elitist tendencies of the left. While insisting that choral music should be tailored to the natures and abilities of amateur singers, Hindemith explained in a 1928 lecture to a group of choral conductors that art should nevertheless avoid political fashion. Rejecting the practice of singing anything and everything which is new, without regard for artistic value, he continues:

What would be almost more condemnable would be the singing of pieces simply because of the stance of their texts, because of their political or any other content. First and foremost, artistic quality should be looked after.[19]

From a wider perspective, it should not be supposed that Hindemith's association with the Jugendmusikbewegung implied the complete social determinism of musical activity. In the above-mentioned essay *Forderungen an den Laien* Hindemith doubted that communalism necessarily entailed the proper conditions for quality music-making:

In many organizations [...] one can observe that music is not so important within the community as the community itself thinks. There are all types of communal activity, from the worst sort of clubbability and the usual forms of social entertainment to the most eccentric cliques, all of which have obscured in an alarmingly large number of cases the original pleasure in music-making.[20]

---

[19] Lecture given at the Berliner Musikhochschule, October 1928. Qtd. in Andres Briner, *Paul Hindemith*, Zürich: Atlantis, 1971, p. 309. Translation partly adapted from Stephen Hinton.

[20] Qtd. and trans. in Stephen Hinton, *The Idea of Gebrauchsmusik: A Study of Musical Aesthetics in the Weimar Republic (1919–1933) with Particular Reference to the Works of Paul Hindemith*, New York: Garland, 1989, p. 201.

What Hindemith shared with Brecht a short time later was not, therefore, a desire for socialist agitation; still less did he share the nationalist and reactionary political tendencies of the Jugendmusikbewegung, which, as Hans-Dieter Krabiel points out, owed its appeal in part to the social dislocations brought about by the rise of the modern industrial economy[21]. Rather, Hindemith's activity in the realm of Laienmusik stemmed from a conviction that people should be awakened from cultural passivity and brought together to work as producers of art. A desire for a thoroughgoing renewal of the relationship between artists and audiences was common to Hindemith and Brecht in the late 1920s; as Hindemith so aptly wrote in his 1929 essay *Über Musikkritik*,

In music today there are hardly any technical issues which cannot be overcome. The technical and creative questions are being relegated to the background. What concerns us all is this: the old public is dying away; how and what must we write to attract another, greater, new public; where is this public? [...] *We must consider other forms of music-making and musical enjoyment. The sooner the concert in its present form dies away, the faster we will have the opportunity to renew musical life.*[22]

In this renewal only the final product differed for Brecht and Hindemith: while for Brecht a groundswell of support for the socialist cause was the desired result, Hindemith kept the music, as such, at the forefront. Beyond the obvious differences in the temperaments of the two men, their ultimate disagreement about the true function of art would eventually lead to an irreparable rift.

In the two fruits of this collaboration, *Lehrstück* and *Der Lindberghflug* (the latter of which involved the contributions of Kurt Weill as well as Brecht), Hindemith intended Brecht to furnish works which would

---

[21] Krabiel, *Das Lehrstück von Brecht und Hindemith*, p. 158–159. Hindemith's aversion to the political overtones of the Jugendmusikbewegung, as well as to Brecht's later polemicizing, is also stressed by Dieter Rexroth in *Paul Hindemith und Brechts Lehrstück*, Hindemith-Jahrbuch 1983/XII, p. 41–52.

[22] From Hindemith, *Über Musikkritik*, *Melos* (8) 1929, p. 106.

involve the audience to the greatest extent possible in the performance itself. Although Brecht would later see such an enterprise as an opportunity for agitation and for stressing the bankruptcy of individual idealism severed from collective well-being, in 1929 he was still willing to admit that communal music-making had value, even if not explicitly political in content. For both pieces Brecht used the topical theme of Lindbergh's flight across the Atlantic, but the accomplishment represented for Brecht not an archetype for individual aspiration, but rather an opportunity to exhort the participants and audience to a greater sense of communal interdependence. The friction between Brecht and Hindemith was not necessarily related to the circumstances of the Baden-Baden festival at which the works were performed, but was more directly a result of a disagreement about Hindemith's preface to the Schott score of *Lehrstück* (1930). In it Hindemith stressed the adaptability of the work according to the circumstances of the performers, allowing cuts, additions, and reordering if necessary. Brecht, who by this time had moved considerably to the left, objected to what he perceived to be Hindemith's favoring of purely musical aims:

Even if one expected [...] *that here certain spiritual, formal congruencies come about on a musical basis, it would never be possible for such an artistic and shallow harmony, even for a few minutes, to create on a broad and vital basis a counterbalance to the collective formations which pull apart the people of our times with a completely different force.*[23]

It is certain that Hindemith would not find himself in agreement with this conception, which seemed to sacrifice the act of music-making itself to political ends. As Albrecht Dümling has pointed out, by 1930 Hindemith and Brecht were both interested in a kind of pedagogy (simply the title of one of the works – *Lehrstück* – would seem to have required it), but the ideal aim and audience differed greatly between the two artists: on the one hand, Brecht would conceive of music as a single aspect of

[23] Qtd. in Krabiel, *Das Lehrstück von Brecht und Hindemith*, p. 177.

the larger social function of the work (a process which naturally lent itself to the edification of the proletariat), while Hindemith kept music-pedagogical objectives and the middle class at the center of his intentions[24]. The controversy over Hindemith's preface heightened to the point that his publisher Schott withdrew the piece from stores in 1930[25]. For the festival *Neue Musik Berlin 1930* in June of that year the program committee, on which Hindemith served as a member, rejected a projected work by Brecht and Hanns Eisler entitled *Die Maßnahme*, on grounds of *formal inferiority* of the text[26]. Whatever the purely structural merits of the work, its subject matter, which dealt explicitly with the creation of a popular Marxist consciousness among its performers and audience, probably would have been repellent to Hindemith; in any case, the committee members (which, along with Hindemith, included Georg Schünemann and Heinrich Burkard) seemingly had decided only to accept works which were demonstrably non-partisan with respect to to political issues[27]. Although Hindemith had expressed his hope to his publishers in early 1930 for a new libretto from Brecht, the controversy surrounding the Berlin festival widened and made more explicit the aesthetic and philosophical rift between the two artists[28]. In subsequent years Brecht, without the aid of Hindemith, would make a number of modifications to *Der Lindberghflug* and *Lehrstück*, altering the titles and replacing almost Benn-like textual references to social

[24] Dümling, *Tun ist besser als fühlen. Der pädagogische Aspekt bei Brecht und Hindemith*, p. 92.

[25] Curiously, the preface to *Lehrstück*, which was partially published in *Melos* in 1929, induced Arnold Schoenberg to criticize what he felt to be Hindemith's cavalier attitude regarding the work's adaptability to different performance contexts. Schoenberg saw in this flexibility a surrendering of the composer's creative will. See Hinton, *The Idea of Gebrauchsmusik*, p. 210–211.

[26] See Giselher Schubert, *Paul Hindemith in Selbstzeugnissen und Bilddokumenten*, Hamburg: Rowohlt Taschenbuch Verlag, 1981, p. 73–74.

[27] Hanns Eisler, *Hanns Eisler: Musik und Politik*, ed. Günter Mayer, Leipzig: VEB Deutscher Verlag für Musik, 1973, p. 104–105.

[28] Andres Briner et al., *Paul Hindemith: Leben und Werk in Bild und Text*, Zürich: Atlantis Musikbuch-Verlag, 1988, p. 128.

transformation as »das Unerreichbare« with the more teleological »das Noch-Nicht-Erreichte«, more in keeping with Brecht's drastic move towards propagandistic activity after 1930. Hindemith's refusal to involve himself in this explicit politicization of the Baden-Baden works during this critical period, as well as his behavior on the program committee for the Berlin festival, lends some intelligibility to his subsequent association with Benn beginning in summer of 1930.

Hindemith and Gottfried Benn

While the origins of Hindemith's interest in Brecht are somewhat ambiguous, the composer's differences with the playwright, at least on a superficial level, helped to prepare the ground for his collaboration with Gottfried Benn, the fiercely independent poet who until his association with Hindemith was widely known only in literary circles. Despite the nearly opposite stances of Brecht and Benn in the political realm of the early 1930s, it is important not to assume that Hindemith's new-found interest in Benn represented a move to the political right for the composer personally. Rather, it would come to pass that the ideologies of both writers would prove too extreme for Hindemith, who probably remained a consistent centrist throughout the period[29]. Even Benn himself had not taken an explicit position against the German left before the collaboration with Hindemith; in fact, the poet distrusted the material and technological trappings of capitalism with such fervor that his work was featured regularly in various left-of-center journals during the 1920s, including *Die neue Rundschau*, *Die Weltbühne*, and *Der Querschnitt*[30]. Benn shared with the leftists the idea of society as a collect-

---

[29] Furthermore, no discernable change in Hindemith's compositional style accompanies the shift from Brecht to Benn. As Stephen Hinton points out in *The Idea of Gebrauchsmusik*, p. 203–204, *If the fates and deeds of the poets Brecht and Benn are left aside, then Lehrstück and Das Unaufhörliche indeed have much in common, both musically and textually.*

[30] Reinhard Alter, *Gottfried Benn: The Artist and Politics (1910–1934)*, Bern: Lang, 1976, p. 61–62. Benn's anti-modernist ideas are strongly developed in his *Der*

ive rather than an aggregation of individuals, but while Brecht and his circle focused on the proletariat, Benn conceived of the collective as a common fund of subconscious artistic potential which crossed national and racial boundaries. His later association with the National Socialists would not, in fact, be primarily based on questions of racial purity: in several essays he extolled French culture (*Paris* [1925], *Frankreich und wir* [1930]), and wrote in *Das Genieproblem* (1930) that artistic accomplishment was *most common in regions and landscapes of blood and racial mixture.*[31] Although by 1929 and 1930 he was involved in various controversies with the artistic left, it was not at all clear at this time that his political allegiances would swing so far to the right by 1933.

Yet Benn's work had always something of a mystical, irrational character which flowed more naturally toward the mythos of the right than toward the concrete materialism of the left. A representative example is his 1925 poem *Qui sait*, part of which appears below:

Aber der Mensch wird trauern –	*Yet mankind shall mourn*
solange Gott, falls es das gibt,	*while God – if that exists –*
immer neue Schauern	*moves ever newly born*
von Gehirnen schiebt	*brain waves into the lists*
von den Hellesponten	*from the Hellesponts*
zum Hobokenquai,	*to Hoboken's quay,*
immer neue Fronten –	*opens ever new fronts –*
wozu, qui sait?	*what for? Qui sait?*

Garten von Arles (1920), *Das letzte Ich* (1921), *Medizinische Krise* (1926), *Fazit der Perspektiven* (1930), and *Gebührt Carleton ein Denkmal?* (1932), the last of which questions the value of developing a new, hardy variety of wheat when the prospect of merely living in modern society was, according to Benn, so burdensome. Hindemith would later reject this idea of a »Weizengeschichte« as an opera subject in 1932.

31 Gottfried Benn, *Das Genieproblem*, in Benn, *Sämtliche Werke*, ed. Gerhard Schuster, Stuttgart: Klett-Cotta, 1986, vol. 3: p. 281.

Spurii: die Gesäten
war einst der Männer Los,
Frauen streiften und mähten
den Samen in ihren Schoß;
dann eine Insel voll Tauben
und Werften: Schiffe fürs Meer,
und so begann der Glauben
an Handel und Verkehr.

Spurii: being sowed
used to be men's meed;
women stripped and mowed,
into their womb the seed;
then came an isleful of pigeons
and wharves: ships for the sea,
and thus began the religions
of commerce and industry.

...

Aber der Mensch wird trauern –
kosmopoler Chic
neue Tempelmauern
Kraftwerk Pazifik:
die Meere ausgeweidet,
Kalorien-Avalun:
Meer, das wärmt, Meer, das kleidet –
neue Mythe des Neptun.

Yet mankind shall mourn –
cosmopolitan styles,
temple walls adorn
Pacific power stations;
eviscerated oceans,
calorific Avalon:
sea heat, costuming lotions –
Neptune's new pantheon.

Bis nach tausend Jahren
einbricht in das Wrack
Geißlerscharen,
zementiertes Pack
mit Orang-Utanhauern
oder Kaiser Henry Clay –
wer wird das überdauern,
welch Pack – qui sait?

Until a thousand years later
rabidly penitent
gangs invade the crater,
rabble cast in cement,
ape fangs dripping saliva
of Emperor Henry Clay –
and who'll be the survivor?
Which gang – qui sait?[32]

[32] From Benn, *Qui sait*, in Benn, *Sämtliche Werke*, vol. 1: p. 76–77. Translation adapted from E. B. Ashton, in E. B. Ashton, ed., *Primal Vision: Selected Writings of Gottfried Benn*, New York: New Directions Publishing, 1971, p. 244–247.

Indeed, it was this critique of materialism and its corresponding lack of mythos which brought him into open conflict with the left by 1930 (even if Benn's censure was essentially non-political in intent, it need not be emphasized that anti-materialism was a component of Nazi ideology as well). Benn continued to develop this theme in essays such as *Nach dem Nihilismus* (1932):

Actually all materialism is reactionary today, as much in historical philosophy as it is in attitude: namely looking backwards, acting backwards, for before us already there lies a completely different person, and a completely different goal.[33]

This goal was clearly the renewal of man's spiritual, artistic, and subconscious energies at the expense of materialism and consumerism, which, according to Benn, plagued capitalist and communist alike[34]. Western society, which Benn identified sometimes as northern Europeans, sometimes as the »white race« (a category which begins to appear with some frequency in Benn's writings by 1930, and indeed in the baritone solo within the oratorio itself: *oil rigs, rubber plantations / grave of the myth-less white race*), had lost its spiritual and mythic moorings under the onslaught of modernism, which while pretending to stand for progress in reality was decimating the primeval human spirit:

The white race is at an end. Technical magic, a thousand words of Rebbach, text standardized, score consisting of numbers, that was its last dream. Imports from Asia: bicycles to Ulster, lollipops to Halberstadt, beer warmers for the union building. Farewell, opportunity from the stock market to the psychiatric ward! Land without grain, exhausted mine shafts, empty docks. Who cried for the falling generations – Iliads back and forth! The unceasing [Das Unaufhörliche] *visits the pole, scatters earth over Scott's grave, soon even those in Tierra del Fuego will*

[33] Qtd. in Alter, *Gottfried Benn: The Artist and Politics (1910–1934)*, p. 46.
[34] Qtd. in ibid., p. 62–63.

be able to pick roses. The unceasing, from sea to sea, pre-dawn moonless worlds, up, down.[35]

This nihilistic »Weltanschauung« which Benn developed most broadly in the oratorio »Das Unaufhörliche« would have its dangers by 1933, when his quest for the mythic and subconscious foundations of art would lead him to an approval of Nazi ideology. It was at this time that Benn took his strongest position against intellectualism (particularly on the left) and the materialistic society associated with it: *What must be destroyed*, Benn writes in 1933/1934, *is intellectualism and the civilization which is rooted in it.*[36]

Much more significant from Hindemith's viewpoint than Benn's existential nihilism, however, was the poet's view of the role of art and of artistic creativity, which was rooted not in the *era of consciousness* (»Bewußtseinsepoche«) but in what Benn felt to be pre-historical instinct. In his 1930 essay *Geologie des Ich* Benn developed his notion that the deepest layers of human artistic consciousness are characterized

---

[35] From Benn, *Fazit der Perspektiven*, in Benn, *Sämtliche Werke*, vol. 3: p. 303–304. »Rebbach« is probably a reference to a volume of Jewish humor compiled by Avrom Reitzer entitled *Rebbach: Rituelle Scherze, Lozelech, Maisses und koschere Schmonzes für unsere Leut*, Pressburg: s.n., 1901.

[36] From Benn, *Der neue Staat und die Intellektuellen*, in Benn, *Sämtliche Werke*, vol. 4: p. 394. Benn's position by 1933 is strikingly paralleled in the works of Ernst Jünger, who, like Benn, survived the First World War to become a writer highly suspicious (to say the least) of doctrines of social progress. In writings such as *In Stahlgewittern* (1920) and *Der Kampf als inneres Erlebnis* (1922) Jünger developed the trauma of his wartime experiences into a nihilistic doctrine of spiritual renewal through the catharsis of destruction and chaos. The phenomenon of war is seen to expose the thinness of society's civilized veneer, confronting mankind with the primitive and fundamental roots of its own behavior in the form of untrammeled violence. It is fascinating that Jünger, like Benn, hesitated to lend his explicit support to any of the political movements stirring in Germany by the late 1920s: *Jünger was therefore* [...] *anxious to preserve his distance from the practical manifestations of that ideology, as much because of a distaste for reality itself as out of a dislike of any particular manifestation of his ideology.* See Hugh Ridley's illuminating comparison of the two men in *Irrationalism, Art and Violence: Ernst Jünger and Gottfried Benn*, in *Weimar Germany: Writers and Politics*, p. 26–37.

by their freedom from the laws of time and space, history and causation[37]. In Benn's view, true works of art – those which transcend the time in which they are created – are entirely autonomous objects with universal significance and lacking any transient political content whatsoever. The implication, naturally, is the ideal of the autonomous artist who refuses to be defined by his local political context, but rather creates timeless works originating in the deepest, most universal layers of consciousness which all humans share. Although on a superficial level this ideal appears to be opposed to the communal spirit of Laienmusik, in which music is regarded as an activity rather than as an object of contemplation, its resonance with the Hindemith of 1930 lies in its rejection of the subordination of art to extremist politics. If Laienmusik on the one hand rejects the Romantic idea of transcendent art (and even the metaphysical aspects of Benn's own thought), it does in Hindemith's practice insist on the centrality of the music to the enterprise, rather than the use of music-making for ideological ends[38]. Whether or not Benn's insistence on the non-political nature of art influenced Hindemith's thoughts concerning *Mathis der Maler* (a work which indeed suggests the theme of artistic autonomy), this principle was nevertheless relevant to Hindemith, who struggled with the reconciliation of artistic value and social relevance during these very same years.

It is quite possible that Hindemith, who had kept himself abreast of developments in the German literary world during the 1920s, acquainted himself with Benn during the public controversies in which the poet was embroiled from 1929. In the same month that the Hindemith-Brecht collaboration reached its height in the form of *Lehrstück*

---

[37] Alter, *Gottfried Benn: The Artist and Politics (1910–1934)*, p. 41.

[38] This is certainly Hindemith's intention, which is not to say that such a position could not be consistent with an ideological agenda. We will see that Benn's philosophy, which included such prominent assertions of artistic »autonomy«, was to dovetail rather nicely with the chauvinism of the Nazis by 1933.

and *Der Lindberghflug*, a laudatory article appeared in an issue of *Die neue Bücherschau* by Max Herrmann-Neisse entitled *Gottfried Benns Prosa*. Two Marxist editors of the magazine, Egon Erwin Kisch and Johannes R. Becher, relinquished their posts; Kisch fiercely attacked Benn in his letter of resignation, also criticizing Benn in the magazine itself for his lack of interest in social engagement[39]. In several polemical essays, among them *Über die Rolle des Schriftstellers in dieser Zeit* (1929) and *Können Dichter die Welt ändern?* (1930), Benn refuted the criticisms, stressing his belief in the non-political nature of art and distinguishing between »Dichter«, whose creations are timeless and universal, and the engaged »Schriftsteller« of the left, whose work is irretrievably mired in futile social projects. Asked whether the poet should help to ameliorate society's ills or simply stand back and watch, Benn responded in *Können Dichter die Welt ändern?*:

I don't hesitate for a moment: the poet watches. Not the author of civilization-literature and of an evening's intellectual pretexts for shifting the stage-props, the one who sits next to the minister at the banquet with a carnation in his swallow-tail coat and five wine glasses behind his plate: he signs declarations against the evils of our time. But the other one watches; he knows that the innocent misery of the world will never be removed by welfare measures, never be overcome by material improvements. Hygienic wish-intoxications of short-legged rationalists: with my pension in my heart and a heat-lamp in my house. A creation without horror, jungles without bites, nights without mares that ride their victims – no, the poet watches in the conviction, which is not to be denied in the face of any death, that he alone possesses the substance that can banish horror and reconcile the victims: sink, he cries out to them, sink, but I could also say: rise.[40]

---

[39] See Alter, *Gottfried Benn: The Artist and Politics (1910–1934)*, p. 73.

[40] Benn, *Können Dichter die Welt ändern?*, in Gottfried Benn, *Prose, Essays, Poems*, ed. Volkmar Sander, trans. Joel Agee, New York: Continuum, 1987, p. 102.

Challenged by his interviewer with a list of contemporary woes suffered by the German people – tuberculosis, unemployment, and other ills – Benn offered an unusual solution:

The thought occurs to me whether it wouldn't be far more radical – because more revolutionary and far more demanding of a strong man's hardness and fitness – to teach the human race: this is how you are and you will never be otherwise: this is how you live, how you have lived, and how you will always live. He who has money gets healthy; he who has power swears the right oath; he who wields might determines what's right. That is history! Ecce historia! Here's today, take its body, eat and die. This teaching strikes me as far more radical, philosophically deeper, of far greater psychological consequence than the political parties' prophesies of happiness.[41]

In this fundamental expression of nihilism as well as in his positing of a sub- or pre-conscious basis for human creative potential, Benn seems to echo the thinking of Jung or Schopenhauer, rejecting confidence in the benevolent power of human consciousness and reason while asserting the ultimate inescapability of suffering. Nietzsche's shadow is, of course, perceptible as well.

Heinrich Mann, brother of Thomas Mann and a writer who frequently had espoused socialist ideas in his work, was perhaps the most important catalyst for Benn's propulsion into the realm of explicitly political affairs. On 28 March 1931, Benn gave a speech to the »Schutzverband deutscher Schriftsteller« on the occasion of Heinrich Mann's sixtieth birthday, in which he celebrated the earlier, non-politically motivated work of the author while criticizing him for abandoning his artistry in favor of a socially engaged mediocrity. Having alienated the literary left, Benn's speech provoked another attack by Werner Hegemann in the article *G. B. als Faschist und Adolf Hitler* in the journal *Das Tagebuch* of April 1931. Benn's response appeared shortly thereafter in

---

[41] Ibid., p. 103–104.

Eine Geburtstagrede und die Folgen (*Vossische Zeitung*, 16 April 1931), which contained decidedly anti-Nazi sentiments; however, that Benn had in fact composed his essay before Hegemann's attack demonstrates that his feelings against the Nazis were more genuine than a mere rebuttal of Hegemann would suggest[42]. It is significant that Benn, who at this time was working with Hindemith on *Das Unaufhörliche*, still wished to maintain his disengagement from explicitly political questions to the greatest extent possible.

It was precisely this refusal on Benn's part to become embroiled in political issues (whether or not his stance contained ideological elements of its own) that Hindemith was initially attracted to in the wake of his falling out with Brecht. The increasing commercialization of musical life on the one hand and the political appropriation of his work by Brecht at Baden-Baden on the other resulted, according to his associate and biographer Heinrich Strobel, in an *increasing aversion* to the situation of a modern music *which was primarily determined by non-artistic factors. The modern cultivation of music seemed to him ever more questionable, civilized activity ever more doubtful. The man whose feet were planted so firmly upon the ground of present-day life became more and more conscious of the great questions which lay behind this present.*[43]

Keeping in mind Strobel's tendency for hyperbole, his comment generally rings true. In this polarized cultural atmosphere Benn represented for Hindemith not a retreat into nihilism but rather an affirmation of the autonomy of the artist in the face of deteriorating circumstances. Since the bulk of the public controversies surrounding Benn in 1929 and 1930 revolved around his lack of political engagement rather than his metaphysics, it is possible that Hindemith was either unaware of or unconcerned with the irrational and mystical streak which had been a

[42] See ibid., p. 76–77. See also Augustinus P. Dierick, *Gottfried Benn and his Critics: Major Interpretations 1912–1992*, Columbia, SC: Camden House, 1992, p. 92–93.

[43] Heinrich Strobel, *Paul Hindemith*, [3]Mainz: B. Schott's Söhne, 1948, p. 73.

prominent factor in Benn's poetry. Hindemith probably made contact with Benn after having heard his radio essay *Können Dichter die Welt ändern?* in the early months of 1930, in the midst of the heightening tensions with Brecht. That the initial approach was, in fact, a response to Benn's essay is further suggested by Gertrud's writing the words *Anlass* z[um] *»Unaufhörlichen«!* on a 1961 reprint of Benn's essay[44]. In contrast with Brecht, Benn must have appeared to Hindemith *as a guarantor of art understood as a true metaphysical activity, which is not subordinated to political interests, but rather claims its autonomy and obeys the demand for freedom.*[45] Apart from their mutual distaste for certain aspects of modern culture Hindemith and Benn shared a conception of art as an activity with ethical value unto itself rather than in the service of extra-artistic goals[46].

Benn may have interested Hindemith before this time, however, for the three settings of Benn's poems *Vision des Mannes*, *Fürst Kraft*, and *Du mußt dir alles geben* were completed by April 1930. There is not neces-

---

[44] Qtd. by Giselher Schubert, liner notes for Paul Hindemith, *Das Unaufhörliche*, Rundfunk-Chor Berlin, Rundfunk-Kinderchor Berlin, Rundfunk-Sinfonieorchester Berlin, Lothar Zagrosek, Wergo compact disc WER 6603-2.

[45] Rexroth, *Wiederklang des Dichterischen*, p. 177.

[46] Yet the ethics of art, in Benn's view, has its root in a nihilistic vision that Hindemith surely did not share. Asked by his interviewer whether he subscribes to a nihilistic conception of poetry, Benn responds, *Let all the works of art which history has bequeathed you pass by in a pageant. Nefertiti and the Dorian temple, Anna Karenina or the song of Nausikaa in the Odyssey – there's nothing in these works that points beyond the work itself, nothing requiring any explanation, nothing that seeks to affect anything outside. It is this procession of silent shapes and images sunk into self-contemplation – if you want to call that nihilistic, it's the special nihilism of art.* From Benn, *Können Dichter die Welt ändern?*, in Benn, *Prose, Essays, Poems*, trans. Joel Agee, p. 101. It is also important to add that Hindemith's compositions of the 1920s demonstrate a fascination with technological means not shared by Benn: thus, one may usefully distinguish between Hindemith's rejection of the modern politicization of art and Benn's rejection of modernism as such. Examples of the use of technological devices in Hindemith's OEuvre include the siren in *Kammermusik No. 1* (1922), the percussive typewriters of *Neues vom Tage* (1929), and the exploitation of the medium of radio in the collaborations with Brecht.

sarily a contradiction in Hindemith's setting an existential text like *Du mußt dir alles geben* for men's chorus (»Männerchor« - an ensemble which carries the implication of Gebrauchs- or Laienmusik) if one recognizes the distinction between the social activity of music and the service of music to an overtly ideological program[47]. Yet it is clear that by 1932 Hindemith would not be willing to follow Benn very far down the path of nihilism (much less Benn's embracing of rightist ideology in the following year), even if the poet was an attractive alternative to Brecht in 1930 on the basis of his essentially anti-political view of art. The first extant correspondence between Hindemith and Benn with respect to the oratorio dates from early July of 1930. Despite Benn's initial hesitation to begin the new project (on 8 July 1930 he writes, *Your invitation to write a text* [...] *is very honorable for me.* [...] *But at the moment I am physically and spiritually so fatigued that I can not think about work.*[48]) his enthusiasm for the association quickly developed and it seems that he put aside other work to concentrate on the oratorio exclusively[49]. The concept of *Das Unaufhörliche* was not a new one for Benn; the term had occurred in several of his previous writings as far back as 1916 and Benn continued to use it after the completion of the oratorio in 1931[50]. In a letter to Hindemith on 29 July Benn defines the concept of *Das Unaufhörliche* as a law of perpetual change:

This text, called »das Unaufhörliche«, is not a Lehrstück but rather a poem. The name should reveal the perpetual senselessness, the ebb and

[47] Rexroth implies that the ideological conflict contained the settings of Benn's poems was far more significant for Hindemith's work in the 1930s. See ibid., p. 179–180.

[48] Benn to Paul and Gertrud Hindemith, 8 July 1930, in Benn, *Briefwechsel mit Paul Hindemith*, p. 15–16.

[49] Fehn, *Das Unaufhörliche: Gottfried Benns Text in der Vertonung von Paul Hindemith*, p. 45.

[50] Examples include his poem *Strand* (1916), his essays *Kunst und Staat* (1927), *Fazit der Perspektiven* (1930), *Die neue literarische Saison* (1931), and *Nihilistisch oder positiv?* (1953). See ibid., p. 61. I prefer the translation of »Das Unaufhörliche« as »The Unceasing«, since this lends Benn's term greater agency than the commonly-encountered »The Perpetual«.

flow of history, the transience of greatness and glory, the perpetual accident and variation of existence.[51]

It would appear from this comment that Hindemith may have intended Benn to produce a Lehrstück, a didactic text similar to Brecht's in form if not in content. Even if Benn's philosophy excluded the possibility of human improvement through man's own endeavors, it is not necessarily the case that the oratorio (which as a genre carried a didactic implication) was meant by Benn to be free of pedagogical intent altogether. This intention, however, did not involve the improvement of society (which for Benn was a futile enterprise) but rather mankind's realization of the perpetual instability of existence. *What follows, therefore, from this lesson* [*Lehre*]*?*, Benn asks. *Das Unaufhörliche nourished by day and night, watching over individuals, peoples, races and continents in its course through galaxies and millions of years – how shall man meet it?*[52]

Benn also provides this metaphysical grounding for *Das Unaufhörliche* in the foreword intended for the libretto for the premiere:

We know nothing of creation, apart from its continual change – and das Unaufhörliche should be an expression for this ultimate background of life, its elementary principle of transformation and the ceaseless upheaval of its forms[53].

In the text of the oratorio itself Benn defines this concept of »unceasing« most clearly at the opening and at the closing in large-scale choral settings (note here the resemblance to the previously-cited quotation from Benn's *Fazit der Perspektiven*):

Das Unaufhörliche:	*The Unceasing:*
Großes Gesetz.	*great law.*

[51] Benn to Hindemith, 29 July 1930, in Benn, *Briefwechsel mit Paul Hindemith*, p. 16.

[52] Benn's preface to *Das Unaufhörliche*, qtd. in Fehn, *Das Unaufhörliche: Gottfried Benns Text in der Vertonung von Paul Hindemith*, p. 45–46.

[53] Qtd. in ibid., p .47–48.

Das Unaufhörliche	*The Unceasing*
mit Tag und Nacht	*with day and night*
ernährt und spielt es sich	*sustained and plays itself*
von Meer zu Meer,	*from sea to sea,*
mondlose Welten überfrüht,	*pre-dawn moonless worlds,*
hinan, hinab.	*up, down.*
Es beugt die Häupter all,	*It bows all heads,*
Es beugt die Jahre.	*It bends the years.*

Although Benn's antagonism to the left would suggest that his concept of unceasing flux was intended as an antidote to European socialism and modernism, he was careful not to undermine his view of the universal validity of *das Unaufhörliche. With the theme das Unaufhörliche, Großes Gesetz,* Benn writes to Hindemith,

we can not take a position for Asia or against Europe, against civilization or for collectivism – the U[naufhörliche].*-motif must transcend all historical events: purely mythic, unsympathetic and contemplative.*[54]

It is certainly valid to ask why Hindemith, the composer of *Hin und zurück*, *Neues vom Tage*, and *Lehrstück*, would have turned at this time to the oratorio with its distinctly metaphysical overtones. Although a detailed answer to this question is beyond the scope of this article, it should be stressed that the genre of the oratorio was, in fact, entirely consistent with Hindemith's continuing belief in the non-individualistic roots of artistic creation, his search for the universal laws of musical theory and practice eventually embodied in such works as *Ludus tonalis* and *Die Harmonie der Welt.* As Wolfgang Rathert has suggested recently, Hindemith's interest in these broader issues after 1930 finds analogues in the work of Georg Grosz and Otto Dix, both artists who distanced themselves from their original realistic and social-critical concerns and

[54] Benn to Hindemith, 2 May 1931, in Benn, *Briefwechsel mit Paul Hindemith*, p. 28–29.

embraced instead historical and even religious motifs in their work[55]. Again, the rift between *Das Unaufhörliche* and the *Plöner Musiktag*, for example, was less wide than one might suppose: both approaches share an insistence on music as a collective activity or utterance rather than as the unique expression of an individual creator. In this respect Hindemith's turn to the oratorio seems less surprising than it commonly has been made out to be[56].

Work on *Das Unaufhörliche* continued through the remainder of 1930 and into 1931, not without some hesitation on the part of Benn, who clearly felt out of his element as a librettist and seemed to have difficulty in constructing his text in musical rather than in purely poetic terms. Upon receiving two portions of the musical setting of the oratorio from Hindemith in early October 1930, Benn states that *it almost depresses me that you would devote your work and time, not to mention genius, to such a questionable figure, to such a shadowy talent as myself.*[57] He was, nevertheless, grateful for the opportunity to disseminate his work and ideas to a larger audience than he had previously enjoyed. Hindemith, after all, possessed the greater reputation in German cultural life, especially after his appointment to the Berliner Musikhochschule in 1927. On 6 March 1931 Benn wrote a telling letter to Hindemith which illustrates the poet's feelings concerning the collaboration:

---

[55] See Wolfgang Rathert, *Was wird mit Hindemith geschehen? Stand und Perspektiven des Hindemith-Bildes*, Hindemith-Jahrbuch 1996/XXVII, p. 24–27.

[56] Extant statements by Hindemith concerning the subject matter of the oratorio are few. One comment appears in a letter to Willy Strecker dated 28 June 1931: *Benn's introduction, which is to appear at the beginning of the libretto as well as in the score, I find to be very good; it makes many things clear which otherwise might remain obscure.* In Benn, *Briefwechsel mit Paul Hindemith*, p. 106.

[57] Benn to Hindemith, 5 October 1930, in Benn, *Briefwechsel mit Paul Hindemith*, p. 19. Benn was unable to achieve the same notoriety as figures like Thomas Mann, Gerhard Hauptmann, and Stefan George in the German literary world of the 1920s; his frustration with this situation is developed in his essay *Kunst und Staat* of 1927 and may have been one of the pillars of his discontent with Weimar culture as a whole. See Alter, *Gottfried Benn: The Artist and Politics (1910–1934)*, p. 59–60.

I am so terribly sorry if my text causes you any difficulties, whether musical or philosophical in nature. Please be frank with me. I would gladly change everything to avoid seeming stubborn or thick-headed to you. I find our collaboration so agreeable and interesting that I do not wish to be a burden to you. I am enormously grateful that you understand so spontaneously and immediately everything intellectual, linguistic, and literary about my text. I am amazed by this.[58]

While it is not possible to know what Hindemith might have said to Benn to provoke this reaction, the letter strongly suggests Benn's enthusiasm for the project, at least by the time the collaboration was well underway. Some time after the ending of the collaboration Benn would write a letter to Ernst Nef (the letter is undated) in which he would assert his artistic independence vis-à-vis Hindemith, while remembering the project fondly:

The theme, the idea »Das Unaufhörliche«, is mine [...]. *At the time Hindemith and I were good friends, both lived in Berlin, and worked closely together. Once he said to me: »I cannot compose this* [text]*; you must change it, then I will do it.« At times I said, »You must learn to compose better, for I cannot change this on poetic grounds.« Then he did it. For example, the soprano solo was a piece which Hindemith did not like at first, but let remain according to my wishes. It was a very friendly collaboration piece by piece, line by line; Frau Hindemith, this charming and clever woman, was always around and often drove us by car through the villages of my homeland on Sundays, and we spoke of many things as we went. Long, long ago!*[59]

This final exclamation (written by Benn in English) implies that the letter probably postdates the collaboration by quite a long time, and therefore cannot supersede the correspondence more contemporary with the oratorio which puts Benn in a somewhat different position with respect to Hindemith.

[58] Benn to Paul Hindemith, 6 March 1931, in Benn, *Briefwechsel mit Paul Hindemith*, p. 24.
[59] Benn to Ernst Nef (undated), in ibid., p. 88.

On 21 November 1931 *Das Unaufhörliche* was premiered in Berlin by the Berlin Philharmonic Orchestra and Chorus under the direction of Otto Klemperer; the oratorio received somewhat mixed reviews in the press despite the warm public reception[60]. By this time, Hindemith and Benn were already considering subjects for an opera, but the less-than-enthusiastic reaction of the press to the oratorio renewed Benn's reservations about the problematics of setting poetry to music. Writing to Ewald Wasmuth in December, Benn confessed that

This occupied me greatly: namely, the senselessness of finding good texts to set to music, the lack of understanding of poetry, the direct and injurious attacks of the provincial press, and the fundamental error of being engaged with the music world and music criticism, which are not responsible for me and for whom I am not responsible. Hindemith is pressing me for an opera, but I cannot decide on anything.[61]

Nevertheless, Benn pressed on, and during the later stages of work on *Das Unaufhörliche* as well as subsequently the two exchanged numerous ideas for possible subjects. One of the most striking topics – almost certainly suggested by Benn – seemed to deal with what Benn enigmatically referred to in his correspondence with the letters »W. R.« From the context in which the abbreviation was used it seems clear that Benn meant »die weiße Rasse« (the white race), which he felt was in its last

---

[60] See ibid., p. 193–194. Hindemith, who was on hand for the southwest German premiere of the work three days later in Mainz, may have referred to his Berlin critics when he wrote Gertrud that *everything* [in Mainz] *is nicer, happier, and easier than in Berlin. One should never premiere such things in Berlin.* Paul to Gertrud Hindemith, 24 November 1931, in Hindemith, *»Das private Logbuch«. Briefe an seine Frau Gertrud*, ed. Friederike Becker and Giselher Schubert, Mainz: Schott, 1995, p. 85–86. Benn, who was probably more sensitive to the reviews than Hindemith, was pilloried in the *Frankfurter Zeitung*, which called his text *ein klagendes Lied vom Katzenjammer der vom Daseinapparat eingestampften Menschen.* Qtd. in Werner Rübe, *Provoziertes Leben: Gottfried Benn*, Stuttgart: Klett-Cotta, 1993, p. 284–285.

[61] Benn to Ewald Wasmuth, 17 December 1931, in *Benn, Briefwechsel mit Paul Hindemith*, p. 85–86.

throes of existence, thoroughly separated from metaphysical grounding and drowning in a sea of industrialization, modernity, and economic collapse. By August 1931 this idea was at the forefront of Benn's mind, and the prominence of the subject in his letters to Hindemith in August and September suggests that Hindemith must not have been opposed to the idea, at least initially. Writing to Gertrud Hindemith on 15 August, Benn describes his feelings about the topic:

Now to the spiritual, poetic, textual, thematic, dramatic, librettistic [Librettistische] –, *the W. R. With this too I have been idle. It is actually very close to me as a theme, preoccupies me constantly,* [it] *is the theme, the next which I actually have in mind, the only framework for my next work and thoughts. But the execution is still inadequate.*[62]

Benn's most comprehensive – if muddled – exposition of his intentions concerning the »weiße Rasse«, however, comes in a letter to the Hindemiths written approximately one month later:

W. R. If we want to work on it this winter, I would be for it. I can hardly begin on it alone. Too many questions which we must discuss. We will have to approach it bit-by-bit and gradually build it up (with suggestions from Mrs. Hindemith). Above all the fundamental question: revue or what not? Revue with Commère and Compère, a couple to which everything relates, [...] *the starting-point could be the question between the two: should we propagate ourselves, should we propagate this race* [underlining Benn's], *what does it* [this race] *look like, where does it come from, where is it going, what are its ideas, its ideals, its body (ballet! you must – I am so physically oriented – write the most beautiful ballet music, beautiful women, that is the only thing that will work, beautiful white women!) we must reveal the foolishness, the absurdity, the impulses and finally the narrowness of the race. We would have to grasp its specifics: the technical-industrial, the intellectual, the race in tails, the race as Titans* [die Rasse im Titanen] [...]. *untouched by the mystery of*

[62] Benn to Gertrud Hindemith, 15 August 1931, in ibid., p. 43–44.

being, the inexplicability of its origins and of its goals (but everything very material and objective).[63]

Due to Hindemith's frequent absence from Berlin in the late fall and winter of 1931–1932 the idea was seemingly abandoned, for Benn does not mention it further. Its significance lies, however, in Benn's increasing interest in the application of the principle of *Das Unaufhörliche* to specific rather than to abstract aspects of the world: to nation, to race, to European civilization. As Hindemith became more and more engaged with the friction between artistic individuality and social responsibility, Benn's continuing insistence on treating metaphysical rather than specifically artistic matters must have evoked a cool response from the practice-oriented composer. Although the philosophy expounded in *Das Unaufhörliche* was, perhaps, appropriate to Hindemith in 1930 as a reaction against the extreme social engagement of Brecht and Eisler, his interest in Benn was based more on aesthetics than politics.

That Hindemith and Benn were by 1932 moving in different directions is evident from their inability to reach agreement on a suitable subject for an opera. In January of that year he reported to Schott that discussions with Benn were underway for a *serious and proper* subject, but that things were moving slowly[64]. In late May Benn finally suggested a subject dealing with an unfortunate figure by the name of Rönne who is portrayed as a victim of economic and social catastrophe. As his situation becomes more and more desperate Rönne is forced to question the very rationality of society. *It will probably be shown*, Benn explains, *above all that no other response to this question exists apart from that toward the inner, that everything which exists in natural life: history, socialism, philosophy, is completely hopeless, tragic and inadequate, and*

[63] Benn to the Hindemiths, 20 September 1931, in ibid., p. 50–51.

[64] *Mit Benn*, Hindemith writes, *berate ich immerzu weiter. Es geht langsam, wird aber vielleicht was Ernstes und Richtiges. Man kann ja mehrere Eisen im Feuer haben.* Hindemith to Schott, 22 January 1932, qtd. in Angela Zabrsa, *Hindemiths Opernprojekte*, Hindemith-Jahrbuch 1971/I, p. 54.

must be according to its nature, that no other solution exists apart from the arrangement of one's life according to one's spiritual self, as the absorption of life and its hopeless laws into that spirit which witnesses them, struggles with them, suffers from them, and finally accepts them with heroic patience. No greater things exist for human beings.[65]

Benn's idea for a tragic opera about the Rönne character seems to have been short-lived; the last mention of the subject is made in a letter to Hindemith in early June[66], and on 16 July Hindemith explained in a letter to his publisher Schott that Benn *produces vehemently, but has not yet shown me anything*[67]. Benn's next proposals involved two novels by Paul de Kruif, namely *Der Mikrobenjäger*, in which a doctor asks himself whether his work is still relevant in the context of the present »Weltuntergang«, and *Bezwinger des Hungers*, part of which concerns the societal implications of the development of a new resistant type of wheat. Both projects demonstrate, again, Benn's present concern with the application of the abstract ideas of *Das Unaufhörliche* to concrete situations. Hindemith was clearly not convinced of the efficacy of any of these subjects, and the input of Gertrud certainly played a part in his decisions. A letter from Benn to Paul Hindemith dated 17 August demonstrates the poet's frustration at the possibly premature criticism of his ideas. *I have considered the sharp opposition of your wife, and she has much instinct for these things, and I have told myself that she is*

[65] Benn to Hindemith, 29 May 1932, in Benn, *Briefwechsel mit Paul Hindemith*, p. 57–58. This is by no means the first appearance of Rönne in Benn's œuvre; as Benn explained in his 1934 essay *Lebensweg eines Intellektuellen*, *Periodisch verstärkt, das Jahr 1915/16 in Brüssel war enorm, da entstand Rönne, der Arzt, der Flagellant der Einzeldinge, das nackte Vakuum der Sachverhalte, der keine Wirklichkeit ertragen konnte, aber auch keine mehr erfassen, der nur das rhythmische Sichöffnen und Sichverschließen des Ichs und der Persönlichkeit kannte, das fortwährend Gebrochene des inneren Seins und der, vor das Erlebnis von der tiefen, schrankenlosen mythenalten Fremdheit zwischen dem Menschen und der Welt gestellt, unbedingt der Mythe und ihren Bildern glaubte.* See Benn, *Doppelleben: Zwei Selbstdarstellungen*, Stuttgart: Klett-Cotta, 1984, p. 22.

[66] Benn to Hindemith, 8 June 1932, in Benn, *Briefwechsel mit Paul Hindemith*, p. 59–61.

[67] Hindemith to Willy Strecker, 16 July 1932, in ibid., p. 119.

probably correct. She is incorrect, in my opinion, only in that there is no material and no plot. [...] *It is difficult to work when every idea is criticized from the outset and objected to.*[68]

Replying on 20 August, Hindemith gives Benn little encouragement:

If you believe that you shouldn't continue with the Weizenstück [referring to *Bezwinger des Hungers*] *I will not encourage you to do so. The advantages of this material are surely great – but it has disadvantages as well and you shouldn't be too angry about a premature criticism of these disadvantages.* [...] *If you were completely convinced by the Weizengeschichte, you would have created it despite the sharpest criticism; and in the first surge of enthusiasm I don't believe it is your way or my way to work* [on it].[69]

In the same letter Hindemith also dissuades Benn from a reworking of Knut Hamsun's novel *Viktoria*, for he is *fearful of things which have already found a good solution in another genre*[70]. In the meantime Hindemith had been developing some ideas of his own, but in contrast with Benn's insistence on a concrete realization of his nihilistic philosophy, Hindemith turned his attention to historical figures and subjects. It is clear, however, that Hindemith intended to select a subject with relevance to the contemporary political situation, which by 1932 was becoming critical. Three subjects appear with some frequency in Hindemith's surviving correspondence from this period: one dealing with issues of cultural colonization at a monastery school in medieval St. Gall, another dealing with the printer Gutenberg, and another concerning the painter Mathias Grünewald. The fact that both Gutenberg and Grünewald were active in Mainz, not far from Hindemith's own

---

[68] Benn to Hindemith, 17 August 1932, in ibid., p. 64.

[69] Hindemith to Benn, 20 August 1932, in ibid., p. 77–78.

[70] Ibid., p. 78. As a response to what he felt to be the overriding influence of the Russian literary commissars Benn writes in his essay *Die neue literarische Saison* of 1931 that *To create art, whether it be Egyptian falcons or the novels of Hamsun, means from the standpoint of the artist to exclude life, to narrow it down, yes, to combat it, in order to give it style.* Translated by Eugene Jolas, in E. B. Ashton, ed., *Primal Vision: Selected Writings of Gottfried Benn*, p. 42.

place of origin, suggests that from an early stage in his operatic deliberations Hindemith sought a topic relevant to him personally[71]. His initial enthusiasm for the St. Gall project is evident from a letter he penned to Schott on the very same day as the letter to Benn above; after dismissing Benn's Weizenprojekt as not *rich* [*ergiebig*] enough, Hindemith goes on to mention, tongue-in-cheek, *a promising idea, which in its Germanic, upright* [*biederen*], *highly-tragic and deeply felt manner would be perfect to quicken heartbeats in your publishing house, from the youngest errand-boy to the oldest shopkeeper.*[72] Although he had not yet decided on its musical efficacy, Hindemith assured Benn at the end of August that the subject presented *a theme which today is not irrelevant*[73], *Charlemagne, the confrontation of the waning Roman culture and that of the barbarians.*[74] St. Gall interested Benn at first, but by September he was questioning Hindemith's concern with historical topics:

Concerning your last letter I have not yet found a good answer, neither St. Gall nor Charlemagne have come to me yet. Something modern would be better. In a time when so many interesting things are happening – to be historic, is that good?[75]

In the figure of Mathias Grünewald Hindemith was also able to find correspondences with the present day. On 26 September his publishers advised Hindemith that *With Grünewald the peasant wars and the Renaissance would be possible as good parallels to the present time.*[76] Since

---

[71] Rudolf Stephan, *Zum Verständnis der Oper Mathis der Maler*, Hindemith-Jahrbuch 1990/XIX, p. 16–17.

[72] Hindemith to Ludwig and Willy Strecker, 30 August 1932, in Benn, *Briefwechsel mit Paul Hindemith*, p. 120.

[73] Hindemith to Benn, 20 August 1932, in ibid., p. 79.

[74] Hindemith to Benn, 31 August 1932, in ibid., p. 80.

[75] Benn to Hindemith, 15 September 1932, in ibid., p. 67.

[76] Willy Strecker to Hindemith, 26 September 1932, in ibid., p. 121–122. The original idea seems to have been that of Franz Willms, a reader for the Schott firm. Hindemith's own roots in the area around Frankfurt am Main also may have increased his enthusiasm for the Grünewald story, which is set in nearby Mainz; see Rudolf Stephan, *Zum Verständnis der Oper Mathis der Maler*, p. 16–17.

there is a gap in Benn's correspondence to Hindemith from September 1932 to October 1933, it is impossible to say for certain what the poet's position on this subject might have been. Nonetheless, Hindemith's communications to Schott indicate that Benn was unreceptive to any of Hindemith's suggestions, and the tone of his writing demonstrates that Hindemith was quite upset at the poet's lack of interest:

A man of good breeding does not indeed say »It's enough to make me throw up«, but all the same it is. I sit here like a dried-up spinster. Benn just won't catch fire. By being so overcritical he gets nowhere. He is straining for all he's worth, and something will doubtless emerge, but how long will one have to wait for it? The St. Gallen affair apparently doesn't appeal to him strongly enough, and it's the same with Gutenberg and Grünewald. He is still racking his brains – one must just wait and see what happens. In desperation I have decided to lay the eggs for myself. After all, I know what I want, and these poets have never been able to write the words until I have written out in minute detail what they need to do.[77]

Thus Hindemith concluded to compose his own libretto, but not before exploring the possibility of working with other poets, notably Carl Zuckmayer and Ernst Penzoldt[78]. Yet the cooling of relations with Benn

---

[77] Hindemith to Ludwig and Willy Strecker, 10 October 1932, in Hindemith, *Selected Letters of Paul Hindemith*, p. 63. The fact that Benn was even given a monetary advance in expectation of a text must have sharpened the frustration of Hindemith and his publishers. Negotiating with Willy Strecker nearly two years later for a similar advance for *Mathis der Maler*, Hindemith would have to assure his publisher that there would be no repeat of the Benn episode: *If you consider what trouble and expense we would have had with a »proper« librettist before being so far advanced with a text as we now are with ours, this concession should not fall too hard on you. True, in expectation of a text on a previous occasion we flung an unduly large sum of money into Benn's jaws (shame on him), and owing to the political climate this sum cannot be recovered through »Das Unaufhörliche« (its turn will come again!) – that is regrettable. But the new opera will of course make up for that and, besides, I am writing the opera score myself and delivering the piano arrangement complete – this will save a few thousands.* Hindemith to Willy Strecker, 29 July 1934, in ibid., p. 81.

[78] The correspondence between Hindemith and Zuckmayer (artists who developed a close relationship in later years) has been published and annotated by Giselher

must have been disagreeable to Hindemith in light of their close professional and personal association over the previous two years. His disappointment in Benn's lack of enthusiasm is understandable, for Hindemith surely felt that an opera subject concerning the artist and his relationship to society would have been highly appropriate for a writer who had made artistic autonomy a central concern of his prose.

In the early months of 1933 Benn embraced the newly risen Nazi regime. As he began in April to issue a flurry of polemical essays for radio and for print declaring his allegiance to the new government, Hindemith wrote to Gertrud of his worry that Benn would follow in the tracks the pianist Wilhelm Backhaus, who also had declared himself

---

Schubert and Gunther Nickel in *Paul Hindemith – Carl Zuckmayer: Briefwechsel*, Zuckmayer-Jahrbuch (1) 1998, p. 9–118. Hindemith had considered a collaboration with Zuckmayer as early as 1927 (his address appears in Hindemith's pocket diary shortly after he had relocated to Berlin from Frankfurt am Main), although the first concrete evidence of serious discussion between the two comes from January of 1932, during the period in which the composer and Benn were seemingly unable to agree on a suitable subject for an opera. Ludwig Strecker had reported to Hindemith on 18 January that Zuckmayer has *a burning desire to write a stage work with you and only with you.* On 22 January Hindemith replied that *Naturally, I would gladly undertake something with Zuckmayer (despite the doubts, who doesn't have these!). That it has not happened yet is surely not my fault, for I again eagerly pressed him about it last summer – however he gave no reaction. I will look for him soon in Berlin.* The conversation mentioned by Hindemith was probably that which took place two days after he had seen Zuckmayer's *Hauptmann von Köpenick* on 13 July 1931. See Schubert and Nickel, *Paul Hindemith – Carl Zuckmayer: Briefwechsel*, p. 13–15. Letter from Hindemith to Ludwig and Willy Strecker, 22 January 1932, in Benn, *Briefwechsel mit Paul Hindemith*, p. 116. It is possible that Hindemith toyed with other ideas for operatic projects as far back as 1931, in the midst of work upon *Das Unaufhörliche*. A letter of 1 May 1931 from Ludwig Strecker (on a business trip in the United States) to Hindemith suggests that Strecker was on the lookout for possible librettists, and had obtained a favorable response from John Erskine. That Erskine's offer of a text was not taken seriously by Hindemith comes across in the composer's reply to Strecker later that month: *Mit dieser Isolde ist natürlich nichts anzufangen.* Qtd. in Zabrsa, *Hindemiths Opernprojekte*, p. 52–53. For the collaboration of Hindemith and Ernst Penzoldt see Gunther Nickel/Susanne Schaal, *Die Dokumente zu einem gescheiterten Opernplan von Paul Hindemith und Ernst Penzoldt* in this volume, p. 88–253.

for the new government early in the year: *Benn seems to have lost his wits* [...] *After a couple of months I would like to see his disappointment. Perhaps he will go as far as Backhaus, who has suddenly turned up in America under the name William Bachhaus and announces on his concert-posters: »At the special request of the Chancellor of the Reich. The Chancellor has endorsed his appearance.«*[79] Hindemith concludes by denigrating Benn as a *Leibhautundharnpoet* [roughly, skin-and-urinary-tract-poet, a sarcastic reference to Benn's medical background].
The resignation of such prominent figures as Heinrich Mann and Käthe Kollwitz from the Prussian Academy of Arts, to which Benn had recently been appointed, only magnified Benn's resentment against those who in his view were threatening the autonomy of the artist[80]. Upon receiving a letter from Klaus Mann, the older son of Thomas Mann and one of the exiled literary émigrés, which questioned Benn's decision to accommodate the new regime, Benn responded decisively in an open letter entitled *Antwort an die literarischen Emigranten*:
First, I have to tell you that many experiences in the past weeks have convinced me that German events can be discussed only with those who have witnessed them in Germany [...] *but the refugees who went abroad cannot. For they have missed the opportunity to feel the concept of »the people« – a concept so alien to them – grow within themselves, not as a*

[79] Paul to Gertrud Hindemith, 25 May 1933, in Hindemith, *»Das private Logbuch«*, p. 100–101. Benn read his essay *Der neue Staat und Die Intellektuellen* on the radio on 24 April 1933, which was reprinted in the *Berliner Börsen-Zeitung* the next day; a further essay on art and national duty appeared in the *Berliner Tageblatt* on April 30, and the famous *Antwort an die literarischen Emigranten* followed on May 25. As for Backhaus, he gave a concert in Berlin on June 1 of music by Schumann, Beethoven, Chopin, Schubert, and Liszt; posters containing the cited propaganda appeared advertising this event.

[80] Mann and Kollwitz had supported a proclamation agitating for a union of the socialists and communists to oppose the Nazis in the elections of 5 March. Under pressure from the Nazis, the Academy accepted their resignations on 15 February, and on 20 February Benn participated in a discussion of the resignations with the remaining members in which he stressed the need to purge the Academy of political motivations. See Alter, *Gottfried Benn: The Artist and Politics (1910–1934)*, p. 79–81.

thought but as a living experience, not as an abstraction but as condensed nature. They have missed their chance to perceive the concept of nationalism – which your letter, too, employs so derogatorily and scornfully – in its true motion, as a genuine, convincingly expressed phenomenon; they have missed seeing history, form-laden, image-laden, at its conceivably tragic but surely fated work. And here I do not mean the spectacular side of events, the impressionistic fascination of torchlight and music, but the inner process, the creative impact that tended to cause a goading, human transformation even in the initially restive observer.[81]

The crucial moment, perhaps, came on 13 March when at a meeting of the literary section of the Prussian Academy Benn suggested that all members sign the following statement:

Are you prepared, under recognition of the changed historical situation, to place yourself further at the disposal of the Prussian Academy of Art? An affirmative answer to this question excludes public, political activity against the government and obliges you loyally to work for the missions of the nation which statutorily devolve upon the Academy.[82]

Although Benn's anti-Marxist bias and concern for the overt politicization of art assisted in his drift toward the right, the sometimes subtle tendencies in his work toward a type of transcendent, mystical purity of expression were not incompatible with the National Socialists' undeniable power to frame identity in anti-intellectual, chauvinistically national terms. Benn's principle of artistic autonomy, which always had concerned itself with metaphysical purity rather than the concrete, prevented him from recognizing the direct social implications of the new state.

At first, Hindemith's willingness to continue his work under the new regime had less to do with his indifference than with his conviction that

[81] Benn, *Answer to the Literary Emigrants*, translated by E. B. Ashton, in E. B. Ashton, ed., *Primal Vision*, p. 46–47. The letter (originally dated 24 May 1933) was subsequently published in the German press and disseminated over the radio under the direction of Goebbels.

[82] Qtd. in Alter, *Gottfried Benn: The Artist and Politics (1910–1934)*, p. 83.

the Nazi government, like most of the previous Weimar governments, would be short-lived. He could still teach on a limited basis, his music was still published, and he was allowed to travel abroad. As the new government consolidated its hold on power, Hindemith did not feel his position to be endangered; he even envisioned the possibility of influencing German music education and performance through the official Nazi organs. In early 1934 Hindemith felt confident enough to expect a commission for a far-reaching restructuring of music education in Germany. A letter addressed to Willy Strecker in February 1934 illustrates Hindemith's paradoxical desire at this time to cooperate with, and even participate in, the new government's cultural program while preserving a degree of artistic freedom for himself:

Quite a lot is going on in Berlin. I am still »conferring« with all sorts of higher-ups in the Arbeitsfront, the Dopolavoro and the Arbeitsdienstlager. The outcome will be that I shall make suggestions for a very far-reaching musical education system for the German people and, if things continue as they have now begun and these people continue to show goodwill towards me, I hope to provide the impetus for vast plans and to cooperate in putting them into effect [...] [I did not] *show any enthusiasm for a kind of propaganda concert Havemann wanted to promote, because I am very much against seeing my music constantly used as a cover for one bungler after another, and altogether against always presenting contemporary music separately, as if it were something extravagant and off the beaten track. They come up creeping from all sides, but I am in favour of selling my carcase dear.*[83]

A few days later Hindemith reported having had a discussion with an official of the Arbeitsdienst about his educational proposal. *Our whole conversation will probably be rushed through all the newspapers at*

---

[83] Hindemith to Willy Strecker, 5 February 1934, in Hindemith, *Selected letters of Paul Hindemith*, p. 76. He goes on to report that he is preparing to give a concert in Lübeck which is being organized by the »Kampfbund für deutsche Kultur«, led by party members and involving the performance of some Hitler Youth.

home and abroad, he boasts, *and I believe that this and subsequent discussions, and written proposals still to follow, will provide the basis for the most ambitious programme of popular musical education (together with appropriate composer training) the world has ever seen. One can literally have the musical enlightenment of millions in one's hands. I myself intend, as before, to steer clear of any official position, trusting to achieve all the more from the background* [...][84]

In this year Hindemith was even nominated to the advisory committee for the Reichsmusikkammer, an organ which he still felt capable of conducting its business with a degree of independence[85]. *I intend*, Hindemith tells Willy Strecker in November,

before long to see what I can do with the Kammer. At the moment, unfortunately, all the Kammer is doing is seeking to ingratiate itself with the party, and on that account one does not wish to be too active. But I am very much in credit, and the worst that can happen is that we shall have to wait a little while[86]. He did not have to wait long before the very public controversies surrounding the premiere of his *Mathis der Maler* symphony damaged his prospects for further government undertakings[87]. Even if the idea about Grünewald had been only one of several possibilities for an opera in 1932, it is clear that in later years Hindemith would come to identify himself with the artist who felt himself buffeted on all sides by social conflict and in the end retreated into his art.

---

[84] Hindemith to Willy Strecker, 9 February 1934, in ibid., p. 77.

[85] Kemp, *Hindemith*, p. 28–29.

[86] With some weariness, Hindemith reports in the same letter that *The missing Benn rang me yesterday. He is apparently seeking to renew contact. After all his carefully nurtured plans have come to grief, he now intends to hire himself out to the Reichswehr.* Hindemith to Willy Strecker, 11 November 1934, in *Selected Letters of Paul Hindemith*, p. 82–83.

[87] The events surrounding Furtwängler's conducting of *Mathis* and the ensuing controversy are too well-known to be recounted here. A good summary of the principal events with reproductions of significant press coverage is in Andres Briner, et al., *Paul Hindemith: Leben und Werk in Bild und Text*, p. 140–148. See also Zenck, *Zwischen Boykott und Anpassung*, for a detailed account of Hindemith's continued attempts to regain his standing in German musical life before his permanent departure for Switzerland in September 1938.

Conclusions

It is tempting, perhaps, to suggest that the theme of artistic autonomy and »inner emigration« (to use a well-worn phrase) developed in *Mathis der Maler* was one result of Hindemith's association with Benn, in whose works similar themes had been prominent. It is undeniable that the futility of temporal political struggles forms an important thread of the narrative of Mathis; one might consider, for example, Ursula's entreaty to Albrecht in the fifth tableau of the opera:

Like no other prince you have the power and wisdom
to lead the world of the new belief with strength. You can bring together the quarrelers,
bring form out of confusion.
An end must come to this unprofitable war.
Among the people hate increases daily.
You see how obstinacy rises out of faith.
Where words no longer suffice, the sword shall prevail.
The most peaceable men are caught up in the struggle.
To that they see as Truth they give themselves over blindly, looking neither left nor right.
They abandon what is of most value on this earth and go off to war.

Mathis himself comes to this realization in the conclusion to the sixth tableau, as Albrecht (in the guise of St. Paul) reproves him (in the guise of St. Anthony) for his abandonment of the artist's mission. *Sit down with me*, Paul tells him, *and I shall tell you where you went wrong.*

You lived in the house of your work, and there you were sheltered.
You were led by mastery, study of your forefathers.
To see farther than others you soon stepped out of the fold which would have confined you. Because you stood alone you began to falter.
You were touched by a new, sweeter art from foreign lands which held out new promise.

Stormy winds blew through our holy Church which nearly ripped you from the earth.
You fled to penury, doubts plagued you.
You surrounded yourself with misery and sickness.
Faith and inconstancy struggled ever greater within you.
Where there is only war and blood, art can have no place.
The infirmity of the times possessed you, and you felt yourself responsible and threw yourself into the fray.

Anthony (Mathis):
Yes, in order to serve my God I was willing to sacrifice my life and blood for my people.
Why was it all in vain?

Paul (Albrecht):
You were given the extraordinary gift of painting.
You were ungrateful, unfaithful, as you brazenly betrayed your godly gifts.
You betrayed your people even as you went to them, renouncing your mission.
Return then to both: let all that you create be an offering to the Lord, and he shall be present in all of it.

While the above dialogue certainly contains suggestive parallels with themes of artistic autonomy prominent in Benn's writings, it would certainly be disingenuous to argue that the poet alone directly inspired Hindemith to compose an opera with these ideas in mind. Hindemith's disillusionment with the political appropriation of art by the left had already set in by the summer of 1929 (especially with respect to *Lehrstück* and *Der Lindberghflug*) and would simmer for nearly a year before he sought any serious collaboration with Benn. Furthermore, the professional relationship between Hindemith and Benn was a lopsided one: even with regard to the content and structure of the poetry to *Das Unaufhörliche*, Benn comes off in his correspondence as being clearly the subservient partner, despite his later suggestions to the contrary. What Hindemith sought in the summer of 1930 was not a philosophical guide but rather an artist who already shared some of Hindemith's views concerning the nature of the relationship of art to politics. Yet Hindemith in all likelihood was initially familiar only with the public, prosaic Benn of 1929–1930, the Benn of *Können Dichter die Welt ändern?* and the controversies with the left, the Benn who disdained the subjugation of art to politics; not necessarily with the private, poetic Benn of *Geologie des Ich* and the proposed *Die weiße Rasse*. That the two artists would drift apart was inevitable in light of the fundamental difference between them: while they shared a common interest in the centrality of art and its independent status, Hindemith could not participate in Benn's nihilistic vision.

What, then, was the true significance of the Benn collaboration to Hindemith's artistic career? Was Benn for Hindemith a latter-day Grünewald, a visionary artist who embodied the political aloofness epitomized in *Mathis der Maler*? Or was the association little more than a convenient and temporary reaction against the excesses of the left? The answer, I believe, lies between the two extremes. If we consider the possibility that two parallel concerns exist in the Hindemith of the early 1930s, on the one hand a distaste for the political appropriation of art, and on the other a real compulsion for relevance to society, then we may conclude that with respect to the former Benn was particularly important to Hindemith as a voice against the politicization of the artist[88].

[88] That Hindemith may have harbored these potentially contradictory tendencies simultaneously has been suggested to me by David Neumeyer. Dieter Rexroth, in a similar vein, argues that both tendencies can be found in Hindemith's stage works extending from the first version of *Cardillac* (1926) through *Mathis der Maler*, *Die Harmonie der Welt*, and the revised version of *Cardillac* (1952). The latter revision is a particularly good example of Hindemith's continued concern with the social position of the artist well after the chaotic events of the 1930s had played themselves out. Specifically,

Most importantly, Benn seemed to place art itself at the center of his efforts, an art which was unanswerable to the demands of the partisans of right and left. This is the common thread which links such exceedingly different works as *Das Unaufhörliche* and the *Plöner Musiktag*: Hindemith's desire to keep music and the act of music-making, not politics, at the heart of his enterprise. It may be argued, naturally, that this centrality of art within the context of Hindemith's political centrism represents an ideology of its own, a vision of society which, while distinct from the collectivism of the left and the chauvinism of the right, is not different from these in kind. Yet in a political and cultural atmosphere characterized by well-defined fault lines between various ideologies, the vision of art shared by Hindemith and Benn in the early 1930s was clearly one of autonomy from the brutal political struggles of the late Weimar Republic.

---

the inserted material from Lully's *Phaeton*, notably Phaeton's fatal fall from the heavens in Apollo's chariot, can be seen not only as an oblique reference to the thematic of *Lehrstück* and *Der Lindberghflug*, but also as a symbol of the disastrous consequences of an artist having contempt for the society of which he is a part. See Rexroth, *Paul Hindemith und Brechts Lehrstück*, p. 51–52.

Andres Briner

Im Zeichen Friedrich Nietzsches

Zur Zusammenarbeit von Gottfried Benn und Paul Hindemith für das Oratorium *Das Unaufhörliche*

Paul Hindemiths und Gottfried Benns Oratorium *Das Unaufhörliche*, 1931 entstanden und von Otto Klemperer in Berlin uraufgeführt, ist ein vielschichtigeres Werk, als die meisten Zeitgenossen glaubten. Hinter dem Schwung und der Konstruktivität der Musik verbergen sich Probleme. Anläßlich der Schweizer Erstaufführung unter Volkmar Andreae, 1932 in Zürich, waren sie noch nicht sichtbar. Die erste gültige Wiedergabe des Werks auf Tonträger, um eine von Benn selbst gelesene Einführung bereichert, ermöglicht neue Sichten.

Gegen Ende des Ersten Weltkriegs erhielt der 1895 in Hanau geborene, spät einberufene Komponist Paul Hindemith, der in diesem Gemetzel seinen eigenen Vater und einen engen Freund verloren hatte, von seinem Militärkommandanten einen Nietzsche-Band zu Geschenk; das war in jenen Tagen, in denen eine Vergeistigung der bereits deutlichen Niederlage gesucht wurde, nichts Außergewöhnliches. August Strindberg, dessen Dichtungen er als Schüler zu imitieren versuchte, Friedrich Nietzsche und zeitgenössische Dichter des Expressionismus, vor allem Else Lasker-Schüler, Ernst Wilhelm Lotz und Georg Trakl, waren Leitsterne über seinen Gedanken und frühesten Vertonungen. Bertolt Brecht, mit dem in Zusammenarbeit 1929 das *Lehrstück* entstand, brachte eine kurze Erweiterung; sie barst bald an grundsätzlichen Meinungsverschiedenheiten über Sinn und Zweck von Kunst in (jener) Gegenwart.

Enttäuscht von Brecht und seinem Gesinnungsgenossen, dem Komponisten Hanns Eisler, wandte sich der Komponist Benn zu. Er kannte des

Dichters Gegenposition zur sozial »engagierten« Literatur. Er hatte alte und neuere Polemiken gegen Benn verfolgt und dessen Antworten geschätzt. Nun fühlte er sich ihm verbunden und wünschte, mit ihm zu arbeiten. Hindemith war damals 35jährig, Benn 44jährig und, trotz Hindemiths Erfolgen als Bratschensolist, Organisator und auflüpfischer Komponist, in Deutschland der bekanntere.

Tagessituation und Hintergrund

Die im weitern Sinn »politische« Konstellation der Zusammenarbeit Hindemiths mit Benn ist deutlich. Weniger sichtbar sind Rückverbindungen, die sie beide, auf verschiedenen Geleisen, hatten und die sie sich wechselseitig kaum eingestanden. Ihnen nachzugehen, wird dadurch erschwert, daß die Wirkung der Schriften Friedrich Nietzsches, vor allem der Spätschriften, in den zwanziger Jahren bereits weit verästelt war und daß schon damals Vereinfachungen geläufig waren, in denen der indirekte Einfluß den direkten überwiegt. Im Mai 1939 komponierte Hindemith drei Männerchöre auf Nietzsche-Texte, ohne für sie ein neues Idiom zu entwickeln. Er brauchte es deshalb nicht zu tun, da er indirekt Nietzsche mehrfach begegnet war.

Im Bestreben, Gottfried Benn für einen Text zu gewinnen, vertonte Hindemith drei Gedichte des Dichters für Männerchor a cappella. Welche sind es? *Fürst Kraft* (1926), *Vision des Mannes* (1927) und *Du mußt Dir alles geben* (1929). Alle drei thematisieren männliches Selbstgefühl, das erste allerdings satirisch. Alle drei gehen nicht auf alltägliche Fragen und Aufgaben ein, sondern zielen auf Unalltägliches, Übergeordnetes. Offenbar versuchte der Komponist, den Dichter in dieser Richtung zu unterstützen, ja zu lenken.

Diese drei Gedichttexte erhellen sich in ihrem zeitlichen Umfeld. Eng zu ihnen gehören die Gedichte *Regressiv* (1927), *Was singst Du denn* (1927), *Mediterran* (1927), *Die hyperämischen Reiche* (1928), alle drei vor dem für und mit Hindemith geschriebenen Text *Das Unaufhörliche* entstanden, sowie die Gedichte *Mann*, *Dennoch die Schwerter halten* und *Sils Maria* (diese drei von 1933) – das letzte ein wenig verschlüsselter Nietzsche-Hommage.

Im kurzen Vergleich mit der Lyrik Benns aus den zehner und frühen zwanziger Jahren wird es sofort deutlich: Der offene Kampf und Krampf, die bare Not, die Geilheit von Männern und Frauen, das Makabre von Totensärgen und Krankheiten sind gewichen; der Arzt Benn, der soviel unsäglich Trauriges sah und behandelte, hat sich vom Schriftsteller (der von 1916 an als »Dr. Rönne« schrieb), getrennt. Benns Lyrik erfuhr eine thematische und stilistische Verschiebung, die sich sicher aus seiner eigenen Entwicklung, auch aus der Jugend in seine mittleren Jahre, herleitete. Diese Lyrik ist seit etwa 1926 gezähmter, aber auch hintergründiger, ja hinterhältiger. Weil die Motive nicht mehr jener Tagesrealität entstammen, die für Benn sekundär geworden ist, sind die Gedichte mehr aufeinander angewiesen. Mythologisches will verstanden, Anspielungen wollen geklärt werden.

Der Arzt Benn bezeichnete den dichterischen Rückzug von der Tagesrealität selber mit »Regression«; er verstand sie nicht nur negativ – das macht schon die hohe Produktivität deutlich –, aber als Zeichen eines (oft zurückblickenden) Eintauchens – das Bild des »Tauchens« drängt sich schon deshalb auf, weil im Umkreis dieser Vorstellungen fließendes Wasser, aber vor allem das Meer als Bildmotiv häufig wird.

Schon das Gedicht *Regressiv* von 1927 besingt das Dunkel der »Thalassischen Regression«, also das Eintauchen ins Dunkle des Unbewußten. In den beiden ersten Strophen nimmt der Text Abschied von Menschen, Göttern und Tieren, *von Muscheln wachsen die Augen zu*. An die Stelle der kleinen Szenen und Grotesken des täglichen Lebens sind *Spaltungen* und *Niederbrüche* getreten, die nicht so leicht zu orten sind, die aber unzweifelhaft in der Vergangenheit liegen. In der letzten Strophe ist der Styx, der Eingang zur griechischen Unterwelt, erreicht; der Mensch der Gegenwart geht in ein (sein?) mythisches Präteritum ein.

Im Gedicht *Was singst Du denn* nimmt der Rückschritt des Individuums

einen dramatischeren Gang an (auch in den Gedichten *Trunkene Flut* und *Sieh die Sterne, die Fänge*). Das regressive Subjekt ist jetzt deutlich männlich. Auch hier endet die innere Reise in Meerattributen, in Fjorden, Sunden und *der See*. Daß die imaginäre Szene das klassische Griechenland ist, macht schon die zweite Zeile deutlich; zu Beginn der zweiten Strophe tritt mit der *Sage* die überlieferte Mythologie ins Blickfeld. In der dritten Strophe wird *des Mannes Qualenlied* nicht gesungen, aber genannt; der leidende Heros scheint der König Tantalus zu sein, der seinen eigenen Sohn (Pelops) schlachtete und deshalb dazu verdammt ist, im Wasser stehend zu dürsten. Durch sein Verbrechen an sich selber gekettet, erleidet er unaufhörliche Qual; der Leser vernimmt den *Fluch- und Felsenschrei, die alte Sage der See.*
Zwar waren Gottfried Benn und Paul Hindemith 1927 noch nicht miteinander bekannt, aber beide hatten sich bereits mit dem seit dem Kriegsende hochaktuellen Thema der Rechtfertigung von Morden beschäftigt (in der Weimarer Republik nahm es gelegentlich, aber nicht bei Benn und Hindemith, die Züge des Verdachts einer »Ermordung« Deutschlands, also der »Dolchstoßlegende« an). Hindemith hatte in der Erstfassung der Oper *Cardillac* auf einen Text von Ferdinand Lion das Problem auf seine Weise »gelöst« – nach dem Zweiten Weltkrieg wollte ihm diese Art der Mordrechtfertigung nicht mehr behagen.
Unverkennbar lebt in den Vorstellungen von der Rechtfertigung der Gewalt auch Friedrich Nietzsche fort. Benns Lyrik der späten zwanziger Jahre hatte sich, in ihrer »Regression«, den *Betrachtungen eines Unzeitgemäßen* und den *Dionysos-Dithyramben* angenähert (die kurzgliedrigen Zeilen der letztern kehren in vielen Gedichten wieder, auch im *Unaufhörlichen*). Gedanklich wurden die Ideen um die *Moral als Widernatur* wichtig. Das Antichristliche dieses Vorstellungskreises liegt auf der Hand. Der Abschnitt *Zur Psychologie des Künstlers* aus den *Betrachtungen eines Unzeitgemäßen* mag auf Benn einen besonders großen Einfluß ausgeübt haben. In diesem Abschnitt wird *der Rausch* als Vorbedingung des *aesthetischen Tuns und Schauens* geschildert. Jene Rauschzustände,

die sich aus geschlechtlicher Erregung, aus Fest und Sieg herleiten, gehen dort ohne moralische Skrupel in den *Rausch der Grausamkeit* und den *Rausch der Zerstörung* über. Ferdinand Lions Libretto des *Cardillac* hatte die Mordtat des Goldschmieds aus solchen Verbindungen in Friedrich Nietzsches *Unzeitgemäßen Betrachtungen* heraus gerechtfertigt. Der den Cardillac als Mörder identifizierende Goldschmied zeigt auf ihn mit den Worten: *Trinker, kommt zum Rausch des Bluts!*

Von »hyperämischen Reichen«

Das räuberische Verhalten, wie es der von Lion entworfene *Cardillac* aufzeigt, wird bei Nietzsche, allerdings ausgesprochen dichterisch, mit der Gier von Raubtieren verglichen. In den *Dionysos-Dithyramben* sind *des Dichters Sehnsüchte* sowohl *adlerhaft* wie *pantherhaft*. Das Motiv der Tierähnlichkeit des einsamen Menschen, besonders des Künstlers, wird bei Benn in mehreren Gedichten aufgegriffen. Im Beginn von Nietzsches *Dithyramben* liest man vom Dichter als *Tier, ein listiges, raubendes, schleichendes, nach Beute lüstern*. Hier öffnet sich jene Frage nach dem »Übergang« vom Tier zum Menschen, auf die Gedichte und Prosa eine Antwort suchen.
Im Gedicht *Das hyperämische Reich* steht der *kunstverkündende Mann*, wie beim Philosophen, in südlichen Gefilden, von *Tiernacht* und *Mythenmeer*, auch von einem (ebenfalls von Nietzsche übernommenen) Löwen umgeben. Die Gesetze der Wüste haben jene der westlichen Zivilisation abgelöst. Allerdings ist dieses Gedicht, wie mir Thomas Ehrsam mitteilt, dem Kunsthändler Alfred Flechtheim gewidmet, der Henri Rousseau und Paul Klee propagierte, sodaß sich Urwaldmotive auch aus einer persönlichen Beziehung herleiten. Nach dem Zweiten Weltkrieg stellt Benn *Steppenleben* mitten im verwüsteten Berlin fest; die Zeit der großen Projektionen in die Ferne ist dann, aber nur fürs erste, vorbei.
Benns Vorstellung von Ländern mit *Hyperämie*, also Menschen, die den *Rausch des Blutes* verstärkt wahrnehmen, ihm vielleicht unterworfen

sind, entstammt heidnischen Vorstellungen, wie sie vom Philosophen gepflegt wurden. Das *Restgehirn* dieses Gedichts ist jenes, welches das Christentum im Menschen zurückgelassen hat. Das Individuum mit solch reduziertem Denkorgan bedarf der Stimulantien, die es über seine Beschränkungen hinausheben. Das Triumphierende in solcher an sich desperater Lage ist, im Vorgriff auf den Text des *Unaufhörlichen*, das *Immer und Nie*. Die *Übergänge mit monistischem Ziel* in der dritten Strophe der *Hyperämischen Reiche* beziehen sich, wie Benns autobiographische Schriften zeigen, auf die Frage nach einem gemeinsamen Prinzip für Tiere und Menschen, also hier: für den *kunstverkündenden Mann* und den Löwen. Die Frage streifte, wenige Jahre vor dem Barbarentum des Nationalsozialismus, gefährliche, übergeordnete Probleme. Auch in dem von Paul Hindemith vertonten Gedicht *Vision des Mannes* liest man eingangs die Zeichen von Nietzsches Idee der Dekadenz in der Zivilisation: *stumm und namenlos* ist er, *im Fluch des Bannes morbider Züge* groß geworden. Dieser Mann ist, zivilisatorisch und kulturell, auf dem *Abstieg*; er verklärt ihn selber als *Abstiegsglück*. Er schwelgt in Träumereien vom Herbst des Jahrs, von Trauben, Kelter und Zaum, und zerschellt dann *im namenlosen Raum*.

Dieses Gedicht kann aus der Perspektive von Benns Pessimismus, aber auch seines Optimismus gelesen werden (Hindemith tat das letztere). Zwar sind die *Häupter* auf diesem Erdenrund *todeswund*, und einen (christlichen) Glauben kennt dieser Mann nicht mehr, aber gerade diese Eigenschaften zeichnen ihn aus und verschaffen ihm eine Aura des Kühnen. Die Bildmetaphern gewinnen in der zweiten und dritten Strophe an Größe. Dieser einesteils von Morbidität geschlagene Mann verbündet sich andernteils mit den Elementen Feuer und Wasser und vermag so der Erde *Antipod* zu werden. Ein Heroismus des Untergangs ergibt sich, wie er auch in Oswald Spenglers Hauptwerk *Der Untergang des Abendlands* beschworen wird.

Im gleichen Ideenkreis bewegt sich ein anderes der (teilweise) von Hindemith vertonten Gedichte, *Du mußt dir Alles geben* von 1929. Der Einzelne, *der große Verlasser*, ist zugleich der vom fürsorglichen Gott und von Hoffnung auf ein Jenseits Verlassene. Er soll zurücknehmen: *nimm die Olivenhaine, dir die Säulen zurück*; jener Einzelne, der die *süße Stunde* des Alterns erreicht, soll bewußt sich alles, auch den südlichen Horizont, selbst verdanken. Hindemith hebt, indem er nur die zweite Strophe komponiert, die Gottferne hervor (*Götter geben dir nicht*); die Verlassenheit des empfindenden Menschen hebt er in zarten Melismen hervor.

Das *Altern* ist bei Benn in diesen Jahren assoziiert mit der Spätzeit der westlichen Kultur. Benn hegte die Hoffnung, aus dem Niedergang seiner eigenen Umwelt und Zeit werde ein neuer, anthropologisch besserer Menschentyp entstehen – wobei die Attribute, die er ihm zudichtete, wechseln. *Der grosse Verlasser* dieses Gedichts scheint dem Untergang geweiht, aber diesen zugleich, wohl im Sinn von Hindemiths Vertonung, zu sublimieren.

Ganz anders dagegen das ebenfalls von Hindemith vertonte Gedicht *Fürst Kraft!* (im Originaldruck *Krafft*) von 1926, das noch Benns früher Lyrik, zeitlich und inhaltlich, nahesteht. In diesem Gedicht mokiert sich Benn, fast mit einem Augenzwinkern zu Brecht, über das, was Ibsen eine *Stütze der Gesellschaft* genannt hätte. Die letzten Zeilen, *neben der Industrie alles Schöne, Gute und Wahre* sprechen Hohn auf das, was diese *Nachrufpersönlichkeit* darstellte oder darstellen wollte. Anne Clark Fehn, die Herausgeberin von Gottfried Benns Briefwechsel mit Paul Hindemith im Limes-Verlag, 1978, deutete im Hindemith-Jahrbuch 1976 auf jene zeitkritischen Aspekte, die Hindemith bereitwillig aufgreifen konnte. Sie schildert auch die reziproke, zeitlich eng gestaffelte Arbeit der beiden Künstler am *Unaufhörlichen*.

Das Überindividuelle und seine Gefahr

Im Briefwechsel von Paul und Gertrud Hindemith mit Benn über *Das Unaufhörliche* wird Nietzsche wenig genannt; (im Brief des Dichters an

Gertrud vom 15. April 1931 kommen in Anspielungen die Namen von andern Dichtern vor). Allerdings erwähnt Benn am 6. März 1931 ein kleines Buch über *Nietzsches Zusammenbruch* und meint, daß er daraus *die Stelle in Abteilung Kunst* entnommen habe, die im fertigen Text Nr. 9 betrifft. Aber die Bilder des Librettotextes stammen teils indirekt vom Dichter-Philosophen, teils direkt aus der Lyrik der dreißiger Jahre. Besonders die *Chöre des Rauschs* (Nr. 10), die Benn im April 1931 in der *Götterpartie* vorschlägt, lassen ihre Herkunft leicht erkennen. Im gleichen April spricht Benn in einem andern Brief aus, daß die Worte *Vergänglichkeit von hellen Himmeln* aus *Zarathustra* stammen könnten. Auch dort, bereits bei Nietzsche, *versank das Individuelle.*

Vor dem Nietzsche-Hintergrund wird jenes Terzett (Nr. 15) verständlich, das Benn in seinem Schreiben vom 12. Juli an Hindemith ein *Individualterzett* nennt. In Benns Entwurf noch auffälliger als in der von Hindemith vertonten Fassung, wird die Nähe zu Gedichten wie *Du mußt dir alles geben* und *Vision des Mannes* deutlich. Da hat die *späte Art* des weißen Menschen sich *durchgekämpft durch Tier- und Vormenschmassen* – (Gibt es ein *monistisches Prinzip?*) –, da sind die ausrangierten *Schöpfungsmythen*, die unterschwellig auf ihre Rehabilitierung hoffen (und in jenen Jahren tatsächlich hoffen konnten), da sind dann, in Nr. 16, die Ablehnung des bürgerlichen Wohlbefindens, der bloßen *Geschäfte* und der ausgewaschenen Sentenzen wie: *Edel sei der Mensch, hilfreich und gut.*

Hindemith wollte, als er eine *zynische Figur* als Sänger vorschlug, die Akzente noch heftiger gegen die zerschlissene Bürgermoral setzen, aber offenbar war er mit Benns Text dann doch einverstanden. Die Abwertung des auf relative, also auch auf demokratische und bürgerliche Werte bauenden Menschen, wird auch so deutlich – ohne daß die Autoren diese Konsequenzen bedacht haben.

Die bürgerliche Sattheit wird anschließend in den Zeilen des Männerchors persifliert: *So sprach das Fleisch zu allen Zeiten; nichts gibt es als das Satt- und Glücklichsein!* Wie verhält sich dieser Ausfall gedanklich

zu Nr. 8, zum *Kleinen Marsch*, für den Hindemith aus seiner eigenen Musik zum *Lehrstück* mit Brecht zitiert? Benns Text mit seiner *objektiven* Erwähnung der *Fortschritte der modernen Technik* steht seinem Gedicht *Zwischenreich* nahe, das die Vergnügungen des Normalbürgers nennt und ironisiert. Aber, wie es im Gedicht heißt: *die Massenglücke sind schon tränennah*. Die Zeit der ungestörten Erholung der Stadtmenschen (Benn versuchte, Stadt- und Landmenschen gegeneinander auszuspielen) in Natur und Zivilisation sind vorbei; der *unaufhörliche* Wandel, *Verfall und Wende* (wie es in Nr. 1 heißt), haben für die Auflösung der lebensnotwendigen Ergänzung von Arbeit und Erholung gesorgt. *Kein Ding hat Frieden vor seinem Schwert*: die Gewalt der Wendezeit hat den Frieden illusorisch gemacht. *Das Unaufhörliche* ist auch ein Klagelied auf den verlorenen Frieden bürgerlicher Beschaulichkeit.
Gelegentlich, vor allem im Schreiben Benns an Hindemith vom 20. September 1931, dringt der Jargon der Berliner Umwelt, auch der (früher von Benn so geschätzten) Unterwelt in den Briefwechsel. Da wird von der Frage geschwafelt: *Sollen wir uns fortpflanzen, sollen wir diese Rasse fortpflanzen?* Benns medizinische Praxis für Haut- und Geschlechtskrankheiten und zeitgenössische Schlagworte gehen da eine üble Verbindung ein. Allerdings sinkt dann der Anspruch so tief (*schöne Frauen, das ist doch das Einzige, was wirkt, schöne weiße Frauen*), daß weder durch den Dichter noch den Komponisten die Ausschweifung der Phantasie ernst genommen werden konnte. Kurz darauf, am 19. Mai 1932, spielte Benn mit einem intellektuelleren Gedanken, nämlich für Hindemith eine Rönne-Oper zu schreiben. Dazu ist es nie gekommen. Auch der Plan eines Librettos mit der Prosafigur »Carleton«, eines nach Amerika emigrierten Deutschen, fiel ins Wasser. Darauf spielen der Brief Hindemiths an Benn vom 10. August 1932 und der Brief Benns an Hindemith vom 17. August 1932 (über den *Weizentraum*) an.
Das Libretto zum Oratorium *Das Unaufhörliche* vereinigt etliche gedankliche Strähnen. Zwar kann man seine Haltung als *mythischen*

Idealismus (Heinrich Strobel, 1948) beschreiben, aber dabei bleibt einiges, auch Gefahrenreiches, unerwähnt. Auch Gottfried Benn spricht in einer jetzt auf der Wergo-Aufnahme des Oratoriums enthaltenen Einführung, gelesen 1932 anläßlich einer Aufführung von Teilen des Werks in der Berliner Funkstunde, nicht davon. Der Text berührt sympathisch, er hält aber von jenen Fragen, die Benn damals in seiner Dichtung beschäftigten, einige Distanz. Er hatte zwar mit dem Komponisten nicht den gesamten, teils vulkanischen gedanklichen Hintergrund des Texts besprochen, aber immerhin jene Fragen um Gewalt, um Fortpflanzung, um Entwicklung und *Unaufhörlichkeit* angetönt, die in seinen Gedichten Gestalt gewonnen haben. Von Stalins *Herrschertyp* schreibt er im gleichen etwas saloppen Brief, der die *schönen weißen Frauen* empfiehlt. Offenbar hatte Benn in jenem Zeitpunkt die Witterung verloren für die enormen Gefahren, die jetzt anstanden. Im Brief an Hindemith vom 25. August 1931 meint Benn: *Unaufhörlichkeit wird das Menschheitsgefühl des kommenden Jahrhunderts sein.* Eine vage, aber oft seltsam heroische, wenig kontrollierte Erwartung packt jetzt Benn gelegentlich, die ihn dann für einige Monate dem Nationalsozialismus zugänglich machte.

Angesichts dieser nicht unbedenklichen Lage ist es gut, auf jene Dauerhaftigkeit von Benns Ideen hinzuweisen, welche sich nicht der Zeitlage verdankt. Die Erwartung auf einen Menschen, welcher einem neuen Zeitalter gewachsen sein wird, gab er auch nach dem Zweiten Weltkrieg nicht auf. Noch 1949 schrieb er in der Schrift *Doppelleben*: *Es ist ein neues Erdzeitalter, und Typen, die dieser Mutation nicht gewachsen sind, werden ausscheiden.* Benn sah sich dann, was sicher auch seine Fragwürdigkeit hatte, wieder als Mediziner und Biologen. Wieder laborierte er gedanklich an der ungelösten Frage des *monistischen Prinzips*. Er erkannte, ebenfalls im *Doppelleben*, die Unmöglichkeit eines Verharrens in einem *animalischen* Entwicklungsgedanken. An Nietzsche anknüpfend argumentierte er: *Der europäische Nihilismus: der animalische Entwicklungsgedanke ohne die Ergänzung durch eine anthropologische*

Herrschaftsidee, aber auch dann wollte er auf den eigentlichen Gehalt und damit das Bedenkliche der *Herrschaftsidee* nicht eingehen.
Der Becher Nichts, der dunkle Trank, der Nietzsche-Refrain im *Unaufhörlichen*, klingt heute, in der weniger von Ambivalenzen geprägten Musik, positiver, als er vom Dichter gemeint war. Einen von Benn absichtlich als versöhnlichen Abschluß bereitgestellten Choraltext wollte Hindemith allerdings nicht vertonen. Er mag gespürt haben, daß der Text mit einem christlichen Choral nichts als die strophische Form, aber auch diese nicht eigentlich, gemeinsam hat.

Wolfgang Rathert

Das Unaufhörliche – ein verkanntes Hauptwerk Hindemiths?*

Die Neubewertung des Werkes von Paul Hindemith, die Ende der 1970er Jahre einsetzte und teilweise, so beim Frühwerk, einer Wiederentdeckung gleichkam, ist immer noch nicht abgeschlossen: Denn es hat sich herausgestellt, daß die stilistischen und satztechnischen Konzeptionen Hindemiths komplexer und die Bestimmung ihres geschichtlichen Orts schwieriger zu beurteilen sind, als es seine Anhänger wie seine Verächter zu wissen meinten. Viele der allzu pauschalen Urteile haben sich inzwischen als fragwürdig und oftmals haltlos erwiesen, und das Bild des naiven Handwerkers und anti-intellektuellen Gegenspielers der Wiener Schule trifft nicht einmal mehr die halbe Wahrheit. Doch immer noch gibt es Werke Hindemiths, die sich einer sicheren Beurteilung entziehen, und unter diesen nimmt das Oratorium *Das Unaufhörliche* aus den Jahren 1930/31 zweifellos eine Sonderstellung ein: Zwar ist seine Entstehungsgeschichte durch die Veröffentlichung des Briefwechsels zwischen Hindemith und seinem Textdichter Gottfried Benn gut dokumentiert und seit längerer Zeit bekannt; doch die Komposition selbst ist trotz ihres offensichtlichen Anspruchs immer noch ein relativ »unbekanntes« und vielleicht auch »verkanntes« Hauptwerk Hindemiths.

Man kann eine ganze Reihe von Gründen anführen, warum *Das Unaufhörliche* nicht nur von anderen Kompositionen Hindemiths aus seiner Berliner Zeit verdrängt, sondern in der Rezeption nach 1945 als problematisch empfunden wurde. Der gewichtigste Grund betrifft die Zusam-

* Leicht überarbeitete Fassung eines am 9.11.1996 an der Lübecker Musikhochschule gehaltenen Vortrags.

menarbeit mit Gottfried Benn. Als führender Vertreter einer nachromantischen, jungen Generation von Komponisten der Weimarer Republik, der sich zu einem direkten, gleichermaßen unprätentiösen wie sozialreformerisch engagierten Musikbegriff bekannte, vollzog Hindemith damit eine unvermutete Wendung: Noch 1929 hatte er mit Bertolt Brecht das Baden-Badener *Lehrstück* konzipiert, aufgeführt und damit einen Kulturskandal in der bürgerlichen Presse hervorgerufen; unmittelbar daran anschließend schlug er sich scheinbar unmotiviert auf die Seite des Außenseiters und Nihilisten Gottfried Benn, dessen Poetologie jede soziale Anteilnahme und Relevanz des Kunstwerkes abstritt. Gegen die lapidar-aggressive, ihren Mitteln nach anspruchslose Sprache des *Lehrstücks* setzte Hindemith nun einen »hohen« Tonfall und Gestus, der als Konservatismus oder sogar – wie durch Hanns Eisler – als »bourgeoise Dekadenz« interpretiert und attackiert werden konnte. So leitete *Das Unaufhörliche* noch vor *Mathis der Maler* Hindemiths vieldiskutierte Stilwende ein, und gerade dieses Werk konnte von Teilen der nationalsozialistischen Musikkritik zwanglos als Zeichen der musikalischen und moralischen »Läuterung« Hindemiths begrüßt werden. Vergegenwärtigt man sich zugleich die politische Position Benns, sein kurzzeitiges, aber folgenschweres Bekenntnis zum neuen Regime 1933/34, so gerät *Das Unaufhörliche* in den Ruch einer ideologischen und künstlerischen Verirrung, die Hindemiths ästhetische und politische Desorientierung ausdrückte. Während Hindemith auch nach 1945 ungeachtet seines längst abgekühlten Verhältnisses zu Benn am *Unaufhörlichen* festhielt und es immer wieder aufführte, war für die Kritik im Gefolge Adornos das Werk, sofern es überhaupt noch Beachtung fand, durch das Stigma totalitärer Anfälligkeit moralisch unhaltbar und in seinem stilistischen Ansatz obsolet geworden.

Das Unaufhörliche besitzt zweifellos wesentliche Merkmale eines entschiedenen kompositorischen und ästhetischen Paradigmenwechsels, der über seinen Platz in Hindemiths Oeuvre hinaus die Tendenz der älteren, noch expressionistisch geprägten deutschen Moderne der Zwischenkriegszeit widerspiegelt, romantische Kategorien von »Ausdruck« und »Tiefe« wieder zuzulassen und gleichzeitig auf eine avancierte Klangsprache zu verzichten, so daß Hindemith in den dreißiger Jahren in die künstlerische Nähe des von ihm durchaus geschätzten Hans Pfitzner rücken konnte. (Hindemith ist daher immer auch als Expressionist der »zweiten Generation« zu lokalisieren.) Doch sind die lieb gewordenen Zuordnungen und Klischees – hier der »fortschrittliche« Hindemith im Verbund mit Brecht, dort der »reaktionäre« Hindemith im Verbund mit Benn – ohne weiteres zu rechtfertigen? Versucht man, Hindemiths Übergang von Brecht zu Benn aus der Situation um 1930 zu interpretieren, so verliert der Widerspruch seine attraktive Folgerichtigkeit und macht vielschichtigeren Überlegungen Platz: In ihnen wird sichtbar, daß den Unvereinbarkeiten zwischen Brecht und Benn, zwischen marxistischer Gesellschaftskritik und anti-bürgerlicher Provokation auf der einen und spätbürgerlicher, pessimistischer Zivilisations- und Fortschrittskritik auf der anderen Seite wichtige gemeinsame Positionen gegenüberstehen. Benn wie Brecht sind gleichermaßen scharfe Kritiker der bürgerlichen Kultur der Weimarer Republik in ihrer Attacke des Etablishments der *Börsenbullen und Bänkeljulen* (so Benn in dem Gedicht *Verlauste Schieber* von 1922); beide propagieren die Exklusivität des Künstlers und sein antipodisches Verhältnis zum Staat, und beide reagieren unmittelbar auf die Faszination von Technik und Masse. Kaum zu betonen braucht schließlich die gemeinsame, aus intensiver Nietzsche-Rezeption sich herleitende Ablehnung des Christentums, die Brecht zum Atheisten und Benn zum Nihilisten macht.

Vergleicht man die Texte des *Lehrstück*s und des *Unaufhörlichen* im einzelnen, tritt ein weiteres gemeinsames Motivfeld in der Thematisierung des Individuums hervor, wobei die zentrale Definition der Rolle des Individuums sofort wiederum das Ende der Parallelen markiert: Brecht übt eine politische, von rational-aufklärerischem Anspruch getragene Kritik des dekadenten bürgerlichen Individuums in der Form einer Parabel, die das Kollektiv als geschichtlich notwendige Ablösung fordert. Benn entwirft eine »Geologie« oder »Biographie« des Ich, die den romantischen Gedanken der absoluten Autonomie des Ich stärkt und gleichzeitig irrationalistisch zur »Selbstvernichtung« stilisiert. Benns erster, an Gertrud Hindemith gerichteter Brief vom 22. Mai 1930 berührt diesen Zusammenhang scheinbar en passant, doch in frappierender literarischer Zuspitzung, deren anti-aufklärerischer Impetus durch die Sonnenlicht-Metapher unübersehbar ist:

Oh, gnädige Frau, ferner habe ich manchmal die Empfindung gehabt, als ob man auf die Natur nicht direkt zufahren soll, im Vorbeigehn sieht man an ihr das Beste [...] *Auch ist in ihr ein Licht, das Sonnenlicht, verbreitet, das einem die Augen ungeheuer schwer macht, wenn dazu noch Gespräche kommen, kann sich ein Strom von Vernichtung durch die Persönlichkeit bewegen.*[1]

Während Brecht das »Absterben« des bürgerlichen Individuums, das im *Lehrstück* ja auf drastische Weise praktiziert wird, als Voraussetzung gesellschaftlicher Veränderungen sieht, besteht Benn demgegenüber auf dem Ich als einer Instanz, die durch die Errichtung einer ästhetischen Fantasie- und Gegenwelt gestärkt und gegen eine unerträgliche gesellschaftliche Verdinglichung verteidigt werden muß. Die Dichotomisierung des Ich-Begriffs, die sich in beiden Konzeptionen zeigt, bildet damit gewissermaßen das Panorama eines ideologisch wie ästhetisch gleichermaßen polarisierten geistigen Klimas. Interessanterweise hat Hindemith in den *Männerchören* aus den Jahren 1929/30, die seine erste Vertonung von Gedichten Benns darstellen (*Fürst Krafft*, *Du mußt Dir alles geben* und *Vision eines Mannes*), diese mit Gedichten Brechts und Whitmans gekoppelt und damit das weltanschaulich Disparate musikalisch neutralisiert.

---

1 Gottfried Benn, *Briefwechsel mit Paul Hindemith*, hrsg. von Ann C. Fehn, Wiesbaden 1978 (*Gottfried Benn, Briefe*, 3. Band), S. 14.

Auch das *Lehrstück* und *Das Unaufhörliche* stehen in diesem antipodischen Spannungsfeld, und zwar nicht allein aufgrund der symbolischen Anwesenheit des *Lehrstücks* in der Verwendung der Musik aus der berühmt-berüchtigten Zerstückelungsszene im Oratorium. Grundsätzlich man kann *Das Unaufhörliche* als metaphysischen Gegenentwurf zum *Lehrstück* lesen, da es auf dessen Gesellschaftkritik mit Weltentsagung antwortet. Geblieben ist das Selbstverständnis einer von pädagogischem Ethos und Volksnähe erfüllten Moderne. Auf Brechts und Hindemiths Idee eines »Volks-Oratoriums«, das die umfassende Beteiligung von Laien ermöglichen soll[2], nimmt der von Benn und Hindemith gewählte Gattungsbegriff direkt Bezug; im Briefwechsel spricht Benn weiter davon, ihr Werk solle im Sinn der *Maßnahme* und des *Lehrstücks* demonstrieren, *wie das U.*[naufhörliche] *arbeite*[3]. Daß Hindemith den geistigen und weltanschaulichen Überzeugungen Benns zu folgen bereit war, ist durch seinen Konflikt und Bruch mit Brecht sicherlich gefördert worden. Schon unmittelbar nach der Uraufführung des *Lehrstücks* wurden die Mißverständnisse deutlich: Hindemith verteidigte sein funktionalistisches Konzept, wonach die Form des *Lehrstücks* durch die jeweiligen Aufführungsmodalitäten bedingt sei, während Brecht dadurch die Wirksamkeit des Textes und damit den Primat der politisch-moralischen Aussagekraft entschärft sah. Anläßlich des Festivals *Neue Musik Berlin 1930*, das die Tradition der Donaueschinger und Baden-Badener Festivals auf dem Höhepunkt der Wirtschaftskrise beendete, führte die Ablehnung des von Brecht und Eisler geschriebenen Lehrstücks *Die Maßnahme* durch das Programmkomitee, dem Hindemith angehörte, zum Bruch. Aus dieser Entscheidung konnte Brecht folgern, daß Hindemith – der seit 1927 die Kompositions-Professur an der Berliner Staatlichen Hochschule für Musik innehatte – sich nun zum Protagonisten staatlicher Zensur gemacht hatte. Daß ihm dieser Eklat

2 Vgl. Klaus Dieter Krabiel, *Das Lehrstück von Brecht und Hindemith*, in: Hindemith-Jahrbuch XXIV/1995, S. 168.
3 Benn/Hindemith, *Briefwechsel*, S. 29.

vor der sich radikalisierenden politischen Gesamtsituation und damit zur Profilierung seiner eigenen Position recht kam, ja von ihm teilweise sogar provoziert worden war, steht auf einem anderen Blatt. Die damit verbundene Diskussion und Polemik, die in den entsprechenden Jahrgängen von *Melos* nachgelesen werden kann, bedarf noch einer gründlichen Auswertung und Deutung.

Hindemiths Interesse an Benn resultierte zweifellos aus einem Überdruß an sich zuspitzenden kulturpolitischen Konflikten, in denen er auch eine Instrumentalisierung seines eigenen Komponierens sah. Er glaubte, dadurch jener Politisierung des Künstlerischen entgegenwirken zu können, welche das geistige Klima der Weimarer Republik von Anfang geprägt und an der Hindemith selbst – wenngleich so von ihm nicht intendiert – im *Lehrstück* mitgewirkt hatte. Stattdessen bezog er in der Vertonung des Bennschen Textes eine spiegelbildliche Position, die zu jener Ästhetisierung des Politischen beitrug, die Walter Benjamin 1935 als Kennzeichen faschistischer Herrschaft analysiert hat. (Daß diese Ästhetisierung als fortschrittliche Konzeption gedacht werden konnte, zeigt u.a. das Plädoyer des jungen Wolfgang Koeppen für den Futurismus, den er als genuine Ästhetik des Neuen Deutschland erhoffte, in einer der letzten Nummern von *Melos* Anfang 1934.) Diese für Hindemith wohl kaum vorhersehbare Entwicklung bestimmte die kurze Rezeptionsgeschichte des *Unaufhörlichen* nach 1933 in hohem Maße. Gerade *Das Unaufhörliche* wurde von den »fortschrittlichen« nationalsozialistischen Apologeten Hindemiths, die sich um Goebbels gruppierten, während der Furtwängler-Affäre als Zeichen seiner angeblichen Läuterung herangezogen, um Hindemith damit als führenden Vertreter einer neuen deutschen Musik empfehlen zu können. Im *Unaufhörlichen* erkannte man jene einer erneuerten deutschen Musik immanenten Attribute von »Tiefe«, »Reife« und »Ernsthaftigkeit«, die den Werken der »Systemzeit«, d.h. der zwanziger Jahre, aufgrund einer weltanschaulichen Abirrung des Komponisten noch gefehlt hätten. Hindemith hat zu dieser Bewertung des *Unaufhörlichen* geschwiegen – wohl auch schweigen können, weil das Werk aufgrund seiner eigenen Stigmatisierung und spätestens mit Benns Abwendung von den neuen Machthabern keine Zukunft mehr besaß und damit nicht mehr politisch zu mißbrauchen war.

Gottfried Benn stellte, schon von den äußeren Bedingungen her, den Gegentypus zu Brecht dar: Dem überaus erfolgreichen Dramatiker, der die aktuellen politischen und gesellschaftlichen Entwicklungen auf- und angriff, stand der nur einem kleinen intellektuellen Publikum bekannte Gelegenheitsschriftsteller gegenüber, der beruflich als eher erfolgloser Venerologe agierte, sich oft genug am Rande von Existenzkrisen bewegte und ein abgeschirmtes, teilweise von seltsamen Obsessionen bestimmtes Privatleben führte[4]. Brechts Themen und politische Gesinnung waren ein Anathema für den Nihilisten und Solipsisten Benn, dessen Bekenntnis zum Nationalsozialismus – wie die spätere Auseinandersetzung mit Klaus Mann offenbarte – auch Ausdruck seines vehementen Anti-Kommunismus war. Was Hindemith an Benn interessierte und anzog, beruht sicherlich auf dessen demonstrativem Außenseitertum und einer Dichtung, in deren Suggestivität und Radikalität Hindemith Erfahrungen und Prägungen seiner Generation – vor allem die Zäsur, die der Erste Weltkrieg bildete – wiederfand. Mit der Entscheidung für den Außenseiter Benn blieb Hindemith also auch in gewisser Weise seiner eigenen Lust an der Provokation treu. Andererseits reagierte er auf ein neues Publikumsbedürfnis, das er mit der ihm eigenen Nüchternheit und unter dem Eindruck des großen Erfolgs von Strawinskys *Symphonie des Psaumes* gegenüber Willy Strecker mit der Bemerkung registrierte, daß *jetzt allmählich wieder eine Welle für ernste und große Musik käme*[5]. Die Rätselhaftigkeit des scheinbar unvermittelten Schwenks Hindemiths von Brecht zu Benn relativiert sich: Er reflektiert

---

[4] Vgl. dazu Werner Rübe, *Provoziertes Leben. Gottfried Benn*, Stuttgart 1993, S. 260 ff.

[5] Benn/Hindemith, *Briefwechsel*, S. 95.

vielmehr unter den gesellschaftlichen Auflösungserscheinungen Deutschlands im Schatten der wirtschaftlichen Depression jene umfassende Wertkrise, durch die Benns ästhetischer Nihilismus eine brauchbare Alternative zu Brechts schließlich offen klassenkämpferischem Standpunkt werden konnte. *Das Unaufhörliche* ist aber auch Ergebnis des über die Musik hinaus auch die Bildenden und Gebrauchs-Künste erfassenden Stilwandels um 1930, der für wenige Jahre zentrale Ideen der Moderne im öffentlichen Bewußtsein tragfähig macht. Als Kulmination und Verdichtung von gestalterischen Möglichkeiten, die in den zwanziger Jahren entwickelt worden waren, besitzt die Physiognomie des *Stils 1930* – wie der Kunsthistoriker Klaus-Jürgen Sembach formulierte, einen *Anhauch von Klassik* und eine *formale Reife*, die zwischen klassizistischen und avantgardistischen Tendenzen einen Ausgleich schafft und – im Angesicht der fortschreitenden gesellschaftlichen Destabilisierung – das utopische Gegenbild einer gewissermaßen *stillgestellten* kulturellen Klärung und Ordnung entwirft[6].
Der konkrete Anlaß für Hindemiths Idee, Benn für ein Oratorium zu gewinnen, war das Rundfunkgespräch *Können Dichter die Welt ändern?* von 1930, in dem Benn zugleich die Autonomie und Zweckfreiheit des Künstlertums verteidigte wie den missionarischen Anspruch von Kunst als Korrektur gesellschaftlicher Mißstände ironisch infrage stellte, also Schriftsteller wie Alfred Döblin, die für die *Neue Musik Berlin* ihre pädagogisch orientierten Lehrstücke und Hörspiele vorlegten, verspottete. Um die gedankliche Intention des *Unaufhörlichen* zu verstehen, muß es im Kontext von Benns gesamter essayistischer Produktion am Ende der Weimarer Republik gesehen werden. Dazu gehören in erster Linie die Arbeiten *Der Aufbau der Persönlichkeit*, *Fazit der Perspektiven* und *Zur Problematik des Dichterischen.* In ihnen entwirft Benn auf Grundlage der Wahrheitskritik Nietzsches das ebenso grandiose wie fragwürdige Tableau einer »Geologie des Ich«, das Regressions- und

[6] Klaus-Jürgen Sembach, *Stil 1930*, Tübingen [2]1984, [S. 1ff.].

Untergangsphantasien mit Spenglerscher Zivilisationskritik, Jungscher Archetypenlehre und einer spekulativen Phylogenese-Theorie des Menschen verschmilzt. Benns Diagnose begreift das moderne Ich als Endstadium einer fortschreitenden »Verhirnung« und »Materialisierung« der menschlichen Gattung, als letztes, quartäres Stadium einer Millionenjahre umfassenden Entwicklung, die zur Krise und Auflösung des Individuuums führt. Die Entdeckung der unter dem dünnen Firnis zivilisatorischen Fortschritts wirkenden uralten und unveränderlichen »Substanz« von Magie und Kosmogonie weist den Weg aus dieser Krise. Das *Fazit der Perspektiven* von 1930, das den fundamentalen »Umbau des Ich« fordert, schließt mit den Worten:

Die weisse Rasse ist zu Ende. Technische Magie, tausend Worte Rebbach, Text genormt, Partitur aus Zahlen, das war ihr letzter Traum. Import aus Asien: Fahrräder nach Ulster, Lutscher nach Halberstadt, Bierwärmer fürs Gewerkschaftshaus. Farewell, Opportunismus von der Börse bis zur Psychiatrie! Kornloses Land, erschöpfte Schächte, leere Docks. Wer weinte um die fallenden Geschlechter – Illiaden hin und her! Das Unaufhörliche besucht den Pol, streut Erde auf Scotts Grab, bald werden die Feuerländler dort Rosen ziehen. Das Unaufhörliche, von Meer zu Meer, mondlose Welten überfrüht, hinan, hinab.[7]

Dieter Wellershoff hat darauf hingewiesen, daß Benn den Dichter damit zum *Organ des archaischen Phantasiegrundes*, zum *Magier ohne Stamm* erhoben hat, der *fremd* [ist] *in einer Zeitgenossenschaft, die sich durch den Aufklärungsprozeß von der uralten, schöpferischen Substanz emanzipiert hat*[8]. Diese Abkehr von aller aufklärerischen Rationalität vollzieht gleichzeitig eine radikale Verschiebung der Perspektiven, die sich von der Zukunft ab- und auf eine in phantastische Urzeiten ver-

---

[7] *Fazit der Perspektiven*, in: Gottfried Benn, *Gesammelte Werke in acht Bänden*, hrsg. von D. Wellershoff, München 1975, Bd. 3, S. 690.

[8] Dieter Wellershoff, *Gottfried Benn. Phänotyp dieser Stunde*, München 1976, S. 112.

längerte mythische Vergangenheit zuwenden und eine negative Utopie der Regression formulieren. Die Kategorien des sozialen, gesellschaftlichen und technischen Fortschritts werden verworfen und durch »statische« Metaphysik und Introspektion ersetzt. Das Motiv des »Unaufhörlichen«, das Benn vom Ende des *Fazits der Perspektiven* direkt in den Text des Oratoriums übernommen hat, wird zum Chiffre eines archaischen Weltbildes und einer Gegenmoderne, die an die Stelle historischen Bewußtseins, überhaupt von Geschichtlichkeit »asiatische Weltentsagung« setzt, und an die Stelle des Fortschritts die Idee des ziellosen Wandels. (Welche Anziehungskraft diese Vorstellungen in den zwanziger Jahren entfaltete, zeigt nicht zuletzt Paul Bekkers 1926 erschienene *Musikgeschichte als Geschichte der musikalischen Formwandlungen*, deren historiographisches Modell hierauf in freilich entschärfter Form aufbaut.)

Der Vorwurf der Regression, der Benn gemacht werden kann, findet freilich in seinen poetischen Verfahrensweisen keine Entsprechung. Es gehört zu den Paradoxien der Bennschen Poetologie und Persönlichkeit, daß Benn sein extremes Weltbild in eine Sprache und Artistik faßt, deren Originalität und künstlerische Rigidität in der deutschen Lyrik der ersten Jahrhunderthälfte einzigartig ist. Benn zieht aus Nietzsches Lebens- und Kunstphilosophie die Konsequenz, Dichtung als Eigenwirklichkeit und *höchste Steigerungsform des sich selber wollenden Lebens*[9] zu radikalisieren. Nietzsches Kritik des abendländischen Wahrheitsbegriffs, den er für gescheitert erklärt, führt Benn zu der Einsicht, daß Sprache nicht mehr ein anderes Medium der phänomenalen Welt, sondern eine eigene autonome Seinsweise darstellt. Die Diagnose der modernen Welt, der Dissoziation des menschlichen Bewußtseins und der Ununterscheidbarkeit von Sein und Schein spiegelt sich in Benns

[9] Theo Meyer, *Kunstproblematik und Wortkombinatorik bei Gottfried Benn*, Köln 1971 (*Kölner germanistische Arbeiten*, Bd. 6), S. 74.

avantgardistischer Montage- und Assoziationstechnik, die aus den Resten der empirischen Wirklichkeit ihre eigene artifizielle Realität erzeugt. Benns Sprachbilder erbauen eine a-mimetische, konstruktive Welt der »Simultanperspektiven«, die absolute formale und ästhetische Autonomie besitzt. Diese *konstruktivistische Integrationsform* auf der Grundlage literarischer Techniken des Expressionismus und Surrealismus erkennt keine Sinnstiftung durch die alte Metaphysik mehr an, bekennt sich aber emphatisch zur Idee des *absoluten* Kunstwerks als deren Ersatz[10]. Aus der abrupten Folge von disparaten Einzelheiten, von Fragmenten und Stimmungen, die aus völlig unverbundenen historischen, geographischen oder zeitlichen Kontexten assoziiert werden, erwächst eine Form, die Nietzsches Verständnis der Kunst als ein *perspektivischer Zugriff auf die Welt*[11] verpflichtet ist und aus der dialektischen Konstellation der Bruchstücke eine neue, nur ästhetisch gerechtfertigte Einheit von »Leben« und »Form« beschwört. Das Ende des *Fazits der Perspektiven* zeigt dieses Verfahren auf der Ebene des Essays, im *Unaufhörlichen* wird es als Oratorium in eine dichterische Gattung übertragen, dessen Aura den Anspruch formaler Repräsentanz, ja Erhabenheit erhebt. Die Formtendenzen in Benns Lyrik der zwanziger Jahre, die zur Vereinfachung und Abstrahierung führen, erfahren hier ihren vorläufigen Höhepunkt, der andererseits durch den Verlust der Fragmentation und der epischen Verbreiterung einen problematischen Zug zur pathosgeladenen Affirmation erhält.

Die episch-narrative Grundlage der Großform »Oratorium« stellte Benn, dessen Lyrik gerade aus der elliptischen Verknappung der Bilder ihre Wirkung bezog, also vor konzeptionelle Probleme, die – wie der Briefwechsel mit Hindemith zeigt – den langwierigen, von Krisen charakterisierten Produktionsprozeß wesentlich mitbedingten. An die

[10] Meyer, *Kunstproblematik und Wortkombinatorik*, S. 272 f.
[11] Bruno Hillebrand, *Gottfried Benn und Friedrich Nietzsche*, in: *Nietzsche und die deutsche Literatur*, hrsg. von B. Hillebrand, Bd. 2, München 1978, S. 190.

Stelle der wuchtigen Nominalismen, der paradoxen Substantiv-Komposita der Gedichte treten jetzt die »Stimmen« bzw. »Nummern« des Oratoriums, also dialogische Prinzipien in wechselnden antiphonalem oder responsorialen Konstellationen, die den gedanklichen Zusammenhang vor allem durch Wiederholung befestigen. Dem konstruktivistischen Integrationsprinzip wird in der Projektion auf die Großform ein Teil seiner Wirksamkeit genommen. Der gesamte I. Teil des Oratoriums dient nun der Exposition des Zentralmotivs des »Unaufhörlichen« und dessen Entfaltung in archaischen und arkadischen Bildern. Ihnen gegenüber stehen im II. Teil die »relativen«, vergänglichen Werte der Gegenwart – Familie, Wissenschaft, Technik, Kunst, Religion und Liebe als Repräsentanten des modernen bzw. aufgeklärten Menschen. Das eingeworfene Nietzsche-Zitat *Schmeckt ihr den Becher Nichts, den dunklen Trank* gibt dazu den nihilistischen Refrain und Kontrapunkt, gewissermaßen ein säkularisiertes »Memento mori«.
Der dritte Teil bringt angesichts dieses »statischen«, nicht eigentlich dramatisch ausbaubaren Gegensatzes lediglich eine formale Abrundung. Er ist im wesentlichen Zusammenfassung der ersten beiden Teile und Bekräftigung von zentralen Motiven, von »Asien« über den »Ackertag« als Gegenbild der großstädtischer Degeneration (übrigens mit unverkennbarer Verwendung der Metaphorik der von Benn verachteten »linken« Arbeiterlyrik) bis hin zu den »Schöpfungsmythen«, die der mythenlosen „Weißen Rasse« als Ziel und Ausgangspunkt zugleich gewiesen werden. Noch einmal kommt die Gegenwart in Gestalt des »Relativisten« zu Wort, der diesen »Tiefsinn« attackiert, wobei Benns Montageprinzip durch die unmittelbare Zuspitzung der Gegensätze hier überzeugt. Benns Nihilismus zeigt sich in der immanenten Kritik der »Metaphysik«, die durch die Worte des »Relativisten« selbst als Ideologie demaskiert wird. Daran wird sein zutiefst der Moderne verhaftetes poetologisches Denken deutlich, das Ambivalenzen anstelle von eindeutigen Bekenntnissen schafft, indem die Motive spielerisch auf ihre literarische Verwendbarkeit als Formfaktoren und Kontraste geprüft

werden. Das bekenntnishafte und 1930 schon etwas abgegriffene Pathos der Beschwörung der ewigen Gesetzmäßigkeiten, in denen *Das Unaufhörliche* gipfelt, ist aber nicht als Ausdruck eines zynischen ästhetischen Kalküls mißzuverstehen, sondern ist ein lebensphilosophisches (und darin vor dem Hintergrund der Zeitsituation auch zwangsläufig politisches) Bekenntnis: Benns Artisten-Metaphysik träumt vom Anbruch eines »post-ideologischen« und »post-nihilistischen« Zeitalters und mit Spengler von einem neuen »Cäsarentum«, das mit gesetzmäßig-biologischer Zwangsläufigkeit in die Geschichte eintritt. Der Appell an die *Kräfte der Ordnung und des individuellen Verzichts*[12], den Benn am Ende der Einleitung zum Textbuch des *Unaufhörlichen* ausspricht, erscheint daher zwiespältig: Einerseits ist er deutbar als Wunsch nach geistiger Askese und Reinigung, andererseits kann er als Signum des von Helmut Lethen[13] im Bild des »Radar-Typus« gefaßten Depersonalisierungsprozesses gelesen werden und damit Beitrag zu jener Entwicklung, an deren Ende 1933 – wie Dieter Wellershoff formulierte – die *anthropologisch Tieferen die Macht ergriffen* und Benns Anschauungen unvermutet politischen »Bodenkontakt« bekamen[14]. Es bleibt Spekulation, ob Hindemith sich nicht auch gegen diese Tendenzen in Benns Denken wehrte, als er nach dem *Unaufhörlichen* zu keiner weiteren Zusammenarbeit mit ihm fand. Vordergründig endete die Zusammenarbeit durch Benns Unfähigkeit, ein geeignetes Opernlibretto zu schreiben, da er – wie Willy Strecker an Hindemith schrieb – weder die *Menschen noch die Bühne* liebte[15]. Aber Hindemith ließ sich auf Benns ästhetischen Radikalismus und Irrationalismus nicht mehr recht ein, der in dem von Benn vorgeschlagenen »Rönne«-Stoff forciert wurde. (Benn

---

[12] *Das Unaufhörliche.* Oratorium. Text von Gottfried Benn, Musik von Paul Hindemith. Textbuch, Mainz: Schott, 1931, S. 6.

[13] Vgl. Helmut Lethen, *Verhaltenslehren der Kälte. Lebensversuche zwischen den Kriegen,* Frankfurt/Main 1994.

[14] Wellershoff, *Gottfried Benn*, S. 134 ff.

[15] Hindemith/Benn, *Briefwechsel,* S. 127.

griff in dieser Figur bezeichnenderweise sein literarisches Alter Ego aus dem 1. Weltkrieg wieder auf, das nun auf die Situation der Weltwirtschaftskrise übertragen wurde.) Benns Sujets, die ja immer einen Weg nach »Innen«, in eine rein ästhetische Lebensform beschrieben, blieben Hindemith, der durch den Nietzscheanismus nicht wirklich durchgreifend geprägt worden war, letztlich mental und intellektuell fremd. Sein Erstaunen über Benns Bekenntnis zum Nationalsozialismus mag zwar seinerseits aus einer Haltung unpolitischer Distanz geübt worden sein, doch besiegelt es das irreversible Ende einer künstlerischen Partnerschaft, die 1925 noch nicht und 1933 nicht mehr möglich gewesen wäre.

Es erscheint verführerisch und naheliegend zugleich, die Musik zum *Unaufhörlichen* direkt vor dem problematischem Gehalt des Bennschen Textes zu beurteilen und damit jene Polemik von Adorno bestätigt zu finden, wonach Hindemith – teils in der *Anhortung von Bildungsgütern* bei der Wahl seiner Texte, teils durch *naives Musikantentum* – genau jener Bennschen *Regression* Vorschub leiste, statt ein kritisches Verhältnis zum Text zu gewinnen und damit kompositorischen *Widerstand* zu leisten[16]. Dabei wird wohl allzu leicht verdrängt, daß dieser Blickwinkel nachträglich durch den geschichtlichen Verlauf, insbesondere die Katastrophe des Nationalsozialismus determiniert ist, und die Ideen Hindemiths und Benns damit in einem anderen Licht erscheinen als zum Zeitpunkt der Entstehung des Werkes. (In diesem Zusammenhang ist übrigens anzumerken, daß Adornos 1932 an Hindemith gerichteter Vorwurf der *Inhumanität und Brutalität* des Musikantentums sich von der Diagnose des unaufhaltsamen *gesellschaftlichen Rationalisierungsprozesses* ableitet, den auch Benn bekämpft. Hier bestehen also Affinitäten, die durch großzügige ideengeschichtliche Konstruktionen übersehen werden können.) Man muß daher versuchen, dem *Unaufhörlichen* auch hinsichtlich seines kompositorischen Ansatzes aus der Situation der

---

[16] Theodor W. Adorno, *Ad vocem Hindemith*, in: ders., *Impromptus*, [4]1973, S. 69.

Entstehungszeit heraus gerecht zu werden, zu der die gedankliche Problematik des Sujets gehört.

Die Entscheidung Hindemiths, ein Oratorium zu komponieren, resultierte aus mehreren Überlegungen, die nicht nur dem Folgen einer Modeerscheinung, der »Welle für ernste und große Musik«, und damit auch ökonomischen Gesichtspunkten geschuldet waren. Sie sollte sicherlich zunächst dazu dienen, Hindemiths enzyklopädischem, von ihm beharrlich verfolgten kompositorischen Gesamtplan um eine weitere wichtige Gattung ergänzen, die nach der Oper als historisch gewichtigstes »vokal-instrumentales« Genre gelten konnte. Zudem konnte Hindemith die 1927 von ihm programmatisch formulierten Forderungen einer »zeitgemäßen« Chormusik und Erneuerung des a-cappella-Ideals in repräsentativer Weise umsetzen, und schließlich sollte die Wahl – vielleicht auch bedingt durch Schönbergs Vorwurf, Hindemith habe im *Lehrstück* den Kunstanspruch an sich preisgegeben – demonstrieren, daß er jederzeit zur großen Form zurückfinden und den emphatischen Begriff des Kunstwerks erfüllen könne. Die Wahl des Stoffes von Benn bedeutete aber mehr und zugleich weniger, als eine *das Werk beherrschende ethisch-religiöse Idee* gefunden zu haben, die Arnold Schering als Kern des geistlichen Oratoriums bezeichnet hatte[17]. Durch den Bezug auf die Lebenswirklichkeit, auf Technik und Wissenschaft, »Raketenautos« und »Staatsanleihen« wird der traditionelle Motiv-Rahmen des geistlichen und weltlichen Oratoriums entschieden überschritten. Vor dem Hintergrund der Weihnachtslegenden, Christus-Stoffe und biblischen Mysterien oder der »offiziellen« Sujets der germanischen oder griechischen Mythologie, die das deutsche Oratorium der Kaiserzeit dominiert hatten, wie sie etwa Bruch im Zuge des Wagnerismus vertont hatte, erscheint *Das Unaufhörliche* (und darin wieder dem *Lehrstück* ähnlich) als ein Skandalon, das Hindemiths funktionalistischem Stil-Verständnis durch die darin liegenden parodistischen und

---

[17] Arnold Schering, *Geschichte des Oratoriums*, Leipzig 1911, S. 5.

karikierenden Möglichkeiten einen idealen Ausgangspunkt bot. Doch der Ansatz der »Musik nach Maß«, die für die Herausbildung und Legitimation von Hindemiths kompositorischen Selbstverständnis in den zwanziger Jahren von so eminenter Bedeutung ist, erweist sich für die Umsetzung der metaphysischen Grundidee Benns im Gewande einer geläuterten »Neo-Klassik« als zwiespältig: Denn das klassizistische Paradigma soll nun nicht mehr nur die bloße Stil-Haltung eines »Als ob« abgeben, sondern metaporisch den Textgehalt abspiegeln. Diese durch die Dichtung vollzogene Nobilitierung der musikalischen Sprache leitet damit eine »konservative« Wende durch die Aufhebung des bloßen Funktionalismus in Hindemiths Stil ein, wodurch freilich auch ein neuer Autonomie-Anspruch des musikalischen Kunstwerks formuliert wird. Mit der phantastischen Vergangenheit Benns, die Räume und Epochen einer imaginären Menschheitsgeschichte entwirft und durchstreift, korrespondiert eine archaisierende musikalische Sprache Hindemiths, die ebenfalls ihre eigene, von Assoziationen und Erinnerungen durchzogene Vergangenheit formt, gegenüber den Werken der zwanziger Jahre jedoch in einer enormen stilistischen und satztechnischen Differenzierung. Der retrospektiven Grundausrichtung – die insbesondere für die großen Rahmensätze gilt – stehen die parodistisch-pointierten Nummern entgegen, die der Sphäre der Gegenwart, des modernen Menschen, zugeordnet sind. Insofern entspricht die stilistische Variabilität der musikalischen Gesamtkonzeption – einschließlich ihrer Selbstbezüglichkeit, d.h. der Kontrafaktur in der Übernahme des »Kleinen Marsches« aus dem *Lehrstück* oder der Anlehnung an den kapriziös-satirischen Ton von *Neues vom Tage* – der literarischen Montagetechnik Benns. Hindemith hat, etwa durch die von ihm selbst angeregte Einführung des »Relativisten«, die dramaturgischen Möglichkeiten der Gegenüberstellung von »Nihilismus« und »Technik« sogar noch forciert.
Hindemiths Ansatz, für den monumentalen weltanschaulichen Aplomb der Dichtung Benns entsprechend mächtige Form- und Klanggesten zu finden, bewirkt zwangsläufig auch die Rückbindung an geschichtliche

Vorbilder. Diese Tendenz ist Kritikern der Uraufführung nicht entgangen. Robert Oboussier schrieb, daß Hindemith *gregorianisches Melos, Bachsche Passionsarchitektonik, Mahlers Stimmungslyrik, sogar Beethovens Rhythmik mit den stilistischen Elementen der Gegenwart, der eigenen Tonsprache*[18] verbinde; Alfred Einstein konstatierte eine Bindung an den *altklassischen Stil*: *Die beiden großen oratorischen Ecksätze haben den objektiven oratorischen Stil und die oratorische Schwere schon durch den Machtklang der Orgel.*[19] Mit diesem Objektivierungsstreben, zu dem auch Attribute wie die Großzügigkeit der Form und das Al-Fresco der Klangflächen gehören, die sicherlich auch eine Beeinflussung durch die Händel-Renaissance der zwanziger Jahre zeigen, ist Hindemith im *Unaufhörlichen* schon jenem erweiterten Stilbegriff nahe, der jenseits von »Klassizismen« und »Modernismen« einen dritten Weg seines Komponierens ab den dreißiger Jahren bedeutet. Zwischen den »energetischen«, im Geist des Neobarock geschriebenen Kompositionen der zwanziger Jahre – etwa den *Serenaden* op. 35 – und den satztechnisch differenzierteren, aber stilistisch konventionelleren Werken der mittleren Phase und Teilen des Spätwerks nimmt *Das Unaufhörliche* eine zentrale Vermittlungsrolle ein. Insbesondere in den großen Rahmensätzen und dem orchestralen Vorspiel zum III. Teil entfaltet sich eine expressive, auch vor Pathos nicht scheuende Klanglichkeit, die Hindemith in *Mathis der Maler* weiterentwickelt und in der *Harmonie der Welt* zum Abschluß bringt, wobei gerade dieses Werk ja auch verschiedene Bennsche Motive aufgreift, wie bereits Geoffrey Skelton feststellte[20].

Man kann diesen Wandel – der durchaus frühere Konzeptionen (etwa im Melos und Kontrapunkt des *Marienleben)* aufgreift – wiederum vor

---

[18] Kritik vom 25. November 1931 in der Frankfurter Zeitung. Nachweis in Christiane Lehnigk, *Paul Hindemiths Oratorium »Das Unaufhörliche«. Kritische Neuausgabe und Werkgeschichte*, Phil. Diss. Bonn 1995, S. 58.

[19] Kritik vom 23. November 1931 in der Berliner Abendzeitung. Nachweis ebd., S. 60.

[20] Geoffrey Skelton, *Paul Hindemith. The Man behind the Music*, London 1977, S. 100.

der ästhetischen Diskussion und Zuspitzung in Deutschland um 1930 sehen, in der die ethischen Aufgaben und Ordnungsansprüche von Kunst im Mittelpunkt stehen. Es ist an dieser Stelle der Hinweis auf Oskar Schlemmer notwendig, dessen künstlerische Entwicklung und Physiognomie ja in vielerlei Hinsicht Parallelen zu Hindemith besitzt: Auch Schlemmers Stil durchläuft – exemplarisch zu nennen ist hier der zwischen 1928–31 entstandene Zyklus der Folkwang-Wandgemälde – einen vergleichbaren Prozeß. 1929 schrieb Schlemmer in einem Beitrag für die Darmstädter Ausstellung *Der schöne Mensch in der neuen Kunst*: *Wenn die Zeichen nicht trügen, so bereitet sich eine Renaissance der Menschendarstellung in der Kunst vor.* [...] *Nach* [dem] *Expressionismus müßten eigentlich notwendigerweise die Ideale wieder aufleben, die einen Hans von Marées ein Leben lang beherrschten, Ideale, die sich um den hohen Stil in der Kunst bemühen.* [...] *Es werden immer Formungen sein, die im Goetheschen Sinne »antikisch« sind, Schöpfungen, entsprungen aus der Verbindung und dem idealen Gleichmaß von Abstraktion, Maß, Gesetz einerseits, andererseits aus Natur, Gefühl, Idee.*[21]
Wenn Schlemmer davon spricht, daß Kunst mit den *Mitteln von Formen und Farbe* ein Gleichnis, eine *Sonderwelt* schaffe – also keine naturalistische Aufgabe besitze, daß der menschliche Körper nicht als seelischer Ausdrucksträger, sondern als geformter Organismus zu begreifen sei, dessen *Baugesetzlichkeit und plastisches Bildungsprinzip* herausgearbeitet werden müßten, wird eine Parallele zur Idee des *Unaufhörlichen* sichtbar. Die der Kunst zugeschriebene Aufgabe, objektive Werte und Ordnungen zu repräsentieren, für die Schlemmer wie Hindemith auf geschichtliche Urmuster zurückgreifen (hier Ägypten und Babylonien, dort auf über den Barock hinaus die Gregrorianik), bildet eigentlich einen Reflex der mentalen Lage der Weimarer Spätphase. Schlemmer rechnete sich, wie Karin v. Maur schreibt, zu den Künstlern, die *der*

[21] Zit. nach Karin v. Maur, *Oskar Schlemmer. Der Folkwang-Zyklus. Malerei um 1930*, Stuttgart 1993, S. 43.

disparaten und desolaten Wirklichkeit fiktive Ordnungsbilder als Ortungsmodelle entgegenzuhalten versuchten und schließlich, d.h. 1933 zu einer Gleichung von *Staatskomposition und Kunstkomposition* gelangten, die gewissermaßen die ultima ratio dieses Ordnungs- und Rettungsversuchs vor dem sozialen und politischen Chaos darstellte[22]. Und es war wiederum Benn, der in seinem Briefwechsel vom Herbst 1933 an Schlemmer von dem *jedes Chaos ausschließenden Absolutismus* der Kunst schrieb, den es nun zu vertreten gelte[23]. Von diesem »Absolutismus« des Stils und der reinen Form, die als Korrektiv des Amorphen, Unreinen errichtet wird, ist auch das *Unaufhörliche* – auf seiner literarischen wie musikalischen Seite – geprägt.

Ungeachtet der Ambivalenzen, die diese normativen ästhetisch-ethischen Ansprüche Hindemiths, Benns und Schlemmers 1933 durch das totalitäre Denken mißbrauchbar machten, ist der künstlerische Eigenwert des Zyklus der *Folkwang*-Wandbilder wie der Musik zum *Unaufhörlichen* unbezweifelbar. Ähnlich Schlemmers Versuch einer Vermittlung von konstruktiver Strenge, elementaren Raum- und Farbwirkungen und einer impulsiveren gelockerten Malweise (die Schlemmer selbst mit dem Formgefühl des Barock in Verbindung brachte) zielt auch Hindemiths Verfahren im *Unaufhörlichen* auf eine Synthese und Intensivierung bisheriger Techniken. So staunenswert an sich schon das satztechnische und stilistische Spektrum ist, das sich von gregorianischer Hymnik bis hin zur latenten Zwölftönigkeit, vom Accompagnato-Rezitativ bis zur virtuosen Chorfuge erstreckt, so scheint doch die zentrale, freilich eher im Hintergrund zugreifende Leistung in der Vereinheitlichung der konstitutiven Satzparameter zu liegen. Dieser Vereinheitlichungsprozeß bezieht seine Dynamik aus einer strukturellen Reduktion. Die harmonische Grundlage des *Unaufhörlichen* ist modal, nicht tonal ausgerichtet; die Modalität bleibt kein bloß archaisierender

---

22 v. Maur, *Oskar Schlemmer*, S. 39

23 Zit. nach v. Maur, *Oskar Schlemmer*, S. 40.

Farbwert, sondern wird der tonsystematische Ausgangspunkt, von dem die Tonalität, etwa als Bestimmung der tatsächlichen Tonhöhe des jeweiligen Stückes, abgeleitet wird. Der überwiegenden Beibehaltung des authentischen lydischen Modus als strukturellem Klanggrund steht der Wechsel der Tonstufen innerhalb und zwischen einzelnen Nummern bzw. Abschnitten gegenüber, wobei Hindemith mit Vorliebe chromatische Rückungen verwendet (am auffälligsten vom Vorspiel des III. Teils, dessen Tonalität auf C steht, zur anschließenden Nummer 16, dem Wechselchor, der auf Cis gelagert ist) und der Chromatik damit eine formal-gliedernde Aufgabe zuweist. Bezogen auf den durchgängigen Gegensatz von Beharrung und Wandel, der im Motiv des »Unaufhörlichen« eingeschlossen ist, kann Modalität als die gleichbleibende strukturelle Substanz, Tonalität aber als Träger expressiven und klanglichen Wandels gefaßt werden.

Der Reduktion auf Modalität entspricht die motivische Beschränkung, die zu Beginn des Werkes in der Intonation des zentralen Sekund-Terz-Motivs signalisiert wird und dem eigentlichen Anfang des Werkes vorangestellt ist. Dieses Leitmotiv scheint zwar einer gregorianischen Formel nachgebildet, kann aber durch die Labilität der zweiten Stufe – die durch ihre Alteriertheit eine Umdeutung nach Moll, also zur »modernen« Tonalität eröffnet und die Integration in polyphone Satzstrukturen zuläßt – keine wirkliche Authentizität beanspruchen, ebensowenig wie es den Status thematischer Qualität erlangt. Seine eigentliche Funktion scheint in dem zu liegen, was die mittelalterliche und barocke Musiktheorie als »motus«, als Bewegung des Intervalls im Tonraum, bezeichnet hätte. Hindemiths Technik im *Unaufhörlichen* betont das Intervall und die damit verbundenen Möglichkeiten klanglicher Hierarchiebildungen. (Man kann hier, unabhängig von der physikalisch-akustischen Herleitung der »Reihe I« der *Unterweisung im Tonsatz*, eine Wurzel für Hindemiths Theorie des harmonischen Gefälles finden, die im wesentlichen auf der Hierarchie von Intervallqualitäten beruht.)

Diese Hervorhebung der Intervallqualitäten sollte nicht voreilig als Rückfall in »vorthematisches« Denken abqualifiziert werden, sondern steht im Zusammenhang mit Hindemiths entschiedener Hinwendung zu elementaren satztechnischen Fragen, mit der er sich im *Unaufhörlichen* zum ersten Mal deutlich Bruckner nähert. So werden der Satzaufbau und seine Ausdifferenzierungen im *Unaufhörlichen* im wesentlichen weder durch thematisch-motivische Prozesse noch durch parataktische Variantenbildungen im Sinne des Neo-Barock gesteuert, sondern durch die harmonischen und klanglichen Möglichkeiten, die sich aus dem Spannungsfeld von Modalität und Dur/Moll-Tonalität bzw. Diatonik und Chroma ergeben. In seinem polyphonen Grundaufbau folgt Hindemiths Satz der – nach Georgiades – für den Generalbaßsatz charakteristischen Aufgabenteilung zwischen einem »konstruktiv-synthetischen« instrumentalen und einem »analytisch-reihenden« vokalen bzw. melodischen Part[24]. Die diversen satztechnischen Verfahren im *Unaufhörlichen* auf der Grundlage von Gerüstsatz-Modellen – zu nennen sind vor allem Passacaglio- und Ostinato-Strukturen (vgl. Nr. 9), das Arbeiten mit Orgelpunkten und natürlich die Fugen – liefern verschiedene Konstellationen und Konkretionen dieser Grundstrukturen, die über neoklassizistische Stilisierungen hinausgehen. So führt die erwähnte Ambivalenz einzelner Stufen, die durch Alteration entweder einen modalen, dur/moll-tonalen oder freitonalen klanglichen Kontext schaffen, mitunter zu einer eigentümlich verfremdeten »Musica ficta«. So könnte die Sopran-Arie mit Chor Nr. 12 (*Frühe Stunde der Menschheit*) ihrer klaren Formgestaltung nach zwar einer Kantate Bachs entnommen sein, doch ihr Klangbild und Gestus schlagen um in eine »Musik über Musik« und werden zu einer magischen Invokation des Vergangenen aus dem Geist der Moderne, wie sie Benn vorgeschwebt haben mag.

Melos, Harmonik und Metrik sind im *Unaufhörlichen* in einen metaphorisch-programmatischen Zusammenhang gestellt, den Hindemith in

[24] Thrasybulos Georgiades, *Musik und Sprache*, Göttingen 1954, S. 77.

späteren Kompositionen, etwa der zweiten Fassung des *Marienleben* und ihrer dezidierten Tonarten-Symbolik, weiter ausgebaut hat. So sind die kleinschrittigen, chromatischen Intervalle, allen voran das bestimmende Intervall der kleinen Terz, der »dunklen« pessimistisch-nihilistischen Bedeutungssphäre des Textes zugeordnet, während die Konsonanzen Quart und Quinte die »hellen«, mythisch-ekstatischen Elemente (vgl. im Wechselchor Nr. 14 *Uralte Völker singen Asiens dämmerndes Lied*) repräsentieren. Auch der Wechsel von zusammengesetzten und Alla-Breve-Taktarten, der den temporalen Konstruktionen des *Flieder-Requiems* vorgreift, orientiert sich an bestimmten Bedeutungsschichten des Textes, so an der »dionysischen« Formvorstellung Benns von Kunst als einer rauschhaften Wirklichkeitsüberschreitung. Das stilisierte »tempus perfectum« (9/4) des Schlußsatzes und die durch den C-Dur-Schluß gleichsam ins »Weiße« (Lichte) diatonischer Reinheit gewendete Klangapotheose sind das Gegenbild zum All-Einheits-Traum der Schlußverse Benns.
Die satztechnischen Mittel des *Unaufhörlichen* zeigen den Komponisten Hindemith am Scheideweg. Trotz der gleichzeitig experimentellen Werke, die für die Rundfunkversuchsstelle an der Hochschule oder das Festival *Neue Musik Berlin* entstanden sind, deutet sich in ihnen Hindemiths Entscheidung an, in der musikgeschichtlichen Vergangenheit die Antworten für die Lösung der künstlerischen Fragen zu suchen, die ihn interessierten. Die Weiterentwicklung seiner musikalischen Sprache ist für ihn mit und seit dem *Unaufhörlichen* nicht mehr mit dem Fortschrittsmodell einer gesellschaftlich vermittelten »Zukunftsmusik« verknüpft; an deren Stelle tritt ein Innehalten, eine mehr und mehr retrospektive und im Spätwerk schließlich verinnerlichte Auseinandersetzung mit dem musikalischen Material und den historisch gegebenen Modellen sinnvoller Satzbildung. Der äußere, der Gattungstradition geschuldete Glanz des *Unaufhörlichen* sollte aber nicht darüber hinwegtäuschen, daß das Werk auch Dokument einer vom Avantgardismus der zwanziger Jahre sich abwendenden ästhetischen »Innerlichkeit«

und eines »Ordo«-Denkens ist, durch das Hindemith, aber auch Komponisten wie Schönberg und Webern nun in die Rolle von »Traditionalisten« gerieten. Hindemiths tonale Sprache wird klanglich in dem Maße einfacher und konventioneller, wie sie strukturell vielschichtiger wird – bisweilen bis hin zur oft kritisierten Neutralität des Ausdrucks. Aus dem problematischen ideen- und mentalitätsgeschichtlichen Kontext, der diese Tendenzen befördert hat, kann das *Unaufhörliche* weniger gelöst werden als andere, künstlerisch geringere Kompositionen Hindemiths. Größe und Grenze seines Komponierens treten darin aber umso klarer hervor und geben dem *Unaufhörlichen* den Rang eines schwierigen, verfremdeten Hauptwerks Hindemiths und der deutschen Moderne vor der Zäsur des Jahres 1933.

Gunther Nickel / Susanne Schaal

Die Dokumente zu einem gescheiterten Opernplan von Paul Hindemith und Ernst Penzoldt

Einleitung

Noch nie in meinem Leben habe ich so viel Briefe geschrieben wie um diese Oper, seufzte Hindemith am Ende eines Schreibens an seinen Verleger Willy Strecker vom 26. Januar 1933. Trotzdem wurde nichts aus dem Projekt, das nur wenige Monate zuvor, am 7. Oktober 1932, bei einem Treffen zwischen Carl Ebert und Paul Hindemith aus der Taufe gehoben worden war. An diesem Tag amtierte Franz von Papen, der – wie ihn Harry Graf Kessler charakterisierte – *ewig lächelnde, leichtsinnige Dilettant*[1], noch als Reichskanzler und bereitete sich darauf vor, der Koalitionsregierung unter dem Sozialdemokraten Otto Braun in Preußen – dem letzten Bollwerk der Republik – den Garaus zu machen. Auch wenn der Staatsgerichtshof seinen sogenannten Preußenschlag vom 20. Juli 1932, mit dem er eine gewählte Landesregierung absetzte, im Oktober 1932 als Verstoß gegen geltendes Verfassungsrecht verurteilte, so schwand doch immer mehr die Zahl derjenigen, die glaubten, die Rückkehr zu einer parlamentarischen Demokratie sei denkbar. Schon seit dem Rücktritt des sozialdemokratischen Reichskanzlers Hermann Müller am 27. März 1930 wurde Deutschland faktisch nicht mehr demokratisch, sondern nur mehr mit Hilfe von Notverordnungen regiert. 1932 machten die Wahlerfolge, die die NSDAP für sich verbu-

[1] Harry Graf Kessler, *Tagebücher 1918–1937*, hrsg. von Wolfgang Pfeiffer-Belli, Frankfurt/Main 1982, S. 742 (Eintrag vom 18. November 1932).

chen konnte, und das Scheitern von Kurt von Schleichers Bemühungen, ein Querfrontbündnis aus Sozialdemokraten, Gewerkschaftern und dem linken Flügel der NSDAP um Gregor Strasser zu bilden, immer wahrscheinlicher, daß Adolf Hitler auf legalem Wege nicht mehr dauerhaft von der Macht fernzuhalten sein würde. Anders als Schleicher, der deshalb – gestützt auf die Überlegungen von Carl Schmitt in *Legalität und Legitimität* – eine Regierungsbeteiligung der NSDAP um den Preis eines Verfassungsbruchs verhindern wollte, hegte Papen die Hoffnung, Hitler werde sich »zähmen« lassen.

Bekanntlich folgte Reichspräsident Hindenburg nicht den Vorschlägen Schleichers, sondern dem Rat Papens und berief Hitler zum Reichskanzler. Damit war auch das Schicksal der von Hindemith und Penzoldt begonnenen Arbeit besiegelt. Denn eine Oper zu inszenieren, in der eine Deutsche während des Ersten Weltkriegs einen flüchtigen französischen Soldaten versteckt und dieser Vorgang nicht eindeutig als schändlich gebrandmarkt wird, war nach der »Machtergreifung« der Nationalsozialisten, die sie als nationale Revolution bezeichneten, undenkbar geworden. Auch die Umwandlung des Franzosen Etienne in den Russen Stepan, die aufgrund eines Vorschlags des Verlegers Ludwig Strecker Anfang Januar 1933 vorgenommen wurde, hat daran nichts ändern können.

Möglicherweise hätte es zum Abbruch der Arbeiten nicht kommen müssen, wenn Hindemith sich dafür entschieden hätte, eine Erzählung von Penzoldt zu vertonen, die zunächst ebenfalls im Gespräch war: *Die Portugalesische Schlacht.* Aber er votierte aus Gründen, die durch ihre Korrespondenz nicht erhellt werden, gegen diesen historischen Stoff aus dem 16. Jahrhundert und mit *Etienne und Luise* für eine Geschichte von Penzoldt, die politisch brisant war. Wie brisant sie war, zeigte sich kurz nach dem Erstdruck der Novelle in der *Vossischen Zeitung*, der vom 7. Juni 1929 an in Fortsetzungen erschienen war. *Am 27. Juni 1929*, so schilderte es Ulla Penzoldt, *geht in der Postzentrale des Ullstein Verlags Berlin ein Schreiben aus Erlangen vom 21. Juni 1929 ein. Darin bittet der Studienprofessor a.D. Lorenz Ludwig Loch, ihm die Zeitungsausgaben zu schicken, »welche einen Roman eines früheren Schülers von mir [...] enthalten, in dem von der Familie Loch die Rede sein soll, wie ich von Bekannten erfahre.« Die Redaktion der »Vossischen Zeitung« leitet diesen Brief an Penzoldt weiter, der sich darauf direkt an seinen früheren Lehrer wendet. Er schickt ihm die gewünschten Belege und schreibt dazu etwa folgendes: »Es muß sich um ein Mißverständnis handeln. Sagen Sie Ihren Gewährsleuten, daß ich mich gegen diese Unterstellung verwahre. Ich habe lediglich aus klanglichen Gründen den Namen Loch gewählt. Sie können sich vergewissern, daß Sie nicht gemeint sind.«*

Der aber fühlte sich »gemeint« und bemüht sich nun, seinem literarischen Namensvetter immer ähnlicher zu werden. Außerdem trägt eine seiner Töchter auch noch den Namen Luise, und manche Attribute, die der Autor sich für seine Geschöpfe ausgedacht hat, stimmen mit der Realität überein.

Der Erlanger Studienprofessor würdigt seinen ehemaligen Schüler keiner Antwort. Statt sich bei ihm direkt zu beschweren [...] *bereitet der Pädagoge den gerichtlichen Angriff vor. In dem Bewußtsein »Konrad Loch in der Novelle ist ein Ehrenmann und sein Name nicht schlechtgemacht«, reinen Gewissens also, reist der Autor inzwischen nach Wien. Er hatte – so unverständlich das scheinen mag – die Gefahr, die ihm drohte, überhaupt nicht erkannt.*[2]

Drei Klagen wurden von Lorenz Loch eingereicht. Und man darf davon ausgehen, daß seine »nationale Gesinnung« den SA-Mann zu diesem Schritt ebenso bewogen hat wie das Empfinden, persönlich verunglimpft worden zu sein. Zwei der angestrengten Verfahren endeten für ihn erfolgreich: Zunächst wurde aufgrund einer Unterlassungsklage die Verbrei-

[2] Ulla Penzoldt, *Ernst Penzoldts Novelle »Etienne und Luise«. Verhängnisvolle Folgen einer Namenswahl*, in: *Ernst Penzoldt. Kunst und Poesie. Katalog zur Ausstellung im Palais Stutterheim, 3. Mai bis 14. Juni 1992*, bearbeitet von Gertraud Lehmann unter Mitarbeit von Jürgen Sandweg, Erlangen 1992, S. 103–109, hier S. 106f.

tung der Novelle mit dem Namen des Klägers am 8. Januar 1930 verboten; die im September 1929 erschienene Buchausgabe in der Reclam Universalbibliothek mußte daraufhin eingestampft werden (sie erschien 1930 in einer revidierten Neufassung[3]). Dann, am 4. März 1931, wurde Penzoldt wegen Beleidigung zu insgesamt 1100 Mark Geldstrafe verurteilt. Das entsprach etwa vier Monatsgehältern eines Arbeiters und überstieg bei weitem das Honorar von 200 Mark, das ihm der Reclam-Verlag gezahlt hatte. Penzoldt legte gegen das Urteil Berufung ein, ebenso Loch, der eine Gefängnisstrafe erwartet hatte. Um die Auseinandersetzung zu beenden, vereinbarten beide Parteien 1932 schließlich einen Vergleich, der Penzoldt zu einer Zahlung von 5000 Mark verpflichtete. Nur das Meineidsverfahren wegen Penzoldts eidesstattlicher Versicherung, er habe Lorenz Loch nicht gemeint, endete am 17. März 1931 mit einem Freispruch für den Autor[4]. Doch abgesehen von diesem Teilerfolg, war das Ergebnis im Ganzen für Penzoldt eine bittere Niederlage, denn wegen der erheblichen finanziellen Folgen entging er nur knapp einem Offenbarungseid. Dabei hatte sogar der Publizist Josef Hofmiller (1872–1933), dem man sicher nicht Unrecht tut, wenn man ihn einen stockkonservativen, durch und durch nationalistischen Publizisten nennt, als Gutachter der Anklage zwei Expertisen zugunsten Penzoldts abgegeben[5]. Hofmiller, für Kurt Tucholsky der Typus eines deutschen

[3] Ebenfalls 1930 veröffentlichte der zu Ullstein gehörende Arcadia-Verlag Penzoldts Dramatisierung des Stoffs als Bühnenmanuskript. Aus dem Turnlehrer Loch wurde nun der Hilfslehrer Konrad Arminius.

[4] Zu den angegebenen Zahlen und Daten vgl. Ernst Penzoldt. Kunst und Poesie, a. a. O., S. 108f.

[5] Auch der durch zahlreiche Veröffentlichungen zur Klassischen Philologie hervorgetretene Oberstudienrat Eduard Stemplinger (1870–1964) trat als Sachverständiger Lochs auf und stellte fest, Penzoldt habe den Namen Loch nur aus künstlerischen Gründen gewählt. Die weiteren (von Penzoldt bestellten) Gutachter waren: der von 1922 an in München lebende Schriftsteller Paul Alverdes (1897–1966; vgl. auch Anm. 37 in der Dokumentation), der Feuilletonredakteur der *Münchener Zeitung* Hanns Braun (1893–1966), der leitende Redakteur der *Münchner Neuesten Nachrichten* Tim Klein (1870–1944) sowie der Literatur- und Theaterwissenschaftlier Artur Kutscher (1878–1960).

Professors, der an guter Gesinung noch mit dem letzten Feldwebel wetteifert[6], ausgerechnet Hofmiller empfand Penzoldts erzwungene Änderungen am Text der Novelle als künstlerische »Abschwächung«: *Vor allem, daß Penzoldt in der 2. Fassung den Loch zum Schreiblehrer macht, ist ein viel zu weitgehendes Entgegenkommen. Der Turnlehrer ist gleichberechtigtes Mitglied des Lehrerrats einer Anstalt, er hat Sitz und Stimme in jeder Sitzung. Der Schreibunterricht wird fast überall namentlich erteilt, oft vom Aktuar oder Sekretär. Der Turnlehrer gehört zum Kollegium, der Schreiblehrer zum Personal. Außerdem kann nur der Turnlehrer im gesellschaftlichen Leben der kleinen Stadt Mössel an der Maar diese Rolle spielen; nie der Schreiblehrer. Und so mache ich mich anheischig, Ihnen an jedem einzelnen Zug zu zeigen, daß Herr Penzoldt vor lauter Entgegenkommen gegen Herrn Prof. Loch sogar seine Novelle künstlerisch zu ihrem Nachteil verändert hat.*[7]
Wenn nach Penzoldts Tod, vermutete Hofmiller, *die Novelle* Etienne und Luise *in seinen Gesammelten Werken erscheint, wird nur die Urfassung gedruckt werden.* Und tatsächlich findet sich im fünften Band der Jubiläumsausgabe, die zu seinem 100. Geburtstag veröffentlicht wurde, eine erweiterte Fassung des Erstdrucks[8].
Daß es auch bei der geplanten Oper nach der Novelle *Etienne und Luise* zu Änderungen des Textes kam, hatte dagegen weder persönlichkeitsschutzrechtliche noch politische Gründe. Selbst im März 1933 glaubte Hindemith überraschenderweise, wegen des Stoffs *keinerlei Bedenken*[9]

6 Vgl. Kurt Tucholsky, *Kriegsdienstverweigerer*, in: *Kurt-Tucholsky-Gesamtausgabe*, Bd. 5, Reinbek 1999, S. 357.
7 Josef Hofmiller, *Ernst Penzoldts »Etienne und Luise«*, in: *Süddeutsche Monatshefte*, Jg. 28, 1930/31, S. 602–607, hier: S. 604.
8 Vgl. Ernst Penzoldt, *Jubiläumsausgabe zum 100. Geburtstag*, Frankfurt/Main 1992, Bd. 5, S. 66–119. Den leichten Vergleich zwischen der Erst- und der Neuausgabe aus dem Jahr 1930 ermöglicht ein von Wulf Segebrecht in der Fränkischen Bibliophilengesellschaft Bamberg herausgegebener Faksimiledruck der Erstausgabe mit Penzoldts handschriftlichen Änderungen.
9 Vgl. Dok. Nr. 55.

haben zu müssen. Er behielt zwar durchaus im Blick, den Text von *irgendwelche[n] irgendwen anstoßende[n] Stellen*[10] freizuhalten, und auch der Verleger Ludwig Strecker beschäftigte sich mit dem Problem, ob das Libretto »im Sinne der vaterländischen Zuverlässigkeit« einwandfrei sei. Aber die erste entscheidende Veränderung, die Verlegung der Handlung auf einen Bahnhof, geschah keineswegs aus politischen Rücksichtnahmen. Vielmehr sah der Eisenbahn-Narr Hindemith, der in seiner Berliner Wohnung gemeinsam mit Musiker-Kollegen und Kompositionsschülern ganze Sonntage lang mit einer großen Märklin-Eisenbahnanlage zu spielen pflegte, endlich die Gelegenheit gekommen, seine Liebhaberei in einer Oper zum Ausdruck zu bringen. Penzoldt war damit sofort einverstanden und das – so darf man mutmaßen – nicht nur, um Hindemith einen Gefallen zu tun: Schon in seinem ersten, 1927 erschienenen Roman *Der Zwerg* hatte er neben dem Automobil, dem Flugzeug und dem Telephon leitmotivisch die Eisenbahn als einen Indikator für eine Technisierung menschlichen Verkehrs in der Moderne eingesetzt.

Helmut Lethen bezeichnete den Verkehr als einen zentralen Topos neusachlicher Literatur, als ein neues Paradigma, das eine entschiedene Abwendung vom Gemeinschaftsmythos der Lebensideologie mit sich brachte[11]. In Gestalt eines Bahnhofs, auf dem Menschen verschiedener Generationen, ungleicher Herkunft und differierender Meinungen zusammentreffen, sollte dieser Topos nun in einer Weise Eingang in die geplante Oper finden, die auf den ersten Blick vermuten läßt, daß Penzoldt und Hindemith auf die von Lethen bei Arnolt Bronnen und Ernst Jünger beobachtete Militarisierung des Verkehrs-Paradigmas zu Beginn der dreißiger Jahre mit einem Gegenentwurf reagieren wollten. Doch tatsächlich sind die wesentlichen Momente bereits in Penzoldts Novelle ausgeführt, denn die Rettung Etiennes durch Luise führt keinesweg zu einer idyllischen Romanze. *Was als Romeo-und-Julia-Geschichte be-*

[10] Vgl. Dok. Nr. 39.

[11] Vgl. Helmut Lethen, *Verhaltenslehren der Kälte. Lebensversuche zwischen den Kriegen*, Frankfurt/Main 1994, S. 44–50.

ginnt, beschrieb es Magnus Reitschuster, *entwickelt sich zu den* Szenen einer Ehe *und endet schließlich als Strindbergscher* Totentanz: *Die beiden jungen Menschen, die den Krieg ihrer Nationen zunächst privat überwinden, bekämpfen sich im eingeengten Alltag bald bis aufs Messer, und das nur von außen bedrohte Idyll des Anfangs wandelt sich zum verbissenen Stellungskrieg der Geschlechter. Der Mensch, dem Menschen zunächst ein Helfer, wird ihm zum Wolf: Luise erwägt ernsthaft, Etienne selbst anzuzeigen; sie holt sich einen deutschen Soldaten aufs Zimmer und veranstaltet im Angesicht des versteckten Etienne eine Liebesszene; auch Etienne läßt keine Gelegenheit mehr ungenutzt, seinerseits zu verletzen; selbst die nationalistischen Vorurteile der bedrohlichen Außenwelt werden gegen den anderen ins Feld geführt. Der private Raum kann sich nicht als Insel der Humanität behaupten, er wird zum Gefängnis, zum Grab der Gefühle. Zwei, die einmal eins waren, werden sich fremd und feind. Am Ende stirbt jeder für sich allein.*[12]

Im Gegensatz zu Ernst Jünger, der einen gesellschaftlichen Kriegszustand ontologisiert und lediglich die Freiheit zuerkennt, ihn zu verkennen oder ihm in einem heroischen Realismus entgegenzutreten, stellt Penzoldt konkrete Gründe dar, die einer Verwirklichung von Humanität entgegenstehen. Zugleich aber unterscheidet sich seine illusionslose Darstellung menschlicher Verhaltensweisen von einer pazifistischen Literatur, die – wie es etwa bei Leonhard Frank in seinem 1917 publizierten Novellenzyklus *Der Mensch ist gut* zu beobachten ist – das ersehnte Ideal kurzerhand zur Wirklichkeit erklärt.

Welche Vorstellungen Hindemith hatte, um Penzoldts Text kompositorisch umzusetzen, ist nur in Ansätzen erkennbar. Die Arbeit an dem Projekt wurde eingestellt, noch bevor Hindemith mit der musikalischen Ausarbeitung hatte beginnen können. Einige spärliche Andeutungen lassen jedoch zumindest eine grobe Einordnung des geplanten Werks in

[12] Magnus Reitschuster, *Zur Aufarbeitung des an Penzoldt statuierten Exempels*, in: Programmheft zur Szenischen Ermittlung *Der Prozeß des Ernst Penzoldt* von Magnus Reitschuster, Stadttheater Erlangen 1992, unpaginiert.

das Schaffensumfeld zu. *In der Musik werden viele alte Soldaten- und sonstige Lieder vorkommen, auch irgendein russischer Nationaltanz, Mundharmonika- und Zieharmonikastücke* – so hatte Hindemith seinen Verlegern Ludwig und Willy Strecker im Januar 1933 erläutert. Überlieferte Melodien (vorzugsweise Volkslieder) kompositorisch zu verarbeiten, war 1933 für Hindemith nicht mehr neu und wurde auch in den folgenden Jahren und Jahrzehnten von ihm häufig praktiziert. Schon 1930 hatte er in der *Konzertmusik für Klavier, Blechbläser und Harfen* op. 49 erstmals ein Volkslied zur Grundlage eines Satzes autonomer Musik gemacht. Da hier nur eine in der Partitur eingetragene Bemerkung auf das Zitat hinwies, blieb es von Kritikern wie Publikum noch weitgehend unbemerkt. Anders verhielt es sich mit der *Symphonie »Mathis der Maler«* (1933/34) und der gleichnamigen Oper (1934/35) sowie mit dem Bratschenkonzert *Der Schwanendreher* (1935), auf deren Volkslied-Hintergrund Hindemith nun eigens aufmerksam machte[13]. Welche weitreichenden Konsequenzen dieser Hinweis hatte, wurde im Verlauf der von März 1934 an öffentlich geführten kulturpolitischen Auseinandersetzung um Hindemith deutlich, die sich an der umjubelten Uraufführung der *Symphonie »Mathis der Maler«* durch Wilhelm Furtwängler entzündet hatte. Hindemiths wohlmeinende, vielleicht auch allzu naive Verteidiger konnten darauf verweisen, daß von »Kulturbolschewismus« oder »entarteter Musik« doch nicht bei einem Manne die Rede sein könne, der deutsches Liedgut in seine Werke aufnimmt. Sie lieferten damit aber dem kulturkonservativen Lager innerhalb der NS-Bewegung den Beweis dafür, daß sich der Komponist der nationalistischen Stimmung nach 1933 habe andienen, im Sinne der NS-Ideologie »populär« sein wollen. Hindemith geriet in das Kreuzfeuer dieser Debatte, die 1936 schließlich in einem offiziellen Aufführungsverbot seiner Werke endete. Zusammen mit der seit 1933 äußerst eingeschränkten,

[13] In einem Einführungstext für das Programmheft der Uraufführung der *Symphonie »Mathis der Maler«* hatte Hindemith die Volksliedmelodien vorgestellt; das Bratschenkonzert *Der Schwanendreher* trägt den Zusatz *nach alten Volksliedern*.

nur noch im Ausland möglichen Konzerttätigkeit bedeutete dieses Aufführungsverbot für Hindemith ein faktisches Berufsverbot, dem er sich nur durch die Emigration entziehen konnte. Es ist nicht auszuschließen, daß seine in späteren Jahren merkliche Scheu, über programmatische wie autobiographische Bezüge seiner Kompositionen Auskunft zu geben, unmittelbar mit diesen Erfahrungen zusammenhing[14].

Es steht zu vermuten, daß Hindemith sich bei der musikalischen Ausgestaltung des Penzoldt-Stückes den ins Auge gefaßten »Soldaten- und sonstigen Liedern« an geeigneter Stelle auch in parodierender Absicht nähern wollte. Bereits seine Parodiekomposition für Streichquartett *Minimax Repertorium für Militärorchester* (1925) zeigte, wie vertraut er mit dem einschlägigen Repertoire war, das er sich während seiner Soldatenzeit im Ersten Weltkrieg angeeignet hatte. Das letzte Kriegsjahr verbrachte er an der Westfront, wo er als Regimentsmusiker die Große Trommel rührte[15]. Auch der Schlußsatz des 1927 entstandenen Bratschenkonzerts *Kammermusik Nr. 5* op. 36 Nr. 4, eine virtuose Persiflage des »Bayerischen Defiliermarsches«, kann eine ungefähre Vorstellung davon geben, wie Parodien in der Penzoldt-Oper geklungen hätten. Insgesamt jedoch hätte die Oper wohl kaum in der Nachfolge der satirischen, inhaltlich wie musikalisch den Geist der zwanziger Jahre atmenden Zeitoper *Neues vom Tage* (1929) gestanden, deren Text vom

---

[14] In diesem Zusammenhang ist auch der Umstand zu sehen, daß Hindemith in seinem 1945/46 entstandenen *Requiem For Those We Love* eine jüdische Weise zitierte, ohne jemals direkt darauf hingewiesen zu haben. Das Zitat entschlüsselte erst vor wenigen Jahren der amerikanische Musikwissenschaftler Kim Kowalke; siehe dazu seinen Beitrag *For Those We Love. Hindemith, Whitman, and »An American Requiem«*, in: *Hindemith-Jahrbuch* 1998/XXVII, S. 102–154.

[15] Noch in den fünfziger Jahren war Hindemith die Vorliebe für Militärmusik nicht verloren gegangen: Rudolf Hartmann, der als Intendant der Münchner Staatsoper die dortige Uraufführung von Hindemiths Oper *Die Harmonie der Welt* (1957) mitverantwortete, berichtet von einem *vergnügten Abend mit Paul Hindemith, mit dem zusammen ich im kleinen Nebenzimmer der Maximilianstuben alle uns bekannten Märsche sang (sehr zum Ergötzen der beiden anwesenden Frauen), wobei wir eine gemeinsame Vorliebe für den »Mussinan-Marsch« entdeckten.* Vgl. Rudolf Hartmann, *Das geliebte Haus. Mein Leben mit der Oper*, München 1975, S. 9.

Berliner Kabarett-Autor Marcellus Schiffer verfaßt worden war. Denn bereits das in Zusammenarbeit mit Gottfried Benn entstandene Oratorium *Das Unaufhörliche* (1931) steht in deutlicher Distanz zum neusachlichen, bisweilen auch experimentellen Charakter vieler früherer Kompositionen und dokumentiert damit Hindemiths »konservative« Wende zur emphatischen Kunstmusik des 19. Jahrhunderts. Da die 1933 in Arbeit genommene *Symphonie »Mathis der Maler«* und auch die gleichnamige Oper an dieser neuen Stilrichtung anknüpfen, ist mit einiger Wahrscheinlichkeit auszuschließen, daß das von Hindemith selbst ins Spiel gebrachte Eisenbahn-Milieu des Entwurfs ähnlich »zeitopernhaft« umgesetzt worden wäre wie etwa bei Ernst Krenek, in dessen Jazzoper *Jonny spielt auf* (UA Leipzig 1927) nicht nur Requisiten wie Taschenlampe, Telephon, elektrische Klingeln und ein Automobil, sondern auch eine Szene in einer Bahnhofshalle mit einfahrender Lokomotive für großes Aufsehen gesorgt hatten.

Trotz des Fehlens musikalischer Zeugnisse lassen die überlieferten Dokumente der Zusammenarbeit mit Penzoldt Einblicke in Hindemiths Schaffensweise zu. Dies ist um so bemerkenswerter, als sich Hindemith zu seinem eigenen Komponieren sonst nur sehr selten konkret geäußert hat. Am Beginn des Arbeitsprozesses für eine Oper stand danach der von Komponist und Textdichter gemeinsam erarbeitete Handlungsablauf, der freilich ganz *von der Musiknummer her aufgestellt und durchgearbeitet* sein mußte[16]. Die eigentliche dichterische Arbeit konnte erst dann beginnen, *wenn ich mir für die einzelnen Szenen ziemlich feststehende musikalische Gerüste gemacht habe, an die wir dann Musik und Worte anpassen*[17]. Hindemith begründete sein Beharren auf dem Primat der Musik damit, daß *man Musikstücke ja nicht komponieren kann wie Wortsätze und Szenen, sondern die Töne eher wie Backsteine aneinandersetzen muß und genau ausrechnen muß, wieviel jeder trägt und wie*

[16] Vgl. Dok. 39.
[17] Vgl. Dok. 44.

weit ein Bogen zu spannen ist[18]. Die hier angedeutete Vorgehensweise nimmt die in Hindemiths späteren musiktheoretischen Schriften dargelegte Beschreibung des kompositorischen Schaffensprozesses »aus dem Großen ins Kleine« bis in Einzelheiten der Metaphorik vorweg: *Aus dem unbestimmten, fast räumlichen Gefühl des zu bildenden Werkes heben sich langsam die Umrisse, nach und nach gliedert sich die Masse, den tragenden Teilen folgen die Verbindungen und schließlich das schmückende Beiwerk. Es ist offenbar, daß hier der Ablauf der Klänge, die Bewegungen und damit auch die Themen und Motive gebildet werden müssen, indem wir die Proportion der Bauteile bis in die letzten Verästelungen erfassen und den Eigenschaften des Materials entsprechend jeweils das Fehlende einsetzen.*[19]

Die Zusammenarbeit von Hindemith und Penzoldt endete Mitte 1933 vor dem Hintergrund der sich weiter zuspitzenden politischen Situation in Deutschland. Hindemiths durchaus ernst gemeinter Vorschlag von Anfang März 1933, statt der politisch brisanten Novelle *eine heitere Oper über die Eröffnung der ersten Eisenbahnen*[20] zu schreiben, stieß bei Penzoldt zwar auf Interesse. Doch ebenso wie Hindemith die zunehmende Unterdrückung durch die Nationalsozialisten als lähmend empfand, fühlte sich auch Penzoldt *gehemmt in seiner Arbeit, in der freien Entwicklung seiner Ideen, und äußerte das Gefühl »stiller Ausschaltung, literarisch gemeint«*[21]. Der Kontakt zwischen Komponist und Schriftsteller brach im November 1933 schließlich ab. Es gibt keine Dokumente, die darauf hinweisen, daß es in späteren Jahren noch einmal zu einer Begegnung oder einem brieflichen Austausch gekommen ist.

---

[18] Vgl. Dok. 44.

[19] Paul Hindemith, *Komposition und Kompositionsunterricht* [1933/35], in: ders., *Aufsätze – Vorträge – Reden*, hrsg. von Giselher Schubert, Mainz/Zürich 1994, S. 51.

[20] Vgl. Dok. 55; 1935 jährte sich die Inbetriebnahme der ersten deutschen Eisenbahnlinie Nürnberg-Fürth zum hundertsten Mal.

[21] Gertraud Lehmann, *Ernst Penzoldt - Künstler, Poet, Liebender. Eine biographische Skizze*, in: *Ernst Penzoldt. Kunst und Poesie*, a.a.O. (Anm. 2), Erlangen 1992, S. 63.

Editorische Notiz

Alle ermittelbaren Quellen zur geplanten Oper in den Nachlässen von Paul Hindemith (im Hindemith-Institut, Frankfurt am Main) und Ernst Penzoldt (im Deutschen Literaturarchiv Marbach) sowie im Archiv des Musikverlags Schott (Mainz) wurden in chronologischer Reihenfolge und ungekürzt wiedergegeben. Orthographie, Zeichensetzung und Stileigentümlichkeiten sind dabei gewahrt, Schreibversehen stillschweigend korrigiert worden. Textergänzungen der Bearbeiter wurden in spitze Klammern gesetzt.

Dank

an Ulla Penzoldt, die nicht nur dem Abdruck der Briefe ihres Vaters zustimmte, sondern auch mit Auskünften bei der Lösung einer Reihe von Kommentarproblemen half, sowie an Jürgen Sandweg, der uns seine umfangreichen Vorarbeiten zu einer Edition des Briefwechsels zwischen Penzoldt und Hindemith zur Verfügung stellte.

Dokumentation

1 Paul Hindemith an Ludwig[1] und Willy Strecker[2]

Berlin, <7.> Oktober 1932

Verehrte Brüder,
ich begebe mich gerade zur Schmiedung eines neu eingelegten heißen Operneisens[3]. Machen Sie sich noch nicht zu große Hoffnungen, umso weniger werden Sie enttäuscht. Ich berichte Ihnen bald über die Aussichten. – Können Sie mir für mich einen Satz Plöner Musiktag-Stimmen[4] schicken? Ferner bitte ich Sie, mir möglichst gleich, damit ich die Sendung bis spätestens Montag früh habe, auf Rechnung der Hochschule (die Sie mir mitschicken können) zu senden: *Morgenmusik*[5]: 3 x Oberstimme, je 2 x 2.3.4. Stimme.
Kantate[6]: Orchesterstimmen hoch 3 x, mittel 3 x, tief 2 x, 10 Chorstimmen, 1 Solo Sprechstimme.

---

[1] Ludwig Strecker (1883–1978) war Mitinhaber des Musikverlags B. Schott's Söhne in Mainz.

[2] Willy Strecker (1884–1958) war Mitinhaber des Musikverlags B. Schott's Söhne in Mainz und mit den Hindemiths in jahrelanger Freundschaft verbunden.

[3] Hindemith hatte am Nachmittag des 7.10.1932 eine Verabredung mit Carl Ebert (1887–1980), einem gebürtigen Frankfurter, mit dem er wahrscheinlich von den frühen zwanziger Jahren an in Verbindung stand. 1931–1933 war Ebert Intendant der Städtischen Oper Berlin. Unter seiner Regie wurde am 31.1.1931 (parallel zu Inszenierungen am Residenz-Theater in München und in Oldenburg) Penzoldts erstes Theaterstück *Die Portugalesische Schlacht* am Hessischen Landestheater in Darmstadt uraufgeführt. Bei dieser Gelegenheit haben sich Ebert und Penzoldt kennengelernt. Nach Hitlers Ernennung zum Reichskanzler wurde Ebert entlassen und arbeitete als Regisseur an ausländischen Bühnen.

[4] Gemeint ist Hindemiths Komposition *Plöner Musiktag* (1932). Das vierteilige Werk war für die Schüler der Staatlichen Bildungsanstalt Plön in Holstein entstanden und wurde dort im Juni 1932 in Zusammenarbeit mit dem Komponisten einstudiert und aufgeführt.

[5] Erster Teil des *Plöner Musiktag*: Drei Stücke für Blechbläser.

[6] Dritter Teil des *Plöner Musiktag*: Kantate *Mahnung an die Jugend, sich der Musik zu befleißigen.*

Am Montag Nachmittag spiele ich diese Sachen mit den Gesangsvereinsdirigenten, die bei uns an der Schule[7] einen Kursus mitmachen. Sicher ist das eine gute Propaganda.
Schnell Schluß für heute und besten Gruß Ihr
Paul H.
Auch vom Philh. Konzert[8] hätte ich gerne einige kleine Partituren. Gieseking[9] hat das Klavierkonzert herrlich gespielt. Es war in Anbetracht der Tatsache, daß lauter vermutlich sich abwechselnde Rundfunkhörer im Saale waren, ein guter Erfolg.

2 Carl Ebert[10] an Ernst Penzoldt

Berlin, 8. Oktober 1932

Lieber und verehrter Herr Penzoldt!
Ich falle gleich mit der Tür ins Haus, weil ich seit gestern ganz erregt über eine mir vorschwebende Möglichkeit bin, die Sie – wie ich hoffe – interessieren wird.
Sie kennen mindestens dem Namen nach meinen Freund, den Komponisten Paul *Hindemith*. Seit Jahren sucht Paul Hindemith einen »ihm liegenden« Textdichter für eine neue Oper. Seine bisherigen Werke litten fast ausnahmslos unter dem Nachteil einer undichterischen und zu flüchtigen Textbehandlung, sodaß er – zum Bersten angefüllt mit Tatendrang – nunmehr einen wirklichen *Dichter* sucht und keinen Librettisten, der zusammenhanglos neben ihm herläuft.

---

[7] Gemeint ist die Staatliche Akademische Hochschule für Musik in Berlin, an der Hindemith von 1927 an als Kompositionslehrer tätig war. Am 10., 12. und 13.10.1932 nahm er bei einem dort veranstalteten Chordirigentenkurs als Dozent teil.

[8] Hindemiths *Philharmonisches Konzert. Variationen für Orchester* (1932) war ein Auftragswerk der Berliner Philharmoniker aus Anlaß ihres 50jährigen Bestehens.

[9] Walter Gieseking (1895–1956) war dt. Pianist, den Hindemith spätestens von Sommer 1925 an kannte. Gieseking war am 5.10.1932 der Solist bei einer Konzertaufführung der *Konzertmusik für Klavier, Blechbläser und Harfen* op. 49 im Rahmen der Berliner Funkstunde. Das Funkorchester wurde von Eugen Jochum dirigiert.

[10] Vgl. Anm. 3.

Beim öfteren Durchsprechen dieses Problems fiel gestern von seiner Seite Ihr Name. Mir ging es wie eine Erleuchtung auf, und als ich ihm den Inhalt der »Portugalesischen Schlacht« und von »Etienne und Luise« erzählte, waren wir uns beide einig, daß der Komponist Hindemith mit dem Dichter Penzoldt eine gewisse Seelenverwandtschaft besitzen muß, die vielleicht noch einmal fruchtbar gemacht werden kann.
Ich frage also deshalb heute mit Hindemith's Einverständnis bei Ihnen an, ob Sie überhaupt grundsätzlich einem solchen Gedanken nähertreten würden. In diesem Fall wäre ein baldiges Kennenlernen und Aussprechen zwischen Ihnen Beiden notwendig und Hindemith würde Sie mit Freuden einladen, als sein Gast baldigst nach Berlin zu kommen.
Zum zweiten könnten Sie sich vielleicht überlegen, ob die »Portugalesische Schlacht« von Ihnen als Operntext hergegeben wird, was ich persönlich als durchaus möglich hielte, da mir dieser Stoff grade wegen seiner gegensätzlichen Elemente der musikalischen Interpretation entgegenzukommen scheint.
Ich habe bei dieser Kuppelei ein so gutes Gefühl wie es selten ist, und möchte schon heute sagen, daß ich als Kenner der beiden Potenzen Penzoldt und Hindemith auch der Nutznießer dieser Verbindung sein möchte, wie es einem ordentlichen Kuppler zukommt.
Bitte durchdenken Sie die ganze Angelegenheit und geben Sie mir und Hindemith, der Ihnen direkt schreiben wird, baldigst Nachricht. Über ein Wiedersehen, noch dazu in so aktiver Art, würde sich ganz besonders freuen, Ihr Sie und Ihre Frau herzlich grüßender
Carl Ebert

3 Paul Hindemith an Ludwig und Willy Strecker

Berlin, 10. Oktober 1932

Verehrte Brüder,
der vornehme Mann sagt zwar nicht »es ist zum Kotzen«, es ist aber

wirklich so. Ich sitze da wie eine trockene Jungfrau. Benn[11] funkt eben gar nicht. Er kommt vor lauter Überkritik zu nichts. Er plagt sich sehr und sicher kommt auch etwas zum Vorschein, aber wie lange soll man darauf warten? Die St. Galler Sache[12] reizte ihn anscheinend nicht genug, Gutenberg[13] und Grünewald[14] ebenso. Nun knobelt er weiter – man muß halt sehen, was passiert. In meiner Verzweiflung habe ich beschlossen, selbst Eier zu legen. Schließlich weiß ich, was ich will und die Worte haben diese Dichter doch immer nur machen können, wenn ich ihnen ganz genau vorgeschrieben habe, was sie tun sollen. Für Gutenberg habe ich mir eine Menge Material gesammelt. Die Zeit ist interessant, in Mainz und Straßburg passiert um 1440 allerlei, nur der Mann selbst gibt so gar nichts her. Beim besten Willen sprüht er keine Funken, so sehr man auch draufhaut. Er scheint ein ziemlich trockener Herr gewesen zu sein. Möglich wäre es, die Buchdruckerkunst selbst in den Mittelpunkt der Handlung zu stellen, aber dazu gehört ein Dichter mit »Visionen« – und wo sind die? Grünewald wäre gut, wenn er nicht gerade Maler wäre. Wesen und Zweck einer Oper um Grünewald könnte doch nur die Malerei sein und man käme ja gar nicht drum herum, den Mann in Begeisterung malen zu lassen; ein für die Musik sehr dürftiges und für meine Begriffe komisches Motiv. Erinnern Sie sich an die »Gezeichneten«[15], wo die exaltierte Dame vor der Staffelei in Ver-

---

[11] Mit Gottfried Benn (1886–1956) hatte Hindemith 1931 das Oratorium *Das Unaufhörliche* geschrieben und verhandelte mit ihm seitdem über die Zusammenarbeit an einer gemeinsamen Oper. Diese Pläne wurden jedoch nicht realisiert.

[12] Hindemith hatte Benn vorgeschlagen, am Beispiel der Klosterschule von St. Gallen den kulturellen Kolonisationsprozeß zum Thema einer Oper auszuarbeiten (vgl. Gottfried Benn, *Briefwechsel mit Paul Hindemith*, hrsg. von Ann Clark Fehn, Frankfurt/Main 1986, S. 67f.).

[13] Vom Plan, den Mainzer Buchdrucker Johannes Gutenberg zum Thema der neuen Oper zu machen, ist in einem Brief Willy Streckers an Paul Hindemith vom 26.9.1932 die Rede.

[14] Matthias Grünewald (d.i. Mathis Neithardt, um 1460/70–1528) war Maler des *Isenheimer Altars* und Protagonist in Hindemiths Oper *Mathis der Maler* (1933–1935).

[15] Oper von Franz Schreker (1878–1934), die 1918 in Frankfurt/Main uraufgeführt wurde. Dirigent der Uraufführung war Hindemiths späterer Schwiegervater Ludwig

zückung gerät? Etwas Ähnliches müßte wahrscheinlich auch hier passieren. Vielleicht finden Sie noch andere Stoffe. Ich überlege auch hin und her. Zur Übung und zum Zeitvertreib wollte ich einstweilen eine Oper machen, die man für Kinder spielen kann als Weihnachtsmärchen. Ich dachte an eine Variante des Andersen-Märchens »Der kleine und der große Klaus«, hatte es auch schon ziemlich weit entwickelt, aber man kann es doch nicht machen[16]. Entweder man macht es so naiv, wie es geschrieben ist, dann kann man es nicht auf die Bühne stellen, oder man stellt es in ein anderes Milieu, dann passen die Motive nicht mehr. Vielleicht finde ich noch einen anderen Vorwurf. Einiges schwebt mir vor. Es ist ein dämlicher Zustand. Ich bin geladen und könnte jeden Tag mit einer Theatermusik loslegen. So kann ich nur getreu dem Wahlspruch hier sitzen »Verzweifeln und nicht arbeiten«. Zum Trost erscheint nachher Herr Menge[17] bei uns. Besseres weiß ich heute nicht. Vielleicht kann ich Ihnen nächstens trostreichere Dinge schreiben.
Einstweilen schönste Grüße Ihres
Paul H.

4 Ludwig Strecker an Paul Hindemith

Mainz, 10. Oktober 1932

Lieber Herr Hindemith,
die Opern-Angelegenheit ist wirklich verzweiflungsvoll und der Offenbarungseid, den ich in dieser Sache Ihnen gegenüber ablegen muß, beschämt mich.
Eventuelle Anregungen, die ich Ihnen vielleicht geben könnte, sind schriftlich ziemlich zwecklos. Bei einer mündlichen Aussprache fällt schon eher manchmal ein Samenkorn auf fruchtbaren Boden.

Rottenberg. Hindemith, der Schreker auch persönlich gut kannte und schätzte, spielt auf die dritte Szene im zweiten Aufzug an.

[16] Von diesem Projekt sind keine Dokumente überliefert.

[17] Lektor beim Verlag B. Schott's Söhne.

Die Sache mit dem kleinen und großen Klaus hatte mich selbst schon einmal beschäftigt, ich bin aber aus den gleichen Gründen wie Sie zu keinem Ergebnis gelangt. An den gleichen Erwägungen scheiterte ja auch das Faust'sche Puppenspiel[18].
Daß Sie aus Gutenberg[19] keinen Funken schlagen können, erstaunt mich weiter nicht. Ein besonderer Nachteil dieses Stoffes scheint mir das Fehlen jeder Frauenrolle zu sein, ohne die es nun mal bei der Bühne nicht abgeht. Ich hatte an Gutenberg seinerzeit auch in Verbindung mit Faust gedacht, der ja nach verschiedenen Sagen mit Faust identifiziert wird. Mir schien schon bei diesem Stoff dieses Sagenhafte und Mystische der ergiebigste Teil zu sein. Die Klosterleute waren damals diejenigen, die Gutenberg in den Ruf der teuflischen Schwarzkunst bringen wollten, aus Angst ihren Verdienst durch Abschriften der Bücher zu verlieren. In dieser Richtung müßte man m.E. am ehesten suchen. Aber wer besitzt die Phantasie hierzu? Der historische Gutenberg ist notwendig langweilig.
Hinsichtlich Grünewald[20] teile ich durchaus Ihre Bedenken. – Von all den zwischen uns besprochenen Plänen scheint mir das Stück vom Rhein[21] immer noch das amüsanteste zu sein. Die Strauß-Wirtschaften in den feudalen Schlössern und die Tragikomödie zwischen der heutigen und der vergangenen Zeit war ein Thema, welches auch Zuckmayer[22] als ergiebig erkannt hat. Aber auch hier brauchen wir den Gestalter.

---

[18] Hindemith zog 1923 in Erwägung, das im Insel-Verlag (Nr. 125) erschienene *Puppenspiel vom Doktor Faust* als Sujet für eine Oper zu verwenden. In seinem Nachlaß findet sich der *Entwurf einer Filmoper »Faust«* von Franz Blei, dem Autor von Hindemiths Einakter *Das Nusch-Nuschi* (1920). Der Plan wurde nicht weiter verfolgt.

[19] Vgl. Anm. 13.

[20] Vgl. Anm. 14.

[21] Von diesem Bühnenprojekt, das Hindemith und Ludwig Strecker vermutlich nur mündlich erörterten, sind keine Dokumente überliefert.

[22] Gedacht war offenbar an eine Umarbeitung oder Fortsetzung des Erfolgsstücks *Der fröhliche Weinberg* von Carl Zuckmayer (1896–1977), das am 22.12.1925 am Theater

Die Ankündigung eines allerneuesten Planes setzt mich in begreifliche Erwartung. Gleichwohl verspreche ich Ihnen nicht allzu sehr enttäuscht zu sein, wenn das Problem auch noch nicht durch diesen Streich fällt. Jedenfalls bitte ich Sie, mich sehr auf dem Laufenden zu halten, denn es ist doch immerhin möglich, daß die vereinigten Bemühungen unserer Phantasie das Problem fördern können.
Bruder Willy ist zu Schiff nach England und begibt sich von dort zu Schiff nach Frankreich und mit der Eisenbahn wieder zurück.
Herzlichste Grüße Ihnen beiden
Ihr getreuer <Ludwig Strecker>

5 Ernst Penzoldt an Carl Ebert

München, 11. Oktober 1932

Sehr verehrter lieber Herr Professor Ebert,
Ich habe mich schon gefreut ehe ich Ihren Brief las und gelesen noch mehr. Ich bin gern bereit mitzuhelfen (nach Kräften) und bitte Sie Herrn Hindemith, dessen Namen ich natürlich kenne (und einige Arbeiten, die ich sehr gerne habe) dies zu sagen. Auch die Portugalesische Schlacht[23] als Text ist durchaus zu erwägen. Ich glaube aber, ich kann Ihnen noch einen anderen Vorschlag machen[24]!

---

am Schiffbauerdamm in Berlin unter der Regie von Reinhard Bruck uraufgeführt wurde. Kontakte zwischen Hindemith und Zuckmayer bestanden von Beginn der zwanziger Jahre an. Spätestens 1926 gab es auch erste Überlegungen zu einer gemeinsamen Oper, die jedoch nicht realisiert wurden; erst 1961/62 schrieben sie die Kantate *Mainzer Umzug*. Vgl. dazu: *Zuckmayer - Paul Hindemith: Briefwechsel. Ediert, eingeleitet und kommentiert von Gunther Nickel und Giselher Schubert*, in: *Zuckmayer-Jahrbuch*, Jg. 1, 1998, S. 9–118.

[23] Vgl. Anm. 3.

[24] Penzoldt beschäftigte sich mit der Lebensgeschichte des Prinzen Eugen von Savoyen (1663–1736) und hatte vor, ein Stück über ihn zu schreiben. Dieser Plan wurde nicht ausgeführt.

Ich bin ab 20. Oktober jederzeit abkömmlich und nehme Herrn Hindemiths Einladung zum Kennenlernen und Aussprechen gerne an, wobei ich auch Sie wiederzusehen hoffe.
Mit herzlichen Grüßen an Sie und Ihre Frau
Ihr
Ernst Penzoldt

6 Paul Hindemith an Ernst Penzoldt

Berlin, 14. Oktober 1932 [Poststempel]

Sehr geehrter Herr Penzoldt,
Herr Ebert schickte mir heute Ihren Brief. Ich freue mich, daß Ihnen der Gedanke, eine Oper mit mir zu schreiben, nicht unangenehm ist. Es wird sicher keine leichte Arbeit sein, denn die Kritik, die man den leicht etwas lächerlichen Eigenheiten der Oper gegenüber hat, machen die Stoffwahl und die Herstellung des Textes zu einer etwas mühseligen Arbeit und sicher wird vom Dichter wie vom Musiker ein reichliches Maß Selbstverleugnung aufzubringen sein einer Kunstgattung gegenüber, die ja weder reine Dichtung noch reine Musik ist. Wenn Sie die Schwierigkeiten nicht scheuen und einen ja immerhin möglichen Fehlschlag des Versuchs auch mit in Kauf nehmen wollen, wäre ich sehr froh, wenn Sie Ende dieses Monats für ein paar Tage hierher kommen würden. Über das genaue Datum können wir uns ja noch verständigen. Wenn Sie sich einen Stoff (oder sogar einige zur Auswahl) schon vorher überlegen könnten, hätten wir für unsere Unterredungen schon eine gute Grundlage, von der aus man sicher leicht in die Materie sich einarbeiten könnte. Für unpraktisch hielte ich es aber, wenn Sie mittlerweile schon anfangen würden, einen Text in Szenen auszuarbeiten, da ja die Worte, die dem Dichter lieb sind, meistens nicht die sind, die sich gut komponieren lassen. Am schönsten wäre es, wenn Sie kurze Aufrisse und vielleicht Szenenfolgen von Handlungen mitbrächten, über deren szenische, musikalische und textliche Gestalt wir uns dann ausführlich

unterhalten könnten. In der Zeit zwischen 21. und 27. Oktober habe ich gut Zeit. Wären Ihnen da einige Tage recht? Und welche?
Mit bestem Gruß
Ihr Paul Hindemith

7 Ernst Penzoldt an Paul Hindemith

<München>, 15. Oktober 1932

Sehr geehrter Herr Hindemith,
auch ich bin mir der großen Schwierigkeiten bei der Herstellung eines guten Textes wohl bewußt. Aber ich will es versuchen. Eine Aussprache wird die für Ihre Pläne nötigen Voraussetzungen sicher bald klären. Vielleicht lassen sich an Hand meiner *Portugalesischen Schlacht* Ihre Wünsche (und meine Möglichkeiten ihnen zu dienen) praktisch abgrenzen. Ich schlage vor, daß ich am Samstag den 22.X. in Berlin eintreffe (vormittags). Prof. Ebert schrieb davon, daß ich bei Ihnen wohnen dürfe, ich bitte Sie aber mir ganz ruhig zu sagen wie es Ihnen am besten paßt. Ich wohne sonst immer bei einem Freund[25], wo ich auch diesmal unterkommen kann. Ich werde rohe Skizzen der Stoffe die mich beschäftigen mitbringen. Sie sind alle sehr verschieden voneinander.
Mit den besten Grüßen
Ihr
sehr ergebener
Ernst Penzoldt

---

[25] Gemeint ist Wilhelm Foerst (1898–1986). Er war Redakteur der Zeitschriften *Angewandte Chemie* und *Die chemische Fabrik* und stammte wie Penzoldt aus Erlangen, wo sich beide 1918 befreundeten. Foerst verhalf Penzoldt während der NS-Zeit zu Werbeaufträgen. Für die von Foersts Bruder Kurt geleiteten Albertwerke in Wiesbaden gestaltete Penzoldt unter dem Pseudonym Fritz Fliege Werbegrafiken für Schnupfen-, Schlaf- und Abführmittel.

8 Paul Hindemith an Ernst Penzoldt

Berlin, 18. Oktober 1932

Sehr geehrter geehrter Herr Penzoldt,
seien Sie bestens bedankt für Ihre Zusage. Ich freue mich, daß Sie zu einer (oder mehreren) ausführlichen Besprechung herkommen wollen. Sicher werden wir uns gut über alles verständigen und es sollte mich ehrlich freuen, wenn Sie in einer gemeinsamen Arbeit gute Möglichkeiten sehen und darum den Versuch nicht zu ungern unternehmen würden. – Herr Ebert schrieb Ihnen wohl, daß ich Sie einladen wollte und aus Ihrem Brief ersehe ich, daß Sie das mißverstanden haben: Zum Wohnen kann ich Sie leider nicht einladen, da wir teils wegen Platzmangels, teils wegen des vielen Betriebes, in dem ich leider stecke[26], nicht für Besuche eingerichtet sind. Für alle Auslagen Ihrer Reise und Ihres hiesigen Aufenthaltes sollten Sie aber natürlich mein Gast sein. Bitte richten Sie alles so ein, wie es Ihnen am liebsten ist. Auf jeden Fall bitte ich Sie aber, mich nach Ihrer Ankunft bald anzurufen (Nummer siehe oben[27]; verlieren Sie sie nicht, wir stehen nicht im Telefonbuch!). Ich bin den ganzen Samstag und den Sonntag auch vollkommen frei und ich denke, wir werden dann genügend Zeit haben, alles zu besprechen. Eben telefonierte ich mit Frau Ebert: sie meint, wir sollten Sonntag nachmittag zu ihnen kommen.
Also einstweilen bis Samstag herzlichen Gruß.
Ihr
Paul Hindemith

[26] Neben dem Unterricht an der Berliner Musikhochschule, an der Anfang Oktober das Semester wieder begonnen hatte, bereitete sich Hindemith auch auf Konzerte mit den Berliner Philharmonikern unter der Leitung von Wilhelm Furtwängler vor, vgl. Anm. 51.

[27] Hindemith verwendete Briefpapier mit einem gedruckten Briefkopf.

9 Ernst Penzoldt an Paul Hindemith

München, 20. Oktober 1932

Sehr geehrter Herr Hindemith,
vielen Dank für Ihren Brief! Ich rufe Sie am Samstag vorm. an und stehe ganz zu Ihrer Verfügung. Auch zu Eberts komme ich sehr gern.
Ich wohne bei Dr. W. Först[28]
B.-Friedenau Wilhelmshöherstr. 18^{III}
(Amt: Rheingau 8037)
Alles Übrige mündlich.
Mit den besten Grüßen
Ihr
Ernst Penzoldt

10 Ernst Penzoldt An Ernst Heimeran

<Berlin, 24. Oktober 1932>

Lieber Ernstle[29],
ich habe das Gefühl schon eine Woche lang fort zu sein. Es ist leider sehr anstrengend und ich habe das Gefühl: keine neuen Leute mehr! Der erste Tag: Früh nach kurzem 2. Frühstück mit William[30] bei Sulzbach[31],

---

[28] Vgl. Anm. 25.

[29] Ernst Heimeran (1902–1955) studierte nach einer Schlosserlehre Kunstgeschichte und Philosophie. Penzoldt begegnete ihm erstmals am 18.6.1920 bei einem Konzert, kannte aber bereits die von 1917 an von Heimeran herausgegebene Schülerzeitschrift *Der Zwiestrolch*. Penzoldt und Heimeran wurden Freunde. Am 26.8.1922 heiratete Penzoldt Heimerans Schwester Friedi. Wenig später gründete Heimeran einen Buchverlag, der am 27.10.1922 handelsgerichtlich eingetragen wurde. Bei seiner ersten Publikation handelte es sich um Penzoldts Gedichtband *Der Gefährte*. *Man muß*, so Ulla Penzoldt, *sich vergegenwärtigen, was das bedeutete: Ein blutjunger, völlig unbekannter Verleger brachte die ersten Äußerungen eines völlig unbekannten Schriftstellers und Graphikers heraus.* (in: Ulla Penzoldt/Volker Michels [Hrsg.], *Ernst Penzoldt. Leben und Werk in Bildern und Texten*, Frankfurt/Main 1988, S. 225).

[30] D.i. Wilhelm Foerst, vgl. Anm. 25.

[31] Ernst Sulzbach (1887–1954) war Lektor im Theaterverlag Arcadia, der zum Ullstein-Konzern gehörte.

wo ich mit Hindemith und andern telephonierte. S. redete mir zu die Oper zu machen, ab die port. Schlacht von Kukhoff[32] bearbeiten zu lassen, da »ihre Zeit zu Ende sei«. Weil Samstag konnte ich sonst niemanden erreichen. Mittag mit William war Roberts[33]. Ich sagte: heute ist in München Föhn. Nachm. 4h bei Hindemith kleiner Frankfurter Nichtjude, der eine Kindereisenbahn mit 4 Garnituren und endlosen Geleisen besitzt und zuweilen damit spielt. Macht sehr lustige und selbständige »Telephon« Zeichnungen[34]. Er habe zwar Gefallen an dem Schulplan[35], hält es aber für den Stoff zu einer Kinderoper, vielleicht ein andermal. Eugen[36] gefiel ihm besser. Von sich aus schlug er – Etienne und Luise vor in Bahnhofmilieu spielend. Wir verstanden uns ganz gut. Er ist sicher der härtere Kopf. Auch scheinen die Musiker ganz anders zu arbeiten als wir. Abends mit Paul[37] Prinz von Homburg[38]. Recht gut. Sonntag ab 11^{h} vorm. bei Hindemith Spaziergang im Grunewald. Die Füße tun mir heute noch weh. Nachm. Ebert[39]. Zieht nicht recht für E. u L. Möchte lieber Port. Schlacht. Der Schulstoff interessierte ihn gar nicht. Vielleicht sind wir auf dem Mond. Abends mit Helgo[40] und William bei Kempinski[41].

---

32 Möglicherweise der 1930–1932 als Dramaturg und Regisseur in Berlin engagierte Schriftsteller Adam Kuckhoff (1887–1943).

33 Nicht ermittelt.

34 Vgl. Susanne Schaal/Angelika Storm-Rusche, *Paul Hindemith. Der Komponist als Zeichner*, Mainz/Zürich 1995.

35 Nicht ermittelt.

36 Vgl. Anm. 24.

37 Paul Alverdes (1897–1979) war in den zwanziger und zu Beginn der dreißiger Jahre mit Penzoldt befreundet. Danach führte Penzoldts Befremden über Alverdes' Entwicklung als Herausgeber der Zeitschrift *Das Innere Reich* zum Ende der Verbindung.

38 Eine Neuinszenierung von Heinricht von Kleists *Der Prinz von Homburg* am Staatlichen Schauspielhaus Berlin hatte am 19.10.1932 Premiere. Regie führte Max Reinhardt.

39 Vgl. Anm. 3.

40 Helgo Krüll. Nähere Angaben konnten nicht ermittelt werden.

41 Großes Weinrestaurant der gehobenen Kategorie in der Leipziger Straße 25.

Heute werde ich im Verlag sein. Abends bei Zucker[42]. Nachm. will ich versuchen die andern Leute zu erreichen. Hoppenheit[43] hat mich telephonisch mehrmals verfehlt. Er hat kein Telephon.
Bernd[44] kommt Freitag zurück. Helgo sagte ich solle nach Lübeck fahren. Aber ich merke, daß ich vierzig bin. Ich komme voraussichtlich Mittwoch Abend. Lies zwischen den Zeilen stundenlanges Gerede. Ich vermisse Dich überall. Ich habe nur Dich. Alles andere ist mir so gleichgültig geworden. Mehr Ehrgeiz müßte ich haben!
Leb wohl! Hoffentlich erreiche ich Schmahl[45] noch. In München ist das alles so leicht mit dem Selbstwählverkehr.
Vielen Dank für die Kuschekarte[46] und den Brief[47]. Die Rechnung geht mit gleicher Post ab. Helgo ist ein erfreulicher Mensch. Morgen muß ich nochmal zu Hindemith.
Herzlichst Dein E.
Montag früh

11 Gertrud Hindemith an Ludwig Strecker

Berlin, 25. Oktober 1932

Lieber Herr Doktor,
jener geheimnisvolle Herr, von dem ich Ihnen sprach, heißt Ernst Penzold. Kennen Sie ihn? Ich lege Ihnen der Einfachheit halber seine beiden

---

[42] Wolf Zucker (geb. 1905), war 1924/25 Volontär von Siegfried Jacobsohn, des Herausgebers der Wochenzeitschrift *Die Weltbühne*. Zwischen 1927 und 1931 veröffentlichte er zahlreiche Beitrräge in der *Weltbühne*, von 1928 bis 1931 auch in der von Willy Haas herausgegebenen *Literarischen Welt*.

[43] Nicht ermittelt.

[44] Bernd Nitschke. Nähere Angaben konnten nicht ermittelt werden.

[45] Möglicherweise Eugen Schmahl (1892–1954), der Feuilletonredakteur des *Berliner Lokal-Anzeigers* war.

[46] Gemeint ist eine verschollene Karte des Komponisten und Musikschriftstellers Ludwig Kusche (1901–1982), ein Schulfreund von Ernst Heimeran (vgl. Anm. 29) und Mitarbeiter an dessen Schülerzeitschrift *Der Zwiestrolch*. Kusche komponierte die Bühnenmusiken zu Penzoldts *Die Portugalesische Schlacht* und *Die verlorenen Schuhe*.

[47] Nicht ermittelt.

Briefe bei und schicke Ihnen die Portugalesische Schlacht.[48] Er war 2 Tage hier und wird eine moderne Sache machen. Ebert[49] hat die Sache vermittelt und auch einen ganzen Nachmittag hier bei uns verbracht und seinen Senf als Theatermann dazu gegeben. Heute treffen wir P. noch einmal und dann fährt er ab und will einen Entwurf schicken.
Sie hören dann bald. Benn[50] hat sich vergraben. Paul hat Furtwänglerkonzert[51] diese Woche hier und Hamburg, darum wenig Zeit. Er berichtet Ihnen aber nächste Woche, bis dahin hat er auch vielleicht schon eine Skizze. Die Idee ist glänzend, ich will aber nichts vorwegnehmen, lesen Sie erst das Buch, vielleicht auch die berühmte »Powenzbande«[52], die ist auch von ihm. Er hat auch Ideen für Kinderstücke.
Viele Grüße, sehr hastige, ein Bogen muß noch zum Beziehn heute früh
Ihre G. Hindemith

12 Ernst Penzoldt an Paul Hindemith

München, <26. Oktober 1932>

Lieber Herr Hindemith,
die lange Eisenbahnfahrt war eine gute Gelegenheit und Anregung das Besprochene noch einmal durch zu denken. Ich fange morgen an. Heute schicke ich den versprochenen Chatterton[53] und die Novelle (zweite

---

[48] Vgl. Anm. 3.
[49] Vgl. Anm. 3.
[50] Vgl. Anm. 11.
[51] Hindemith spielte mit den Berliner Philharmonikern unter der Leitung von Wilhelm Furtwängler am 27.10.1932 in Berlin und am 28.10.1932 in Hamburg das Bratschenkonzert *Harold en Italie* von Hector Berlioz. Auf dem Programm stand außerdem die *Sinfonia Concertante* KV 364 von Wolfgang Amadeus Mozart, die Hindemith gemeinsam mit Simon Goldberg, dem Primgeiger der Berliner Philharmoniker, interpretierte. Am 30. und 31.10.1932 fanden unter Furtwänglers Leitung zwei weitere Konzerte mit den Berliner Philharmonikern statt, bei denen Hindemith erneut als Interpret von *Harold en Italie* engagiert war.
[52] Penzoldts Roman *Die Powenzbande*, der 1930 im Propyläen-Verlag erschienen war.
[53] Penzoldts Roman *Der arme Chatterton*, der 1928 im Insel-Verlag erschienen war.

Fassung[54]). Es wäre nett von Ihrer Frau wenn Sie sie lesen würde und vielleicht auch Sie. Es wird Sie bestimmt nicht irritieren, dagegen mir den Anfang erleichtern, falls etwas dabei mit Ihren Vorstellungen zusammengeht. Es ist ja schließlich nur der Stoff. Manches was da nur angetippt ist kann Ihnen wichtig und komponibel (sicher gibt es das Wort gar nicht!) erscheinen. Man kann sich über die unverbindlichere Grundlage der Novelle praktisch verständigen. Ich danke Ihnen für alle Freundlichkeit. Ich habe mich, das ist ganz wichtig, wohl und gar nicht fremd gefühlt und das Kompott wie den Trebergeist in *dankenswerter Erinnerung*. – Könnten Sie rausbekommen, ob Frau oder Frl. Ebert den Chatterton besitzt?
Mit den besten Grüßen vor allem an Ihre Frau und Alfi[55].
Ihr
Ernst Penzoldt

13 Ludwig Strecker an Gertrud und Paul Hindemith

Mainz, 28. Oktober 1932

Bravo, liebe Hindemiths, zu Penzoldt und seiner »Portugalesischen Schlacht«[56]. Endlich einmal kein Würstchen; bezaubernde Details und echte Phantasie und zwar dramatische Phantasie. Wenn es sich hier nicht um einen einmaligen Wurf handelt – ich bin vorsichtig geworden – so darf man wirklich wieder einmal hoffen. Hat er also eine Idee und Lust zur Zusammenarbeit, so ... toi, toi, toi!
Ich diktiere diese Zeilen im Bett, ohne Wissen des Arztes und gegen seinen Willen – ich habe se nämlich eine dumme Gallengeschichte – aber ich bin ja so glücklich und gespannt auf weitere Nachrichten.
Am 21. Oktober hatte ich eine Sitzung in Berlin, die meinetwegen abgesagt werden mußte. Ich hatte mir vorgenommen, am 22. Oktober

---

[54] Gemeint ist die wegen der Rechtsstreitigkeiten mit dem Erlanger Pädagogen Lorenz Loch (1863–1957) angefertigte zweite Fassung der Novelle *Etienne und Luise.*
[55] Hund von Gertrud und Paul Hindemith.
[56] Vgl. Anm. 3.

Sie zu besuchen, wäre dann also mit Pentzold zusammengetroffen. Dies merkwürdige Zusammentreffen fasse ich als irgend einen Hinweis auf. Kurzum, in guter Hoffnung mit einem besonders herzlichen, aber verbotenen Gruß aus dem Bett
Ihr aufrichtiger
L.E. Strecker
i.A. Sekretärin

14 Gertrud Hindemith an Ludwig Strecker

Berlin, 30. Oktober <1932>

Lieber Herr Doktor,
wir hoffen sehr, daß Sie inzwischen ganz gesundet sind. Wie kommt denn Ihre Galle dazu, sich mehr als berechtigt bemerkbar zu machen? Die Arbeit mit Penzold geht aber gut weiter (sie haben schon einen bestimmten Stoff, ich will nur Paul nicht vorgreifen, der Ihnen dann berichten will), er ist abgefahren und nun müssen die Männer schriftlich arbeiten. Das ist aber ganz gut, schwarz auf weiß ist sicherer und ergiebiger als gedankengeschwängerte Lüfte. Sowie etwas akut ist, hören Sie. Inzwischen nur die allerbesten Wünsche von uns beiden, vielleicht erscheinen Sie bald bei uns.
Viele Grüße für Sie und Ihre ganze Familie
Ihre Hindemiths

15 Paul Hindemith an Ernst Penzoldt

Berlin, 2. November 1932 [Poststempel]

Lieber Herr Penzoldt,
schönsten Dank für Ihren Brief und die beiden Bücher. Ich habe sie schon beide hinter mir; sowohl die Novelle[57] als auch der Chatterton[58]

---

[57] Vgl. Anm. 54.
[58] Vgl. Anm. 53.

haben mir große Freude gemacht. Es sind schöne Bücher, und da sie mir als fast notorischem Nichtbücherleser (meine Lektüre besteht ja fast nur aus Büchern über Mistkäfer, Musik, Geschichte und so) so gut gefallen haben, hat das sicher seine Bedeutung. Die Novelle hat mich nicht irre gemacht: der Stoff ist nach wie vor großartig und in der dramatischen Bearbeitung muß ja notgedrungen vieles anders aussehen. Auf Ihre praesumptiven Sendungen bin ich schon sehr neugierig, möchte aber nicht, daß meine Neugier Ihnen wie ein Sporn in den Weichen (da wir doch beim Bahnhof verblieben sind!) sitzt. Trebergeist ist alle, auch sonst mangelt's bei mir an Geist, deshalb für heute nichts mehr. Zu Ebert's werden wir Asbjörn Krag[59] oder sonst einen befähigten Detektiv schicken des Chatterton wegen und Ihnen das Resultat seiner geheimen Erkundungen dann durch unseren Privatsender WC00 auf der Riesenwelle 34769 zusprechen lassen. Inzwischen wünschen wir Ihnen zu Ihrer schweren und verantwortungsreichen Mission der Einführung des Rumkompotts einen unbestrittenen Erfolg, ja, wir hoffen Sie auf diesem Gebiete mindestens als Crack, wenn nicht gar als Champignon wiederzusehen. Von meiner über die Novelle begeisterten Frau einen schönen Gruß, vom Alfi ein Pfotchen. Von mir auch.

Ihr

Paul Hindemith

16 Ernst Penzoldt an Paul Hindemith

München, 3. November 1932

Lieber Herr Hindemith!

Heute sende ich Ihnen die erste Fassung für den Operntext[60]. Ich habe absichtlich manche der besprochenen Möglichkeiten noch außer acht gelassen. Ferner habe ich auch schon (nur an manchen Stellen!) Worte

---

[59] Detektiv in Kriminalromanen des norweg. Schriftstellers Sven Elvestad (1884–1934); Krag war in den zwanziger Jahren so bekannt wie Sherlock Holmes.

[60] Vgl. Dok. 17.

gegeben, wo es für mich leichter war, so den Ablauf mancher Szene deutlich zu machen. Ich habe mich bemüht, möglichst einfach zu sein und ich hoffe, daß ich trotzdem deutlich genug war. Sie werden ohne Weiteres erkennen, wo ein Duett, wo der Chor oder die Arie am Platz ist. Mit meinem Laienverstand könnte ich mir ganz gut denken, daß der Krieg musikalisch, namentlich in den ersten Szenen deutlich werden kann. Das erste Bild gibt, glaube ich, genügend klar die Exposition. Das Bahnhofs-Milieu läßt sich leicht noch bunter illustrieren.
Ich glaubte richtig zu handeln, wenn ich dem Geschehen etwas von seiner tragischen Schwere genommen habe. Trotz dem Sie in Berlin dafür nicht recht zu haben schienen, habe ich im zweiten Bild das Haus im Querschnitt gebracht. Erschrecken Sie nicht über den nächtlichen Spuk, vielleicht gelingt es, das halb ernste, halb komische der träumenden Hausbewohner und den Fieberparoxismus Etiennes in einer großen Ensemble-Nummer wirksam zu machen. Bei den Stellen, wo Luise lyrische oder balladenhafte Gesangsnummern haben könnte, bin ich etwas ausführlicher geworden.
Ich habe vorläufig dem Stück ein gutes Ende gegeben, das meiner Meinung nach einen allzu grausigen Ausgang glaubhaft umgeht. Luise hat sich zwar für den Durchschnittsbeschauer schuldig gemacht, aber sie verdient ebenso wenig wie Etienne dafür den Tod, es genügt völlig, daß sie Etienne verliert. Ich weiß wohl, daß da und dort noch manches eingefügt werden kann z.B. Etienne's Entschluß, trotz seiner Liebe zu Luise, zu entfliehen, auch ist die Figur des Vaters nicht völlig durchgeführt.
Ich habe von diesem Entwurf einen Durchschlag hier, sodaß Sie für Ihre Wünsche zur weiteren Ausgestaltung des Textes nur die Seitenzahlen, Bild und Szene angeben brauchen. Ich darf noch sagen, daß der Stoff für die Bühne spröder ist, als ich es mir zuerst vorgestellt habe. Es ist nicht leicht, auf einigermaßen natürliche Weise z.B. Volk mit dem Geschehen in Verbindung zu bringen. Vielleicht ist in mancher *Andeutung* für Sie eine große musikalische Gelegenheit enthalten und umgekehrt. Ich würde mich aber freuen, wenn dieser erste Entwurf im Großen und Ganzen als

zuversichtliche Grundlage dienen könnte. Die von Ihnen als entbehrlich empfundene Mutter, glaubte ich nicht entbehren zu können.
Ich erwarte mit Spannung Ihre Antwort und werde mich bemühen, alle Ihre Wünsche zu erfüllen oder mit neuen Vorschlägen einen für beide Teile überzeugenden Ausweg zu finden.
Mit den besten Grüßen, auch an Ihre Frau
Ihr
Ernst Penzoldt
Vielen Dank für Ihren Brief, der eben kam. Ich freue mich, daß Ihnen die Bücher gefallen. Meine Frau hat leider noch keinen Rumtopf angesetzt.
Der Obige

17 Erster Entwurf der Oper von Ernst Penzoldt

Etienne u. Luise
1. Entwurf zu einer Oper
(unter Zugrundelegung der Erzählung Etienne und Luise) von Ernst Penzoldt
Die Oper spielt auf dem Streckenbahnhof der kleinen deutschen Stadt Querfurt während des letzten Krieges.

I. Bild.
Bahnhofswirtschaft und Warteraum das übliche Büffet mit Vitrine für Schokolade und Zigaretten. Syphon. Künstliche Blumen auf den Gasttischen. Fahrpläne. Große Karte der Kriegsschauplätze, ziemlich hoch an der Wand broncierte Büste Wilhelms des Zweiten auf einer Konsole. Man sieht und spürt durch die Fenster und Schwingtüre den Betrieb auf dem Bahnsteig.

1. Szene.
Am Büffet wirtschaftet Frau Schmidt, eine brave gute Frau, die aussieht, als könnte sie hervorragend Apfelstrudel backen. Sie ist der Alltag und

Haushalt in Person, betulich und ängstlich. Ihr Großer steht vor Ypern im Feld.

Der Wirt, Herr Schmidt, ist ein großes Kind. Er besitzt eine poetische Ader und hat gewaltige Rosinen im Kopf. Als Soldat ist er nicht genommen worden »er hat zuviel Fläche«. Aber er dient auf seine Weise der großen Sache. Er steckt Fähnchen auf der großen Kriegskarte. Denn er ist ein verkannter Stratege und arbeitet freiwillig an einem fabelhaften Plan zur raschesten Niederwerfung sämtlicher Feinde. Er rollt die Westfront auf, treibt die Engländer zu Paaren und wirft die »Vettern« ins Meer, marschiert getrennt und schlägt vereint. Er wird das Ganze ins Reine bringen. Kurz er hat Horizont, er muß es selbst zugeben. Seine Frau versteht das eben nicht, wenn Männer reden.

Schmidt's Publikum ist sein kleiner Sohn Fritz, der Pikkolo, sowie Herr Koppholzer Dienstmann Nr. 1, der vergeblich auf den vornehmen Fremden wartet und auf das fürstliche Trinkgeld. Die Querfurter tragen ihr Gepäck selbst. Koppholzer ist Schmidt's Gegner im Kriegsspiel mit dem die Szene anhebt. Er führt die Feinde und besiegt Schmidt auf dem Papier. »Viele Hunde sind des Hasen Tod«, »Wir müssen und wir werden siegen«. Es geht herrlich vorwärts draußen. Täglich fahren Gefangenentransporte durch Querfurt, weiße und farbige Franzosen, Engländer, Inder, Russen, Italiener. Die Feinde halten es keine vierzehn Tage mehr aus.

Frau Schmidt ist weniger zuversichtlich: es gießt seit drei Tagen in Strömen, es ist Herbst, es wird ja schon um fünf Uhr Nacht. Man wird bald heizen müssen. Drüben in den Telegraphendrähten hängt ein nasser Papierdrache. Man könnte schwermütig werden.

2. Szene.

Der Postzug Querfurt-Köppen-Kaula wird abgerufen. Zehn Minuten Aufenthalt. Nach X umsteigen. Die Wartegäste fragen tausend Dinge, ob der Zug Anschluß nach Schönwitz hat, ob er Speisewagen hat, »Wie komme ich am Besten nach Y, ich muß dort eine Tante besuchen«, der Bahnbeamte gibt nach allen Seiten Auskunft.

Koppholzer eilt freudig an die Arbeit, die Pflicht ruft. Fritz, der Pikkolo hat sein Tragbrett vor den Leib genommen. Man hört ihn draußen rufen: wahme Wühstchen, Bier, Schokolade, Keks, Obst.
Urlauber, die wieder ins Feld müssen benutzen den Aufenthalt rasch mal einen zu heben, Zigaretten zu kaufen. Der Wirt hält sie frei. Wohin sie wohl kommen? »Streng geheim! Sämtlichen Unteroffizieren und Mannschaften bekanntzugeben«. Am liebsten gingen sie nach Italien. Ja die alte deutsche Sehnsucht nach dem Süden! »Im Westen kämpft das tapfere Heer, im Osten steht die Feuerwehr!« »Um ein Drittel Parras gehen wir nicht nach Arras. Wenn wir nicht einen halben kriegen, lassen wir den Tommy siegen«. Der Krieg ist eine herrliche Sache, wenn man ihn gesundheitlich aushält.

3. Szene.
Jetzt kommt Fritz, der Pikkolo, mit einer großen Neuigkeit. Ein französischer Kriegsgefangener ist im nahen Tunnel aus dem Transportzug entsprungen. Die Soldaten nehmen es nicht sehr wichtig. Der kommt nicht weit. Hinter Fritz treten die drei alten Bahnhofstanten auf, rechte Vogelscheuchen mit nassen Schirmen. Sie fabeln: man habe den Franzmann bereits tot auf den Schienen gefunden, in schauderhafter Zerstükkelung. Der Zug sei ihm gerade durch das Gesicht gefahren. Man sagt es sei ein Prinz aus Napoleons Geschlecht. Der Bahnwärter will ihn mit eigenen Augen auf einem Schimmel westwärts reitend gesehen haben. Schließlich es sei gar nicht nur einer entkommen, sondern ihrer zwölfe gefährliche Kerle, die nun nachts die Dörfer heimsuchen würden, brandschatzend, weder Frauen noch Kinder verschonend.
Frau Schmidt ist nun in ernster Sorge um Luise, ihre Tochter. Sie ist eine kranke Freundin besuchen gegangen über den Tunnelberg. Wenn ihr bloß nichts zustößt, wo der fremde Unhold die Gegend unsicher macht. Ein Gendarm fordert die Bevölkerung auf wachsam zu sein und die Behörden tatkräftig zu unterstützen. Wer einem Kriegsgefangenen forthilft oder gar Unterschlupf gewährt, macht sich des Landesverrates schuldig.

Jetzt ist Herrn Schmidt's großer Augenblick gekommen. Man muß den Flüchtling dingfest machen. Schmidt fühlt sich berufen, die Verfolgung zu organisieren.

4. Szene.
Indem kommt Luise, ein Mädchen von sechzehn Jahern, ein Kind fast, unansehnlich und hager von Gestalt, mit einem Gang noch ohne Anmut. Sie trägt die Zöglingstracht eines Mädchenstiftes, schwarzes Kleid von keuschem Zuschnitt und weißem Liegekragen und himmelblauem Lackgürtel. Sie neigt zu Sommersprossen.
Luise ist verstört und totenbleich. Man bestürmt sie mit Fragen ob sie etwas Verdächtiges wahrgenommen drüben am Tunnel. Sie beteuert übertrieben: nein gar nichts, sie habe niemanden gesehen. Sie hat nur einen Zug von Norden kommen sehen, sie hörte sein Zischeln weither und wartete wie so oft, daß er nun schneller und schneller komme, lauter und immer größer werde bis er schwarz und schmetternd unter ihr in den Berg fuhr, der lange nachzitterte. Es fielen aber die Blätter von den Bäumen ihren Schatten entgegen, es donnerte aus den Tiefen und der Qualm zerriß im Wind und geiferte über die Hänge.

5. Szene.
Die Soldaten machen Luise den Hof. Sie ist unnahbar. Vielleicht hat sie schon einen »Schatz«. Herr Schmidt behauptet: nein. Sein Töchterchen erzähle ihm alles, sie habe kein Geheimnis vor ihm. Sie ist noch ein rechtes Kind, noch nicht erwacht.
Frau Schmidt wäre es freilich lieber, Luise ginge auf ihr Zimmer, aber Vater besteht darauf, daß sie nett zu den Feldgrauen sei. Wer weiß ob sie wiederkommen. Sie soll sich nicht zieren, in Züchten die Tapferen küssen. Auch den mit dem roten Bart? Der küßt ihr galant die Hand. Nur einer, der schwer hinausgeht, küßt sie stürmisch wie ein Liebender. Luise reißt sich los und weint am Büffet. Die Alten: was hat das Mädchen, da stimmt was nicht! Da stimmt was nicht!

6. Szene
Einsteigen! Höchste Eisenbahn! (wie vorhin) Die Urlauber lärmen hinaus »Siegreich wolln wir Frankreich schlagen« »Drum Mädchen weine nicht und sei nicht traurig, mach deinem Grenadier das Herz nicht schwer«. Zugsabfahrt.
Vater Schmidt waffnet sich. Auch Fritz rüstet sich indianisch. Bäckerlehrlinge, Gymnasiasten, Schornsteinfeger usw. bilden ein kleines Heer. Auch Koppholzer geht mit. Herr Schmidt hält eine kleine anfeuernde Ansprache, dann ziehen sie aus zum Franzosenfang. Frau Schmidt: Ach die Männer!

II. Bild
Das Wohngebäude des Bahnhofs im Querschitt. Unten rechts der Warteraum, unten links Schlafgemach der Eltern Schmidt; darüber Luisens »Mädchenstübchen«, rechts gegenüber Zimmer der Alten. In der Mitte das Stiegenhaus mit Fenstern nach hinten.

1. Szene.
Luise in ihrem Zimmer am Fenster. »Lieber Gott mach finster um ihn, daß sie ihn nicht finden!«
Die drei Alten auf der Treppe. »Was siehst du Schwester?« »Ich sehe nichts, die Straße ist leer, es ist eine schwarze nasse Nacht.« »Was ist los, was redet ihr da, ich verstehe kein Wort.« »Wir können doch nicht so brüllen, Urschwester.«
»Ach Gott warum muß ich auf der Treppe sitzen, mich friert.« Die Schwester guckt. »Herr Schmidt ist ausgezogen, den entsprungenen Franzmann zu fangen.« »Ist noch immer Krieg, Schwester?« »Ich sehe etwas.« »Was siehst Du Schwester?« »Ich sehe die Lichter von der Knaben Taschenlampen drüben am Tunnelberg geistern. Still! Manchmal höre ich auch ihre Stimmen. Sie rufen einander zu.« »Sie fürchten sich natürlich. Sie werden ihn schon nicht finden. Der ist doch längst über alle Berge.« »Nein, Schwester, o nein, er ist nicht über alle Berge,

oh nein!« »Sie redet aus dem Schlafe, sie ist nicht bei Trost, ich fürchte, wir werden sie nicht mehr lange haben.«
Luise: lieber Gott mach finster um ihn, daß sie ihn nicht finden.
Die Alten: Siehst du was Schwester? »Regen, Nacht und mein Gesicht in der Scheibe.« (Es fallen ein paar Schüsse, man hört Rufe in der Ferne.)
Luise: Allmächtiger Gott, jetzt haben sie ihn totgeschossen!
Die Alten: Jetzt haben sie ihn totgeschossen!
Frau Schmidt in ihrem Zimmer: Jetzt haben sie ihn totgeschossen!
Die Alten: Nun laufen die Lichter hin und her wie eine verirrte Rotte von Sternen. (Man hört eine Knabentrompete, jetzt sammeln sie sich, sie treten den Rückmarsch an.)

2. Szene.
Luise öffnet oben die Tür und schaut die Stiege hinab.
Die Alten: Ei sie sind noch auf, Fräulein Luischen?
Luise: Haben sie es gehört, man hat geschossen da drüben. Sicher ist etwas Entsetzliches passiert.
Die Alten: Warum entsetzlich? Sie werden halt den Franzmann umgebracht haben. Was ist mit ihnen? Sie sind ja leichenblass.
Luise: Ich bin so furchtbar erschrocken.
Die Alten: sie kann nicht einmal das bißchen Schießerei vertragen. Die Geschichte ist aus, gehen wir schlafen.

3. Szene.
Kläglicher Gesang der Heimkehrenden.
Schmidt: (Hinter der Szene) Abteilung halt! Gewehr ab! Rührt euch!
Kleine Ansprache: Leider ist infolge der Ungunst der Witterung dem Unternehmen ein Erfolg versagt geblieben. Weggetreten!
Fritz, der Pikkolo, kommt die Treppe herauf, schnatternd vor Kälte.
Luise: Habt ihr ihn?
Fritz: Ach wo! Papa hat sich vor einem Baum erschrocken und dreimal blindlings in die Nacht geschossen.

Luise: (wirft ihm eine Schachtel Zigaretten zu, Fritz wundert sich)
Vater Schmidt geht auf sein Zimmer, ebenso die Alten.
Luise: (hat rasch ein paar Sachen einen Mantel und dergleichen zusammengepackt und schleicht die Treppe hinab)
Zwischenmusik.

III. Bild

Mitternacht. Szene wie vorhin. Anfangs nur das Stiegenhaus erleuchtet. Luise kommt mit dem flüchtigen Franzosen Etienne, einem todmüden jungen Menschen, er hat einen deutschen Soldatenmantel um, er sieht fremdartig und verwildert aus, seine Haut ist gelb, sein rabenschwarzes Haar ungekämmt und voller Sand, die Füße nackt und blutig. Er kann nicht mehr vor Erschöpfung. O mon Dieu!
Luise: (sie spricht sehr schlecht französisch) Still doch! Taisez-vous Monsieur (sie hält ihm die Hand vor den Mund, er will hinsinken vor Müdigkeit) Courage! Monsieur, Courage!
Man hört abläuten: Bim bam. Etienne und Luise erschrecken sehr. Sie beginnen die Treppe hinaufzusteigen, sehr langsam mit oftmaligem Ausruhen.
Still! Hier schlafen die Eltern, hier die drei Alten, sie sind zusammen 250 Jahre alt, es sind Gespenster.
Jetzt sieht man die Zimmer das Ehepaar Schmidt friedlich schlafend, die Alten in Großvaterstühlen sitzend und eingenickt, unten im Warteraum schläft der Dienstmann, vielleicht auch der Pikkolo. Die Lichter der Züge wandern umher.
Etienne und Luise sind oben angelangt. Etienne muß eine Zigarette haben, er bekommt sie. Luise will ihn zu Bette bringen, er weigert sich »J'ai des poux«, er hat Läuse, sie versteht ihn nicht. Er erklärt es ihr, jeder Soldat hat sie zu hunderten, die Deutschen wie die Franzosen.
Luise: Puh, ich verstehe nicht. Etienne sucht etwas in seinem Hemd und hält es zwischen den Fingerspitzen Luise hin. »Allmächtiger Gott eine Laus.« Etienne fast erfreut: Oui, Oui Melle. Eine Laus! Parfaitment. O

viele Laus, undert, sweiundert. Luise holt einen Eimer entkleidet Etienne, nimmt den Teetopf vom Ofen übergießt die Kleider, daß es nur so dampft. Etienne sitzt frierend und sehr unglücklich auf dem Bett. Olala. Luise bettet ihn auf eine sachliche, schwesternhafte Weise. Die armen blutigen Füße. Etienne lobt das Bett, ein Bett wie ein Himmel. Er fängt an zu phantasieren.
Die Alten schrecken auf: Ist jemand da? Ich dachte es sei jemand die Treppe hinaufgegangen.
Schmidt's: Ich habe doch jemand die Treppe hinaufgehen hören.
Koppholzer: (wie oben)
Die Alten sehen ins Stiegenhaus, sie haben wohl schwer geträumt. Alle haben geträumt!
Während oben Etienne zu singen beginnt, im Fieberdelirium (Sous les ponts de Paris) und Luise außer sich ihn zu beruhigen sucht (Willst Du endlich ruhig sein, du weckst mir noch das Haus auf) ja endlich mit dem Kopfkissen ihn am Singen hindert, erzählen die andern, was sie geträumt. Schmidt hat geträumt, der Kaiser hat mit ihm gesprochen: Durchbruch im Westen. Calais ist unser und Paris, das große Sündenbabel. Frau Schmidt will schlafen.
Die Uralte hat geträumt vom Untergang der Welt, friedliche Städte werden an den Mond gesprengt, Häuser kreisen gleich Gestirnen, brennend im Weltall. Die andern Alten wollen schlafen. Der Dienstmann träumt von Gold und Glück, der Pikkolo fürchtet sich und will schlafen. Der Kanon der Träumer endet, Luise ist allein wach: Wenn er nun stirbt, hier in meinem Zimmer, hier in meinem Bett, was fange ich dann nur an? Dann werde ich ihn fortschleppen müssen bei finsterer Nacht in einem Sack über die Treppe hinab und ihn in den Fluß oder in einen tiefen Brunnen werfen mit einem großen Stein um den Hals. Oder seine Leiche stückweise verbrennen oder heimlich verscharren im Walde.

IV. Bild
Luises Zimmer. Wintersonne.

1. Szene.

Mutter und Luise. Der Haushalt verschlingt entsetzlich, woher das nur kommt? Die Alten sagen, daß der Krieg ein schlimmes Ende nehmen werde. Sie haben sich rechtzeitig eingedeckt, sind bei der Mobilmachung in einer Droschke von Laden zu Laden gefahren, um ordentlich einzukaufen, Kaffee vor allem säckeweis, gebrannt, und ungebrannt, Zuckerhüte, Mehl, Rosinen, sogar Salz. Denn so sagen sie, man muß handeln, als ob man ewig leben werde. Es heißt, der entsprungene Franzmann sei noch immer in der Gegend. Man hat einen französischen Militärknopf gefunden und ein blutiges Schnupftuch drüben am Tunnelberg. Er muß ein zäher und verwegener Bursche sein. Luise soll nicht mehr allein spazieren gehen. Sie sei ein junges hübsches Mädchen, wer weiß, was so ein fremder Unhold alles im Schilde führt.

Luise: Ach wo, der ist ja doch längst über alle Berge.

Die Mutter geht.

Luise öffnet den großen Schrank. Etienne kommt heraus. Solange Luise fortgewesen sei, sei er fast gestorben vor Einsamkeit.

Er solle nicht so melancholisch sein. Etienne: Ich bin sehr traurig immer. Ich habe eine große, wie sagt man (er macht eine sehnsüchtige Gebärde) eine große – nach ein Tier, ein 'und oder eine Kuh, ich habe Lust endlich wieder mit einem Mann zu reden und über eine Wiese zu gehen.

Luise hat ihm alles Mögliche mitgebracht: eine Zahnbürste und Rasierzeug, sie lobt ihn, daß er schon so gut deutsch gelernt hat. Er ist glücklich darüber. Er redet ihr vor: Der Sonn scheint. Sie verbessert ihn: die Sonne. Oh wirklich, ich dachte Sonne sei ein Mann, Mond eine Frau. Der Sonn und die Mondin. Luise hat einen Baedecker mitgebracht, damit Etienne ihr zeigen kann, wo er her ist. Hier dieser kleine schwarze Punkt, da ist er geboren worden. In Mont St. Michel. Es ist eine Insel, ein Fels im Meer, ganz wunderbar. Aber in die Schule ist er in Paris gegangen, hier hat er gewohnt, in der Rue Montmartre, bei der dicken Madame Archenpault. Er erzählt von der Fontaine im Tuillerien Garten, wo sie die Segelschiffe haben schwimmen lassen.

3. Szene.
Luise hat etwas gehört, sie versteckt Etienne im Schrank, es war nur der Schornsteinfeger, er bringt Glück, in Deutschland wie in Frankreich. Etienne kommt wieder heraus. Luise zeigt ihm durch das Fenster ihren Bruder Fritz, den Pikkolo und ihren Vater (un monument). Etienne steht dicht bei ihr, sie zeigt ihm das finstere stille Wasser mit dem blauen Kahn, es ist der Weiher, darin sich manchmal verliebte Dienstmädchen ertränken. Im Winter wimmelt er von Schlittschuhläufern. Luise merkt, daß Etienne sie ansieht, er nennt sie beim Vornamen: Luise! Luise will nichts merken und erzählt weiter: in dem Weiher soll eine Kirche versunken sein, jetzt schwimmen die Fische durch die Fenster und da drüben ist der Tunnel, da muß jeder Junge einmal allein hindurchgegangen sein, ganz allein und bei Nacht, man darf eine Kerze mitnehmen. Luise ist auch einmal durch den Tunnel gegangen und da kam ein Zug und blies ihr Licht aus und sie hat sich schrecklich gefürchtet.
Etienne streichelt schüchtern ihr Haar. Luise entzieht sich ihm, immer heftiger weitererzählend.
Die Mutter ruft von unten. Etienne traut sich noch nicht. Luise sagt, daß sie hinunter muß. Etienne befangen: Au revoir Melle! Luise zögernd: Au revoir Monsieur! Sie geht langsam zur Türe, Etienne folgt ihr. Flehend: Luise! Sie wendet sich traurig lächelnd ihm zu und schüttelt den Kopf. Etienne umarmt sie ungeschickt, mit Innigkeit: Louise je t'aime. Luise: (ganz rein) Ich liebe dich Etienne! Die Mutter ruft, sie braucht Luise, ein Zug ist angekommen, man hört die Beamten rufen und den Pikkolo: Bier, Schokolade, Keks. Soldaten singen: Drum Mädchen weine nicht usw.

V. Bild
1. Szene.
Luises Zimmer.
Etienne allein. Er geht wie ein gefangenes Tier im Käfig auf und ab, vor dem Fenster hält er inne. Er ist so unvorsichtig es zu öffnen und einer Katze zu rufen: Minni, Minni! Er nimmt die Katze herein und spricht

mit ihr französisch und deutsch. Er fragt sie, ob sie Schokolade ißt und streichelt sie und bittet sie bald wieder zu kommen.
Luise kommt: Du hast doch gerade mit jemand gesprochen? Er erzählt von der Katze und von seiner Langeweile, er hat stundenlang am Fenster gestanden, immer fahren Züge vorbei, er hat Sehnsucht. Sie sagt: er werde fett. Etienne wird ärgerlich, er hat keine Bewegung, das Zimmer zu klein. Dann soll er sich etwas beschäftigen. Er täte ja nichts wie Zigarettenrauchen und Kaffee trinken den ganzen Tag. Oh, er wolle schon etwas tun. Er schlafe schlecht, er möchte einmal wieder herzhaft müde werden, er will turnen, Freiübungen machen. Luise soll gut zu ihm sein. Er küßt sie. Aber er hat auch an ihr etwas auszusetzen. Sie soll nicht mehr so viel in die Küche gehen. Ihr Haar habe einen Geruch von Sauerkraut, dem unsterblichen deutschen Sauerkraut, nach Wirsing und schlechtem Fett. Natürlich, das ist der Dank, daß Luise so gut für ihn sorgt. Was kann Etienne dafür, daß das deutsche Brot so miserabel ist. Es schmeckt nach Sägspänen und nach Sand. Er kann es nicht gut vertragen mit seine französische Bauch. »Eure deutschen Mahlzeiten sind schrecklich, das mußt du mir nicht übelnehmen Mädchen. Ihr essen Brot, das ist aus Mehl, ihr essen Suppe mit Nudel, die sind aus Mehl, an die Sauce tut ihr Mehl und an die Gemüse, eure Schnitzel sind paniert und hinterher gibt es eine Mehlspeise natürlich.«

2. Szene.
Luise reißt die Zöpfe zur Seite und horcht angespannt. Die Fräuleins! Etienne schlüpft in den Schrank. Luise öffnet das Fenster, schaut sich um, ob alles in Ordnung ist und geht an die Türe.
Die Alten: Recht guten Abend Fräulein Luischen. Luise erwidert kühl. Als die Alten gestern zufällig vorbeikamen, wollen sie eine Männerstimme bei Luischen gehört haben. Eine Männerstimme, wie unpassend, das wird Papa gewesen sein. Nein das wird Papa nicht gewesen sein, der war unten in der Wirtschaft, es war eine fremde Männerstimme.
Luise hat eine Idee. Ach so natürlich, ob sie sie hören wollen? Darf ich bitten, Platz zu nehmen.

Die Alten schnüffeln herum, Fräulein Luischen: hier riechts nach Mann. Luise dreht hohnlächelnd das Grammophon auf. Eine Stimme trägt mit edlem Pathos Schillers Taucher vor: Wer wagt es Rittersmann ...
Die Alten: Ein Grammophon! Ein Grammophon? Kein Grammophon! Die Alten verlassen tückisch das Zimmer, Luise (süß) Gute Nacht, meine Damen, auf Wiedersehen! Sie schließt die Tür, Etienne kommt aus dem Schrank, sie lachen beide lautlos unbändig.

3. Szene.
Siegesglocken, Böllerschüsse. Eine Fahne wird vor dem Fenster aufgezogen und weht ins Zimmer.
Luise: Oh Etienne, ein großer Sieg. Von wem? Von den Deutschen natürlich. Wir haben einen entscheidenden Sieg erfochten. Etienne: Wir, wir, das sind doch wir zwei. Luise: Ich meine wir Deutschen. Gegen wen? Gegen euch, gegen die Franzosen natürlich. Sie spricht aus dem Fenster mit ihrem Vater. Etienne gedrückt: Ist es ein großer Durchbruch im Westen? Ja fünfzigtausend Gefangene, dreihundert Kanonen und viele tausend Tote. Etienne: Ma pauvre France. Luise: Freu dich doch, dann ist der Krieg bald aus. Hör die Glocken läuten, wie sich die Fahnen im Winde blähen! Etienne ist sehr traurig. Luise: Du verdirbst mir noch alle Freude. Etienne: Wie kannst du dich freuen, wenn ich traurig bin. Du hast ein gläsernes Herz und keinen Geschmack. Luise: Was kümmert uns im Grunde der dumme Krieg. Diese Stube ist unser Vaterland und wir lieben uns, was geht uns die Welt an. Etienne: (beharrlich) Wir haben nicht angefangen. Die Deutschen sind wie Räuber in das friedliche Belgien eingefallen, sie haben die Bibliothek von Löwen verbrannt, sie haben kleine Kinder massakriert. Luise: Ob er wohl endlich still sein wolle, er sei verrückt. Das ist ja alles nicht wahr, das lügen die Zeitungen. Aber eure Weiber haben deutsche Verwundete mit Sägmehl erstickt.
Sie werden immer giftiger. Nein, nein Melle, das ist nicht wahr, die Deutschen sind die Barbaren. Luise: Was sagst du, Barbaren sagst du, was seid ihr? Grausam feige Affen seid ihr! Ihr seid Tiere! Etienne: (sehr böse)

Boche! Luise: Du, du (sie bricht in Tränen aus). Etienne beginnt zu bereuen. O Louison nicht weinen, verzeihe mir, wir wollen nicht mehr sprechen von dieser grausamen Politik, nie mehr, nie mehr. Verzeihe mir halt meine liebe, kleine Frau. Luise: Sonst werden auch wir schließlich noch Feinde. Sie küssen sich lange zärtlich. Etienne: O unsere Münder sind bitter von die böse Worte von vorhin. Luise: Ja ganz bitter.

VI. Bild
Bahnhofswirtschaft wie anfangs.
1. Szene.
Herr Schmidt und Luise. Schmidt mit seinen Generalstabskarten hantierend. Luise (flüsternd) Glaubst du Papa, daß der Krieg noch lange dauern wird? Schmidt: Kaum mein Kind, wohl kaum. Luise: Wirklich, wie lange, ach wie lange noch? Schmidt: Das hinge von gewissen Ereignissen ab, an denen er nicht unbeteiligt sei. Seltsam, wenn man so bedenke, er und diese kleine Stadt hier und daß von hier aus Deutschlands Glück komme. Seit acht Tagen regt sich nichts an der Front, das gibt zu denken, völlige Stille, ein gutes Zeichen so scheint es. Vermutlich will man den Gegner einlullen. Luise: Einlullen? Schmidt: Aber dann auf einmal. Hier bei Ypern oder hier bei Verdun, plötzlich mitten aus der Totenstille werden tausend Kanonen aufbrüllen und die Stunde unseres Sieges ist gekommen. Endlich ist sie da. Luise: (ungläubig) Die Fräuleins denken anders und sie haben schon so oft recht behalten.

2. Szene.
Die Familie setzt sich zu Tisch. Herr und Frau Schmidt, Fritz, Luise. Man spricht von dem entsprungenen Gefangenen. Es muß schon ein ganz besonders verwegener und zäher Bursche sein. Luise lacht nervös. Sie solle sich gefälligst etwas beherrschen, das sei nicht zum Lachen, das sind ernste Dinge. »Ich bitte um Kartoffeln«.
Luise (flüsternd): Sie habe in der Zeitung gelesen, in Sachsen irgendwo sei auch ein Gefangener entsprungen. Alle sehen sie befremdet an. Fritz:

Warum flüsterst du? Schmidt: Warum flüsterst du? Luise, räuspert sich erschrocken, dann laut: Ja, denn in Sachsen oder so sei auch ein Kriegsgefangener entsprungen. Sie glaube ein Franzose, es könne auch ein Engländer gewesen sein. Sie wisse das nicht mehr so recht. Sie meint es sei in Crimmitschau gewesen. Da war ein Fräulein aus gutem bürgerlichem Hause, das spazierte so ein wenig vor die Stadt hinaus, ahnungslos, sie denkt an gar nichts. Da begegnet ihr ein Mensch ganz erschöpft und hungrig, das Haar voll Sand und die Füße blutig. Der hat so verdächtige rote Hosen an. Er sagt zu ihr: Hunger Mädchen, Hunger. Das Fräulein ist natürlich furchtbar erschrocken und sie wäre am liebsten auf und davon gelaufen. Doch weil er gar so elend war, erbarmte er sie. Da hat sie ihm ein bißchen Schokolade gegeben. Es kann auch ein Apfel gewesen sein. Ja und schließlich, weil er so schön war und entsetzlich Fieber hatte, da hat sie ihn heimlich auf ihr Zimmer genommen und er hat in einem alten Schrank gewohnt, wochenlang (die drei Alten erscheinen am Fenster) und sie hat ihn gepflegt und ernährt bis er gesund war und dann (erleichtert) ja dann entkam er heil in die Schweiz. Fritz: Donnerwetter ja. Vater Schmidt: (ernst) Dieses gottlose Mädchen aus Crimitschau hat den Tod verdient. Luise (erschrickt sehr, nimmt sich aber zusammen) Wirklich Papa, meinst du wirklich? Den Tod? (Alle ab, bis auf Fritz, der sich hinter dem Büffet versteckt.)

3. Szene
Die drei Alten kommen hereingeschlichen. Sie sind auf dem Wege zur Polizei, zur Gendarmerie. Die werden Augen machen. Ironisches Bedauern mit den armen Eltern. Wer hätte das gedacht. Das brave Luischen! Luischen ist noch nicht erwacht! Die werden sich wundern! (Die Alten ab)
Luise kommt wieder. Fritz erzählt ihr, was er gehört hat. Die drei Fräulein wissen alles, sie sind auf die Polizei gegangen und verraten euch. Luise: (verliert die Fassung) Nein, das kann doch nicht wahr sein, allmächtiger Himmel, sie töten uns, oh sie töten uns ganz bestimmt.

Fritz: Ihr müßt fliehen Luise, ich helfe euch. Luise: Oh Gott, was habe ich getan, sie töten uns ganz bestimmt.

4. Szene
Die Gendarmerie, die Fräuleins, Herr und Frau Schmidt, Volk.
Luise: Jetzt ist alles aus.
Vater Schmidt: Luise sagt mir alles. Gehen sie hinauf meine Herrn überzeugen sie sich. Sie werden sehen, es ist alles Verleumdung. Die Gendarmen tun nur ihre Pflicht. Es liegt eine Anzeige vor, umso besser wenn nichts vorliegt. Luise gibt den Schlüssel her. Sie gehen nach oben. Luise bleibt allein unten. Sie erlebt die ganze Qual der Entdeckung: Jetzt sind sie an der Tür, jetzt öffnen sie, sie machen den Schrank auf, Etienne, ach Etienne!

5. Szene.
Fritz: (der mit nach oben gegangen war, kommt wieder, er ist außer sich vor Freude) Sie haben nichts gefunden, der Schrank war leer, er ist fort, er ist über alle Berge, sie sollte doch froh sein, er halte seinen Mund. Die Gendarmen kommen herunter. Die Alten haben sich getäuscht. Man bittet tausendmal um Entschuldigung. Luise ist glänzend gerechtfertigt. Man hat ihr bitter unrecht getan. Man beglückwünscht sie von allen Seiten und beschimpft die Hexen, die kleinlaut abgehen. Alle ab. Luise ist allein. Etienne ist fort. Sie wird ihn nie mehr wiedersehen. Sie wird ihn nie vergessen können.
Ende.

18 Paul Hindemith an Ernst Penzoldt

<Berlin, zwischen 4. und 8. November 1932>

Lieber Herr Penzoldt,
Sie sind ein prompter Lieferant, das freut mich sehr und ich danke Ihnen herzlichst für Ihre Sendung. Als Grundlage für die Herstellung der Oper

ist Ihr Entwurf sehr brauchbar und wenn ich nicht mit allem einverstanden bin so ersehen Sie daraus, wie ernst es mir mit dieser Sache ist und für wie gut ich den Stoff halte. Ich habe Ihnen ausführlich alles aufgeschrieben, was ich zu Ihren Vorschlägen denke, und ich glaubte, das mit aller Offenheit tun zu dürfen. Zum Entgelt dafür dürfen Sie mich nachher bei der Herstellung der Musik fortwährend beschimpfen und verbessern. Eine solche Angelegenheit läßt sich nicht über's Knie brechen und ich bitte Sie darum, über meine vielen Einwände nicht ungeduldig zu werden. Auch meine Vorschläge für neue Szenen nehmen Sie bitte nicht als frivole Einmischung in Ihr Handwerk, sondern als wohlgemeinte Beihilfe zu der Arbeit. Ich bin der festen Überzeugung, daß wir eine richtige und gute Oper auf diese Weise fertigbekommen werden. Sobald der Text schon etwas mehr Gestalt angenommen hat, wollen wir uns wieder treffen, um die endgültige Fassung der Handlung festzulegen. Hoffentlich haben Sie immerzu weiter recht viel Lust an dieser Arbeit. Ich ja!
Leben Sie also für heute wohl und seien Sie nochmals herzlichst bedankt. Schicken Sie bald wieder was
Ihrem
Paul Hindemith
Gruß von der ganzen zwei- und vierbeinigen Familie.

19 Anmerkungen/Korrekturen von Paul Hindemith zum 1. Opernentwurf von Ernst Penzoldt

S. 1 »Querfurt« dürfte Ihnen eine Klage der gleichnamigen Stadt am Harz einbringen. Vielleicht tut sie's aber billiger als der Erlanger Herr Loch.
I. Bild ist gut und fast restlos brauchbar.
1. Szene: Herrn Schmidt müßte man mit nur wenigen Sätzen im Dialog mit Herrn Koppholzer entwickeln.
2. Szene: Bemerkung eines Bahnfachmannes: bei Querfurt fährt kein Zug mit Speisewagen vorbei. »Warme Würstchen, Bier, Schokolade,

Keks, Obst« komponiert sich nicht sehr gut im Ernstfall. Über den Dialog überhaupt müssen wir uns nach Festlegung des Handlungsplanes ganz genau und ausführlich verständigen.

3. Szene. »Drei Bahnhofstanten« sind nicht ungefährlich. Die Dreizahl von irgendwelchen charakteristischen Personen ist in der Oper schon reichlich viel dagewesen und ich finde, man kann sie mit gutem Gewissen nicht mehr auftreten lassen. (In der »Zauberflöte« die drei Damen, die drei Knaben; im »Ring« die drei Rheintöchter, die drei Nornen; bei Schreker in der »Irrelohe« die drei Zündler; bei Weill in der »Bürgschaft« auch drei bessere Herren.) Kann man die drei nicht zusammenschmelzen und eine alte und geheimnisvolle Vogelscheuche daraus machen? Auch zwei wären gut, die in Oktaven tiefsinnige Lieder singen könnten.

4. Szene.

Die Luise dürfte m.E. nicht zu jung sein. Eine ausgewachsene Sängerin kann das meistens nicht ganz glaubhaft darstellen. Es gibt wohl Fächer, die man mit blutjungen Sängerinnen besetzt, aber diese Anfängerinnen geben nichts her. Es muß schon eine Rolle sein, die man der Jugendlichen geben kann; deshalb wäre es gut, wenn Sie Luisen etwa 17–18 Jahre zubilligen würden.

5. Szene.

Ich glaube, daß man sich bei der endgültigen Fassung vor zu viel Einzelheiten hüten muß. Aber das findet sich wohl.

6. Szene

Vielleicht verdirbt Herrn Schmidts Abgang mit seiner Truppe den schönen Aktschluß der Zugsabfahrt mit Soldatenchor. Er faßt vielleicht besser laut hörbar den Entschluß, auf die Franzosenjagd zu gehen.

II. Bild.

Drei Räume im Querschnitt halte ich für ein Schauspiel für ganz gut, aber nicht für eine Oper, wenn diese Aufteilung nicht die Grundlage für ein großes und zwingendes Ensemble bildet, wie im Rigoletto zum Beispiel. Papa und Mama Schmidt haben ja in diesem Bild wenig zu sagen, man könnte sie das auch im Treppenhaus tun lassen. Ich glaube auch, daß die Alte (oder die [2!] Alten) viel unheimlicher sein könnten, wenn sie kein eigenes sichtbares Zimmer haben, sondern auf den Treppen herumgeistern. »Jedem seine Wohnstätte« ist sicher als Motto für die Sozialversorgung gut, aber in der Oper etwas zweifelhaft.

1. Szene.

Wenn nur zwei alte Damen übrig bleiben, müßten sie andere Dinge reden. Könnte die Szene nicht Luise's Zimmer mit anschließendem obersten Treppenpodest des Hauses sein? Wäre viel besser. Die Ollen quäken auf dem Podest und durch das rückwärtige Treppenfenster könnten sie ja gut die Lichtwirkung von Papa Schmidt's Jagdzug sehen. Frau Schmidt sollte also hier vielleicht nicht mitkonstatieren, daß sie ihn totgeschossen haben. Was soll sie nämlich die ganze übrige Zeit machen, während die anderen doch immerhin nicht unbedeutende Dinge singen?

2. Szene }
3. Szene } halte ich für nicht bedeutungsvoll genug, geben wenig für Musik her.

III. Bild.

Vielleicht könnte man dieses Bild mit dem vorigen zusammenziehen, so daß man erst die Alte[n] auf dem Podest sieht, das Licht draußen sieht und das Schießen hört. Wenn die Alten fortgegangen sind, könnte Luise Etienne heraufbringen. (Dann folgt die Szene.) Zum Schluß könnte ja der Pikkolo Luisen berichten (durch die geschlossene Türe), daß man den Franzosen nicht gefangen hat. Diese Fassung schiene mir dramatisch wirksamer zu sein.

Das Französischsprechen scheint mir heute noch unmöglicher als neulich. Solche Sachen sind sicher in der Novelle oder im Schauspiel gut. Können Sie sich eine Musik dazu vorstellen?

Auch mit den Läusen wüßte ich musikalisch nur sehr wenig anzufangen. Kleiderübergießen und Ausziehen – auch dazu wird kaum Zeit sein. Durch die Musik zieht sich doch alles auf die zehnfache Länge auseinander, man kann also nur Wichtiges singen lassen.

Wie wäre es, wenn diese Szene als bloßes Duett zwischen Luise und Etienne etwa so vonstatten ginge:
Sie bringt ihn mit großer Angst herauf. Da er sehr müde und fiebrig ist, sagt er zunächst gar nichts. Sie redet etwas überbetont auf ihn ein, teils um ihn aufzumuntern, teils um ihr etwas böses Gewissen zu beruhigen, teils aus einer Art Stolz, etwas Verbotenes zu tun. Ihr Charakter könnte in dieser arienartigen Musik schon gut entwickelt werden.
Sie legt ihn mit Mantel und allem aufs Bett, kocht Tee, zieht ihm die Stiefel aus.
Er fängt im Fieber an zu phantasieren und zu singen. Sie bekommt schreckliche Angst, hält ihm den Mund zu und hält ihn mit Gewalt auf dem Bett fest. Jetzt könnte ein kurzer Dialog kommen, in dem er fragt, wo er ist und während dessen sie mit einer Art mütterlichen Stolzes anfängt, sich in ihn leise zu verlieben. Während er einschläft, könnte sie darüber einen Monolog singen. Hier könnte jetzt der Pikkolo an die Tür klopfen und berichten über die Jagd. Sie antwortet ihm in höchster Angst und nachdem er weggegangen ist, singt sie etwas derartiges, wie Sie es auf Seite 9 in den letzten 6 Reihen ausgeführt haben. So hätte doch Luise eine große Szene, und die muß sie natürlich haben.

———

Jetzt sollte nicht gleich wieder Luisen's Zimmer kommen. Wie wäre es mit Schmidt's Zimmer: Duett zwischen Schmidt und der Alten. Beide spinnen, nur jeder anders. Könnte doch sehr schön sein: zwei Leute, die erfüllt sind mit ihren Angelegenheiten, sich unterhalten wollen und stets aneinander vorbeireden.

IV. Bild.
Hier müßte Etienne seine Szene haben, eine Oper ohne große Tenorarie geht doch nicht. (Mutter Luise könnte man sich umso eher schenken, als in der vorigen Szene genügend Gelegenheit wäre, alles was Sie auf Seite 10 ausführen, zu erwähnen.
Wenn Luise kommt, müßten, finde ich, belangvollere Sachen geschehen

als die etwas idyllenhaften Begebenheiten. Könnte hier nicht ganz große Liebeskiste sein? Die ganzen angeführten Einzelheiten, die sich in der Novelle sehr schön machen, kann ich mir nicht in der Oper vorstellen.

———

Auch jetzt sollte wieder ein anderer Schauplatz kommen, damit nicht immerzu das Zimmer erscheint. Vielleicht könnte man hier das VI. Bild einschieben. An dieser Stelle wäre es auch plausibler, da Luise gerade die große Szene mit Etienne gehabt hat und daraufhin einiges zu riskieren gesonnen ist.

V. Bild.
Scheint mir auch ein wenig zu novellenhaft geworden zu sein. Könnte aber in der Anlage wohl so bleiben. Die Sache mit dem Grammophon halte ich nicht für gut. Ich finde es scheußlich, wenn zu organischen gesungenen und gespielten Tönen oder Worten plötzlich das anorganische Getön eines Apparats kommt. Aber da findet sich sicher eine Lösung.
S. 15. Wäre es nicht besser, die Szene statt auf patriotische Gegensätze auf einen aufkeimenden dumpfen Haß zu stellen, der durch die patriotischen Dinge wohl ausgelöst wird, sich aber nicht in lautem Streit äußert sondern durch die Enge, den Zwang, stille zu sein und durch die Verbundenheit, die durch das beiderseitige Verbrechen gegeben ist, allmählich die Beiden sich fürwider werden läßt. Draußen könnten dazu Soldatenchöre gesungen werden und der Bahnhofsbetrieb könnte sich von seiner schönsten Seite zeigen.
Von S. 17 an finde ich die vorgeschlagene Fassung nicht mehr gut. (Entschuldigen Sie!) Es geht aus wie das Hornberger Schießen. Bei einer Oper muß doch der ganze Aufwand einen Zweck gehabt haben. Diesen hier (nämlich daß drei alte Damen etwas verraten, das augenscheinlich nicht stimmt und daß die Heldin durch einen glücklichen Zufall aus allem Schlamassel heraus ist) wird kaum Einer glauben. Dramatisch ist die Lösung sicher nicht brauchbar. Darf ich noch einige Vorschläge machen?

VI. Bild.
Bahnhofsbüffet. Hier müßte man endlich erfahren, welches Herrn Schmidts große Pläne sind. (Vielleicht könnte er sich mit einem Aufenthalt habenden hohen Offizier unterhalten.) Man bekäme jetzt gesagt, daß der Frieden bald ausbrechen würde. Die Lage könnte durch die etwas bedepperten Ansichten des Offiziers und durch Herrn Schmidts unentwegtes Draufgängertum gut geschildert werden. – Die Alte könnte in der Zimmer-Duettszene evtl. gelauscht haben und jetzt wie eine Hexe herumgehen und geheimnisvolle Andeutungen machen. – Luisens früherer Schatz kommt mit einem Urlauberzug an. Große Begrüßung. Luise etwas betreten. Duett mit ihm. Er muß ihr allmählich wieder besser gefallen als der eingesperrte Franzmann, man (und er) sieht, sie ist ihm nicht abgeneigt.

VII. Bild.
Luisens Zimmer. Luise & Etienne. Ausbruch des Hasses. Sie werfen sich gegenseitig ihr Verbrechen vor. Sie rechnet ihm vor, daß sie ihn aufgenommen hat, er beweist, daß es für ihn besser gewesen wäre, draußen umzukommen. Er wirft ihr ihren schlechten und eigennützigen Charakter vor. Sie sagt, er sei überhaupt ein Waschlappen. Es wird dunkel. Draußen auf dem Bahnhof tut sich allerlei: Truppen- & andere Transporte rückwärts. Es klopft. Etienne wird in den Schrank gestopft. Luisen's früherer Liebhaber kommt, die beiden machen eine ausführliche Liebesszene, die wahrscheinlich Etienne im Schranke unangenehm sein wird, was Luise gerade recht ist. Als wir diese Art Szenenfolge damals hier besprachen, meinten Sie (oder Karl Ebert), daß hier Etienne aus dem Schranke herausspringen müßte. Das ist nicht nötig, wenn man der Szene durch das Zwiegespräch Luise – Liebhaber einen anderen Dreh gibt. Etwa: Sie genießt den Gegensatz zwischen dem verweichlichten Gefangenen und dem frischen Musko; lobt die »Helden«. Er findet den Ausdruck »Helden« lächerlich und behauptet, daß es keine Helden gibt, daß in vielen Fällen der Heldenmut entweder Dummheit oder letzter Ausweg sei.

Wenn dieser Gedankenzug kräftig genug ausgeführt würde, wäre Etiennes Verbleiben im Schrank durchaus erklärlich.
Letztes Bild. Bahnhof außen. Friedensschluß, großer Klamauk. Friedensproklamation kann verlesen werden. Herr Schmidt sieht seine letzten Felle davonschwimmen. Man geht ins Haus. Etienne kommt verstohlen, er weiß nicht, daß der Frieden ausgebrochen ist und will auf jeden Fall fliehen. Luise entdeckt ihn. Sie kommen noch einmal kurz in Wortwechsel, sie erschießt ihn im Dunkel der Nacht außerhalb der Bühne. – Alle kommen wieder aus dem Bahnhof. Luise kommt zurück, es ist alles nicht geschehen, sie hat ihr Verbrechen durch ein größeres aufgehoben, sie hat außerdem eine patriotische Tat getan. Sie wird ihren früheren Liebhaber heiraten. Schluß. Feuerwerk. Trommelwirbel.

Könnte natürlich auch anders schließen, aber nicht schwächer. Diese Lösung hätte den Vorteil, daß neben Luisen's & Etienne's Handlung noch eine große Entwicklung herliefe: der Krieg in seinem letzten Stadium, Zusammentreffen der Kulmination beider Handlungen am Schluß. Durch die Haßszene (wirklich mal was Neues: man hat noch nie eine große Haßszene geschrieben, und sicher sollte man es tun, denn der Haß ist doch sicher ebenso wichtig wie die Liebe) würden die beiden Hauptfiguren besser profiliert. Einstweilen stehen sie ein bißchen fleischlos auf der Bühne. Luise ist vielleicht in dieser Fassung nicht so restlos sympathisch, aber großartiger ist sie auf jeden Fall; und da schon der Held infolge seiner Eingesperrtheit nicht viel Großes begehen kann, muß die Sopranistin schon etwas Größe bekommen. Durch den Text kann Luise sicher sehr sympathisch gemacht werden, vielleicht kann man sie hier ausarbeiten, dort abschwächen; alles, was an Schauerlichem passiert, durch die übrigen Umstände so arrangieren, daß ihr kaum etwas übrig bleibt, als so zu handeln wie sie tut. Etienne müßte auch mehr Profil bekommen, was natürlich durch ein ausführliches Liebes- und durch ein ebensolches Haßduett leicht geschehen könnte.
Warum wollen Sie eigentlich keinen grausigen Ausgang? Dieses Stück

mit all den großartigen Vorbedingungen wirkt mit dem vorläufigen Schluß wie ein General mit einem Strohhut. Solche Nummern wie die Traumgeschichte halte ich für gefährlich. Es kommt auch sicher beim Singen nicht heraus, was gemeint ist. Luise in Ihrer Schlußszene ist m.E. viel zu matt, es ist ja offenbar im ganzen Stück nichts mit ihr vorgegangen, als daß sie einen fremden Herrn im Schrank hatte und nun ängstlich ist, daß alles entdeckt wird. Das ist doch zu wenig.

20 Ernst Penzoldt an Paul Hindemith

München, 9. November 1932

Lieber Hindemith!
Sie haben auf meinen Entwurf fast genau so reagiert wie ich es erwartet habe. Sie haben ihn benützt wie einen Tonklumpen, weggenommen und hinzugefügt. Man sieht wirklich jetzt schon etwas wie ein Gesicht. Schon jetzt kann ich sagen, daß mir Vieles im Einzelnen sehr einleuchtet z.B. aus den *drei* Alten *eine* zu machen. Geradezu erleichtert bin ich über den Umstand, daß Sie keine Scheu vor Szenen- und Dekorationswechsel haben. Ich glaube, daß gerade dieser Umstand meiner Art zu schreiben entgegenkommt.
Daß Sie einen blutigen Ausgang meinem sanften Hornberger Schießen vorziehen, kann ich verstehen, vor allem, wenn es Ihnen musikalisch größere Gelegenheiten gibt. Die Orts- und Personen-Namen sollten nicht bindend sein. Wenn Sie gerade in diesem Punkt besonders sangbare Wünsche haben, so bitte ich Sie <sie> mir mitzuteilen. Ich habe mich zunächst mit Absicht einer gewissen Trockenheit befleißigt in diesen Äußerlichkeiten.
In der Novelle hat der kleine Bruder eine besondere Rolle gespielt, während er in dem Entwurf eigentlich nur Stichworte serviert. Vielleicht kann man in ihm das Detektivische etwas herausholen?
Eine grundsätzliche Frage, die schon in dem jetzigen Stadium wichtig ist, scheint mir die Festlegung des Stiles. Ich wäre ganz damit einverstanden,

wenn ungeachtet des zeitgenössischen Geschehens und eines mehr oder minder aktuellen Bahnhofbetriebs ruhig nach alten Operngesetzen verfahren werden könnte. Aus Ihren Anmerkungen scheint mir das deutlich hervorzugehen, ebenso aus Ihren früheren Arbeiten. Ich werde also alle Kleinmalerei möglichst ausmerzen, da man sie ja doch nicht sieht und begreift. Ich habe neulich in der Macht des Schicksals auch beinahe übersehen wie es eigentlich zu dem Tod des alten Herrn gekommen ist.
Ich werde nun an Hand Ihrer Einwände versuchen, der Oper Gestalt zu geben, was diesmal naturgemäß einige Zeit erfordern wird. Ich habe selbst auch daran gedacht zwischen den beiden Liebhabern eine Szene herbeizuführen. Das würde aber zu einem andern Ende drängen. Wenn ich an der einen oder andern Stelle gar nicht mehr vorwärts komme werde ich Ihnen Bulletins schicken. Luisens Haltung am Schluß überzeugt mich noch nicht ganz. Ihre eigenen Bedenken über die Handlungsweise dieses seltsamen Mädchens sprechen auch dafür, daß dies ein schwieriger Punkt ist. Sie werden weiter von mir hören!
Ich weiß nicht, ob ich Ihnen schrieb, daß mein Junge in diesem Jahr bereits die zweite Diphterie durchmacht. Er befindet sich zum Glück diesmal leidlich wohl, doch hat es auf uns Eltern nicht eben lebensbejahend gewirkt.
Mit herzlichen Grüßen, auch an Ihre Frau
Ihr
Ernst Penzoldt

21 Willy Strecker an Paul Hindemith

Mainz, 10. November 1932

Lieber Herr Hindemith,
die Gema fragt bei uns an, wer die Aufführungsrechte von Ihrem »Martinslied«[61] besitzt, die Firma Peters oder wir. Soviel ich weiß, hat die Firma

[61] Gemeint ist das *Martinslied* op. 45 Nr. 5 aus der *Sing- und Spielmusik für Liebhaber und Musikfreunde* op. 45.

Peters nicht das Recht, Stimmen herauszugeben und auch keine veröffentlicht, sodaß eigentlich die Sachlage mit Erscheinen unserer Ausgabe vollständig klar liegt. Ich möchte aber der Gema nichts falsches berichten und bitte Sie mir mitzuteilen, wie Ihre vertragliche Abmachung mit Peters lautet, um diese an sich unwichtige Angelegenheit prinzipiell zu klären.
Ferner beabsichtigt der »Weihergarten«[62] einliegendes Foto[63] von Ihnen zu veröffentlichen, das heute sicherlich von »naturhistorischem« Interesse ist. Hätten Sie etwas dagegen?
Sind irgendwelche Neu-Entwicklungen auf dem Operngebiet zu erwarten?
Mit herzlichen Grüßen
Ihr <Willy Strecker>

22 Paul Hindemith an Willy Strecker

Berlin, <circa 15. November 1932>

Lieber Herr Strecker,
so viel ich mich erinnere, habe ich nichts mit Peters seinerzeit ausgemacht. Die ganze Sache schien mir so bedeutungslos, daß ich mich gar nicht darum gekümmert habe. Ich wäre nun sehr traurig, wenn ich dadurch ein Millionengeschäft mit dem Martinslied[64] (besonders jetzt in der Gänsesaison) hintertrieben hätte. Sicher hat Peters keinerlei Rechte auf Stimmen an dem Stück. Irgendwann müßte doch darüber einmal geredet worden sein und ich weiß doch, daß es nicht geschehen ist. Wenn er die Möglichkeit hätte, wären doch sicher längst Stimmen von ihm hergestellt worden und wahrscheinlich hätte er doch mit Ihnen darüber verhandelt, als Sie seinerzeit das Stück übernahmen. Ich glaube also, daß Sie der Gema ruhig

[62] Eine nach der Mainzer Verlagsadresse benannte Broschüre des Verlags B. Schott's Söhne, die von 1932 an monatlich erschien.
[63] Vermutlich handelt es sich um ein Bild Hindemiths in Soldatenuniform; vgl. dazu den Brief vom 22.11.1932 von Willy Strecker an Paul Hindemith (vgl. Dok. 25).
[64] Vgl. Anm. 61.

versichern können, daß Sie das Aufführungsrecht haben. – Muß das interessante Bild erscheinen? Sie wissen ja, daß mir gar nichts an Veröffentlichungen liegt. Die Folge wird natürlich sein, daß nachher dieses Bild in jedem Mistblatt als Attraktion erscheint und das würde ich umso weniger schätzen, als ich mit herzlich wenig Stolz des Kaisers Brennesselstoffrock getragen habe. Aber wenn Sie das Klischee schon haben und meinen, daß so was erscheinen muß, in Gottes Namen denn. – Betreffs der Opernaussichten kann ich nur wie im Kinderspiel sagen: warm, warm, warm! Penzoldt ist der neue Favorit: er war neulich hier, hat auch schon einen ausführlichen Entwurf über ein besprochenes Thema geschickt. Jetzt verbessert er dran, in einigen Wochen spätestens hoffe ich aber einen kompletten Aufriß der Handlung zu haben und den bekommen Sie dann gleich. Ich sehe dieser Sache mit sehr großer Zuversicht entgegen. Irgendetwas kommt sicher dabei heraus.
Nur das für heute. Schönste Grüße derweil ans ganze Haus.
Ihr Paul Hindemith

23 Paul Hindemith an den Schott-Verlag

Berlin, <circa 19. November 1932>

Lieber Verlag,
heute nur wenig. Von Penzoldt hörte ich, daß er eifrig an der Opernhandlung arbeitet. Er hat sich aber etwas Zeit ausbedungen, um nichts überstürzen zu müssen: Ich taxiere, daß in spätestens 14 Tagen wieder eine größere Sendung von ihm kommt. Ullstein ist auf die überaus geniale Idee gekommen, die moderne Musik zu popularisieren. Er will Hefte machen, in denen Biographien und Kostproben je eines Musikers sich befinden, so daß also in Zukunft jeder seine Portion Schönberg sich am Zeitungskiosk mitnehmen kann. Ich vermute, daß dieses Unternehmen als Ersatz für den seinerzeit eingegangenen »heiteren Fridolin«[65] gedacht ist. Mich haben sie

[65] *Der heitere Fridolin. Halbmonatsschrift für Sport, Spiel, Spaß und Abenteuer* ist 1921–1928 im Ullstein-Verlag erschienen.

natürlich auch gefragt, aber ich war in der angenehmen Lage, auf Sie verweisen zu können. Und da die Leute voll Hoffnung waren, Sie herumkriegen zu können, wollte ich ihr Zutrauen nicht ins Wanken bringen. – Können Sie nicht an Frau Lübbecke[66] einen Plöner M.[67] und ein kleines Partitürchen des Philharmonischen Konzerts[68] schicken? Der Musiktag macht anscheinend überall großen Eindruck, ich höre von x Seiten darüber. – Briefe schicke ich auch wieder einige mit. Bitte schicken Sie mir doch den mit dem Säbelduell wieder; so etwas kommt ja nicht alle Tage. Auch den bescheidenen Pfarrer hätte ich gerne wieder.
Alsdann!
Ihr Paul Hindemith

24 Paul Hindemith an Ernst Penzoldt

Berlin, 21. November 1932

Lieber Herr Penzoldt,
Sie mußten lange warten auf eine Antwort. Aber Sie können sich denken, daß ich bei unserem Betrieb hier nicht immer gleich dazu komme, zu schreiben. Ich hatte mir schon gelinde Vorwürfe gemacht, daß ich Ihnen so viel Vorschläge gemacht habe, aber aus Ihrem Brief sehe ich, daß Sie alles richtig aufgefaßt haben. Um die Befolgung der alten Opernpraktiker werden wir wohl kaum herumkommen. Die Musik wickelt die ganzen Geschehnisse doch so sehr ein, daß dadurch für das Verständnis ganz andere Bedingungen geschaffen werden als beim bloßen Wort, und danach muß sich wohl der Text richten. Man hat aber trotzdem eine sehr reichliche Auswahl von Möglichkeiten. Bitte nehmen Sie sich nur Zeit, die Handlung auszuführen. Lassen Sie sich auch nicht zu sehr von meinen

---

[66] Emma Lübbecke-Job (1888–1982), dt. Pianistin, war Hindemith zeitlebens freundschaftlich verbunden. Sie führte als erste sämtliche Kompositionen für Klavier und eine große Zahl von Kammermusikwerken Hindemiths auf und galt in den zwanziger Jahren als Pionierin der musikalischen Moderne.
[67] Vgl. Anm. 4.
[68] Vgl. Anm. 8.

Vorschlägen bestimmen; sie sollen doch nur Vorschläge sein. Daß zwei Leute eine Sache ganz verschieden ansehen, kann hier nur gut sein. Der Schluß ist sicher schwierig. So wie ich ihn vorschlug, geht er auch nicht. Nun, ich erwarte voll Vertrauen Ihre neuen Propositionen. Hängen wir fest, können wir ja wieder eine größere Konferenz einberufen. – Aus der übersandten Eisenbahn entnehme ich, daß es Ihrem Buben[69] wieder besser geht; Sie hätten wohl sonst kaum die Laune aufgebracht, an meine Fimmel zu denken. Sagen Sie jedenfalls der Bahnhofswirtstochter Luise meinen herzlichen Dank! Ihre heimtückische Geburtstagssendung hat mich arg erfreut, wie Sie sich denken können. Schade, daß Sie nicht hier waren, ich hatte einen Teil der Eisenbahn aufgebaut und den ganzen Tag über kamen ernste Männer um zu sehen, wie die Maschinen laufen und um auf dem Boden sitzend Weichen zu stellen.
Herzlichste Grüße einstweilen an's ganze Haus von uns beiden.
Ihr Paul Hindemith

25 Willy Strecker an Paul Hindemith

Mainz, 22. November 1932

Lieber Herr Hindemith,
zunächst in sachlicher Kürze zur Geschäftsordnung:
Peters wird also zum Gänseklein nicht eingeladen; wir fressen das Schmalz selber.
Die Veröffentlichung Ihres Uniform-Bildes wird zunächst bis zur Wiedereinführung der Monarchie oder einer anderen unpassenden Gelegenheit zurückgestellt.
Die Ullsteins sollen sich ruhig an uns wenden; wir werden ihnen die neuesten Nachrichten übermitteln.
Sehr schön ist der Brief des bescheidenen ungarischen reformierten PEN-Club Bruders[70], den ich trotz seiner entwaffnenden Naivität em-

[69] Günther Penzoldt (1923–1997).
[70] Nicht ermittelt.

pörend und unverschämt finde. Sie haben noch Glück, daß er in der Produktion seiner Autographen sammelnden Familie sich noch eine gewisse Zurückhaltung auferlegt hat; unter zwölf Kindern tut es ein Landpfarrer eigentlich doch nie.
Der kampflustige Zeileis[71]-Anhänger gefällt mir immerhin schon besser. Den Rektor von Ulm werden wir direkt behandeln. Es ist ja sehr schön, daß man dort Instrumente und andere Dinge benötigt, aber man verlangt von Ihnen und uns nicht weniger als einen Beitrag zu dieser wohltätigen Sammlung in einer Höhe, die wahrscheinlich kein ansässiger Ulmer geben würde. Mk. 15,– für eine Aufführung ist wirklich nicht viel, zumal wenn man Ihrer Kunst drei ausverkaufte Häuser zu verdanken hat. Aus Dankbarkeit hierfür sollen Sie jetzt noch Mk. 15,– Beitrag für die dortigen wohltätigen Zwecke zahlen. Darauf läuft es doch letzten Endes hinaus und da sich diese Wohltätigkeitsbettelei in allen Städten bei jeder Aufführung wiederholt, so unterstützen Sie ebenso wie wir sämtliche Winterhilfen, Kanalisationen und Entbindungsanstalten in ganz Deutschland und umliegenden Ortschaften. »Hänsel und Gretel«[72] und jetzt »Wir bauen eine Stadt«[73] scheinen die beliebtesten Objekte sämtlicher Wohltätigkeitsveranstaltungen zu sein, Frau Lübbecke wird den Plöner Musiktag[74], sowie das Philharmonische Konzert[75] erhalten.
Man kann noch nicht den Erfolg von Plön beurteilen, aber großes

---

[71] Der umstrittene Laienarzt Valentin Zeileis, Gründer eines Ambulatoriums für elektrophysikalische Therapie in Gallsbach, pries eine Strahlentherapie als Wundermittel an. Von Januar 1930 an berichtete die Presse ausführlich über einen Rechtsstreit zwischen Zeileis und dem Berliner Chefarzt Professor Paul Lazarus (1873–1957), der im Mai 1930 zu einem Sensationsprozeß führte, weil Lazarus die Seriosität von Zeileis bestritt.

[72] 1893 uraufgeführte Oper von Engelbert Humperdinck (1854–1921).

[73] Ein – so der Untertitel – *Spiel für Kinder* nach einem Text von Robert Seitz (1891–1938), das am 21.6.1930 im Rahmen des Musikfestes »Neue Musik Berlin 1930« uraufgeführt wurde.

[74] Vgl. Anm. 4.

[75] Vgl. Anm. 8.

Interesse scheint überall vorhanden zu sein und ich hoffe, daß Kestenbergs Rücktritt[76] nicht ungünstig auf die Jugend-Entwicklung wirkt. Am interessantesten bleibt Penzoldt, auf dessen Entwurf wir alle außerordentlich gespannt sind. Mit seinem Bruder[77], dem Mann von Sigrid Onégin[78] waren wir letzte Woche zusammen.
Schönste Grüße vom ganzen Haus
Ihr <Willy Strecker>

26 Ernst Penzoldt an Paul Hindemith

München, 2. Dezember 1932

Bitte zuerst lesen!

Lieber Herr Hindemith!
Heute sende ich Ihnen den ersten Teil meines zweiten Entwurfes. Ich tue es mit etwas gemischten Gefühlen, weil ich vieles beiläufig niedergeschrieben habe, von dem ich gar nicht weiß, ob es Möglichkeiten hat. Erschrecken Sie nicht vor dem teilweise schon formulierten Text. Ich mußte die Leute reden lassen, wenn ich mir selber einigermaßen klar über den Ablauf werden wollte. Ich bin in der Hauptsache bemüht gewesen, Ihren Anweisungen zu folgen und wenn manches noch reichlich ledern klingt, so ist vielleicht da und dort doch für Sie eine Anregung und Möglichkeit der Entfaltung enthalten. Ich habe den Entwurf

---

[76] Leo Kestenberg (1882–1962) war von Dezember 1918 an Referent für musikalische Angelegenheiten im preußischen Ministerium für Wissenschaft, Kunst und Volksbildung. Er hat die Berliner Musikhochschule durchgreifend reformiert und zur bedeutendsten musikalischen Ausbildungsstätte in Deutschland gemacht. In der Folge des sogenannten Preußenschlags der Regierung Papen vom 20.7.1932 wurde er zum 1.12.1932 in den vorzeitigen Ruhestand versetzt.

[77] Fritz Penzoldt (1888–1959), studierte erfolgreich Medizin, übte den Arztberuf aber nur sporadisch aus und versuchte sich statt dessen als Schriftsteller einen Namen zu machen.

[78] Sigrid Onégin (1889–1943) gehörte zu den bedeutendsten Altistinnen der zwanziger und dreißiger Jahre. Sie war von 1920 an in zweiter Ehe mit Penzoldts Bruder Fritz verheiratet.

vorläufig nur bis zu dem Wiederauftreten des deutschen Soldaten getrieben, weil ich mir über den nach Ihren Vorschlägen (entschuldigen Sie das harte Wort) etwas knalligen Schluß nicht klar werden konnte. Anschließend an die skizzierte Szene am Eisplatz sollte dann die Liebesszene in Luisens Zimmer und vorher vielleicht die Haß-Szene kommen. Wären Sie damit einverstanden, da Sie sich sichtlich für einen unblutigen Ausgang nicht erwärmen können, wenn ich ein ähnliches Ende wie in der Novelle versuchen würde? Ich gebe Ihnen zu, daß die Gestalt der Luise in dem von Ihnen vorgeschlagenen Schluß sehr stark aber vielleicht zu stark werden würde. Sie kann m.E. nicht ungerupft davon kommen. Ich stelle mir so etwas Ähnliches vor: die Szene spielt vor dem Tunneleingang, die beiden Alten, die doch irgend einen Sinn haben müssen, haben Luise angezeigt, der entsprungene Gefangene ist wieder aktuell, es erfolgt die Haussuchung, aber Etienne wird nicht gefunden. Luise stünde nun wie in meinem ersten Entwurf tadellos da. Aber sie hat dennoch Angst, teils vor der Entdeckung, teils für Etienne, der ja nun nicht mehr im engen Zimmer ist, sondern sozusagen auf freier Wildbahn. Man will den Entsprungenen in der Nähe des Tunnels gesehen haben und setzt ihm nach. Luise will Etienne warnen und erreicht ihn vor dem Tunnel. Sie können, trotzdem Luise an dem deutschen Soldaten hängt, nicht voneinander und flüchten gemeinsam vor den Verfolgern in den Tunnel. Der Schluß wäre dann, daß unter dem Kommando Schmidt's Gendarmerie und bewaffnete Zivilisten in die Finsternis des Tunnels hineinfeuern, wobei Etienne und Luise vermutlich den Tod finden. So oder so ähnlich wäre es mir persönlich lieber und bei aller Unerquicklichkeit (die ja dem ganzen Stoff wie ich selbst gestehen muß, eigen ist) schiene mir diese Lösung erträglicher. Es müßte auch gar nicht der Friede richtig ausgebrochen, aber vielleicht der Rückzug und der Zusammenbruch erfolgt sein (Herrn Schmidt zuliebe).

Im Einzelnen: ich habe vorläufig für das Liebesduett Etienne und Luise einfach zwei Gedichte von mir eingesetzt sozusagen als Versuchsballon, ob etwas derartiges komponierbar ist. Wir wissen alle, daß Liebessze-

nen in Wirklichkeit im Wesentlichen prosaischer Natur sind. Es ist also nicht mehr als recht und billig, wenn man für eine Oper lyrisch übertreibt. Wie denken Sie über die (wie so manches nicht ausgeführte) Schlachterzählung des deutschen Soldaten? Ich war so frech, dazu zu schreiben mit Mundharmonika. Sie können mich ruhig auslachen, aber wenn ich an den Krieg denke, so höre ich neben den höchst unmusikalischen Geräuschen immer Mundharmonika oder auch Ziehharmonika. Manches wie Sie sehen werden, so z.B. den patriotischen Streit, habe ich noch gelassen. Auch das Grammophon, das ich mir nie als ein wirkliches Instrument gedacht habe, sondern von Menschenstimme gesungen, habe ich gelassen, da mir kein anderer Ausweg, die alten Tanten zu leimen, eingefallen ist. Dazu gehört auch »Warme Würstchen, Keks, Bier« das für einen Bahnhof so charakteristisch ist und vielleicht zwischen einem Monolog hineingesungen werden könnte.
Ich bin mir wohl bewußt, daß manches noch recht hart aufeinander steht, beinahe so hart und unlogisch wie etwa im Oberon[79] die Bilder aufeinander folgen. Dazu ist, wie Sie ja schon schrieben, unbedingt eine mündliche Aussprache notwendig, zu der ich selbstverständlich immer bereit bin. Ob Sie nach München kommen oder ich nach Berlin, das sind für mich nur wirtschaftliche Fragen.
Ich habe auch diesmal wieder einen Durchschlag dabehalten; es wird sich aber empfehlen, daß Sie nun zum Rotstift greifen und in meinem Manuskript zu wüten anfangen wie ein Oberlehrer, indem Sie streichen oder Auslassungszeichen einfügen oder wie Sie eben gewohnt sind vorzugehen. Denn ich habe ja gar keine Ahnung, ob nicht manche Stelle durch entsprechende Wiederholungen, die wie ich neulich in einer Oper bemerkte, manchmal absolut logisch und verstärkend wirken können viel größer werden und ob sich meine zum Teil noch recht holprige Diktion überhaupt der Musik »anschmiegt«. Ferner weiß ich nicht, ob

[79] 1826 uraufgeführte Oper von Carl Maria von Weber (1786–1826) nach dem gleichnamigen Epos (1780) von Christoph Martin Wieland (1733–1813).

Sie, was mir als Laien durchaus erlaubt erscheint, da und dort Motive aus Soldatenliedern verwenden. Ich weiß aus eigener Erfahrung, daß derartige bewußte Reminiszenzen sehr stark wirken können.
Nun ist mein Begleitbrief beinahe länger geworden als der eigentliche Entwurf. Seien Sie mir deshalb nicht böse, grüßen Sie vielmals Ihre Frau und verlieren Sie nicht die Zuversicht. Ihrer Antwort mit großer Spannung entgegensehend bin ich mit den herzlichsten Grüßen
Ihr
Ernst Penzoldt

27 Zweiter Opernentwurf von Ernst Penzoldt[80]

Zweiter Entwurf
zu einer Oper unter Anlehnung an die Erzählung Etienne und Luise von Ernst Penzoldt.

Personen:
Luise
Herr Schmidt, Bahnhofswirt } Luises Eltern
Frau Schmidt } Luises Eltern
Etienne, ein entsprungener Kriegsgefangener
Fritz, Pikkolo
Koppolzer, Dienstmann
Die beiden Bahnhofstanten
Haubitzen-Gustav

---

[80] Von diesem Entwurf sind zwei Fassungen überliefert: zum einen ein Manuskript Penzoldts von sieben Seiten, das auch die »Tunnelszene« enthält, zum anderen ein dreißigseitiges Typoskript, das in diesem Umfang als Manuskript nicht erhalten ist. Das Typoskript weicht im Wortlaut vom Manuskript leicht ab, die »Tunnelszene« fehlt darin vollständig. Die Edition folgt bis auf die »Tunnelszene«, die nach dem Manuskript wiedergegeben wird, dem Typoskript und vernachlässigt die geringfügigen Unterschiede im Manuskript.

Ein Gendarm
Ein Bahnsteigschaffner
Reisende, Volk.
Die Oper spielt auf dem Bahnhof einer kleinen deutschen Stadt während des letzten Krieges.

I. Bild
Bahnhofswirtschaft und Warteraum mit dem üblichen Büffet (Vitrine für Schokolade und Zigaretten, Syphon), künstliche Blumen auf den Gasttischen. Fahrpläne. An der einen Wand eine auffallend große Karte der Kriegsschauplätze. Ziemlich hoch an der Wand broncierte Büste Wilhelm II auf einer Konsole.
Man sieht und spürt durch die Fenster und die Schwingtüre den Betrieb auf dem Bahnsteig. Es ist Nachmittag im Herbst.

1. Szene
Frau Schmidt: (am Büffet wirtschaftend, sie ist eine brave gute Frau, die aussieht als könnte sie hervorragend Apfelstrudel backen. Sie ist der Alltag und Haushalt in Person, betulich und ängstlich; sie versteht die Welt nicht.)
Herr Schmidt: (ist ein großes Kind. Er ist ein verkannter Stratege und steht auf einer Leiter vor der ungewöhnlich großen farbenprächtigen Karte des Kriegsschauplatzes. Er hat eine Zeitung in der Hand und steckt danach mit jungenshafter Begeisterung Fähnchen.)
O es geht herrlich vorwärts an allen Fronten! In Flandern Polen und in der Türkei. Die Araber haben den heiligen Krieg proklamiert, in Rußland ist große Revolution, Meuterei auf der englischen Flotte. Ja unsere U-Boote, die macht uns keiner nach. Was bringt unser heutiger Heeresbericht? Hurra vor Ypern feindliche Gräben erstürmt, siebzehn Gefangene, zwei Maschinengewehre, ein Minenwerfer erbeutet. Unsere Verluste verhältnismäßig gering. (Er rückt die lustigen Fähnchen viel zu weit vorwärts.)

Koppolzer: (trocken) Unbedeutende Teilerfolge. Ein paar Meter Schützengraben ...

Schmidt: O mir bangt nicht um den Sieg unserer gerechten Sache, wetten in vierzehn Tagen stehn unsre braven Feldgrauen in Paris. Noch einen Winter hält es Frankreich nicht aus. Steht fettgedruckt in der Zeitung.

Koppolzer: Die müssens ja wissen. Ich lese keine Zeitung, wenn der Friede ausbricht spricht sichs schon herum.

Pikkolo (der ebenfalls zuhört): Heute ist schon wieder ein Gefangenen-Transport durch die Station gekommen mit weißen und farbigen Franzosen, Engländer und Inder waren auch dabei, im Ganzen ca. 500 Stück. Sie machten einen ziemlich abgekämpften und müden Eindruck.

Schmidt: In Frankreich heben sie ja schon die Siebzehnjährigen aus.

Reisender: (an einem Tisch) Ober! (Niemand hört)

Schmidt: Ist Calais erst unser, dann bombardieren wir mit der dicken Berta auf die englische Küste. Germanische Waffenfreudigkeit ist aufgewacht. Wir halten durch, wir müssen und wir werden siegen.

Koppolzer: Viele Hunde sind des Hasen Tod.

Reisender: (ungeduldig) Herrr Ober!

Pikkolo: (springt dienstbeflissen herbei) Unser Ober ist leider gefallen schon im August in der Lothringer Schlacht. Was darf es sein?

Reisender: Zwei Kaffee!

Pikkolo: (wiederholt) Zwei Kaffee!

Schmidt: (zum Büffet rufend) Zwei Kaffee!

Frau Schmidt: (nach hinten) Zwei Kaffee!

Reisender: Dauert es lange?

Pikkolo: Nein: der Herr, soeben frisch. Zwei Sekunden. Kuchen angenehm? Gesundheitszwetschgen, Aprikosen?

Reisender: Danke nein.

Schmidt: (tritt zu den Gästen und macht, Blumen, Senf und Zahnstocher ordnend die üblichen Honneurs) Recht guten Nachmittag zu wünschen. Die Herrschaften sind unterwegs? Kein Vergnügen gegenwärtig in den überfüllten Zügen. Viel Verspätung durch die Truppenverschie-

Reichardt: Ja[?] [Herr Wirt] wir leben in einer großen Zeit.

Es dämmert

Frau Schmidt: (macht Licht) Nun wird es schon um sechs[?] Uhr Nacht. Man wird bald heizen müssen. [illegible] Es ist [illegible].

Kittel[?]: Dort in den [illegible] Wäldern[?] fängt ein anderer [illegible] an.

Appolzer[?]: Man könnte schwermütig werden.

Frau Schmidt: (am Fenster) Wo nur Luise bleibt? Sie müsste längst zurück sein.

Schmidt: Wo steckt mein Töchterchen[?]?

Frau Schmidt: Sie ist [illegible] auf ein Sprung zu einer Freundin gegangen, drüben über dem Kanal Berg[?]. Es ist schon ganz düster.

Frau Schmidt: Ich mache mir Sorgen. [illegible]

Schmidt: [illegible] den Regenschirm ab[illegible].

2. Szene

(Ein Zug fährt ein. Man hört Soldaten singen: „Siegreich wollen wir Frankreich schlagen"

Bahnhofsportier[?]: Durchgangszug Zwickau[?] – Hohenstein[?] – Wüstenbrand – Grüna – Rabenstein – Chemnitz zehn Minuten Aufenthalt.

Reichardt: (schreckt sich von dem Fenster, durcheinander) Muss ich nach Frankfurt umsteigen? – Wie komme ich am besten nach Leipzig[?] – ich muss in Weimar[?] baden meine Kräfte erhalten[?]. Habe ich Anschluss nach Köln[?]?

B. P.[?] Nein, Sie können sitzen bleiben. Steigen Sie in Chemnitz um. Nein! Ja! Um 11 h 13.

Schmidt: (stellt Wolle[?] zurück)

bung. (mit seiner Karte kokettierend) Ich glaube im Westen bereitet sich wieder was Großes vor.
Reisender: (gönnerisch) Na Herr Wirt Sie haben ja da eine märchenhafte Karte vom Kriegsschauplatz.
Schmidt: (geschmeichelt) Selbst gemacht, mein Herr, selbstgemacht. Im großen Maßstab, damit man es doch auch ordentlich sieht wie unsere Truppen vordringen. [Hier beginnt der erhaltene Teil von Penzoldts Ms.:]
Reisender: Ja Herr Wirt wir leben in einer großen Zeit.
(es dämmert)
Fr. Schmidt: (die kopfschüttelnd ihres Mannes Reden begleitet, macht Licht) Nun wird es schon um sechs Uhr Nacht. Man wird bald heizen müssen. Draußen gießt es schon wieder in Strömen. Es ist schon wieder Herbst.
Pikkolo: Dort in den Telegraphendrähten hängt ein nasser Papierdrache.
Koppolzer: Ein Sauwetter! Man könnte schwermütig werden.
Fr. Schmidt: (am Fenster) Wo nur Luise wieder bleibt? Sie müßte längst zurück sein.
Schmidt: (Wo steckt mein Töchterchen?
Pikkolo: (etwas naseweis) Das Fräulein Luise ist heute Mittag auf einen Sprung zu einer Freundin gegangen, drüben über dem Tunnelberg.
Fr. Schmidt: Ich mache mir wirklich Sorgen, es ist schon ganz düster.
Pikkolo: (der ein wenig in Luise verliebt ist) Sie wird sich noch den Tod holen bei dem Wetter.

2. Szene
(Ein Zug fährt ein, man hört Soldaten singen: Siegreich wolln wir Frankreich schlagen, sterben als ein tapferer Held)
Bahnsteigschaffner: (ruft aus) Personenzug Köppen-Dingskirchen-Neustadt-Kaula-Rabenstein-Schönwitz zehn Minuten Aufenthalt.
Reisende: (scharen sich um den Beamten, durcheinander) Muß ich nach Frankfurt umsteigen – wie komme ich am schnellsten nach Burlafingen?

– Ich muß in Wiesbaden meine Tante besuchen – habe ich Anschluß nach Köln?
Bahnsteigschaffner: (nach allen Seiten antwortend) Nein Sie können sitzenbleiben. Steigen Sie in Schönwitz um. Nein – Ja. Um elf Uhr dreizehn.
Schmidt: (stellt Stühle zurecht, wedelt mit der Serviette über die Tische)
Pikkolo: (eilt mit Tragbrett auf den Bahnsteig)
Koppolzer: (zu sich) Nun und du Koppolzer, vielleicht – kommt endlich – der reiche Mann gefahren – mit dem großen Portemonnaie – und gibt dir das fürstliche Trinkgeld, damit du dich endlich zur Ruhe setzen kannst mein Alter. Aber diese Knauser tragen lieber ihre Koffer selber als unser einem ein paar Groschen zu gönnen.
Pikkolo: (draußen während des Selbstgesprächs) Warme Würstchen – Wein – Schokolade – Keks –
(Die Reisenden haben das Restaurant verlassen, es kommen nun Rekruten neu eingekleidet und Urlauber mit Schützengrabenpatina, sie hauen ihre Tornister irgendwo hin und machen sich breit.)
Haubitzen-Gustav: Bier her, Bier her oder i fall um, fall um.
Schmidt: (mit Bier) Liebe Herren Kameraden es ist mir eine selbstverständliche Pflicht, euch zu bewirten als meine lieben Gäste.
(Zu den Rekruten) Wohin geht die Reise?
Rekrut: Wir fahren nach Frankreich, nach Lille.
Haubitzen-Gustav: Im Osten kämpft das tapfere Heer, im Westen steht die Feuerwehr.
Rekrut: Wie ist es denn so an der Front?
Haubitzen-Gustav: Mulmig mein Junge, mulmig. Krieg ist eine herrliche Sache, wenn man ihn gesundheitlich aushält.
Schmidt: O ich wollte, ich könnte mit, aber sie haben mich nicht genommen, leider. [Hier ist das überlieferte Ms. Penzoldts unterbrochen.]
Haubitzen-Gustav: Seien Sie froh, ich hätte Angst um Sie dicker Mann. Sie haben so viel Fläche.
Rekruten: (lachen künstlich) Ha, ha er hat zuviel Fläche!
Haubitzen-Gustav: (ernst geworden) Scherz beiseite! Wie es im Kriege

zugeht wollt ihr wissen? Nie werde ich die Feuertaufe vergessen. (Zur Mundharmonika)
Schlacht-Erzählung.

3. Szene

Pikkolo: (stürzt herein) Extrablatt, Extrablatt. Eine große Neuigkeit. Aus dem Kriegsgefangenentransportzug, der heute mittag hier durchgefahren ist, ist ein Franzose entsprungen. Im Tunnel, so wird vermutet, den der Zug in langsamer Fahrt passierte, im Tunnel in Qualm und Finsternis muß es dem Franzmann geglückt sein, ungesehen durchzubrennen.
Haubitzen-Gustav: Im Tunnel, nicht dumm von ihm, nicht dumm.
Andere: Der kommt nicht weit.
Pikkolo: (wichtig) Als der Zug in Karlsburg ankam, fehlte ein Mann, d.h. nicht ganz, seine Stiefel waren noch da, seine Soldatenstiefel waren allein weitergereist. Niemand hatte seine Flucht bemerkt, jetzt ist er natürlich längst über alle Berge.
Haubitzen-Gustav: Der kommt nicht weit. Ein französischer Soldat in Uniform, ganz allein mitten in Feindesland, ohne Karte, ohne Kompaß.
Frau Schmidt: Wenn unsere Luise doch zurück wäre! Wo der fremde Unhold die Gegend unsicher macht.
Schmidt: (Wie immer zuversichtlich) O mein Töchterchen fürchtet sich nicht und wenns der Teufel wäre.
(Inzwischen sind allerlei Stadtbewohner hereingekommen, Schusterbuben, Bäckerlehrlinge, Schornsteinfeger)
Hört meine Freunde der Augenblick ist da, wo auch wir in der Heimat unser bescheidenes Teil zum Wohl des Ganzen beitragen können. Man muß den Flüchtling dingfest machen. Man muß sogleich die Verfolgung aufnehmen. Meine Wenigkeit ist gerne bereit die Führung zu übernehmen.

4. Szene.

Luise: (etwa achtzehnjährig, sehr brav gekleidet und züchtig frisiert kommt ganz verstört hereingeplatzt, nimmt sich aber dann sehr zusammen)

Fr. Schmidt: Luise, gütiger Himmel, wie siehst du aus!
Luise: (künstlich heiter) Ich, o ich bin so gelaufen, es regnet so, ich bin ganz außer Puste. Was ist denn eigentlich los? Was seht ihr mich denn alle so an?
Schmidt: Daß du nur wieder da bist, mein unvorsichtiges Töchterchen. Welchen Weg bist du gegangen?
Luise: (leichthin) Welchen Weg? Wie immer den Birkenweg über dem Tunnelberg natürlich.
Fr. Schmidt: Hast du nichts Verdächtiges wahrgenommen?
Luise: (Betont ahnungslos) Wahrgenommen? Wieso? Nichts, gar nichts. Ich versichere dich Mama, ich bin keiner Menschenseele begegnet.
Pikkolo: (vorlaut) Wir hatten alle so Angst um Sie. Es ist nämlich ein Franzmann entsprungen, heute Mittag im Tunnel.
Luise: (unschuldig) So so ein Franzmann. Nein ich habe niemand gesehen. Doch den Transportzug habe ich gesehen, als ich Mittags über den Berg ging. (sich erinnernd) Von Westen kam der Zug, ich hörte sein Zischeln weither und wartete wie so oft, daß er nun schneller und schneller und immer lauter werde, bis er endlich schwarz und schmetternd unter mir in den Berg fuhr, [Hier setzt das Ms. Penzoldts wieder ein:] der lange nachzitterte. Es fielen aber die Blätter rings von den Bäumen von der dumpfen Erschütterung, wie erschrocken ließen sie die Zweige los und schaukelten ihrem Schatten entgegen, es donnerte aus den Tiefen und der Qualm zerriß im Wind und geiferte über die Hänge. Nein ich habe keine Menschenseele gesehen als ich im Regen über den Berg ging.
Die Bahnhofstanten: (rechte Hexen mit nassen Schirmen, sie haben es ungeheuer wichtig, abwechselnd) Wißt ihrs schon, wißt ihr schon? Die Metzgerin hat mir eben erzählt, man habe den Franzmann bereits maustot auf den Schienen gefunden, in schauderhafter Zerstückelung, da ein Fuß, dort eine Hand, man sagt es sei ein Prinz aus Napoleons Geschlecht. Der Zug ist ihm mitten durch sein Gesicht gefahren. (Sie lachen häßlich)
Luise: (wankend, mechanisch) Der Zug ist ihm mitten durch sein Gesicht gefahren,

Koppolzer: (in aller Ruhe) Unsinn, alles gelogen. Der Bahnwärter Dübel hat ihn mit eigenen Augen auf einem Schimmel westwärts reiten sehen. Gehen wir schlafen Herrschaften, die Geschichte ist aus.
Luise: (leise) Die Geschichte ist aus.
Die Bahnhofstanten: Man munkelt es sei gar nicht nur einer entkommen, sondern ihrer zwölfe, blutdürstige ganz gefährliche Kerle, die nun des Nachts die Dörfer heimsuchen, brandschatzen und weder Frauen noch Kinder verschonen.
Ein Gendarm: (mit amtlicher Würde)
Alle: Hat man ihn?
Gendarm: Nein man hat ihn noch nicht. Die Bevölkerung wird ermahnt, wachsam zu sein und die Behörden bei der Ergreifung des flüchtigen Franzosen weitgehendst zu unterstützen. Derselbe ist etwa 20 Jahre alt, ledigen Standes, hat schwarze Haare und Augen. Wer einem Kriegsgefangenen forthilft oder gar ihm Unterschlupf gewährt, macht sich des Landesverrates schuldig (ab).
Luise: (ganz verschreckt) Macht sich des Landesverrates schuldig. (Sie will gehen)
Haubitzen-Gustav: Halt wohin Mädchen? Komm bleib bei uns! Graust dir am Ende vor uns wilden Feldsoldaten?
Fr. Schmidt: Luischen, es ist besser, du gehst jetzt auf dein Zimmer!
Haubitzen-Gustav: So unnahbar? Sie hat vielleicht schon einen Schatz bei der Infanterie, Artillerie, Kavallerie.
Herr Schmidt: Nein einen Schatz hat sie nicht, das müßte ich wissen. Mein Töchterchen erzählt mir alles, sie hat kein Geheimnis vor mir. (zu Luise) Komm ziere dich nicht, sei nett zu dem Herrn. Gib jedem einen artigen Kuß mit in den Krieg, wer weiß ob sie wiederkommen.
Luise: (sie nickt ergeben und geht von einem zum andern) Auch dem mit dem roten Bart?
Der Bärtige: Ich nehms für genossen Fräulein. (Er küßt ihr chevaleresk die Hand)
Rekrut: Ach Fräulein ich glaube, ich komme nicht wieder.

Luise: (küßt ihn auf die Stirn) Fürchte dich nicht.
Haubitzen-Gustav: Kopf hoch, Kamerad, nicht jede Kugel trifft. Aber verzagte Herzen ziehen das Blei an. (zu Luise) Was mich betrifft, ich komme bestimmt wieder. (Er küßt sie stürmisch wie ein Liebender.)
Luise: (reißt sich los und weint am Büffet)
Die Bahnhofstanten: (taktlos) Mit unserm Luischen stimmt was nicht, da stimmt was nicht, da stimmt was nicht! [Hier ist das überlieferte Ms. Penzoldts unterbrochen.]

5. Szene.
Bahnsteigschaffner: (wie oben) Personenzug Köppen-Dingskirchen-usw. Einsteigen, höchste Eisenbahn!
Soldaten: (singen) Um ein Drittel Parras
Gehn wir nicht nach Arras
Wenn wir nicht einen halben kriegen
Lassen wir den Tommy siegen
(Sie lärmen hinaus, Publikum drängt winkend nach.)
Pikkolo: (draußen wie oben: Warme Würstchen ...)
Soldaten: (draußen im Abfahren) Drum Mädchen weine nicht und sei nicht traurig, mach deinem Grenadier das Herz nicht schwer.
Luise: (ganz allein) Lieber Gott mach finster um ihn, daß sie ihn nicht finden.

II. Bild
Freundliches Jungmädchenzimmer in weiß-rosa-hellblau; darinnen ein großer Schrank, Bett usw. Daneben ein Stück des Stiegenhauses mit Fenster.

1. Szene
Die Bahnhofstanten: (auf der Treppe)
Erste Tante: Was siehst du Schwester?
Zweite Tante: Ich sehe nichts, es ist eine schwarze nasse Nacht.

Erste Tante: Warum muß ich auf der Treppe sitzen? Es zieht so, mich friert.
Zweite Tante: Ich muß doch gucken. Herr Schmidt ist ausgezogen den entsprungenen Franzmann zu fangen.
Erste Tante: Ist noch immer Krieg Schwester?
Zweite Tante: Still, ich sehe etwas.
Erste Tante: Was siehst Du Schwester?
Zweite Tante: Ich sehe die Lichter von der Knaben Taschenlampen drüben am Tunnelberg geistern. Horch manchmal höre ich auch ihre Stimmen. Sie rufen einander zu. Sie fürchten sich natürlich. Sie werden ihn schon nicht finden, er ist doch längst über alle Berge.
Erste Tante: Nein gute Schwester, oh nein, der ist nicht über alle Berge, der ist nicht über alle Berge, o nein. Siehst du was Schwester?
Zweite Tante: Regen und Nacht und mein Gesicht in der Scheibe.
(Es fallen in der Ferne ein paar Schüsse, man hört aufgeregte Rufe und das Signal einer Knabentrompete)
Die Bahnhofstanten: (sehr befriedigt) So nun haben sie ihn totgeschossen. Die Lichter laufen hin und her wie eine verirrte Herde von Sternen; die Geschichte ist aus, gehn wir schlafen.
Erste Tante: Franzmann tot, Geschichte aus, schlafen, schlafen (Sie huschen fort)
Luise: (kommt mit dem flüchtigen Franzosen Etienne, einem todmüden jungen Menschen. E. sieht fremdartig und verwildert aus, er hat nur ein Hemd und rote Hosen an. Sein rabenschwarzes Haar ist ungekämmt und voller Sand, die Füße nackt und blutig.)
Etienne: (er kann nicht mehr vor Erschöpfung) Oh la la.
Luise: Still doch, still doch! (sie hält ihm die Hand vor den Mund)
Etienne: (will hinsinken vor Müdigkeit)
Luise: Vorwärts, vorwärts mein Herr! Nur jetzt nicht nachgeben, sonst sind wir verloren. Gleich sind wir da.
(Man hört abläuten: bim bam, ein Zug fährt draußen vorbei, die Lichter wandern durchs Stiegenhaus und Zimmer)

Etienne und Luise (erschrecken sehr)
Luise: Jetzt aber schnell. (sie schleppt ihn ins Zimmer, setzt ihn aufs Bett und sperrt die Türe zu.) Gott sei Dank wir sind da!
Die zweite Tante: (spioniert auf der Treppe) Ist jemand da? Mir wars doch als hörte ich jemand die Treppe hinaufgehen.
Luise: (horcht atemlos)
Etienne: (hat sich mühsam erhoben, horcht ebenfalls)
Luise: (schnell beruhigt) Jetzt ist wieder alles still, es war der Wind im Kamin oder ein Wurm in der alten Kommode oder ein Ast kratzte am Haus. (Sie macht Licht und sorgt mit großer Umsicht für ihren Gast, plaudernd) Ich habe eingeheizt für Sie mein Herr, der Tee steht unter der Haube. Ihr habt mich ja nicht wenig erschreckt drüben am Berg.
Etienne: (mit mattem Lächeln) Eine Zigarette bitte.
Luise (belustigt) Natürlich rauchen ist immer das Erste, ach ihr Männer! (aber sie gibt ihm eine) Plötzlich standen Sie vor mir, elend lächelnd und krank. Offen gestanden Sie sahen nicht sehr Vertrauen erweckend aus, mehr wie ein Räuber, ungewaschen und ungekämmt, die Füße nackend und blutig. (leise) Sie erbarmten mich. Ich hätte Sie ja eigentlich anzeigen müssen, aber ich hatte wirklich das Herz nicht dazu. Also gab ich Ihnen den Apfel. Da kann ich doch nichts dafür. Morgen vielleicht schon oder übermorgen sind Sie wieder ganz gesund und können weiter, das geht mich dann nichts mehr an. Warum sind Sie den überhaupt entflohen?
Etienne: Unerträglich erschien es mir, ein Gefangener zu sein. Aber nun stand ich auf einmal ganz allein, mitten in Feindesland, im Innern eines Berges im Dunkeln, ohne Ahnung wo in aller Welt ich mich befände, ohne Karte und Kompaß, ohne Speise und Trank, nichts wissend, als daß Frankreich westlich lag. In eine Nische gedrückt stand ich lange, den Kopf zurückgebogen, mit offenem Mund die Tropfen zu trinken, die vom Gestein des Gewölbes fielen. Züge fuhren groß und nah an mir vorbei und erschütterten mir Fleisch und Bein von ihrem gewaltig lärmenden Widerhall. Der Hunger trieb mich aus meinem Versteck. (Er fröstelt)

Luise: (ihn bemutternd) Sie frieren ja, Sie haben Fieber, Sie Ärmster. Kommen sie, ich decke Sie schön zu. Sie müssen jetzt schlafen und schnell wieder gesund werden.
Etienne: Ja schlafen und alles ist wieder gut.
Luise: (sie bettet ihn auf eine sachliche, schwesternhafte Weise)
Etienne: O danke schön! Ein wunderbares Bett, ein Himmel von einem Bett! (Er wird immer lauter) Ist noch immer Krieg?
Luise: Psch, psch schlafen!
Etienne: (richtet sich auf) Nein auf Posten darf der Soldat nicht schlafen. Halt wer da! Parole! – passiert! Zu Befehl Herr Hauptmann! Nein es ist alles still drüben bei den Deutschen. Totenstill.
Luise: (erschrocken) O Gott er redet irr, er redet im Fieber!
Etienne: (aufgeräumt) Kommt Kameraden seid lustig! Trinkt, ich zahle alles. Singen wir eins! (Er singt laut und lärmend) Sous les ponts de Paris ...
Luise: (außer sich) Willst du wohl endlich ruhig sein! Du weckst mir ja noch das Haus auf. Was fange ich bloß mit ihm an? (Sie hält ihm mit dem Kissen den Mund zu)
Etienne: (er beruhigt sich) Wo bin ich denn Kamerad? Hier war ich doch noch nie. Natürlich ich bin in Gefangenschaft. Ich bin ja in deutscher Gefangenschaft.
Luise: (erleichtert) Sie sind in Sicherheit mein Herr. Ich habe Sie gerettet.
Etienne: (aufdämmernd) Gerettet? Aber Sie sind doch eine Deutsche?
Luise: (beinahe trotzig) Und ich habe Sie dennoch gerettet. Ich weiß selbst nicht warum. Vielleicht weil Sie so hilflos waren und so allein und völlig ausgeliefert in Feindesland. Sie müssen aber jetzt ganz ruhig sein, ganz ruhig.
Etienne: (ergeben) Ja mein Fräulein, ganz ruhig. (er schläft ein)
Luise: Hier sucht dich niemand. Bei Luise bist du in Sicherheit, mein heimlicher Gastfreund. Ich habe dich gefunden, ich bin verantwortlich für dich, damit dir nichts Schlimmes geschehe. Du hast dein Leben mir anvertraut, drüben am Berg, als du mich anrührtest wie den heiligen Herd, daß er dich schütze. Du bist in meine Hand gegeben. Du und ich

wir haben doch einander nie etwas Böses getan. Eigentlich müßte ich dich wohl töten wie einen Feind, aber ich kenne dich ja gar nicht, ich weiß nichts von dir, ich hasse dich nicht, schöner schlafender Fremdling, ich habe gar kein böses Gewissen.

3. Szene

Pikkolo: (bewaffnet, klopft an die Tür)

Luise: Wer ists? Ich schlafe doch schon!

Pikkolo: (zärtlich) Ich bins bloß liebes Fräulein Luise, ich bins, Fritzchen, der Pikkolo.

Luise: (erleichtert) Nur der Pikkolo! Was fällt dir ein Fritzchen zu nachtschlafender Zeit die Leute aufzuwecken.

Pikkolo: (wichtig) Ich komme von der Franzosenjagd.

Luise: (schlau) Habt ihr ihn?

Pikkolo: I wo der Herr Koppolzer hat sich vor einem Baum erschrokken, da hat ihr Herr Papa hurtig geschwind in die Nacht geschossen.

Luise: Ich danke dir Kleiner, nun gehe aber schlafen!

Pikkolo: Ich bin patschnaß und todmüde, aber ich mußte Ihnen doch noch Bescheid sagen. Gute Nacht liebes Fräulein Luise. (Er küßt die Türe zärtlich ehe er geht)

Luise: Gute Nacht kleiner Pikkolo! (Sie setzt sich zu Etienne, der wie vorhin leise zu singen beginnt) Wenn er aber stirbt, hier in meinem Zimmer, hier in meinem Bett, was fange ich dann bloß an, Dann werde ich ihn fortschleppen müssen bei finsterer Nacht in einem Sack über die Treppe hinab und ihn in den Fluß oder in einen tiefen Brunnen werfen, mit einem großen Stein um den Hals, oder seinen lieben Leichnam stückweis verbrennen oder heimlich verscharren im Walde.

III. Bild

Wohnzimmer bei Schmidts, bürgerlich patriotisch eingerichtet, Mittagszeit, seitlich ein Tisch mit Karten, daran Schmidt mit Zirkel und Büchern mit großer Wichtigkeit arbeitet.

Luise: (zu ihrer Mutter) ich habe alles besorgt, Mama.
Frau Schmidt: (die Waren überzählend) Ich begreife das gar nicht, wir verbrauchen zu viel in letzter Zeit.
Luise: (unschuldig) Ja wirklich Mama so ein Haushalt verschlingt entsetzlich.
Pikkolo: (den Tisch deckend) Die Alten sagen, daß der Krieg noch Jahre dauern und ein schlimmes Ende nehmen werde.
Frau Schmidt: Ach diese Alten, diese Hexen. Die haben <sich> natürlich rechtzeitig eingedeckt. Sind bei der Mobilmachung in einer Droschke von Laden zu Laden gefahren ordentlich einzukaufen. Kaffee vor allem säckeweis, gebrannt und ungebrannt.
Luise: Zuckerhüte, Mehl, Rosinen.
Pikkolo: Sogar Salz.
Die Bahnhofstanten: (plötzlich unter der Tür, hämisch)
Ach diese Alten, diese Hexen.
O man muß handeln, als ob man ewig leben würde.
Frau Schmidt: (verlegen) Sie glauben wirklich, daß der Krieg noch lange dauern wird, meine Damen?
Die Tanten: Wir rechnen mindestens mit dreißig Jahren. (zu Luise, ganz verdächtig) Fräulein Luischen es heißt der entsprungene Franzmann sei noch immer hier in der Gegend.
Luise: Was geht das mich an?
Pikkolo: Man hat einen französischen Militärhosenknopf drüben am Tunnelberg gefunden. Und ein blutiges Schnupftuch. Er muß ein zäher und verwegener Bursche sein.
Frau Schmidt: Höre <Luise, du> solltest nicht mehr allein spazieren gehen.
Luise: (die mit gemischten Gefühlen zuhört) Ja Mama.
Die Tanten: Du bist ein junges hübsches Mädchen. Wer weiß was so ein fremder Unhold alles im Schilde führt. (sie huschen davon)
Luise: (unbefangen) Ach er ist ja doch längst über alle Berge (sie geht)

2. Szene

Schmidt: (heiter) Es ist schon seltsam, alle diese hohen Militärs und Generalstäbler, alles gelernte Leute, aber keiner kommt darauf, keiner. Und dabei ist doch alles so einfach. Wenn ich Hindenburg wäre, ich wüßte schon, was ich täte. Du wirst staunen Mathilde ich habe einen Plan ausgearbeitet zur raschesten und völligen Niederwerfung unserer Feinde. Ein gigantisches Unternehmen fürwahr, bombensicher und doch so einfach, so einfach.

Frau Schmidt: Komm jetzt essen! (sie ruft) Luise zu Tische!

Schmidt (versonnen) Kurios, kurios. Wenn man so bedenkt, unsereiner, meine Wenigkeit, hier in diesem dummen kleinen Städtchen, kein Mensch kennt es und dennoch, hier ist die Wiege unseres Ruhmes.

Luise: (kommt zurück)

Pikkolo: Seit acht Tagen rührt und regt sich nichts auf dem Kriegsschauplatz.

Schmidt: Völlige Stille. Das gibt zu denken. Ein gutes Zeichen, vermutlich will man den Gegner einlullen.

Luise: (flüsternd) Einlullen? (sie lacht nervös)

Schmidt: (hat sich zu Tische gesetzt) Beherrsche dich etwas mein Töchterchen, da gibt es nichts zu lachen. Das sind ernste, sehr ernste Dinge. Ich bitte um Kartoffeln.

Luise: (flüsternd) Denkt euch ich habe gehört in Sachsen irgendwo sei auch so ein Gefangener entsprungen.

Alle: (sehen sie befremdet an)

Schmidt: Luise warum flüsterst du?

Luise: (räuspert sich erschrocken) Flüstere ich? Ich bin etwas erkältet vielleicht. (laut und künstlich) Ja denkt euch nur in Sachsen ist auch ein Franzose entsprungen. Es kann auch ein Engländer gewesen sein oder ein Russe, das weiß ich nicht mehr so genau. Ja und denkt euch, ich meine es ist in Crimmitschau gewesen oder so, da war ein Fräulein aus gutem Hause, ein junges hübsches Ding, das spazierte eines Tages ein wenig vor die Stadt hinaus und da begegnet ihr ein Mensch, ganz erschöpft und

hungrig, der hat so verdächtige rote Hosen an. Der sagte zu ihr: Hunger Mädchen ja. Das Fräulein ist natürlich furchtbar erschrocken. Doch weil er gar so elend und hungrig war, erbarmte er sie, sie hatte ein gutes Herz. Da hat sie ihm einen Apfel gegeben oder Schokolade, ja und schließlich, weil er so schön war und entsetzlich Fieber hatte, da hat sie ihn heimlich auf ihr Zimmer genommen, aus lauter Gutherzigkeit. Er hat in einem Schranke gewohnt wochenlang und sie hat ihn gepflegt und ernährt bis er, bis er gesund war und dann entkam er heil in die Schweiz.
Pikkolo: Donnerwetter ja.
Schmidt: (sehr ernst) Meine Lieben dieses gottlose Mädchen von Crimmitschau hat den Tod verdient.
Luise: erschrickt sehr, nimmt sich aber zusammen) Den Tod? Wirklich Papa, meinst du wirklich?

IV. Bild
Luisens Zimmer mit Stiegenhaus wie vorhin. Sonne.

1. Szene
Etienne: (geht im Zimmer auf und ab, aus einem Buche lernend) Wenn ich Geld hätte, würde ich mir ein Haus kaufen. Ich liebe, du liebst, er liebt, wir lieben, ihr liebt, sie lieben. Liebe! Geliebt!
(Er hört jemand kommen und flüchtet in den Schrank)
Luise: (kommt mit allen Vorsichtsmaßregeln, sie ist verdutzt, weil E. nicht da ist) Etienne, wo sind sie?
Etienne: (kommt aus dem Schrank) Guten Morgen Fräulein Luise. Wie geht es Ihnen? Der Sonn scheint.
Luise: (lächelnd) *Die* Sonne.
Etienne: (widersprechend) Nein, nein, Sonne ist Mann, Mond ist Frau. (auf sich und Luise deutend) Der Sonn und die Mondin.
Luise: (ebenso) Die Sonne und der Mond – ich habe Ihnen etwas mitgebracht, eine Zahnbürste und Rasierzeug und einen Baedecker von Frankreich, damit Sie mir zeigen können, wo ihre Heimat ist.

Etienne: (entzückt) Frankreich, ganz Frankreich in *einem* Buch! (Er blättert geschäftig) Hier sehen sie, dieser kleine schwarze Punkt. Das ist meine Heimat, da bin ich geboren.
Luise: Mont St. Michel. O es ist eine Insel.
Etienne: Eine Insel mitten im Meer, wunderbar, ganz wunderbar.
(er beschreibt seine Heimat)

2. Szene
Luise: (reißt die Zöpfe zur Seite und horcht angespannt) Still, die Bahnhofstanten!
Etienne: (schlüpft in den Schrank)
Luise: (öffnet das Fenster, schaut sich um, ob alles in Ordnung ist und geht an die Türe.)
Die Tanten: (klopfen) Ists erlaubt?
Luise: (öffnet) Bitte sehr meine Damen, was steht zu Diensten?
Die Tanten: Recht guten Tag, Fräulein Luischen.
Luise: (kühl) Guten Tag, meine Damen.
Erste Tante: Wir wollten nur eben mal auf den Speicher.
Zweite Tante: Nein wir wollten nicht auf den Speicher. Als ich gestern zufällig hier vorbeikam, hörte ich eine Männerstimme mit Ihnen reden.
Luise: Eine Männerstimme wie unpassend, nicht wahr? (sie lacht gezwungen) Das wird Papa gewesen sein.
Zweite Tante: O nein, das wird Papa nicht gewesen sein. Der war unten am Büffet.
Erste Tante: Es war eine fremde Männerstimme.
Luise: (hat eine Idee) Ach so, natürlich. Wollen Sie sie hören? Darf ich bitten Platz zu nehmen?
Zweite Tante: (laut schnüffelnd) Fräulein Luischen, Fräulein Luischen, hier riechts nach Mann.
Luise: (läßt das Grammophon spielen, eine Stimme trägt mit edlem Pathos Schillers Taucher vor: Wer wagt es Rittermann oder Knapp)
Zweite Tante: (enttäuscht) Ein Grammophon.

Luise: Ein Grammophon!
Erste Tante: (weiß es besser) Kein Grammophon! (Die Tanten verlassen tückisch das Zimmer)
Luise: (höhnisch) Leben Sie wohl, meine Damen! Auf Wiedersehen! (Sie sperrt die Tür ab, Etienne kommt heraus, sie lachen beide lautlos unbändig.)
Luise: (ganz erschöpft vor Lachen lehnt sich an Etienne, faßt sich aber schnell, künstlich) Ich will Ihnen auch meine Heimat zeigen. Da drüben also ist der Tunnel. Da muß jedes Kind einmal allein hindurchgegangen sein, ganz allein und bei Nacht. Man darf eine Kerze mitnehmen.
Etienne: (ist zärtlich zu ihr getreten)
Luise: (immer schneller) Ich bin auch einmal durch den Tunnel gegangen und da kam ein Zug und blies mein Licht aus, da habe ich mich schrecklich gefürchtet.
Etienne: (streichelt schüchtern ihr Haar)
Luise: (entzieht sich ihm, immer heftiger weiter erzählend) Und da drüben, das finstere stille Wasser mit dem blauen Kahn, da ertränken sich manchmal verliebte Dienstmädchen, im Winter wimmelt es dort von Schlittschuhläufern.
Etienne: Luise!
Luise: (will nichts merken) In dem Teich soll eine Kirche versunken sein, jetzt schwimmen die Fische durch die Fenster aus und ein.
Etienne: (nimmt Luisens Gesicht in seine Hände)
Luise: Nein, bitte, nein. Bitte, bitte nein.
Etienne: (umarmt sie ungeschickt, aber mit Innigkeit) Luise, je t'aime!
Luise: (ebenso) Ich liebe dich Etienne!
Beide: Ich will an deiner Seite still über beschneite Wege gehen, tief in das unbekannte Weiße und alle Spuren sollen hinter uns verweh'n. Dir werden Flocken leicht im Haare hangen, in deinem Lächeln sich verfangen, im blauen Atem glitzern und vergehn. Du bist so leise, als könntest du verstehen, daß wir schon lange nur auf Locken schreiten und endlos fallend aus den Ewigkeiten ins Grenzenlose sanft hernieder gleiten.

Luise: Du mußt mir schon einmal begegnet sein vor hundert oder tausend Jahren als wir im Nichts unendlich klein, von Anfang an befreundet waren.
Etienne: Dann flossen wir, noch kaum zu sehen, zur Feuchte in der Gottheit Mund.
Luise: Wir schimmerten, sonst war noch nichts geschehen und viele Monde mußten noch vergehn, dann durften wir als Worte wehen ein Ich, ein Du verbrüdert durch das Und.
Etienne: Nun schon fast Seelen kaum in Gräsern zitternd, in kleinen Vogelherzen ich und du, erschrocken klopfend, später warm gewitternd im Brüllen einer braunen Kuh. Durchgeisterten wir Tulpen und Gazellen, in Möven lebend wie in Jaguaren, bis wir auf einmal Menschen waren. Wenn wir uns einst von hier entfernen, wird man uns zu den Sternen gesellen und die Schüler müssen uns lernen.

V. Bild
Bahnhofs-Büffet, Stammtisch.
Bahnsteigschaffner: (wie am Ende einer Unterhaltung) Meine Herren ich sehe mit großer Sorge in die Zukunft unseres Vaterlandes. Nur ein sofortiges Friedensangebot kann uns retten.
Schmidt: Um Frieden winseln? Lächerlich! Niemals!
Gendarm: (zum Schaffner) Ich dachte du wolltest immer das Becken Briey halb Belgien und natürlich Calais in die Tasche stecken.
Bahnsteigschaffner: Das war wie wir noch siegten. Heute denke ich natürlich ganz anders. Es gibt nur eines: Friede um jeden Preis.
Koppolzer: Viele Hunde sind des Hasen Tod.
Schmidt: (mitleidig) O ihr Kleingläubigen! Ich weiß es besser. Ich durfte es bis jetzt nur noch nicht sagen. (geheimnisvoll) Meine Herren wir stehen vor großen weltgeschichtlichen Ereignissen, an denen meine Wenigkeit nicht ganz unbeteiligt ist. Das Rad der Geschichte läßt sich nicht zurückdrehen. Ich gebe zu, es sieht zur Zeit nicht rosig aus an der Front, wir haben, ich leugne es nicht, unsere Linien etwas zurückge-

nommen, man nennt das elastische Front. Ein freiwilliges Scheinmanöver, den Gegner einzulullen. Das geschieht ganz in meinem Sinn. (großartig) Man befolgt nur meine Befehle.
Die übrigen: (sehen sich an) Wie? Was? Seine Befehle?
Schmidt: (napoleonisch) Meine Befehle! Während ihr verzagtet habe ich gearbeitet. Ich habe Tag und Nacht gerechnet, in aller Stille schuf ich den großen Plan zur raschesten Niederwerfung unserer Feinde. Ich habe ihn mit einem höflichen Begleitschreiben ins große Hauptquartier gesandt an Se. Majestät den Kaiser persönlich. Der Rückzug ist die erste Auswirkung meiner Idee. Während wir hier reden, brüllen vielleicht schon im Westen die Kanonen und die Stunde unseres Sieges ist gekommen.
Die übrigen: Armer Narr, der Krieg hat ihn um den Verstand gebracht. Er spinnt vollkommen.
Schmidt: (fanatisch, visionär, er steht auf der Leiter und rückt bündelweise die Fähnchen vor und steckt sie im Halbkreis um Paris) Seht meinen Plan, hier und hier durchbrechen wir in einem artilleristisch tadellos vorbereiteten Angriff die feindlichen Linien, rollen sie auf und bringen uns in den Besitz der Schlüsselstellungen von Ypern und Verdun. Gleichzeitig an zwei Stellen greifen wir an, könnt ihr folgen? Ihr wißt das alte Prinzip; getrennt marschieren, vereint schlagen, es bewährt sich auch hier.
Koppolzer: Ein zweiter Moltke und Klausewitz.
Schmidt: Wenn man meine Gebrauchsanweisung pünktlich befolgt, ist in drei Wochen Friede (er steigt herab).
Die übrigen: Seltsam, daß dies alles Ihnen vorbehalten blieb. (Sie schütteln ihm ironisch die Hand)
Schmidt: (irr, bescheiden) Ja es ist freilich eine besondere Gnade, daß es Gott gerade mir einfallen ließ, der ich doch eigentlich ein Laie bin. Aber wer weiß was Gott mit seinem armen Knechte alles vor hat. Meine Herren! Es sind ungewöhnliche Zeiten. Es kämpfen die Geister der Erschlagenen um den Besitz der Erde, in den blutroten Wolken über dem katalaunischen Schlachtfeld.

VI. Bild
[Hier setzt das Ms. Penzoldts wieder ein:]
Luises Zimmer wie oben.

1. Szene
Etienne: (seine Haare sind länger geworden, er macht einen verweichlichten Eindruck, er geht wie ein gefangenes Tier im Käfig im Zimmer auf und ab; vor dem Fenster hält er inne, öffnet es vorsichtig und nimmt eine Katze herein) Komm zu mir, Mimi, Mimi, komm kleine Freundin. Magst du Schokolade? Ja? Du bist sehr schön, du bist ein liebes Tier. Komm bald wieder zu mir, kleine Freundin.
Luise: (kommt mit Schlittschuhen, leicht gereizt) Mit wem hast du gesprochen Etienne? Du hast doch eben mit jemanden gesprochen?
Etienne: Eine Katze war bei mir. Ich habe entsetzlich Langeweile. Stundenlang stehe ich am Fenster und sehe die Züge fahren. Ich bin dein Gefangener.
Luise: (unfreundlich) Ich kann nicht ewig bei dir hocken und Süßholz raspeln.
Etienne: Ich habe Sehnsucht mit einem Manne zu reden. Ich habe weniger Freiheit als wenn ich im Gefangenenlager wäre.
Luise: (abschätzig) Du wirst fett mein Freund.
Etienne: Das Zimmer ist klein. Ach könnte ich bloß einmal über eine Wiese gehen! Ich habe keine Bewegung.
Luise: (gouvernantenhaft) Du mußt dich eben beschäftigen. Du tust ja nichts als essen, Kaffee trinken und Zigaretten rauchen.
Etienne: (kläglich) O ich will schon etwas tun. Ich schlafe schlecht, ich habe Kopfschmerzen die ganze Zeit. Ach ich möchte einmal wieder herzhaft müde werden. Ich werde turnen. Ich werde Freiübungen machen. [Hier ist das überlieferte Ms. Penzoldts unterbrochen.] (Er macht einen hilflosen Versuch) Komm Luise sei gut zu mir! (Er versucht zärtlich zu ihr zu sein; er streichelt ihr das Haar und zieht die Luft ein) Dein Haar Mädchen, dein Haar hat einen Geruch nach Küche, ich

glaube nach Wirsing und schlechtem Fett und nach eurem unsterblichen Sauerkraut. Du solltest nicht soviel in die Küche gehen.
Luise: Das ist der Dank dafür, daß ich dir extra koche, daß ich dir extra Weißbrot gebacken habe.
Etienne: (nörgelnd) Ich kann doch nichts dafür, daß euer deutsches Brot so miserabel ist. Es schmeckt nach Sägspäne und Sand. Eure deutschen Mahlzeiten sind schrecklich, das mußt du mir nicht übelnehmen. Ihr eßt Brot, das ist aus Mehl, ihr <eßt> Suppe mit Nudeln, die sind aus Mehl, an die Sauce tut ihr Mehl und an die Gemüse, eure Schnitzel sind paniert und hinterher gibt es eine Mehlspeise natürlich.
Luise: (macht einen Kopf)
(Während der Szene hört man draußen vaterländische Weisen zunehmend Siegesglocken und Böllerschüsse; eine Fahne wird vor dem Fenster aufgezogen und weht ins Zimmer.)
Luise (mit Absicht) Hörst du es Etienne? Siehst du die Fahnen? Ein großer Sieg Etienne.
Etienne: Ein Sieg, von wem Luise?
Luise: Von uns natürlich, wir haben einen entscheidenden Sieg erfochten.
Etienne: Wir, wir! Das sind doch wir beide.
Luise: Ich meine wir Deutschen.
Etienne: Gegen wen?
Luise: Gegen euch, gegen die Franzosen natürlich.
Etienne: (gedrückt) Ist es ein großer Sieg?
Luise: Fünfzigtausend Gefangene, dreihundert Kanonen und viele tausend Tote.
Etienne: Armes Frankreich.
Luise. Freu dich doch, dann ist der Krieg bald aus. Dann kannst du fort und alles ist wieder gut.
Etienne: Du willst mich loshaben Luise?
Luise: (kehrt sich nicht daran) Hör die Glocken läuten, wie sich die Fahne im Wind bläht.
Etienne: Ich glaube, du verstehst mich nicht mehr.

Luise: Du verdirbst mir noch alle Freude.
Etienne: Wie kannst du dich freuen, wenn ich traurig bin, du hast entweder kein Herz oder keinen Geschmack. Was kümmert uns im Grunde der dumme Krieg? Wir wohnen in dieser Stube und lieben uns. Was geht uns der Krieg an.
Luise: Ach diese Stube!
Etienne: (böse werdend) Wir Franzosen haben nicht angefangen. Ihr seid wie die Räuber in das friedliche Belgien eingefallen, ihr habt die Bibliothek von Löwen verbrannt.
Luise: Willst du wohl still sein. Du bist ja verrückt. Das ist ja alles nicht wahr.
Etienne: (ebenfalls giftig werdend) Das ist schon wahr. Ihr habt gehaust wie die Barbaren.
Luise: Was sagst du, Barbaren sagst du? Und was seid ihr? Grausame feige Affen seid ihr. Ihr seid Tiere.
Etienne: (böse) Boche!
Luise: (bricht in Tränen aus)
Etienne: (beginnt zu bereuen) Ach Luise nicht weinen. Verzeihe mir. Wir wollen nicht mehr sprechen von dieser verdammten Politik. Nie mehr, nie mehr. Komm sei gut meine kleine Frau.
Luise: (schluchzend) Sonst werden auch wir schließlich noch Feinde. (Sie küssen sich lange zärtlich)
Etienne: (sich behutsam von ihr lösend) O unsere Münder sind bitter von den bösen Worten von vorhin.
Luise: Ja ganz bitter. (Luise gibt sich einen Ruck.) Ich muß jetzt gehen.
Etienne: (von neuem verfinstert) Jetzt in diesem Augenblick. Bleib Luise!
Luise: Ich kann nicht.
Etienne: Wohin Luise?
Luise: (ihre Sicherheit wiedergewinnend, beinahe keck) Ich gehe Schlittschuh laufen.
Etienne: Schlittschuh laufen? Mit fremden deutschen Soldaten?
Luise: (geht munter mit ihren Schlittschuhen)

Etienne: (sieht ihr aussichtslos nach)
(Der Siegestaumel ist immer lauter geworden)

VII. Bild
Eisplatz
Am Ufer des Teiches. Man sieht und hört im Hintergrund Kinder und Erwachsene auf dem Eis sich tummeln, vorn eine Bank. Wintersonne.

1. Szene
Luise: (sitzt auf der Bank, der Pikkolo kniet vor ihr und schnallt ihr die Schlittschuhe an) Fester, fester!
Pikkolo: (strengt sich an) Ist es so recht? Meine Finger sind ganz klamm vor Frost. (Er haucht in seine Hände.)
Luise: (steht auf) Ja so geht es glaube ich. (sie geht unsicher) Ich fürchte ich habe es ganz verlernt.
Pikkolo: (ergreift freudig die Gelegenheit) O ich lerne es ihnen, ich führe sie, liebes Fräulein Luise, ich fahre mit ihnen.
Luise: Der linke Schlittschuh hält nicht. (Sie setzt sich wieder.)
Pikkolo: (vor ihr knieend) Ach Fräulein Luise!
Luise: Was hast du denn?
Pikkolo: Im Knieen kann man es leichter sagen. Ach Fräulein Luise ich liebe Sie nämlich.
Luise: (gar nicht überrascht, sehr freundlich) Lieber kleiner Pikkolo meinst du, ich wüßte das nicht längst, daß du mich liebst. Bin ich nicht auch immer sehr nett zu dir? Aber du bist ja noch so jung.
Pikkolo: O ich verstehe, Sie meinen der Altersunterschied ist zu groß.
Luise: (muß lachen) Ich habe dich gern, kleiner Pikkolo und freue mich, wenn du mich lieb hast. Aber du mußt vernünftig sein, ja? Ich bin dir nicht böse.
Pikkolo: Ich glaube, daß ich sehr unglücklich bin.
Luise: (ihm übers Haar streichend) Das verwächst sich.
Pikkolo: O ich weiß, Sie lieben einen andern.

Luise: (ernst) Nein nicht mehr.
Pikkolo: Doch ich weiß es. Dort kommt er, den Sie lieben.
Luise: (fast erschrocken) Wer?
Pikkolo: Der Haubitzen-Gustav, er ist wieder im Land.
Luise: (verwirrt) Der Haubitzen-Gustav – geh jetzt Kleiner, geh jetzt und nachher darfst du mir die Schlittschuhe ausziehen. (Sie küßt ihn rasch.)
Pikkolo: (selig ab)

2. Szene
Haubitzen-Gustav: (den Arm in der Schlinge, leidenschaftslos) Guten Tag, Fräulein Luise. Da bin ich wieder.
Luise: Ach Herr Gustav sie?
Haubitzen-Gustav: Ja, ich.
Luise: Verwundet?
Haub. Gustav: Heimatschuß.
Luise: Ist es schlimm?
Haub. Gustav: Ein kleiner Kratzer. Ich habe Ihnen versprochen wiederzukommen.
Luise: Ja, das ist nett von ihnen.
Haub. Gustav: Es war nicht immer ganz einfach, mein Versprechen zu halten.
Luise: Ja natürlich.
Haub. Gustav: Seit jenem Abschied drüben am Bahnhof – ich habe immer nur an Sie gedacht.
Luise: Wirklich? Nur an mich? Auch im Schlafe und in der Schlacht?
Haub. Gustav: Immer, auch in der Schlacht.
Luise: (sich innerlich wehrend) Darf man denn das so ohne Weiteres? Immer an jemanden denken, Tag und nacht, ohne zu fragen?
Haub. Gustav: Man darf es.
Luise: Ich habe keinen Augenblick an Sie gedacht. Ich hatte Sie völlig vergessen. Aber jetzt ...

Haub. Gustav: Aber jetzt, Fräulein Luise?
Luise: Nein, nein was rede ich! Nichts.

3. Szene

Die beid. Tanten: (sehr warm angezogen) Guten Tag beisammen, guten Tag Mamsell Luise.
Luise: Ich muß jetzt gehen. Da humpeln die Alten vorbei, die Hexen. Ich habe Angst vor ihnen. (Sie macht ihre Schlittschuhe los) Ich habe gar keine Lust mehr zu fahren.
Haub. Gustav: Kommen Sie Luise. (Sie gehen)
Pikkolo: (kommt wieder) Fräulein Luise, Fräulein Luise! (Er sieht den beiden verblüfft nach) Aber ich sollte ihr doch die Schlittschuhe abschnallen.
Die Tanten: Luischen hat halt jetzt auch ihren Soldaten. [hier endet das Typoskript]

[Nur im Ms. überliefert:] *S. 44*[81]
Vor dem Tunnel
Schwarze Öffnung. Bahnwärterhaus.
Schmidt (mit Koppolzer) Was habe ich gesagt Durchbruch im Westen! Es ist bis auf einige Schönheitsfehler ganz nach meinem Plan gehandelt worden.
Koppolzer: die verdiente Auszeichnung wird nicht ausbleiben.
Schmidt: O darum ist es mir nicht. Ich bleibe gern im Hintergrund.
Postbote: Ich suche Sie Herr Schmidt. Ein Paket, aus dem Hauptquartier.
Koppolzer: das werden die Insignien des roten Adlerordens sein.
Schmidt: Vom Großen Hauptquartier! (Er reißt es auf) Mein Kriegsplan? (Er liest das Begleitschreiben) Mit besten Dank für Ihre frdl. Bemühung. Wir haben leider keine Verwendung.
Koppolzer: (zum Postboten) Was gibt es Neues?

---

[81] Es konnte nicht ermittelt werden, worauf sich diese Angabe bezieht.

Postbote: Rückzug im Westen.

Schmidt: Rückzug im Westen? Keine Verwendung? Ich verstehe die Welt nicht mehr. (Sie gehen)

Etienne: (erscheint) Hier war es. Hier fing es an. Von hier will ich fliehen.

Luise: (stellt sich ihm entgegen) Zurück! Wenn sie dich hier finden! Man wird mich töten, ganz gewiß.

Etienne: Immer denkstu nur an dich. Ich verrate dich nicht. Ich will fliehen. Laß mich.

Luise: Du kannst nicht fliehen. Man wird dich fangen und alles kommt an den Tag.

Etienne: Leb wohl Luise. Ich bin frei! (Er läuft in den Tunnel)

Luise: (zieht eine Pistole und feuert rasch mehrere Schüsse ins Dunkle der Öffnung)

Etienne: O la la.

Luise: Etienne! (Pause) Etienne!

Leute: (laufen zusammen) Wer hat geschossen<?>

Luise: Ich, ich habe ihn totgeschossen.

28 Ludwig Strecker an Paul Hindemith

Mainz, den 5./7. Dezember 1932

Lieber Paul Hindemith,
ich habe »Etienne & Luise« inzwischen gelesen. Das Buch erhalten Sie zurück, wenn es reihum gegangen ist. Ich habe mich mit den anderen Herren noch nicht besprochen; was ich jetzt sage ist daher zunächst nur ein eigenes Urteil. Die geäußerten Bedenken wegen zu befürchtender Einsprüche will ich heute etwas einschränken und zwar dann, wenn aus Etienne ein Iwan wird und Sie die beifolgende Lösung akzeptieren, die m.E. dem Stoff die letzten Giftzähne ausbricht. Ich habe dies, wie ich glaube Kolumbus-Ei in der Bahn gelegt und hoffe, daß Sie die Vorteile einsehen.

Der Stoff ist von Haus aus nicht ganz erfreulich und man müßte alles tun, um das Beste daraus zu machen. Dazu gehört ein mehr oder minder happy end, denn es gibt keinen Menschen der Welt, der, wenn er gegen sich selbst gerecht ist, den Tod eines Theater-Helden ohne gemütliche Belastung hinnimmt. Mit dem von mir vorgeschlagenen Schluß könnte das Ganze als eine Art »Idyll aus einer Kleinstadt« gestaltet werden. Ob man im übrigen das Ganze als einen internationalen Stoff bezeichnen darf, weiß ich noch nicht. Es ist nicht notwendig ausgeschlossen.
Ich wäre Ihnen dankbar, wenn Sie mir das erste Szenarium nochmals schicken wollten. Ich habe es doch viel zu flüchtig gelesen. Vielleicht komme ich auch noch auf ein paar andere Ideen. Jedenfalls halten Sie mich bitte auf dem Laufenden und lassen Sie mich wissen, was Sie von meinem Vorschlag denken. Ich habe gleich einen Durchschlag gemacht, den Sie evtl. Pentzold einschicken können.
Ich habe mich wie stets außerordentlich wohl bei Ihnen gefühlt und bedauere nur, daß ich so selten mit Ihnen zusammen sein kann.
Mit herzlichen Grüßen Ihnen beiden
Ihr getreuer <Ludwig Strecker>

Zu »Etienne und Luise«
Etienne muß ein Russe sein und zwar ein russischer Student, der schon möglichst gut deutsch kann. Man vermeidet auf diese Weise die immer blöde Situation, daß er nach vierzehn Tagen schon fließend deutsch spricht und singt.
Etienne entflieht kurz vor der Nachsuche, aber derart, daß die Spannung bis zum Äußersten vorhanden ist.
Wenige Tage nach dieser Flucht ist Friede, aber nicht der endgültige Friede, sondern Friede mit Rußland. Der einzige deutsche Sieg und der einzige deutsche Friede, von dem man noch sprechen kann, ohne die Hände zu ballen.
Die gefangenen Russen, die ja bekanntlich als Feldarbeiter verteilt waren, werden zusammengezogen, um abtransportiert zu werden.

Etienne findet sich bei dieser Gelegenheit ein. Auf Befragen, wo er die ganze Zeit gewesen sei, verweigert er die Auskunft oder lügt irgend etwas zusammen.
Die Freunde und Freundinnen von Luise rufen diese aus dem Haus, um ihr die Sensation zu melden und ihr den entflohenen Russen zu zeigen. Die beiden sehen sich an ohne sich zu verraten. Die Russen setzen sich mit einem russischen Lied in Marsch, um nach Hause transportiert zu werden; Etienne unter ihnen. Noch ein letzter verstohlener Abschiedsblick; Luise bricht zusammen oder ähnliches.
Diese Andeutungen genügen m.E. um etwas Brauchbares daraus zu machen. Wir haben dann alles, was das Publikum will und was die Geschichte zu einem halbwegs harmonischen Abschluß bringt.
Im Film würde selbstverständlich der Russe nicht wieder in seine Heimat zurückkehren und bitten in Deutschland bleiben zu dürfen: »happiest end«. Bekanntlich sind ja viele Russen, vor allen Dingen als Feldarbeiter in Deutschland auch nach Friedensschluß geblieben und waren herzlich willkommen. Den Russen gegenüber bestand im Gegensatz zu den Franzosen niemals irgendwelcher Haß, sondern immer nur Mitleid; außerdem waren wir die Sieger und den Russen gegenüber moralisch freier, als gegenüber den Franzosen, die ja noch bis in die heutige Zeit hinein als unsere Folterknechte empfunden werden.

29 Willy und Ludwig Strecker an Paul Hindemith

Mainz, 17. Dezember 1932

Lieber Herr Hindemith,
einliegend schicke ich Ihnen einen Brief im Original, wie in einer deutschen Übersetzung von Robert *Mayer*[82] aus London, dem einflußreich-

[82] Der genannte Brief ist verschollen. – Der in Mannheim geborene Musikorganisator Sir Robert Mayer (1879–1985) hatte in England von 1923 an Kinderkonzerte veranstaltet. Für 1933 plante er eine Aufführung von Hindemiths *Plöner Musiktag* (vgl. Anm. 4), die aber nicht zustandekam.

sten Propagandisten und Veranstalter von Kinderkonzerten, der seinerzeit auch die englischen Aufführungen von »Wir bauen eine Stadt«[83] in Oxford organisierte und sich mindestens außerordentlich viel Mühe und Arbeit machte, wenngleich das Verständnis leider nicht dem guten Willen entsprach.
Besagten Herrn Mayer bearbeitete ich bei meinem letzten Londoner Aufenthalt, etwas für den »Plöner Musiktag« zu tun und eine Möglichkeit zu suchen, praktisch zu demonstrieren, nach welcher Richtung sich in Deutschland die Gemeinschaftsmusik-Bestrebungen entwickeln. Ich sagte ihm, daß Sie Ende März sowieso nach London zum »Unaufhörlichen«[84] kämen und man vielleicht bei dieser Gelegenheit versuchen sollte, ein Gastspiel der Plöner Schule mit der dazu gehörigen Musik zu veranstalten. Das Resultat ersehen Sie aus dem einliegenden Brief. Auch der Rundfunk würde evtl. bereit sein, ein solches Konzert zu übertragen und dadurch zu den Kosten beizusteuern. Aufenthalt, Unterkunft und Kosten in England sind, wie Sie sehen bereits gesichert. Es fragt sich, ob man in Deutschland die Reisekosten durch geeignete Schritte stark reduziert oder überhaupt geschenkt erhalten kann. Ich glaube bestimmt, daß man auch auf der englischen Bahn und auf der Überfahrt durch diesen englisch-deutschen Club größtes Entgegenkommen findet. Es wäre bestimmt eine Kulturtat und Propaganda, für die Geld aufzubringen sein muß, da etwas ähnliches überhaupt noch nie da war und die Darbietung bestimmt eine Sensation wäre. Wenn man schon im Auswärtigen Amt Interesse für eine Aufführung des »Unaufhörlichen« in Amerika[85] hat, so müßte ein wesentlich höheres Interesse für dies

[83] Vgl. Anm. 73.
[84] In Anwesenheit des Komponisten fand am 22.3.1933 in der Londoner Queen's Hall die englische Erstaufführung von *Das Unaufhörliche* unter der Leitung von Sir Henry Wood statt. Das Oratorium wurde in englischer Sprache in der Übersetzung von Rose und Cyril Scott mit über 400 Mitwirkenden gesungen. Am 24.3.1933 war Hindemith bei einer Aufführung des *Lehrstücks* bei der BBC zugegen.
[85] Detailliertere Angaben über eine mögliche Erstaufführung des *Unaufhörlichen* in den Vereinigten Staaten während der dreißiger Jahre konnten nicht ermittelt werden.

Unternehmen bestehen. Es fragt sich natürlich auch noch, ob die Plöner Schule hierzu bereit ist, aber ich denke, wir werden da auf keine Schwierigkeiten stoßen. Die Schüler werden glänzend untergebracht, wie ich aus Erfahrung weiß auf das Gastlichste aufgenommen und bei dieser Gelegenheit mehr lernen, wie in den acht verlorenen Schultagen. Es war an sich nicht ganz leicht, wie Sie sich denken können, das nötige Interesse aufzubringen und ich bin auf das Energischste für die Idee eingetreten, die auch Ed. Clark[86] sehr interessierte.
Melden Sie mir nun bitte in Berlin, da mir dort die nötigen Beziehungen fehlen. Jedenfalls müssen wir bald eine Entscheidung herbeiführen und ich glaube eine solche Gelegenheit wird schwerlich wieder kommen. Welches Programm die Jungen darbieten ist ganz einerlei. Ich dachte natürlich an den »Plöner Musiktag«, es kann aber auch »Wir bauen eine Stadt« oder sonst irgend etwas sein.
Sie selbst sind, wie Sie sehen bei besagtem Herrn Mayer als Gast eingeladen.
Mit herzlichen Grüßen
Ihr <Willy Strecker>

Anlagen
NS. des älteren Bruders:
Wie steht es mit »*Luise*«? Sie haben mir leider noch nicht geantwortet, was Sie zu meinem Vorschlag sagen oder ob Ihnen Pentzold irgend etwas neues geschickt hat?
Herzlichst
Ihr <Ludwig Strecker>

[86] Edward Clark (1888–1962), Leiter der Musikabteilung der BBC London.

30 Paul Hindemith an Ernst Penzoldt

Berlin, <Mitte Dezember 1932>

Lieber Herr Penzoldt,
ich habe Ihren Entwurf genau durchgelesen und finde, daß viel Brauchbares darin steckt. Etwas daraus zu machen ist also auf jeden Fall. Nur sind mir einige Bedenken aufgestoßen, die ich für sehr überlegenswert halte.
1.) Mir scheint, die ganze Sache ist in dieser Form eine etwas muffige Kleinbürgersache mit minimalen Affären und einem Übermaß von Philisterkram. Und das kann man ja nicht ernsthaft mit einer Musik von Format versehen. Die Figuren, wie sie jetzt sind, sind für Musik sehr wenig geeignet.
2.) Der Bahnhofswartesaal als große Szene scheint mir nicht gut. Tatsächlich geschieht ja in dieser ganzen langen Szene gar nichts, was zur eigentlichen Handlung des Stückes gehört. Es müßte alles viel konzentrierter sein und wirklich von Belang für das Stück.
3.) Die Gespräche über den Krieg kann ich mir nur sehr schwer komponiert vorstellen.
4.) Herr Schmidt hat wenig Gesicht, finde ich. Er müßte ernster sein. Das bißchen Kriegsdilettantismus macht ihn eigentlich noch nicht zu einer Opernfigur. Er paßt, wie er eben ist, in ein kleinbürgerliches Schauspiel. Da die Musik aber alle Figuren stark stilisiert und Schwächen und Vorzüge außerordentlich vergrößert, müßten natürlich Vorzüge vorhanden sein. Ich bin dafür, aus ihm den Bahnhofsvorstand zu machen und den ganzen nebensächlichen und klein-naturalistischen Betrieb des Bahnbüffetts zu streichen. – Mama Schmidt ist sicher eine sympathische Frau, aber sie tut und sagt im ganzen Stück auch nicht das geringste, das ihr Dasein rechtfertigte. Bitte lassen Sie doch den Vater Witwer sein. Die nötige zweite Frauenrolle könnte sehr gut die Mutter des Geliebten der Luise sein (bei Ihnen: Haubitzen-Gustav). Diesen Geliebten dächte ich mir gern als ruhigen, wehmütigen und etwas resi-

gnierten Jungen, etwa einen kriegsfreiwilligen Primaner – im Gegensatz zu Etienne, der temperamentvoll sein müßte und droben wie in einem Käfig eingesperrt ist. Die Mutter des Jungen müßte eine Zusammenziehung und Verjüngung der 2 alten Tanten sein (die ich nach wie vor nicht gut finde, bitte um Entschuldigung), die wirklich an der Handlung beteiligt ist, da sie an einer Verbindung ihres Sohnes mit Luise doch interessiert ist, und ihr wäre es auch zu glauben, daß sie lauscht und daß damit die Grammophonszene ihren Sinn bekäme. Daß die alten Tanten lauschen und verraten, ist doch eigentlich nur ein kleines Ornament. Wenn Sie die alten Damen umbringen oder einpökeln lassen wollten, würden Sie mich also zu größtem Dank verpflichten. Statt dessen könnten Sie doch Ihre ganze Liebe und Phantasie auf die noch ganz jugendliche (etwa 40!) Mama des jungen Kriegers werfen, sie lohnt es Ihnen sicher! – Koppolzer, Piccolo etc sind wohl für eine straffe Entwicklung der Handlung auch nicht nötig.

5.) Wie in der 3. & 4. Szene die Handlung durch Extrablätter und Unterhaltungen über den Entsprungenen und durch die Befürchtungen um Luise und durch deren Erscheinen angedreht wird, halte ich für ein wenig vereinstheaterhaft.

Im Ganzen glaube ich, daß dieser ganze Realismus nicht geht. Ich denke mir das alles höchst stilisiert; die Leute dürften nicht reden wie auf der Straße, sondern in Gottes Namen in Reimen oder Versen. Das Stück müßte wohl mit realen visuellen Mitteln, aber auf einer Ebene spielen, wo die Musik überhaupt erst ihre Berechtigung bekommt. Einstweilen hat es noch den Charakter eines bürgerlichen Schauspiels. Das kann man aber viel besser ohne Musik machen. Im Allgemeinen stelle ich mir eine gehobene nur sehr konsequent durchgeführte Handlung vor, wie etwa den Wozzeck[87]. Dazu ist es natürlich auch nötig, daß die Szenen nicht so lang, dafür aber prägnanter sind. Ich habe mir erlaubt, einen

[87] 1925 in Berlin uraufgeführte Oper von Alban Berg (1885–1935) nach dem Drama *Woyzeck* von Georg Büchner (1813–1837).

Entwurf für den ersten Akt in dieser Art zu machen. Auch die Zeitdauer der Musikstücke habe ich dazu angegeben, damit Sie ungefähr sehen, wie ich mir die Längenverhältnisse vorstelle. Ihre erste Szene würde, wenn sie komponiert würde, kaum unter einer halben Stunde Dauer abzumachen sein und das ist der eigentlichen Handlung gegenüber viel zu viel. Deshalb glaubte ich Ihnen die empfehlenswerten Zeitlängen angeben zu sollen. Die illustrativen Beigaben dürften getrost wenig Raum einnehmen (in meiner Aufstellung hätten nur die zweite und fünfte Szene mit zusammen 14 Minuten von 41 lockeren Zusammenhang mit der Handlung). Durch die erste Szene könnte schon die ganze miese Kriegsstimmung in einigen Sätzen da sein, die andere, großsprecherische & laute Seite des Kriegsrummels könnte im 2. Akt sein und eine Art größeren Betriebs, die Sache von der heiteren Seite zeigend denke ich mir im 5. Bild. Bei kleineren Szenen ist es sehr empfehlenswert, die Teile, die in der Novelle so schön sind, mit zu übernehmen, so die erste Begegnung Luisens und Etiennes (die meine Frau sehr liebt). Haben Sie Lust, die Sache einmal von dieser Seite zu betrachten oder ist's Ihnen schon langweilig? Können wir uns darüber nicht nächstens sprechen? Da ich über Neujahr für 3 Tage nach Rom und Florenz muß[88], wollten wir vor- & nachher nach Seefeld in Tirol fahren. Dürften wir am 25. (1. Feiertag) bei Ihnen in Minken vorbeikommen und hätten Sie Lust, vom 2. Januar ab für 4 oder 5 Tage nach Seefeld zu kommen? Bei den guten Ansätzen, den Ihre Entwürfe jetzt schon haben und bei dem sehr guten Kern des Stückes kriegen wir sicher in dieser Zeit ein für die Musik geeignetes Buch fertig. Seien Sie mir nur nicht böse über mein Gemecker und über die Rigorosität, mit der ich in Ihrer Arbeit herumpatsche. Aber da ja für die Musik weder die reine Dichtung noch das reine Theater gute Unterlagen bieten, muß man natürlich einige Zeit suchen bis das Richtige gefunden ist.

---

[88] Das Trio Goldberg-Hindemith-Feuermann gab am 30.12. in Rom und am 31.12. in Florenz zwei Kammermusikkonzerte.

Also genug für heute, und verzeihen Sie meine vielleicht lästige aber gut gemeinte Ausführlichkeit. Herzlichste Grüße inzwischen und
Auf Wiedersehen hoffentlich am 25.
Ihr Paul Hindemith
Gruß von Weib und Hund.

31 Anmerkungen/Korrekturen und Entwürfe von Paul Hindemith für den 1. Akt und Skizzen zum 2. und 3. Akt

Personen:
Luise (bin mit Ihrem Plan, sie 16–17 Jahre sein zu lassen, einverstanden, nachdem ich mir die Sache musikalisch etwas klar gemacht habe).
Etienne (wie bisher)
Luisens Vater, Bahnhofsvorstand (nicht Wirt, da der Bahnvorstand viel aktiver sein kann und an der Handlung direkt beteiligt werden kann).
Mutter fällt weg, da sie notgedrungen nur eine vollkommen belanglose Figur sein kann und absolut nichts zur Handlung beiträgt.
Ein junger Soldat (der Luise liebt und eine ziemlich wichtige Rolle spielt).
Seine Mutter (eine seltsame Frau, etwa 40 alt. Sie tritt an die Stelle der Mutter und der 3 Tanten).
Nebenpersonen.

Erster Akt.
I.
Wartesaal im Bahnhof. Alles leer, nur eine Lampe brennt, es ist noch lange bis zur Abfahrt des Zuges. Der junge Soldat muß aus seinem Urlaub ins Feld zurück und kommt, von seiner Mutter gefolgt, um Luise noch einmal zu sehen.
Duett Sohn und Mutter. Die Mutter müßte eine etwas spinnerte Dame sein, (verkrachte Opernsängerin oder hinterlassene Geliebte eines Großfürsten oder ehemalige Flohdresseurin oder sonstwas Abenteuerliches – sie weiß nicht recht, wo sie mit sich hin soll). Der Sohn sehr weich und lyrisch, verliebt in Luise und wehmütig, weil er wieder ins

Feld muß. Die Gegenüberstellung dieser beiden wesensfremden Leute müßte der Inhalt des Duetts sein. Die Mutter verläßt ihn, da sie sieht, daß nichts mit ihm anzufangen ist und daß er auf Luise wartet.
Duett Luise und der junge Soldat. Muß ein sehr wehmütiges Stück werden. Er liebt sie sehr und sagt es ihr, sie mag nicht recht, »wenngleich bedauernd nebigen Betreff«. Draußen auf dem Bahnsteig könnten Chöre eines Urlauberzuges dazu gesungen werden.

II
Bahnsteig. Urlauberzug.
Chor mit Soli, die ganz jämmerliche, mit überdrehter Heiterkeit gemischte Stimmung abfahrender Soldatengruppen zeigen. Müßte auf ein altes Soldatenlied gemacht werden. Trauriger Abschied des jungen Soldaten.

III.
Auf dem Tunnelberg.
Duettino Luise und Etienne, etwa so wie in der Novelle.

IV.
Dienstzimmer im Bahnhof. Luisens Vater; der Ortskommandant; mehrere Offiziere, Bahnbeamte.
Ensemble. Vernehmung über einen aufregenden Fall: ein Franzose ist entsprungen. Könnte ziemlich preußisch zugehen. Luisens Vater bekommt große Schwierigkeiten, da die Flucht in seinem Gebiet geschehen ist. Die Beamten hätten nicht aufgepaßt. Man schiebt die Schuld auf die Landsturmbewachung. Vernehmung dieser. Während die Vernehmung weiter fortschreitet, hört man draußen im Dunkel Schüsse und sieht Lichter der Landstürmer, die die Verfolgung aufnehmen.

V.
Luisens Zimmer (ohne Vorplatz)
Solo. Etienne stürzt herein, berichtet kurz von der Verfolgung und daß er besinnungslos diesen Schlupfwinkel gefunden habe. Fällt auf das Bett in Ohnmacht.

Solo. Luise kommt, entdeckt den Ohnmächtigen. Große Gewissensquälerei, ob sie ihn ausliefern soll etc. Kann ein ziemlich ausgedehntes Stück werden. Etienne bekommt Fieberfantasien.

VI.
Schlußszene des ersten Aktes, könnte in einer Kneipe, im Soldatenheim oder sonstwo spielen. Großer Soldatenrummel. Die Schlachterzählung mit Ziehharmonika kann hier stattfinden, außerdem fände ich, es wäre ausgezeichnet, wenn die Mutter des jungen Soldaten hier eine große Szene vorführen würde, etwa indem sie den Soldaten vorsingt oder aber irgendwas exorbitantes tut oder vorstellt. Müßte großer Aktschluß werden.

Reihenfolge und ungefähre Dauer der Musiknummern des ersten Aktes:

Szene I.	Musik 1. Duett	2 Min
	Musik 2. Duett	4 Min
Szene II	Musik 3. Chor etc	4 Min
Szene III	Musik 4. Duettino	3 Min
Szene IV	Musik 5. Ensemble	7 Min
Szene V	Musik 6. Solo	2 Min
	Musik 7. Solo	9 Min
Szene VI	Musik 8. Chor etc	10 Min
		41 Min

Im weiteren Verlauf des Stückes sind dann noch nötig:

II. Akt

...

Luisens Zimmer. Liebesszene zwischen Luise & Etienne.

...

Wohnzimmer im Bahnhof; die Geschichte mit dem Grimmitschauer Mädchen, aber ohne alte Tanten. Die Mutter des j. Soldaten hat nunmehr ein starkes Interesse daran, herauszukriegen, was mit Luise los ist. Große Duettszene zwischen ihr & Luise.

...

III. Akt

Der junge Soldat ist verwundet worden und sieht Luise wieder. Könnte eine sehr zarte Szene werden, in der er ohne von seiner Liebe zu sprechen sie zart umwirbt. Sie müßte sich allmählich zu ihm bekehren.

...

Solo für Etienne, erinnert sich an die Heimat und überlegt seine jetzige Lage.

...

Haßszene zwischen Luise & Etienne.

...

Liebesszene zwischen Luise & dem jungen Soldaten, während Etienne im Schrank steckt. Nachher könnte Etienne ausrücken, da er sieht, daß alles aus ist und entweder spurlos verschwinden oder erschossen werden (was man ja erzählen lassen könnte) oder sonstwas.
Schluß dann nach Belieben.

32 Ludwig Strecker an Paul und Gertrud Hindemith

Mainz, 23. Dezember 1932

Liebe Hindemiths,
das große Schweigen, das von Ihnen eben ausgeht versetzt mich in die feierliche Stimmung, daß plötzlich etwas ganz unerwartet Großes und Schönes geschieht und auf einmal der weiße Hirsch (nicht der aus Dresden[89]) vor uns steht, in Gestalt des glücklich vollendeten Textbuches.
Im übrigen habe ich die Hoffnung, von Ihnen zu hören, wenn Sie in Frankfurt sind, damit wir dann alles weitere beraten können.
Mit den herzlichsten Grüßen und Wünschen, zugleich im Namen der zahlreichen Familien
stets der Ihre <Ludwig Strecker>

---

[89] Weißer Hirsch ist der Name eines hochgelegenen Stadtteils in Dresden.

33 Gertrud Hindemith an Ernst Penzoldt

Seefeld, 31. Dezember 1932

Lieber Herr Penzoldt,
schreiben Sie doch bitte Ihre genaue Ankunft damit wir Sie in Seefeld vom Zug abholen können. Bringen Sie auch einen Musterkoffer Lyrik mit (für Lieder) wenn Sie haben[90]. Von Schnee keine Spur, herrlichste Sonne.
Viele Grüße
Ihre G.H.

34 Paul Hindemith an Ludwig und Willy Strecker

<Seefeld>, 1. Januar 1933

Prost Neujahr dem ganzen Verein! Ich beginne ganz langsam meinen Kompositionsapparat wieder zu ölen. Morgen tritt hier Penzoldt an, Ihr Verlagsschiff kann also an den längst gewohnten Riffen und Untiefen vorbei einstweilen per terras et maria gondeln, sofern ihm vom Oberkohlenbunker P.H. nicht wieder das neujährlich-appetitanreizende Brikett entzogen werden muß, was hierorts nicht erhoffbar. Beiliegend Post von unerhörter Wichtigkeit, wovon ich die eine an's Dornröschen Walter[91] weiterzuschicken bitte, deren Adresse ich gottlob nicht weiß, obwohl sie ganz in unserer Nähe wohnt. – Schnee haben Sie nicht im Verlag? Wir könnten ihn brauchen. Unsere Ski sind hier so unbrauchbar wie Kompositionen von Schulhoff[92]. –
Herzlichst Schott's ergebener
Paul Hindemith

---

[90] In Hindemiths Nachlaß sind weder Liedkompositionen nach Gedichten von Penzoldt noch Dokumente überliefert, die auf Pläne zu derartigen Gedichtvertonungen hinweisen.

[91] Rose Walter (1890–1962), dt. Konzertsopranistin, die sich in den zwanziger Jahren als Interpretin von Kompositionen Schönbergs, Hindemiths und Strawinskys erfolgreich einsetzte. Sie emigrierte 1933 nach England und später in die USA.

[92] Erwin Schulhoff (1894–1942), in Prag geborener Komponist. Bei der Uraufführung seines *Streichsextetts* (1924) bei den Kammermusiktagen in Donaueschingen (1924)

Preisfrage: Wie kam L.E.Str. seinerzeit nach Seefeld? Christen sind in dieser Saison dort streng verpönt.
Bis 7. hier, dann Berlin.

35 Paul Hindemith an Ludwig und Willy Strecker

<Seefeld>, <5.> Januar 1933

Verehrte Brüder,
ich kann Ihnen die erfreuliche Mitteilung machen, daß ich mit Penzoldt, der gestern von hier wieder abfuhr, sehr gut vorangekommen bin. Wir haben entsetzlich viel geredet und gearbeitet, haben dem Stoff sämtliche Knochen gebrochen und ihn durch den Wolf getrieben, so daß jetzt wirklich ein im wahrsten Sinne deutsches Beefsteak zu Tage kommt, das jedem schmecken dürfte. Befürchtungen jeglicher Art sind nunmehr ganz ungerechtfertigt. Von den 12 Szenen des Stückes haben wir 7 auf die Beine gestellt, gerade die wichtigsten; an den 5 übrigen arbeitet er jetzt eine Weile allein weiter, ich treffe ihn aber vielleicht noch im Januar, spätestens Anfang Februar, außerdem schreiben wir dauernd. Worte haben wir noch gar keine angefangen, nur über den Stil gesprochen. Erst soll die Handlung ganz genau feststehen und die Worte muß er dann Szene für Szene ganz auf die Musik zuschneiden. In der Musik werden viel alte Soldaten- und sonstige Lieder vorkommen, auch irgendein russischer Nationaltanz, Mundharmonika- und Ziehharmonikastücke und so. Ich glaube, Sie werden zufrieden sein können. In den nächsten Tagen schicke ich Ihnen einmal unsere bisherige Arbeit zu einer kurzen Durchsicht (bei der Ihnen vieles allerdings unklar bleiben muß, da ja die Zwischenglieder noch fehlen, die wir schon im Kopfe, aber noch nicht restlos gut durchkonstruiert haben). Sie müßten sie mir aber bald wieder zurückschicken, weil ich mich fortwährend mit der Sache beschäftige. Ich nehme an, daß die Partitur nicht so umfangreich

wirkten neben dem Prager Zika-Quartett auch Paul Hindemith (Viola) und sein Bruder Rudolf (Violoncello) mit.

wird, etwa halb so groß wie »Neues vom Tage«[93], trotzdem wird natürlich eine richtige Oper daraus, ich rechne auf etwa 2½ Stunden. Kommen Sie (oder Einer von Ihnen) bald wieder nach Berlin? Wenn ich Ihnen den Entwurf dort zeigen könnte, wäre es natürlich einfacher.
Herzlichst Ihr Paul Hindemith,
ab Dienstag sind wir wieder in Berlin

36 Zwölf Szenen von Paul Hindemith und Ernst Penzoldt, entstanden bei einem Arbeitstreffen in Seefeld vom 2.1. bis 6.1.1933 (»Mösern-Entwurf«)[94]

{Opernentwurf
Das Stück heißt jetzt nicht mehr »Etienne und Luise«, der neue Titel steht noch nicht fest.

Personen:

... Bahnhofsvorstand in einer kleinen Stadt	(Bariton)
Luise, seine Tochter	(Sopran)
Martin, ein Soldat	(Tenor)
..., seine Mutter	(Alt)
..., sein Freund	(Bariton)
..., dessen Geliebte	(Sopran)
Stepan, russischer Soldat	(Tenor)
Stadtkommandent	(Bass)

Nebenpersonen.

[93] Oper von Hindemith und dem Kabarett-Autor Marcellus Schiffer (1892–1932), die 1929 an der Berliner Krolloper uraufgeführt wurde.

[94] Von diesem Entwurf sind zwei Fassungen erhalten: Die erste, im Nachlaß von Penzoldt überlieferte Fassung, ist mit einem Deckblatt versehen, auf dem eine Szenenübersicht notiert ist. Es handelt sich um ein Manuskript von Hindemith mit handschriftlichen Ergänzungen Penzoldts sowie der handschriftlichen Kennzeichnung »Oper Hindemith« durch Ernst Heimeran (vgl. Anm. 29). Die zweite, im Nachlaß Hindemiths vorliegende Fassung, eine Blaupause der ersten Fassung, ist ohne Deckblatt überliefert, trägt aber Zusätze und Ergänzungen von Hindemiths Hand, die in der ersten Fassung fehlen (sie sind in der Edition in geschweiften Klammern wiedergegeben).

Ouvertüre: wahrscheinlich eine Art Phantasie über einen alten und sehr schönen Militärmarsch (von der Schwester Friedrich's d. Gr. komponiert) Die Worte sollen knappe und ganz prägnante Sätze bilden, wenn möglich etwas wozzeckhaft, aber konzentrierter. Die hier angeführten direkten Reden bleiben natürlich im Text nicht.}

I. *Kasernenhofgitter*
II. *Szene am Tunnelberg*
III. Bahnhofsdienstzimmer x
IV. *Luisens Zimmer I*
V. Fest x
VI. *Luisens Zimmer II*
VII. Szene im Feld
VIII. Szene zwischen Luise, ihrem Vater & Martins Mutter x
[Einschub Hs. Penzoldt:] IX. Sterbeszene
[Hs. Hindemith:] X. Martin zurück, Begegnung mit Luise. Nachher Martin mit seiner Mutter x
XI. *Luisens Zimmer III* Hasszene.
XII. Martin und Stepan
~~XIII Bahnhofsdienstzimmer~~
[Hs. Penzoldt:] XII Fluchtszene und Schluß

[Hs. Hindemith:] ~~Erster Akt, I. Szene~~ *Erste Szene* [Randbemerkung:] Am Abend vor einem grösseren Transport ins Feld
I. *Gitter vor dem Kasernenhof* [Randbemerkung:] ~~Signale im Hintergrund~~

1. Mutter & Sohn (Martin)
2. Mutter, Sohn, Luise
3. Sohn, Luise

Trübe Abenddämmerung.

Dialog Mutter - Sohn:
Wohin der Transport? Mutter kennt alles, Rom, Paris, Petersburg, Al-

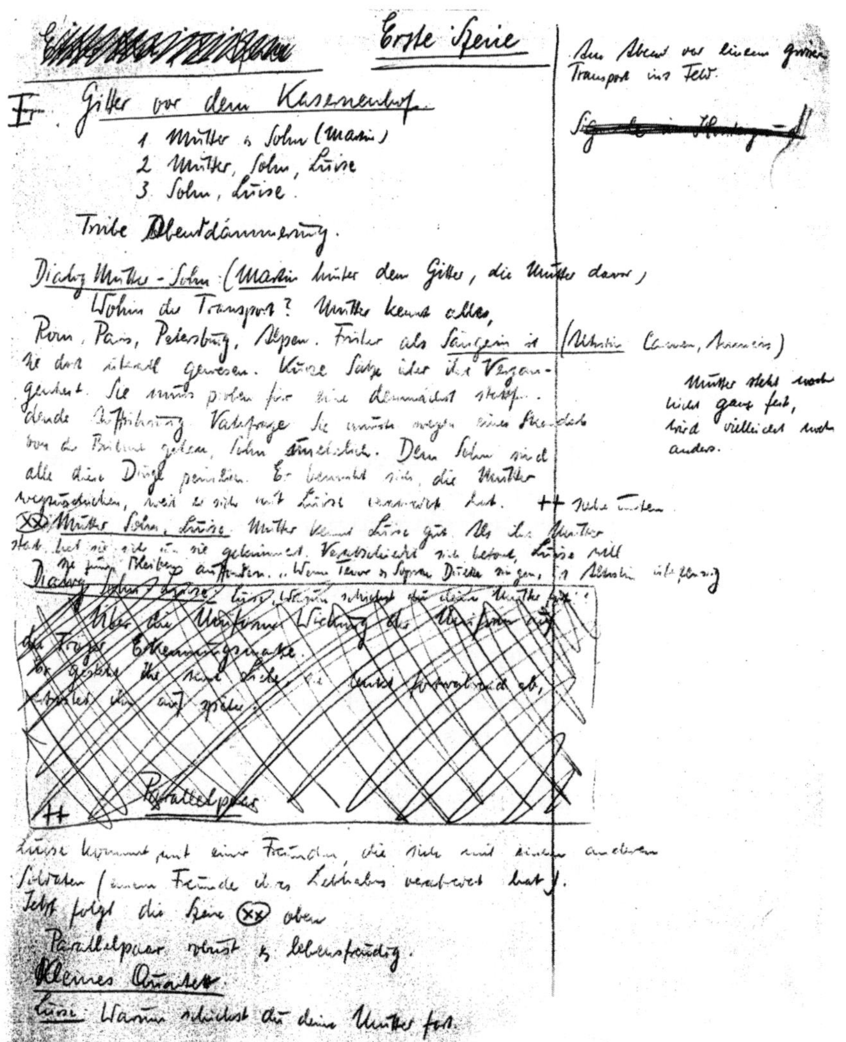

Erste Szene

Am Abend vor einem großen Transport ins Feld.

I. Gitter vor dem Kasernenhof.

1. Mutter u. Sohn (Martin)
2. Mutter, Sohn, Luise
3. Sohn, Luise.

Trübe Abenddämmerung.

Dialog Mutter-Sohn (Martin hinter dem Gitter, die Mutter davor)
Wohin der Transport? Mutter kennt alles, Rom, Paris, Petersburg, Alpen. Früher als Sängerin ist (Altistin Carmen, [illegible]) sie dort überall gewesen. Kurze Sätze über ihre Vergangenheit. Sie muss proben für eine demnächst stattfindende Aufführung. Vaterfrage. Sie musste wegen eines Skandals von der Bühne gehen, Sohn [illegible]. Dem Sohn sind alle diese Dinge peinlich. Er bemüht sich, die Mutter wegzuschicken, weil er sich mit Luise verabredet hat. ++ siehe unten.

Mutter steht noch nicht ganz fest, wird vielleicht noch anders.

(XX) Mutter Sohn, Luise. Mutter kennt Luise gut. Als ihre Mutter starb, hat sie sich um sie gekümmert. Verabschiedet sich betont, Luise will sie zum Bleiben auffordern. „Wenn Tenor u. Sopran Duette singen, ist Altistin überflüssig"

++ Luise kommt mit einer Freundin, die sich mit einem anderen Soldaten (einem Freunde des Liebhabers) verabredet hat).
Jetzt folgt die Szene (XX) oben
Parallelpaar robust u. lebensfähig.

Kleines Quartett

Luise: Warum schickst du deine Mutter fort.

pen. Früher als *Sängerin* [Randbemerkung:] (*Altistin:* Carmen Amneris) ist sie dort überall gewesen. Kurze Sätze über ihre Vergangenheit.
[Randbemerkung:] Mutter steht noch nicht ganz fest, wird vielleicht noch anders.
Sie muß proben für eine demnächst stattfindende Aufführung. Vaterfrage: Sie mußte wegen eines Skandals von der Bühne gehen, Sohn unehelich. Dem Sohn sind alle diese Dinge peinlich. Er bemüht sich, die Mutter wegzuschicken, weil er sich mit Luise verabredet hat. ++ siehe unten
** *Mutter, Sohn, Luise.* Mutter kennt Luise gut. Als ihre Mutter starb, hat sie sich um sie gekümmert. Verabschiedet sich betont, Luise will sie zum Bleiben auffordern. »Wenn Tenor & Sopran Duette singen, ist Altistin überflüssig«
~~*Dialog Sohn - Luise:* Luise: »Warum schickst du deine Mutter fort«?~~
~~Über die Uniform. Wirkung der Uniform auf die Träger. Erkennungsmarke.~~
~~Er gesteht ihr seine Liebe, sie lenkt fortwährend ab, vertröstet ihn auf später.~~
[Einschub Hs. Penzoldt:] Ich weiß wann Mütter überflüssig sind. Mir ist nichts Menschliches fremd.
[Hs. Hindemith:] ++ ~~*Parallelpaar*~~

Luise kommt mit einer Freundin, die sich mit einem anderen Soldaten (einem Freunde ihres Liebhabers verabredet hat). Jetzt folgt die Szene ** oben
Parallelpaar robust & lebensfreudig.
Kleines Quartett:
Luise: Warum schickst du deine Mutter fort.
{*Alle 4* gemeinsam über Uniform, Erkennungsmarke, etc.
Luise & ihr Liebhaber: Gespräch über seine Liebe zu ihr. Sie will ihn auf später vertrösten. Er fatalistisch, glaubt nicht an später.
Das andere Paar rechnet bestimmt mit besseren Zeiten.
Alle 4 Zeit, Abschied zu nehmen (Uhrschlag oder Signal), die Mädchen gehen.

Er sieht Luisen durch das Gitter nach, sein Freund wendet ihn burschikos ab.

Musik: viel Signale und sonstige primitive Musik im Hintergrund.}

II.
Szene am Tunnelberg. Früher Herbstmorgen
Luise allein:
Darf man denn das: einen anderen lieben ohne sein Einverständnis. Es tut ihr leid, Martin so zu kränken, aber sie kann sich nicht vorstellen, wie sie immer mit ihm zusammen leben kann. Es ist ihr unangenehm, für ihn so wichtig zu sein. Wie merkt man überhaupt, daß man liebt? Was muß dazu geschehen?
Stepan erscheint plötzlich. Abgerissen und verwahrlost.
Er bittet sie um etwas zu essen, gestern früh sei er entflohen aus dem Zug im Tunnel, man verfolge ihn. Begründung seiner Flucht: unerträglich, gefangen zu sein.
Sie gibt ihm Schokolade. Sie ist erstaunt, daß er sich ihr ohne weiteres in die Hände gibt. Sie brauchte ja nur hinzugehen, ihn anzuzeigen. Wo er eigentlich hinwolle, was er vorhabe. Er meint, er würde schon irgendwelche Hilfe finden? Es gibt mondhelle Nächte, sicher hie und da auch einen hilfreichen Menschen. Sie: er solle nicht auf Hilfe rechnen, er sei doch ein Feind. Auch sie dürfe ihm ja eigentlich nicht helfen, sie sei seine Feindin. Er: Wieso Feind? Sie hilft ihm ja. Warum tut sie es denn? »Gehn Sie«, sie will nichts mit alledem zu tun haben. Er küßt ihr mit überschwenglicher Dankbarkeit beide Hände.

{III Szene
Dienstzimmer im Bahnhof. Abenddämmerung
Verhandlung über die Flucht. Der Stadtkommandant macht großen Krach, Luisen's Vater hat Unannehmlichkeiten, weil der Mann auf seinem Gebiet entflohen ist. Draußen große Verfolgung, die aber ergebnislos verläuft. Diese Szene ist noch nicht genau festgelegt.}

IV. {*Szene*}
Luisens Zimmer mit Treppenabsatz, Dachstube{. Abenddämmerung.}
Luise steht am Fenster und sieht die Verfolgung. Was hat er eigentlich getan, daß man ihn so verfolgt und schließlich erschießt? Verfolgung kommt näher.
Stepan stürzt die Treppe abends herauf und bricht zusammen. Luise geht hinaus, hebt ihn auf und bringt ihn ins Zimmer, legt ihn auf ihr Bett, schließt die Türe.
Fiebererzählung von der Flucht vor Wölfen
Er wird immer lauter, sie ängstlicher; sie hält ihn mit Mühe nieder.
Einige Landstürmer kommen die Trepp herauf, stehen vor der Türe. Dialog mit Luise. Ob sie den Entflohenen gesehen hätte, er müßte hier im Bahnhof sein. Sie betäubt Stepan mit dem Kopfkissen und antwortet mit gemachter Ruhe. Es sei doch ganz unmöglich, daß er hier ist. Sie geht zur Türe und spricht mit ihnen durch die Türe, ängstlich nach dem Bett lauschend. Mit großem Entschluß reißt sie schließlich die Türe auf, zeigt das Zimmer. Die Landsturmleute wollen nicht sehen, entschuldigen sich und gehen hinunter.
Luise sinkt am Bett zusammen.
Sie hat ihn geschützt, sie weiß keinen Grund dafür.
Er ist in ihre Hand gegeben – auch durch das Öffnen der Tür wurde er nicht entdeckt – sie muß also jetzt durchhalten.
»Um dich muß ich mich sorgen! Was haben wir denn miteinander zu tun? Ich kenne dich doch gar nicht!«

V. {Szene
fehlt noch.
Wird eine größere Szene, in der hauptsächlich Martin's Mutter beschäftigt wird. (Vielleicht wird's eine Art Soldatenfest – ich weiß noch nicht)}
[Hs. Penzoldt:] Theaterszene

II. Akt

VI. *Luisens Zimmer* {Stepan, Luise. Abends}

Luise kommt mit einem Körbchen mit Eßwaren ins Zimmer. Er hat sie voll Spannung erwartet und ist hocherfreut über ihr Kommen. Während sie den Korb abstellt, hängt er sich die Bettüberdecke um. Er heißt sie im Lager des x-Stammes der y-Tscherkessen willkommen und führt ihr Lagerleben vor. Spirituskocher am Boden in der Mitte des Zimmers. Stühle als Häuptlinge ringsum. Er stellt sie den Häuptlingen als seine ausländische Braut vor. Sie bringt als Brautgeschenk russische Cigaretten (die sie irgendwoher geschmuggelt hat), worüber seine Freude sich noch erhöht. Sie halb begeistert, halb vorsichtig – spielt mit. Er zeigt ihr im Zimmer ganz Rußland. Er beginnt, ein Liebeslied zu singen und zu tanzen. Er fordert sie auf, den Refrain mitzusingen. Er singt laut, sie beschwichtigt ihn, worauf sie beiden den Refrain pp singen. Ebenso beruhigt sie ihn immer wieder beim Tanz. Während er aus Spaß einmal übertrieben leise tanzt, hört sie plötzlich Schritte auf der Treppe. Sie räumen schnell alles beiseite, er versteckt sich in der Nische. [Randbemerkung:] {Musik: Phantasie über russische Volkstänze} [Einschub Hs. Penzoldt:] siehe Änderung!

~~*Martins Mutter* kommt. Sie hört gerne Musik und ist gerne bei lustigen Leuten. Wieso Luise so lustig sei. *Luise:* »Man vertreibt sich die traurige Zeit mit mancherlei, man tanzt, man singt.« *Mutter:* »Nicht allein, es sang ein Mann. Auch Cigaretten wurden geraucht. Russische Cigaretten. Und das Lied, das man sang, kenne ich – früher, aus Rußland«, sie singt ein paar Takte daraus. Luise ist sehr verlegen, tut sehr verwundert. Ein Mann? Ach so. Sie legt eine Grammophonplatte auf und spielt ein anderes Männerlied. Während Luise das Grammophon fertig macht, zieht die Mutter einen Brief[x)] hervor: »Es ist ein Brief von Martin an dich gekommen.« Luise steht der Mutter abgewandt und liest den Brief. Zugleich beginnt das Grammophon. Die Mutter: »das ist nicht das Lied ...« Luise, abgewandt lesend: »doch, natürlich ist es das.« Die Mutter: »es ging doch anders«, sie stellt das Grammophon ab, und langsam fällt~~

~~ihr das alte Lied wieder ein »damals – in Rußland – in Moskau –«, sie beginnt langsam Tanzbewegungen zu machen, zu singen und geht etwas markiert ab. Luise steht betroffen mit dem Brief. Bemerkt, daß die Mutter fort ist und steckt den Brief weg.~~
[Randbemerkung:] {Ändert sich wahrscheinlich noch, je nachdem wie die Mutter angelegt wird.
[x)] statt Briefszene wird wahrscheinlich auch anderes eingestellt.}
Luise schließt schnell die Tür, stellt sich mit dem Rücken dagegen. Stepan kommt etwas zögernd aus der Nische, geht auf Luise zu. Küßt sie auf den Mund, kniet vor ihr nieder und neigt den Kopf.

VIII.{VII.}
Im Schützengraben. Die Böschung mit Gewehren im Hintergrund, in der Wand die Eingänge zu einigen Unterständen, mit Säcken zugehängt und trübe beleuchtet. Nach Mitternacht.
Martin auf Posten. Einige Soldaten haben Handgranaten aufgeschichtet und sonstige Vorbereitungen getroffen. Ein Offizier inspiziert die letzten Vorbereitungen zum baldigen großen Angriff. Kurze Ermahnungen: »Machts gut. Haltet Euch bereit. In einer halben Stunde. Wegtreten.« Alle ab bis auf Martin, sein Freund tritt zu ihm. Martin bittet ihn, einen Abschiedsbrief an Luise, den er geschrieben habe (er gibt ihn) zu schicken, falls er fiele. Der Freund wollte ihn um das gleiche bitten: er hat ein größeres Päckchen Abschiedsbriefe, die er an Martin gibt. »Wäre doch traurig, wenn die ganzen Mädchen solche Nachrichten bekämen. Ach was, mir passiert nichts.« Martin meint, daß er selbst bestimmt falle. Es sei doch seltsam, daß er vor etwas Angst habe, das doch für ihn die beste Lösung sei. Luise liebe ihn ja doch nicht. Der Freund findet es lächerlich, daß er sich an Eine hängt und singt zur Mundharmonika einige seiner Liebesgeschichten. Martin will nach einer Weile nichts mehr davon wissen. Der Freund geht ab. »Auf Wiedersehn im Massengrab.« – Martin singt eine Strophe eines alten Soldatenliedes. Die Vorhänge der Unterstände öffnen sich, allmählich

erscheinen in den Löchern immer mehr Soldaten, einige setzen sich auf den Laufgang, alle singen leise das Lied mit. In der 2. Strophe kommen Unteroffiziere und geben leise die letzten Anweisungen, in der 3. ertönten plötzlich von allen Seiten Pfiffe und Befehle. Leuchtkugeln, Maschinengewehre, Kanonenabschüsse. Alles stürmt über die Rückwand des Grabens.
{*Musik*: Der Freund zur Mundharmonika: eine Art Couplet.
Martin und Chor: großangelegte Verwendung eines alten Liedes.

X. Szene
Eislaufplatz, oder *irgendeine Feier* im Freien oder sonstwas mit Chor. Winterabend.
Erst Chorscene. Nachher leert sich der Platz. Martin und Luise bleiben zurück. Martin ist bei dem großen Angriff verwundet worden, trägt den Arm in der Schlinge, sein Freund ist gefallen. Liebeserklärung an Luise, die ihr ihre Schuld und das Urteil des Vaters noch mehr zum Bewußtsein bringt, sie ist vollkommen verzweifelt.}

XI. *Luisens Zimmer*{, nachmittags}
Stepan allein, mißmutig. Er sieht sich im Spiegel, findet, daß er früher ein anderer Kerl war. Alle Bücher hat er schon dreimal gelesen. Züge fahren, er sieht die Welt an sich vorbeilaufen. Ein Sklave ist er geworden. Strümpfe stopft er, Kleider flickt er. Er dient einer Frau, die ihn hält wie ein Haustier.
Luise kommt leise und vorsichtig, will ihn begrüßen.
Er beschwert sich, daß sie so spät und nicht öfter kommt.
Sie hat zu tun, was er denn habe.
Natürlich, für andere, nur nicht für ihn hat sie zu tun.
Er soll nicht ungerecht sein, jede freie Minute sorgt sie für ihn.
Sorgen, ja, daß er faul wird und stumpf.
Er solle sich mit irgendetwas beschäftigen. Was hat sie denn nicht alles für ihn getan?

Ja, das wirft sie ihm vor, dankbar soll er sein! Sie hält ihn gefangen, aus einer Gefangenschaft ist er in eine schlimmere geraten.
Wer kam denn flüchtig hierher?
Wer hat mich denn hier festgehalten und läßt mich nicht fort?
Du bist ein geflohener ~~Feind~~ Kriegsgefangener, ich habe dich vor dem Tode bewahrt.
Du hast einen Gefangenen aufgenommen, du weißt, daß d<as> strafbar ist.
Warum habe ich es denn getan?
Warum? Um mich gefangen zu halten, um mich zu unterdrücken, etc.
Er tadelt ihr Aussehen usw.
So entlarvst du dich also. Das ist der Dank. (Er schüttelt sie) Dank dafür, daß du mich hier zu deinem Vergnügen festgehalten hast. Du bist gemein, ein Barbar, ein Asiat.
In fürchterlicher Wut wirft er sie in die Ecke. –
Großer Umschlag.
Er bittet sie, nicht zu weinen. Er sei halt ein Barbar, ein Asiat.
Sie: »Sprich nie mehr so mit mir, wir werden sonst noch Feinde.«
Er: Wohin ist alles gekommen, ich muß auf irgendeine Weise fort von hier.
Sie: Du müßtest gehen. Aber du kannst es nicht tun, ohne uns beide in die größte Gefahr zu bringen. Bleib, wir wollen uns Mühe geben.
Sie legen traurig den Kopf aneinander & küssen sich.
[Randbemerkung:] {Muß sehr große Steigerung werden.}
{XII.
Kurze Szene zwischen Martin und seiner Mutter.
Ihr Verdacht ist natürlich nicht zerstreut worden, sie teilt dem Sohn davon mit. Er ist von Luisens seltsamem Wesen auch erschrocken. Beschließt, treu zu ihr zu halten, ihr zu helfen und alle Schwierigkeiten zu beseitigen. Vielleicht (sogar höchstwahrscheinlich) kommt diese Szene als Fortsetzung gleich hinter der X Szene, man spart eine Verwandlung und macht die X. Szene wichtiger.}

XII. {Oder XIII} *Bahngleis mit Güterwagen (letzter Wagen eines Güterzugs). Morgennebel im Winter*{, noch dunkel}.
Wagenmeister klopft an die Räder. Der Zugführer kommt mit einem Bremser, der ihm eine Laterne hält. Sie vergleichen die Laufzettel auf den Wagen mit Papieren, die sie in der Hand halten. Der Zug ist für die russische Front bestimmt. Dieser Wagen mit Liebesgaben soll nach Wilna (?). Gleich nach dem überholenden Schnellzug fährt der Güterzug ab – Ab.
Martin und Stepan. Martin hat Stepan aus seinem Versteck herausgeholt, Luise weiß nichts davon. (Sie weiß auch nichts davon, daß Martin vom Vorhandensein Stefans weiß). Martin sagt ihm, er müsse fliehen, der Alb müsse von ihnen genommen werden. Der Zug führe ihn bis kurz hinter die Front, in Rußland seien die Linien jetzt sehr dünn, er könne leicht überlaufen oder sonst sehen, wie er fortkommt. Er gibt ihm Geld und ein Päckchen mit Lebensmitteln.
Stepan: Warum lieferst Du mich nicht aus?
M: Du sollst nicht bestraft werden für Handlungen, die ganz natürlichen Instinkten entspringen.
St: Und das Unrecht, das ich dir getan habe? Ich habe Luise geliebt.
M: Wer könnte Luise nicht lieben? Ich liebe sie über alle Maßen.
Stepan dankt ihm »auf Wiedersehen, Kamerad«. Martin ab, Stepan kriecht in den Güterwagen.
Mittlerweile nähert sich der Schnellzug.
Man hört Warnungsrufe eines Bahnangestellten. Luise läuft herein, um den Güterwagen herum und will sich vor den gerade durchfahrenden Schnellzug werfen. Stepan hat auf die Rufe hin aus seinem Wagen gesehen und erkennt Luise. Im letzten Augenblick errettet er sie und führt sie in den Vordergrund.
L: Kannst du mich nicht einmal ungehindert sterben lassen.
St: Warum hast du das getan? Ich war schon fort.
L: Soll das Leiden wieder von neuem anfangen?
Der Bahnangestellte kommt mit anderen, die er herbeigerufen hat. Darunter Luisens Vater und Martin.

Stepan übergibt Martin die Luise. »Sie lebt. Für dich.« Er wendet sich um und meldet sich dem Vater als der entflohene Gefangene. Der Vater, der den Lärm auf die Ergreifung des Entflohenen bezogen hatte, befiehlt, ihn festzunehmen. Stellt ihn den Begleitmannschaften gegenüber als schweren Verbrecher hin, den man gut bewachen müsse. Wo er denn die ganze Zeit über gesteckt habe? Luise schreit, sie will hindern, daß man ihn ausfragt. Stepan sagt, er habe sich in der Gegend herumgetrieben, habe gebettelt, von Rüben gelebt und zuletzt habe er in den Güterwagen übernachtet. Vater: »Spionage wahrscheinlich auch noch, die Strafe wird schwer werden.« Luise: »Man wird ihn erschießen.« Martin: »Er ist kein Spion, er ist ein harmloser Flüchtling; er hat deine Tochter gerettet.« Stepan wird abgeführt. Vater ergreift die Hände Luisens und wendet sich kurz ab, um dem Transport zu folgen. –
Schlußsätze mit hohen Tönen, Luise und Martin.

37 Willy Strecker an Paul Hindemith

Mainz, 9. Januar 1933

Zur Rückkehr nach dem schönen Berlin, lieber Herr Hindemith, sowie zur Wiedereröffnung unserer erfreulichen Korrespondenz meine entsprechenden Glückwünsche, mit denen ich Sie in den Ferien nicht belästigen wollte.

Sehr erfreulich ist Ihre Mitteilung über Pentzold, dessen Szenario wir mit großer Ungeduld erwarten. Sie sollen es sofort wieder zurückbekommen und mündliche Erörterungen können dann bei einem demnächstigen Besuch voraussichtlich noch bis Ende Januar stattfinden.

Wenn wir durch den Entwurf schon etwas vorbereitet sind, wird eine Aussprache umso einfacher sein.

Darf ich Sie dringend an den englischen Plöner Plan[95] erinnern? Herr Mayer in London platzt vor Ungeduld und es wäre wichtig, mindestens

[95] Vgl. Anm. 82.

wissen zu lassen, ob überhaupt eine Möglichkeit zur Verwirklichung dieses Planes besteht, wie sich die Plöner selbst dazu stellen und welche Anzahl von Mitwirkenden zum mindesten in Betracht käme. Ich glaube nicht, daß er mit mehr als 60–80, höchstens 100 gerechnet hatte. Falls der Plan undurchführbar ist, könnte ich ja immer noch den Gegenvorschlag eines Einstudierens einzelner Stücke durch Sie in einer englischen Schule machen, obwohl ich mir viel mehr von dem Besuch der deutschen Schule verspräche. Was schlügen Sie gegebenenfalls für eine englische Schule vor? Wie lange glauben Sie, werden Sie zu den Proben brauchen?
Einstweilen herzlichst
Ihr <Willy Strecker>

38 Ludwig Strecker an Paul Hindemith

Mainz, 10. Januar 1933

Lieber Herr Hindemith,
Rose Walter schreibt uns, daß sie Ihnen aus Bottrop einen ausführlichen Bericht über die Aufnahme des »Unaufhörlichen« geschickt hat und uns vorschlägt, ihn uns gelegentlich von Ihnen zukommen zu lassen. Es würde uns natürlich sehr interessieren, vor allem mit Rücksicht darauf, ob wir ihn evtl. in unserer Hauszeitschrift »Weihergarten«[96] abdrucken können, Ihr Einverständnis vorausgesetzt. In diesem Falle würden selbstverständlich Adressat und Absenderin unerwähnt bleiben und ich wäre Ihnen daher dankbar, wenn Sie ihn uns übersenden wollten.
Wegen Ihres Opernbuch-Ergebnisses schrieb Ihnen gestern mein Bruder schon. Sie können sich denken, daß ich in allererster Linie auf das Ergebnis gespannt bin und darauf brenne, die Skizze zu erhalten.
Mit besten Grüßen und nachträglich unseren Wünschen zum neuen Jahr für Sie beide
stets der Ihre <Ludwig Strecker>

---

[96] Vgl. Anm. 62.

39 Paul Hindemith an Ludwig und Willy Strecker

Berlin, <11. Januar 1933>

Verehrte Brüder,
heute bekommt jeder von Ihnen eine Spezialsendung. Zunächst für den Operninteressierten den Entwurf, so weit er feststeht. Ich hoffe, Sie werden klug daraus. Einstweilen haben wir die Haupthandlung in großen Zügen fertig gemacht. Die Nebenpersonen, ihre Handlungen und die Verknüpfung mit der Hauptgeschichte ist z.Zt. Penzoldts Arbeit. Es ist natürlich möglich, daß sich dadurch noch einiges am Plane ändert, im allgemeinen aber dürfte er wohl so brauchbar sein. Irgendwelche irgendwen anstoßende Stellen sind wohl kaum noch drin. Vielleicht können Sie sich das Ganze noch nicht so klar vorstellen wie ich, das ist auch nicht zu verlangen, aber ein ungefähres Bild werden Sie wohl bekommen. Die schon feststehenden Szenen können sehr bühnenwirksam werden und musikalisch wirken werden sie sicher, da sie ja alle von der Musiknummer her aufgestellt und durchgearbeitet sind. Die ursprüngliche läppische Kacknaivität und das entsetzliche Kleinstadtmilieu ist, so hoffe ich, nunmehr vollkommen entfernt und durch Besseres ersetzt. Ich hoffe, daß schon zu erkennen ist, daß jetzt Menschen auf der Bühne stehen, die den Zuschauer etwas angehen. Sentimentalität bleibt draußen, deshalb ist gottlob nicht einmal ein Liebesduett drin, obwohl das Ganze doch eine doppelte Liebesgeschichte ist. Der Chor im Schützengraben und der Abschied im ersten und zweiten Bild kriegen natürlich keine Spur von kitschiger Sentimentalität. Durch die starke Verwendung alter Lieder und Märsche und der russischen Lieder hoffe ich das Stück auch für Nichtmusiker interessant machen zu können. Wenn Ihnen dieser Entwurf gefällt und Sie Zutrauen zu Penzoldts weiteren Entwürfen haben (ich erwarte bald die übrigen Szenen und will mich dann bald wieder mit ihm treffen, um das Szenar mit ihm fertigzustellen, den Text selbst soll er dann immer machen, wie ich ihn gerade brauche), meinen Sie nicht, man sollte ihm zur Aufmunterung einen

kleinen Vorschuß geben? Er ist anspruchslos und bescheiden und hat nie davon geredet. –
Rose Walter's[97] Brief haben wir neulich meiner Mutter nach Frankfurt (wir schicken ihr alle abgelegten Ruhmesblätter), damit sie auch sieht, was los ist. Wir haben allerdings geschrieben, sie könne ihn nach Kenntnisnahme zerreißen. Vielleicht hat sie ihn aber noch, was Sie ja durch einen Anruf bei ihr erfahren können, und dann können Sie ihn getrost im Weihergarten[98] veröffentlichen. – Darf ich Sie noch bitten, auch weiterhin noch gar nichts über unsere Opernpläne verlauten zu lassen? –
Zweite Abteilung. Die Antwort des Plöner Direktors Dr. Teichert[99] fand ich erst gestern hier vor, er mußte sein Provinzialschuladhäsionsimmatrikulatinstitut anfragen. Aus den Briefen ersehen Sie, daß trotz meiner Unkereien alles einzurichten ginge. Hundert Kinder sind nötig, und ich würde vorschlagen, die Vorführung in London[100] stattfinden zu lassen, wenn ich selbst dort bin, nämlich in der Märzwoche, in der das Unaufhörliche[101] und das Lehrstück[102] stattfindet, sodaß ich den »Musiktag« selbst leiten kann, was immerhin besser ist. Können Sie von Mayer'n[103] erfahren, wie und wo er die Kinder unterbringen kann, ob freier Hin- und Rücktransport (wahrscheinlich) Southampton-London zu erreichen ist? Schwierigkeiten wird's hier geben. Haben Sie irgendwen bei der Hapag oder beim Lloyd, bei dem man vielleicht die ganz oder teilweise freie Überfahrt erreichen könnte? Eventuell müßte man das Auswärtige Amt

[97] Vgl. Anm. 91.
[98] Vgl. Anm. 62.
[99] Der Oberstudiendirektor Dr. Friedrich Teichert leitete das Gymnasium Plön seit 1928 und wurde nach der Umwandlung der Schule in eine »Nationalpolitische Bildungsanstalt« im Jahre 1933 abgelöst.
[100] Vgl. Anm. 82.
[101] Vgl. Anm. 11.
[102] Hindemith schrieb die Musik zum *Lehrstück* von Bertolt Brecht (1898–1956), das am 28.7.1929 im Rahmen des Festivals »Deutsche Kammermusik Baden-Baden 1929« uraufgeführt wurde. 1930 hat Brecht ohne Beteiligung von Hindemith eine grundlegende Überarbeitung und Erweiterung des Textes vorgenommen, der nun den Titel *Das Badener Lehrstück vom Einverständnis* erhielt.
[103] Vgl. Anm. 82.

dranhetzen, aber die Leute werden wohl kaum etwas zahlen. Die Kinder dürfen natürlich nichts zahlen, ganz abgesehen davon, daß die meisten sehr arm, zum großen Teil sogar Waisen und dergl. sind. Wollen Sie so lieb sein, gleich nach England zu schreiben, vielleicht schreiben Sie dem Direktor auch noch ein paar Worte. Es wäre schön, wenn diese Sache zustande käme. Wenn alles klappt, müssen wir uns dann einmal über die genaue Ausführung des Planes unterhalten. – So, das wär's wohl für heute. Packen Sie mir alles gut ein und legen Sie mir einen Wurstzipfel für den Hund bei. – Wollen Sie mir die Einlagen (dieses Briefes natürlich) wieder zurückschicken? Wann erscheint Einer von Ihnen wieder hier in Berlin? Beiliegende Partitur wurde mir heute früh anonym zugeschickt, ich nehme an, daß sie ein Restbestand von Klemperer's Konzert im Dezember ist. Alleweil Schluß. Schönste Grüße Ihres
Paul Hindemith

40 Ernst Penzoldt an Paul Hindemith

<München>, 13. Januar 1933

Lieber Herr Hindemith!
Mit Ihrer Abreise trat herrliches Skiwetter ein. Trotzdem bemühe ich mich fleißig um den Text. Ich gebe Ihnen heute zwei Szenen[104] zur Probe und halte mit dem Übrigen ein, bis ich Ihre Antwort habe. Ich habe mich bemüht möglichst kurz zu bleiben und bitte Sie um genaue Mitteilung, wo Sie mehr Text brauchen und ob das, was ich mir dachte als Unterlage dienen kann. Ich habe über dem Schreiben einige kleine Aenderungen gemacht. Nicht alle Notizen konnte ich mühelos unterbringen. Trotzdem habe ich das Gefühl mittels der vereinbarten Marschroute besser arbeiten zu können. Es ist unbedingt notwendig, daß ich für die weiteren Szenen genau im Bilde bin, was Sie von dem Text dieser beiden Szenen brauchen können. Lassen Sie sich die Mühe nicht verdrießen, ich tue es auch nicht.

[104] Vgl. Dok. 41.

Mit herzlichen Grüßen, auch an Ihre Frau von mir und den Meinen
Ihr sehr ergebener <Ernst Penzoldt>

41 Zwei Szenen von Ernst Penzoldt auf der Grundlage des »Mösern«-Entwurfs[105]

Auf dem Tunnelberg

Früher Morgen, von ferne der Gesang der Soldaten wie in der zweiten Szene.

Susanne: (Schaut ins Weite, die Hand über den Augen) *1.* Wie klein sie sind aus der Ferne. *2.* Wie Zinnsoldaten von unsichtbarer Hand gespielt und einer davon ist Martin, der sagt, daß er mich lieb hat. *3.* Aber darf man denn das, jemanden lieben nur so vom Sehen, ob man mag oder nicht und ist auf einmal Fleisch und Blut in einem fremden Mann und tut ihm weh und ist dran schuld und kann doch nichts dafür. *4.* Ich habe ja nicht einmal aufgeschaut, wenn er vorüberging und habs ihm dennoch angetan. *5.* Möchte wohl wissen, was er an mir hat. *6.* Ach die Männer! (ausschauend) *7.* Ich kann ihn gar nicht herausfinden aus den vielen. *8.* Jeder könnte es sein. Ein Gesicht ist wie's andere. *9.* Nur ein kleiner heller Fleck. – *10.* Der Zug ist geladen wie ein Geschütz. (ein Pfiff, Läutwerk) Jetzt, jetzt fährt er ab (Abschiedsjubel von ferne). *11.* Noch höre ich sein Zischeln und Rollen. *12.* Der Qualm zerreist im Wind und geifert über die Äcker. *13.* Ferner wird er und ferner, jetzt ist er fort und die sterben sollen sind schon tot. *14.* Man denkt, man müßte ihnen den Tod am Gesicht ansehen, aber man sieht nichts, gar nichts. Ach der Krieg!

Stepan: (verwildert nur in Hose und Hemd, er sieht nicht gerade sehr vertrauenerweckend aus)

---

[105] Diese Szenenentwürfe liegen als Manuskripte sowie als maschinenschriftliche Abschriften mit geringfügigen Änderungen vor. Die Textwiedergabe folgt den Typoskripten und vernachlässigt die Unterschiede in den Manuskripten. Die kursiv gesetzten Ziffern in der ersten Szene stammen von Paul Hindemith.

Susanne: *15.* Allmächt habe ich mich jetzt erschrocken.
Stepan: *16.* Barmherzigkeit Mädchen, mich hungert.
Susanne: *17.* Wer sind Sie denn überhaupt?
Stepan: *18.* (mit Anstrengung chevaleresk) Stepan Micheilowitsch Borodin vom neunzehnten russischen Infanterieregiment Großfürst Alexei.
Susanne: Ein Russe?
Stepan: Ein Flüchtling. *19.* Gestern als der Transportzug den Tunnel passierte entfloh ich ungesehen in Qualm und Finsternis. *20.* Stand ganz allein mitten in Feindesland im Innern dieses Berges im Dunklen ohne Ahnung wo in aller Welt ich mich befände, ohne Karte und Kompaß, ohne Speise und Trank, nur wissend dort im Osten liegt Rußland. *21.* In eine Nische gedrückt, den Kopf zurückgeneigt trank ich die Tropfen, die vom Gestein des Gewölbes fielen, Züge brausten groß und nah an mir vorbei und erschütterten mir Fleisch und Bein mit ihrem gewaltig lärmenden Widerhall. Hunger und Fieber trieb mich aus dem Versteck (er fröstelt).
Susanne: (fast böse) Wenn ich Sie nun anzeige, wenn ich um Hilfe gerufen hätte.
Stepan: (achselzuckend) Ich bin ein Russe.
Susanne: Gehen Sie schnell wenn Leute kommen, so fliehen Sie doch endlich Mensch.
Stepan: Ich kann nicht. Meine Füße bluten, ich habe Hunger.
Susanne: Warum sind Sie denn dann überhaupt geflohen?
Stepan: Unerträglich schien es mir gefangen zu sein.
Susanne: Und geben sich ohne weiteres in einer Feindin Hand.
Stepan: Ach Fräulein warum Feindin? Wir haben einander doch nie etwas böses getan.
Susanne: Nein wir haben einander nie etwas böses getan. (Sie greift entschlossen in ihr Handtäschchen.) Da nehmen Sie und jetzt gehen Sie bitte.
Stepan: (Kindlich) Schokolade (er kniet nieder und küßt überschwänglich Susannens Hände)

Susanne: (macht sich los und enteilt verwirrt)
Stepan: (verharrt knieend, er lächelt)

Straße am Kasernenhofgitter gegen Abend
Gaslaterne. Herbstnebel. Kugel-Akazien ohne Laub, erleuchtete Backstein-Kaserne mit schwarzen Fensterkreuzen. Soldatenlied.
Hinter dem Gitter Martin, Felix und andere Soldaten. Sie sind nagelneu eingekleidet; Mütze ohne Seitengewehr, Schaftstiefel, Hose in denselben. Familienangehörige nehmen durch die Gitterstäbe Abschied. Beim fröhlichen Felix drängen sich nur so die Mädchen, etwa 5 Stück, beim stilleren Martin steht seine Mutter, eine auffallend gekleidete, pompöse nicht mehr ganz junge Dame, die einst bessere Tage gesehen hat. Sie besitzt ein gewisses Etwas. Ihr Mund ist knallrot, das Haar zitronengelb, das Gesicht stark gepudert. Sie ist eine ziemlich penetrante, aber gutherzige Person.
Martin: Ich bitte dich herzlich, liebe Mama, geh' jetzt.
Frau Engel: Laß dich nur erst mal richtig anschauen, mein Heldensöhnchen. Nun sehr kriegerisch siehst du gerade nicht aus in deiner neuen Uniform.
Martin: (unbehaglich) Ja ich ertrinke fast darin, es gab nur noch drei Größen. Man mußte schon Glück haben hineinzupassen.
Fr. Engel: Nein so lasse ich dich nicht gehen, mein lieber Junge. Weißt du was, ich werde einfach deinen Herrn Hauptmann bitten ...
Martin: Um Gotteswillen Mama tu das nicht.
Fr. Engel: Was war da der bunte Rock doch so schmuck, besonders bei den Herrn von der Kavallerie, Ulanen und Husaren. Jetzt sind sie alle so grau, sieht einer wie der andere aus. Nur die Gesichter sind noch verschieden – Wißt ihr schon, wohin ihr kommt? Nach Frankreich, Rußland oder Italien?
Martin: Das weiß kein Mensch. Ich bitte dich herzlich Mama, jetzt zu gehen.
Fr. Engel: (unbeirrt) Wenn ich so daran denke, daß ich dort überall

schon gewesen bin, in Paris und Petersburg und Rom, singender Weise als Carmen, Amneris und Dalila (unvermittelt) Dein Vater, Martin, war ein schöner Mann, eine prachtvolle Erscheinung. Ach ja, tempi passati. Du hast ganz seine Augen und seinen Mund.

Martin: (peinlich berührt) Ich bitte dich herzlich, man hört dir zu!

Fr. Engel: (pathetisch) O ich schäme mich meiner Liebe nicht, aber auf einmal war ich halt allein mit dir. Ja ja ich habe manchen Puff vertragen müssen in dieser Welt des Jammers. (mit lächelnder Bitternis) Jetzt gibt die berühmte Frau Engel Stunden, Gesangunterricht bis zur Bühnenreife an höhere Töchter in einer kleinen unbekannten Stadt. Auch singt sie zuweilen auf Wunsch in Wohltätigkeitskonzerten. Sic transit gloria mundi!

Die Mädchen: Leb wohl, liebster Felix, bleib hübsch gesund und vergiß uns nicht.

Felix: Ich werde mir Mühe geben euch zuliebe.

Martin: Aber verstehst du denn nicht Mama, ich erwarte jemand.

Fr. Engel: Dacht ich's doch! Sei unbesorgt, mir ist nichts Menschliches fremd. Wer ist denn die Glückliche?

Martin: Du kennst sie, sie hat Stunde bei dir.

Fr. Engel: Susanne vom Bahnhof?

Martin: Ja Susanne.

Susanne: (kommt zögernd, sie ist etwa achtzehn Jahre alt, sehr brav gekleidet und züchtig frisiert)

Fr. Engel: (mit Wärme auf sie zu) Ei freilich kennen wir uns. Sie hat recht hübsches Material, sie hat Gold in der Kehle.

Martin: Mama ich beschwöre dich, laß uns jetzt allein.

Susanne: (unschuldig) Warum schickst du deine Mutter fort?

Fr. Engel: Ach gute Kinder, ich weiß sehr wohl, wann Mütter überflüssig sind. Die alte Dame zieht sich diskret zurück (sie geht nicht ohne sich einen Augenblick an dem vermeintlichen Glück der jungen Leute zu weiden).

Martin: (befangen) Ich danke dir Susanne, daß du gekommen bist.

Susanne: Ich hätte dich fast nicht wiedererkannt. Du bist ja jetzt ein richtiger Soldat.
Martin: Ja ein Soldat (sie stehen geniert beisammen).
Felix: (wird reich beschenkt) Pulswärmer!
Erst. Mädchen: Hasenwolle, ich habe sie selbst gestrickt.
Felix: Und Zigaretten, fünfhundert Stück.
Zweit. Mädchen: Es ist deine Lieblingsmarke.
Felix: Eine Taschenlampe, wie praktisch!
Dritt. Mädchen: Sie brennt acht Stunden.
Felix: Und eine Uhr, na aber!
Viertes Mädchen: Mit leuchtendem Zifferblatt!
Felix: Und was ist das? Ein Amulett?
Fünftes Mädchen: Ein Kugelsegen um den Hals zu tragen.
Felix: Jetzt kann mir durchaus nichts mehr passieren.
Martin: Susanne seit ich dich zum ersten Male sah
Susanne: Sprich nicht weiter, Martin, bitte sprich nicht weiter.
Martin: Ich liebe dich Susanne, das weißt du doch.
Susanne: Ich habe dich doch so gebeten, es nicht zu sagen. Und bist du auch deiner ganz gewiß? daß ich es bin, die du lieb hast? Es gibt soviele Mädchen.
Martin: Ich bin es ganz gewiß.
Susanne: Aber wie weiß man es denn? Irgendwie müßt ich's doch spüren.
Martin: Ich liebe nicht so leicht, ich liebe nur dich.
Susanne: Nur mich? Kann man das nur einen Menschen lieben?
(es bläst)
Die Mädchen: Soldaten solln nachhause gehn.
Die Soldaten: (außer Martin) Und nicht so lang beim Mädchen stehn.
Alle: Der Hauptmann hats befohlen.
Martin: Susanne, liebe, liebe Susanne!
Susanne: Nein, Martin, nein! Ich hatte dich so gebeten, es nicht zu sagen nun bist du traurig und ich bin betrübt, ach Martin später, wenn du zurückkommst, später.

Martin: Ich komme nicht zurück. Gute Nacht Susanne!
Susanne: Gute Nacht, Martin! (sie geht)
Martin: (sieht ihr aussichtslos nach)
Die Mädchen: (sind gegangen)
Felix: (mit Paketen beladen) Nun Martin?
Martin: Ich habe halt kein Glück!
Felix: Gräm dich nicht Kamerad, es gibt soviele Mädchen und eine ist wie die andere.

42 Ludwig Strecker an Paul Hindemith

Mainz, 14. Januar 1933

Lieber Paul Hindemith,
Ihren Opernentwurf[106] habe ich verschlungen und muß Ihnen meine rückhaltslose Bewunderung aussprechen für das, was Sie aus dem Stoff gemacht haben, denn der Schwierigkeiten war ich mir vollkommen bewußt. Sie haben, abgesehen von allem anderen die Verfänglichkeit des Stoffes glänzend eliminiert und da ich annehme, daß Sie sich bereits in Ihr Kind verliebt haben, bin ich überzeugt, daß Ihnen auch die Gestaltung derartig gelingt, daß so etwas wie eine Volksoper daraus werden kann. Ich hoffe und glaube, daß der Stoff auf diese Weise Allgemeingültigkeit und Außer-Aktualität gewonnen hat. Ich pflichte Ihnen vollkommen bei, daß die Figuren lebendig sind und, was das Wichtigste ist, alle sympathisch geworden sind.
Etwas lächeln mußte ich über Ihren Triumph, daß Sie jedem Liebesduett aus dem Weg gegangen sind. Ich gebe zu, daß es Ihnen gelungen ist, aber was hat Ihnen denn dies nur Allzumenschliche getan? So lange Menschen leben und auf der Bühne dargestellt werden, wird dies nun einmal von der Natur gewollte Ereignis im Leben wie auf der Bühne, eine – sagen wir – besondere Berücksichtigung verdienen. Seit des para-

[106] Vgl. Dok. 36.

diesischen Adam, Händels und Verdis Zeiten hat die Liebesszene weder im Leben noch auf der Bühne an Wirkung verloren. Ich wage diese Bemerkung selbst auf die Gefahr hin, daß Sie mich für einen perversen Menschen halten.

Der Text ist in unserem Hause herumgewandert und wurde dann in einer 2 Stunden langen Sechs-Männer-Konferenz unter das Mikroskop genommen. Hierbei sind noch einige Momente hervorgetreten, die ich Ihnen mitteilen möchte, da sie Ihnen vielleicht noch weitere Anregungen zu geben vermögen. Da Sie selbst sagen, daß es sich erst um eine Skizze handelt, werden manche unserer Beobachtungen vielleicht überflüssig sein und von Ihnen bei der Ausarbeitung sowieso noch berücksichtigt werden.

Einer unserer Herren bemerkte, daß im Milieu eine gewisse Verwandtschaft mit dem »Sergeanten Grischa«[107] bestünde, der ja auch dramatisiert wurde. Ich habe das Buch allerdings nicht gelesen und daher kein eigenes Urteil. – Aber dies nur nebenbei.

Daß Ihnen der Schluß schwer gefallen ist, glaube ich herauszufühlen. Es liegen noch so einige Schalen der geknackten Nuß herum. Es ist natürlich sehr viel leichter, einen schwierigen Konflikt tragisch zu lösen, als zu einem glücklichen Ende zu führen. Trotzdem bin ich Ihnen dankbar, daß Sie den letzteren Versuch gemacht haben, denn im Sinne des Publikums ist ein solcher Ausgang der einzig richtige.

Am ernstesten beschäftigte uns folgende Frage: Martin, der an sich schon eine etwas weiche und unklare Rolle spielt begeht durch die Freilassung des Russen militärisch gesehen und im Sinne der vaterländischen Zuverlässigkeit ein Verbrechen. Es könnte sein, daß man aus nationaler Gesinnung heraus den Finger auf diese Wunde legt, die man mit dem Fremdwort Pazifismus bezeichnen könnte. Ich muß immerhin darauf aufmerksam machen.

Diese Tatsache gewinnt verstärkte Bedeutung auch vom dramatischen Standpunkt aus. Bei diesem doch offenbar tapferen deutschen Soldaten

---

[107] 1927 erschienener Roman von Arnold Zweig (1887–1968).

dürfte der Konflikt eigentlich nicht unberücksichtigt bleiben. Wir haben uns lange den Kopf zerbrochen, wie dem abzuhelfen sei. Ich gebe Ihnen nachstehend eine Andeutung, die am wenigsten die augenblickliche Endfassung stört, ohne behaupten zu wollen, daß sie die einzig mögliche ist: Der letzten Szene voraus müßte in Luisens Kammer eine Aussprache der drei jungen Menschen gehen, bei der alle Gegensätze aufeinander platzen. Im Höhepunkt – wobei auch ein Eifersuchtsausbruch des Russen nicht unmotiviert wäre, wird Luise aus dem Zimmer gerufen, sodaß die beiden Männer allein bleiben. Martin macht Stepan den Vorschlag zur Flucht, der sofort ausgeführt wird.

Das nächste Bild kann in der Haupt-Anlage so bleiben, nur daß nach vollzogenem Fluchtplan Luise etwa mit Martin zusammentrifft und ihn fragt, was er mit Stepan gemacht habe. Er sagt zu ihr:

»Ich habe meine Pflicht als Mensch erfüllt, Dich von ihm befreit und ihm zur Flucht verholfen. Niemand wird erfahren, wo er sich aufgehalten hat. Ich aber werde jetzt meine Pflicht als Soldat erfüllen und mein Verbrechen sühnen, indem ich mich der Kommandantur stelle.«

In Verwirrung und Erschütterung von allen diesen Erlebnissen kann sie sich dann auf die Schienen stürzen und alles andere weitergehen. Wenn dann unmittelbar darauf der Russe gefangen wird, der Bahnhofskommandeur (oder wer das sein mag) erscheint und Martin sein Geständnis ablegen will, kommt er garnicht zu Wort, weil es ja schließlich nur zum Versuch des militärischen Verbrechens gekommen ist.

Auf diese Weise würde m.E. ein ungeheurer Konflikt gewonnen durch den Zwiespalt in der militärischen, bezw. menschlichen Brust von Martin und der letzte evtl. noch angreifbare Punkt beseitigt. Sollte Sie dieser Gedankengang überzeugen, so werden Sie sicherlich mit der gleichen Kunst den Knoten schürzen und lösen können.

Aus Ihrer Skizze geht für uns nicht klar hervor, warum Luise sich auf die Schienen wirft. Wenn es nur geschieht, weil sie das Leben mit dem Russen nicht mehr ertragen kann, so würde allerdings ihr Selbstmordversuch anders motiviert oder die Szene anders geführt werden müssen. Ein

Gewinn schiene mir jedenfalls auch in der letzten Aussprache zwischen Luise und Martin und ferner auch die weitere »Vermenschlichung« des Martin durch seinen Gewissenskonflikt. Die Begründung des Selbstmordversuches müßte ja sowieso dem Publikum gegeben werden. Ich nehme an, daß dies in der Skizze noch nicht angedeutet werden konnte.
Im übrigen wären noch folgende Punkte zu erwähnen:
Es liegt eine gewisse Gefahr in dem allzu Epischen der vielen Bilder. Es genügt vielleicht schon dieser Hinweis, um jedes einzelne nochmals daraufhin zu untersuchen, ob und wie weit in jedem einzelnen Falle die Handlung vorwärts getrieben wird. In diesem Sinne würde die vorgeschlagene Szene der drei Hauptpersonen im Zimmer der Luise eine Verstärkung der dramatischen Handlung bedeuten können. Bei der Ausarbeitung empfehlen wir auch an den geeigneten Stellen den Humor nicht zu kurz kommen zu lassen. Solche Ruhe- und Erholungspunkte sind immer wirksam.
Hinsichtlich der Schützengraben-Szene möchte ich darauf hinweisen, daß dies Bild natürlich schon etwas verbraucht ist. Ich selbst kenne dieses Milieu aus 3–4 Sprechdramen. Es ist die Frage, ob diese Szene nicht in einem großen Eisenbahn-Transportwagen stattfinden könnte, evtl. auf einem Haltepunkt, die ja bei Transportzügen alle Augenblick, auch auf offenem Felde stattgefunden haben. Den notwendigen Chor könnte man ja auch dadurch erreichen, daß die vielen Soldaten aussteigen, um sich gewissermaßen die Beine zu strecken. Wollen Sie ein Gefahrenmoment hineinbringen, so könnte man an einen Fliegerangriff denken, Kommando: »Lichter aus, alles in den Zug«. – Vorhang.
Und nun noch eine Reihe von Kleinigkeiten:
1.) Erste Szene: Warum muß Martins Mutter unverheiratet sein?
2.) Vierte Szene: Kurze Erklärung, warum er so gut deutsch spricht. Russischer Student? Etwa Balte oder dergleichen? Dies würde dann auch seine Fiebererzählung in »deutsch« in der 5. Szene wahrscheinlicher machen.
3.) Ich nehme an, daß Luise eine jugendlich dramatische Rolle ist.

4.) Um auch juristisch sattelfest zu sein wäre noch zu untersuchen, ob auf Flucht eines Gefangenen, soweit es sich nicht um Ertappung auf frischer Tat handelt, im Militärgesetz-Strafbuch Todesstrafe steht. Im allgemeinen, jedenfalls im normalen Strafgesetzbuch ist Selbstbefreiung eines Gefangenen straflos. Dies hätte den Vorteil, daß zum Schluß das Publikum nicht für das Leben des »Helden« zu zittern braucht.
Und damit will ich für heute Schluß machen. Ich würde mich sehr freuen, wenn diese Anregungen Sie zu einer ernsten Prüfung der verschiedenen Fälle führen würde.
Jedenfalls beglückwünsche ich Sie nochmals, daß Sie bis zu dem Punkt gekommen sind, wo man Land sieht.
Noch eins:
Mein Verlag wäre natürlich gern bereit, Penzoldt sagen wir Mk. 500,– à Konto zu geben. Wir sind durch die Mk. 1000,– an Benn, die wir wahrscheinlich nie wiedersehen, bereits »vorbelastet«.
Ich bin Ende Januar oder Anfang Februar fällig für Berlin, kann aber heute noch keinen Termin bestimmen.
Herzlichste Grüße Ihnen beiden
Ihr <Ludwig Strecker>
NS. Bitte schreiben Sie mal ein paar Zeilen, wie Sie darüber denken. Sie lassen sich doch wohl nicht die wirkungsvolle Abschieds-Pantomime im letzten Bild entgehen, wenn Stepan abgeführt wird?

43 Willy Strecker an Paul Hindemith

Mainz, 16. Januar 1933

Lieber Herr Hindemith,
von unserer Spezial-Abteilung für Operntexte erhielten Sie bereits die Senfsauce zum russischen Salat.
Somit heute nur die Beantwortung des Plöner Planes[108]. Es freut mich

[108] Vgl. Anm. 82.

außerordentlich, daß die Möglichkeit einer Verwirklichung der Englandreise besteht und ich schrieb wie einliegend an Dr. Teichert[109], desgleichen an Robert Mayer[110]. Die Reisekosten in England werden wir bestimmt zusammen bekommen. Auch die Reise in Deutschland müßte man durch das Auswärtige Amt auf deutschen Bahnen ersetzt bekommen und die Englandfahrt durch eine der Hamburger Gesellschaften. Es fragt sich nur, ob die Schiffe von Southampton so günstig hin und zurück fahren, daß es mit der Länge des Aufenthaltes in London klappt. Sobald ich von London näheres höre, werde ich es Ihnen mitteilen.
Die Originalbriefe liegen bei; der »Wurschtzippel« kommt gesondert.
Mit den herzlichsten Grüßen
Ihr <Willy Strecker>

44 Paul Hindemith an Ernst Penzoldt

Berlin, <circa 18. Januar 1933>

Lieber Herr Penzoldt,
herzlichsten Dank für die schnelle Übersendung der beiden Szenen[111]. Sie sind, finde ich, als Szenen gut gelungen, da ich aber zwar mindestens so gutherzig wie Frau Engel, dazu aber auch mindestens so penetrant bin, habe ich einige Bedenken gegen diese Fassung als Opernszene. Diese Art Dialog komponiert sich sehr schlecht, ich wenigstens weiß kaum, wie man ihn einigermaßen erträglich in die Musik einschnüren könnte. Sicher werden Sie auch dafür keine Lösung finden, wenn Sie einmal versuchen, sich eine Art Musik dazu zu denken oder die Worte an Musik anzupassen versuchen, die Ihnen geläufig ist. Wir müßten für die Worte erst einige Proben machen, verschiedene Lösungen einiger Sätze, und ich ich müßte auch erst einige Male musikalisch daran her-

109 Vgl. Anm. 99.
110 Vgl. Anm. 82.
111 Vgl. Dok. 41.

umprobieren können, ehe Sie den Text festlegen. Und diese Proben machen wir, glaube ich, bei nächster Gelegenheit einmal zusammen, denn den Stil für dieses Stück, soweit er das Zusammengehen von Wort und Musik betrifft, kann Einer allein wahrscheinlich gar nicht finden. Eine weitere Schwierigkeit dieser Szenen ist, daß sie gar keine Rücksicht auf den formalen Ablauf der Musik nehmen. Da man Musikstücke ja nicht komponieren kann wie Wortsätze und Szenen, sondern die Töne eher wie Backsteine aneinandersetzen muß und genau ausrechnen muß, wieviel jeder trägt und wie weit ein Bogen zu spannen ist, kann sich natürlich das viel schneller und leichter laufende Wort nur nach dem schwerfälligeren Tonablauf richten. Und dann möchte ich Sie bitten, erst mit den Worten anzufangen, wenn ich mir für die einzelnen Szenen ziemlich feststehende musikalische Gerüste gemacht habe, an die wir dann Musik und Worte anpassen. (Das hindert ja natürlich nicht, daß Sie sich für die Worte schon Notizen besonders schöner oder sehr geeigneter Sätze oder Satzfolgen machen.) Diese Gerüste kann ich aber erst machen, wenn ich die noch fehlenden Szenenentwürfe kenne. Ich weiß ja einstweilen außer den vagen Plänen über die fehlenden Szenen nichts über ihre Länge, ihre Art usw, so daß ich gar nicht Musikpläne für die fertigen Entwürfe aufstellen kann ohne Gefahr zu laufen, sie bei der Ankunft eines neuen Entwurfs wieder umstoßen zu müssen. Daß ich derweil Material sammle, ist klar. Einen schönen Marsch, der Hauptinhalt der Ouvertüre sein soll, habe ich schon, auch an den Volksliedern laboriere ich herum, mehr kann ich aber einstweilen auch nicht tun. Können Sie nicht zunächst einmal die nach unserem Plan fehlenden Szenen entwerfen? Ich halte das für die zunächst wichtigste Arbeit. Die Handlung müßte einmal ganz feststehen, damit man eine genaue Übersicht über alle Formen und Maße hat. Wenn es Ihnen zu langweilig sein sollte, an den fehlenden Szenen herumzudoktern, sagen Sie es mir bitte, vielleicht setzen wir uns dann nächstens wieder dafür zusammen, wenn Sie vom letzten Mal noch nicht genug haben. Einen Teil der Szene aus Tunnelberg erlaube ich mir mit genauen Anmerkungen zu versehen,

damit Sie sehen, in welcher Richtung sich die Überlegungen für die Textierung bewegen müßten. Bitte lachen Sie nicht über diese Kleinlichkeiten, aber der Musiker muß sich mit diesen Dingen herumschlagen. – Wollen Sie also so lieb sein, an die fehlenden Stücke des Torso zu denken? – Daß Frau Engel Susannen Gesangstunde gibt, finde ich nicht gut. Das bringt wieder zu viel Privates unter die Personen – sie waren jetzt gerade so herrlich frei davon. – An Schott habe ich den Mösern-Entwurf[112] geschickt; er gratuliert und ist hocherfreut. Auch Vorschuß will er geben, ich habe ihm bis jetzt allerdings noch nicht geschrieben, daß er selbst gleich an Sie deswegen schreiben solle, weil ich erst hören wollte, wie er sich dazu stellt. Meinen Sie nicht, daß es besser aussähe, wenn wir ihm erst den fertigen Entwurf vorlegten, ehe er zahlt? Ich habe so ein nicht ganz hervorragend sauberes Gefühl, wenn er jetzt gerne zahlt und wir selbst sind uns über einige sehr wichtige Punkte noch nicht klar. Was meinen Sie darüber? Ich werde ihm ganz so schreiben, wie Sie es für richtig halten. Er schrieb von 500 Mk, wäre Ihnen das recht? – Mir geht's mies, ich habe mich vor ein paar Tagen in Hamburg[113] sehr erkältet, habe jetzt im Bett gelegen, huste arg und bin etwas matt. Darum heute nur diese kurzen Anmerkungen[114]. – Was macht der Magneto[115]? Unserer ist groß im Betrieb. Ich habe ganz virtuose Dinge drauf gelernt. Bewegliche und ganz labile!
Na dann Schluß für heute (Sie: +++).
Herzliche Grüße an die ganzen Penzöldte
Ihr Paul Hindemith, Frau auch.

---

112 Vgl. Dok. 36.

113 Am 13.1.1933 spielte Hindemith beim Norddeutschen Rundfunk in Hamburg seine *Sonate für Bratsche und Klavier* op. 11 Nr. 4 (1919) und die *Kammermusik Nr. 5* op. 36 Nr. 4, das sogenannte »Bratschenkonzert«. Begleitet wurde er vom Dirigenten und Pianisten Gerhard Maasz.

114 Vgl. Dok. 45.

115 Gemeint ist ein Magnet, auf dem mit verschiedenen Eisenteilen Figuren aufgebaut werden können, die allein durch die Magnetkraft gehalten werden. Hindemith hatte dieses Spiel Penzoldts Sohn Günther (vgl. Anm. 69) bei einem seiner Besuche in München als Gastgeschenk mitgebracht.

45 · Paul Hindemiths Anmerkungen und Korrekturen zur Tunnelberg-Szene[116]

Szene auf dem Tunnelberg

Satz 1 komponiert sich gut. Einzuwenden wäre nur, daß in allen Opern eine Jungfrau Dinge oder Leute, denen sie nachsieht, so oder ähnlich apostrophiert. Vielleicht findet sich etwas Originelleres. (Oder ganz ohne lange Einleitung: »In diesem Zuge ist Martin, der sagt, daß er mich liebt.«)

Satz 2 ist zu lang. Wenn er komponiert wird, zieht er sich auf die sechsfache Länge und man wird den Zusammenhang verlieren. Also besser zwei getrennte Sätze. Die »Zinnsoldaten, von ...« halte ich für überflüssig, da sie rein literarischer Vergleich sind und für die Musik nichts hergeben. Wenn schon Verzierungen, dann solche, die für die Musik Stimmung, Symbol oder so etwas geben.

Satz 3 hat zu viel kleine und unwichtige Worte, die den Musikfluß hemmen. (man, denn, nur, so, vom, ob, man, oder, und, ist, auf, und, und, und.) Mit ganz wenig Worten müßte das Wesentliche gesagt werden; es wird ja in der Musik doch entsetzlich breit alles.

Satz 4 und 5 gehen. Vielleicht würden sie aus dem Stil fallen, wenn das Ganze in der vorher angewendeten Richtung läuft.

Satz 6 geht nicht. Diese prosaischen Ausrufe sind komisch mit Musik.

7,8,9 Diese kurzen Sätze eignen sich natürlich viel besser. Nicht gut ist, daß die Sängerin, um die Worte deutlich zu machen (»Ich kann ihn nicht herausfinden ...«) nach dem Hintergrund oder in die Kulisse spielen muß, was die Arie stört.

10 Der Vergleich ... wie ein Geschütz ... ist für die Musik Ballast und deshab störend, wie fast alle Vergleiche.

11 Das dürfte sie nicht singen. Entweder es zischt und rollt wirklich, dann stört es die Musik und außerdem hört es der Zuhörer sowieso und man braucht es ihm nicht extra mitzuteilen. Oder es zischt und rollt nicht, so kann man es in der Musik markieren und das ist saudumm oder

[116] Vgl. Dok. 41.

sie singt über eine Sache, die offenbar nicht da ist, was auch nicht gerade in diesem Moment die beste Lösung ist.
12 Auch diese Beschreibung ist vielleicht nicht dringend nötig.
13 »die sterben sollen ...« das ist richtig und
14, das ist gut.
15. Wie bei 6 zu belanglos. Man braucht das nicht zu singen. Schreck ist in der Musik mit einem Akkord gemacht.
16 Vielleicht ohne »Mädchen«, oder statt dessen den Satz etwas dringender und wichtiger.
17. Vielleicht nur »Wer sind sie«. »denn überhaupt« ist zu sehr Umgangssprache, die entweder in der Musik nicht herauskommt oder die Musik bagatellisiert.
18 Eine zu lange Ausführung. Halb so lang ist noch lang genug gesungen.
19 Besser die etwas langen Sätze teilen.
20–21 Gut, vielleicht etwas kürzer fassen
usw.

46 Ernst Penzoldt an Paul Hindemith

München, 20. Januar 1933

Lieber Herr Hindemith!
Vielen Dank für die rasche Antwort mit den außerordentlich wertvollen Hinweisen für die künftige Arbeit. Ich werde also zunächst an den fehlenden Szenen herumdoktern und hoffe, sie Ihnen in der nächsten Woche schicken zu können. – Ich bin auch ganz Ihrer Ansicht, daß man einem Verlag erst den fertigen Plan vor die Nase halten soll, ehe man einen Vorschuß in Anspruch nimmt. Wenn das der Fall ist, habe ich freilich nichts dagegen, einen Vorschuß in Empfang zu nehmen, wenn das nun mal Sitte ist. Ich höre eben, daß meine Hamburger Aufführung[117] im

[117] Im Mai 1932 veröffentlichte das Hamburger Schauspielhaus eine Übersicht über die in der Spielzeit 1932/33 geplanten Stücke, darunter auch Penzoldts *Portugalesische Schlacht* (eine entsprechende Meldung erschien u.a. im *Hamburger Fremdenblatt*, 7.5.1932). Diese Aufführung kam jedoch nicht zustande.

Februar sein soll, den Tag weiß ich noch nicht. Jedenfalls wäre das ein günstiger Augenblick für eine Zusammenkunft.
Es tut mir leid, daß Sie nicht wohl sind und wünsche Ihnen baldige Genesung. Die ganze Familie schließt sich meinen herzlichen Grüßen an Sie und Ihre Frau herzlichst an.
Auf Wiederhören nächste Woche!
Ihr
Ernst Penzoldt

47 Paul Hindemith an Ludwig Strecker

Berlin, 20. Januar 1933

Verehrte Opernabteilung,
schönsten Dank für Ihren ausführlichen Brief. Es freut mich, daß Sie schon mit diesem kargen Entwurf so weit zufrieden sind. Penzoldt hat mittlerweile die erste und dritte Szene fertig ausgeführt geschickt, sie sind als Schauspielszenen sehr gut, aber ihres Dialogs wegen nicht für die Oper zu brauchen. Ich habe ihm geschrieben, er solle erst die im Entwurf fehlenden Szenen herstellen. Um Ihre restlichen Zweifel zu zerstreuen oder wenigstens abzuschwächen, gehe ich jetzt Punkt für Punkt auf Ihren Brief ein.
Das haben Sie falsch verstanden: ich triumphiere nicht über das fehlende Liebesduett. Wenn Sie wollen, werden doch in etwa 6 von 12 Szenen hier Liebesduette gesungen. Ich bin nur entschieden dagegen, daß jedes Duett zwischen Sopran und Tenor stets mit »ich liebe dich« und großer Umarmung verläuft. Daß dieses Ereignis von der Natur gewollt ist, darüber ist nicht zu streiten. Ob die Mutter Natur es so gewollt hat, wie es sich in den meisten Opern abspielt, darüber erlaube ich mir leise Zweifel zu hegen. Also Triumph über das fehlende »Liebesduett«. Liebesduette ohne »« werden Sie genug drin finden.
»Sergeant Grischa«[118] kenne ich nicht. Wenn Ähnlichkeiten vorhanden

[118] Vgl. Anm. 107.

sind, sind sie zufällig und schaden nichts. Übrigens ist meines Wissens Penzoldts Novelle schon eher dagewesen als der »Sergeant Grischa«.
Ihre Befürchtungen, Martin betreffend, halte ich für stark übertrieben. Zunächst mal wird doch seine Handlungsweise im Stück erklärt. Begeht er mit der Freilassung ein Verbrechen, so ist das mehr seinen persönlichen Auseinandersetzungen über Luisens Handlung und sein Entschluß, zu verzeihen und für den Erfolg, menschlich anständig dazustehen, eine Kleinigkeit. Regen sich darüber Leute auf, was sie natürlich gar nicht tun werden, denn es kommt ja (wie Sie durch Vergleich der ersten Fassung des Stoffes überhaupt mit dem jetzigen Plan gesehen haben) gar nicht so sehr auf das Was sondern auf das Wie an, so ist man wirklich machtlos. Schließlich soll doch eine Oper gemacht werden und allen kann es nun mal nicht recht gemacht werden.
Ihre eingeschobene Szene halte ich für ungeeignet. Erstens wird nicht mehr drin gesagt, als was in der Szene davor oder nachher nicht mit einem Satz geklärt werden könnte. Zweitens soll man (finde ich wenigstens) nicht in der Technik von Bloch's Vereinstheater[119] dem Publikum aber auch alles aufs Brot schmieren: daß die zwei sich getroffen haben, geht aus der letzten Szene hervor. Eifersuchtsausbruch beim Russen ist nach der Haßszene auch nicht mehr gerechtfertigt. Drittens würde durch diese neue Szene eine dem Martin zuzuschiebende verbrecherische Handlung um gar nichts gemildert.
So einfach ist doch die Sache wieder nicht, daß er mit Luise die letzten Fädchen zur Befriedigung jedes Idioten im 6. Rang entwirrt. Einen Rest Arbeit kann man dem Publikum doch auch noch lassen. Er wird über diese Sache mit Luise (wenigstens jetzt) gar nichts reden. Und die Ent-

[119] Der frz. Schriftsteller Romain Rolland (1864–1935) entwickelte 1903 in seinem ästhetisch-politischen Manifest *Das Theater des Volkes* den Plan, die Verbindungen zwischen dem Theater und dem Volk zu intensivieren. Der frz. Dramatiker Jean-Richard Bloch (1884–1947), der 1925 gemeinsam mit Rolland die Zeitschrift *Europe* gründet hatte, setzte diese Bemühungen zur Begründung eines engagierten, politischen Volkstheaters fort. So unternahm er mit seinem Stück *Naissance d'une cité* den Versuch, mit Hilfe neuer gestalterischer Mittel in einen direkten Dialog mit dem Publikum zu treten.

scheidung darüber, ob er sich der Kommandantur stellt, wird er nicht fällen, da ja außer ihm allein und dem Russen niemand weiß, daß er über die Geschichte unterrichtet ist. Spräche er mit Luise darüber, wäre er ja nicht weiter als ein blöder Tenor wie etwa Herr Linkerton[120]. Das bißchen Größe, das wir ihm angedichtet haben, wollen Sie ihm auch noch nehmen! Und Luisens Selbstmordversuch, den wir durch Gespräche mit ihrem Vater, mit Martins Mutter, mit Martin (in den noch fehlenden Szenen) und durch die Haßszene mit Stepan so schön unterbauen und als letzte Lösung für sie hinstellen wollten, wollen Sie nun auch bagatellisieren, indem Sie sie durch Martins Eröffnungen noch ein letztes Stößchen bekommen lassen. Wenn ich überzeugter Militarist wäre, würden Sie mich nicht im geringsten mit dieser Lösung überzeugen. Ich halte also nach wie vor die ursprüngliche Lösung für die weit bessere – ohne in sie verliebt zu sein. Kleinigkeiten werden sich natürlich noch viele ändern und vielleicht bekommt auch diese letzte Szene noch hier und da ein anderes Aussehen. Daß in den Dialogen alles bis ins letzte motiviert und nachgewiesen wird, dafür laßt Hans Sachs nur sorgen.
Daß Luise sich auf die Schienen wirft, geht aus der Skizze noch nicht recht hervor. Wie gesagt fehlen ja die beiden großen Szenen, in denen diese Frucht gereift wird.
Die Bilder sollen gar nicht so sehr episch werden. Außer der ersten Szene und der Haßgeschichte ist in jedem Bild Handlung genug drin, selbst die Szene zwischen Luise und Stepan ist durch die russische Lagergeschichte lebhaft genug geworden. – Wie gesagt halte ich die vorgeschlagene Konfrontierung der drei Hauptpersonen in einer weiteren Szene außer der letzten für dramatisch äußerst mangelhaft.
Ansätze zu humorvollen oder wenigstens heiteren Stücken können Sie in der Mundharmonikaszene, am Kasernenhof und im russischen Lagerbetrieb erkennen.

---

[120] Hindemith spielt auf die Opernfigur des F.B. Linkerton aus Giacomo Puccinis Oper *Madame Butterfly* (1904) an.

Schützengrabenszene ist natürlich schon in Sprechstücken gewesen. In der Oper nie und sie würde durch die Verquickung mit der Musik – erst die Verkleinerung aller Gefahr durch die Mundharmonikaszene, nachher durch die Entmaterialisierung der ganzen Sphäre und die starke Spannung durch den leisen Chor bis zum letzten Augenblick vor dem dynamischen Ausbruch des Angriffs – ein gänzlich anderes Gesicht bekommen. Ein Transport mit Fliegerangriff könnte ja nur eine geringfügige Episode sein. Dieser Angriff ist ja für die Hauptpersonen immerhin sehr wichtig. Martin wird verwundet, sein Freund fällt.
Martins Mutter ist unverheiratet, weil nur dadurch ihr seltsames Wesen und Martins Zurückhaltung richtig erklärt wird (Sie konnten aus den bisherigen Szenen wenig darüber sehen, kommt aber noch). Und ein Vater ist durchaus überflüssig. Schon der andere (Luisens) Vater ist ja ganz Nebenrolle.
Warum der Russe deutsch spricht? Er hat es gelernt. Wir sind doch in der Oper. Fräulein Butterfly spricht doch auch mit Herrn Linkerton fließend englisch, obwohl sie aus sehr niederen Kreisen stammt, die es gar nicht so gut können. Wenn es unmotiviert ist, daß er seine Fiebererzählung in deutsch singt, kann er sie meinetwegen getrost in russisch singen; das wäre natürlich noch unwahrscheinlicher, womit ich nur andeuten wollte, daß diese Frage durchaus unwichtig ist.
Luise ist jugendlich.
Ob Stepan bestraft werden muß, steht im Stück nicht zur Debatte, das wird die nachfolgende Verhandlung erweisen. Er wird ja auch nicht verfolgt, weil es strafbar ist sondern wegen der Schauergeschichten, die über ausgebrochene Gefangene umlaufen und wegen der Schwierigkeiten, die der Bahnhofsvorsteher und die Wachen haben.
Über Stepans Abführung war im Entwurf berichtet. Es soll aber gar keine Pantomime werden. Er ist aus dem Stück ausgeschieden und zählt weder für Luise noch für Martin fernerhin mit. Bestenfalls könnte er Hände ringen und Augen bedeutungsvoll aufschlagen, Luise desgleichen und als Zugabe dem Martin noch in die Arme sinken – aber das ist

doch alles zu lächerlich. Ein Mann wird abgeführt – zwei Leute bleiben allein, das ist der Tatbestand und über die dramatischen Verwicklungen hat man vorher genug gehört.
Hoffentlich habe ich Sie über alles beruhigt. Ich will nun sehen, was Penzoldt mir schickt und mich nach Möglichkeit bald wieder mit ihm treffen. Ich hoffe, daß bis Ende Februar spätestens der Entwurf ganz fertig ist und daß ich dann so langsam anfangen kann, die Musik zu entwerfen. Die Hauptarbeit denke ich dann im Sommer zu machen. Hoffentlich komme ich gut voran, was ich wohl glaube, so daß Sie bis zum Winter die Oper haben können. Daß Sie Penzoldt bevorschussen wollen, ist sehr freundlich von Ihnen. Aber ich glaube, Sie sollten ihm erst etwas geben, nachdem der Entwurf komplett vorliegt; ich bin etwas abergläubisch, besonders nach den Erfahrungen mit Benn[121]. Er hat nie mehr etwas von sich hören lassen und ich melde mich natürlich auch nicht. Mir ist selten solch eine Chuzpe vorgekommen. Ich weiß nicht, was in ihn gefahren ist. Ich kann mir nur denken, daß er in dem Augenblick, wo er das Geld in Händen hatte, bei seiner Überempfindlichkeit durch einen psychologischen Dreh seinen Nöten freien Lauf ließ, sie aber nach außen in Unverschämtheit projizierte. Was kann man tun? Ich kann gar nichts anfangen, aber Sie hätten natürlich immerhin die Möglichkeit, ihm klar zu machen, daß er 1000 Mk eingesteckt hätte ohne sich fürder zu mucksen. Ich möchte nicht, daß Sie diese Sache mehr verschnupft als nötig, deshalb schlage ich Ihnen folgenden Ausgleich vor: Mit Ihrem Bruder besprach ich schon damals beim Erscheinen des »Unaufhörlichen« die Möglichkeit, Benn später ein Zuschlagshonorar für den Text zukommen zu lassen. Vielleicht können Sie 500 Mark auf dieses Konto buchen. Die restlichen 500 ziehen Sie bitte mir bei der nächsten größeren Abrechnung ab. So ist Ihr Verlust nicht groß. Ich selbst werde mir die 500 als Strafsumme für Leichtgläubigkeit einem Dichter gegenüber auferlegen. Mit Penzoldt war ich von vorneherein

[121] Vgl. Anm. 11.

vorsichtiger und ich mache auch alles mit ihm zusammen, so daß er nicht ausspringen kann, und das Resultat dieser Arbeitsweise (die mich freilich teuer zu stehen kommt, da ich ihm ja Reisen und Aufenthaltskosten zahlen muß, bezw. zu ihm reisen muß) sehen Sie ja in diesem gut ausgearbeiteten Entwurf, so weit er Ihnen vorlag.
Also schnell Schluß für heute und herzlichen Gruß Ihres Paul Hindemith

48 Ludwig Strecker an Paul Hindemith

Mainz, 23. Januar 1933

Lieber Paul Hindemith,
die »Opern-Abteilung« dankt Ihnen herzlich für Ihr so ausführliches Eingehen auf die verschiedenen Anregungen; sie ist beschämt, daß sie Ihnen soviel Mühe verursacht hat. Wenn man aus diesem Brief auf Ihre übrige Korrespondenz in Textfragen Rückschlüsse ziehen darf, so muß man allerdings zugeben, daß diese Arbeit beinahe so groß ist, wie die ganze Fertigstellung des Textes.
In den Liebes-Angelegenheiten haben wir uns also richtig gefunden. Kein Mensch wird von Ihnen offizielle »Liebes-Duette« erwarten. Sie müssen nur verstehen, wenn wir eine gewisse Besorgnis haben, Sie könnten aus Ihrer Gefühls-Askese heraus allem aus dem Wege gehen, was nun einmal das Opern-Publikum erwartet, zumal wenn es sich um einen solchen volkstümlichen Stoff handelt. Eine gewisse Bestärkung erhalten unsere Bedenken, wenn Sie am Schluß Ihres Briefes allzu menschliches als »lächerlich« bezeichnen und schreiben: »Ein Mann wird abgeführt – 2 Leute bleiben allein, das ist der Tatbestand.« Wenn Sie auf diese Weise das Publikum in eine kalte Zugluft setzen, so fürchte ich, daß gerade das zum Teufel geht, was das Publikum warm gemacht hat und der Oper Erfolg bringen kann.
Es besteht m.E. doch noch ein Unterschied zwischen Kitsch und natürlichem menschlichem Empfinden. Verstehen Sie uns bitte nicht falsch,

wenn die »Opern-Abteilung« auf gewisse Möglichkeiten einer verstärkten Theater-Wirkung hinweist. Für alles übrige »lassen wir Hans Sachs gern sorgen«.

Die vielen kleineren Punkte haben Sie durch Ihren Brief geklärt, und dem Hinweis auf das Skizzenhafte des Entwurfes. In der Hauptsache, hinsichtlich des soldatischen und menschlichen Konfliktes bei Martin werden wir wenigstens vorläufig zweierlei Meinung bleiben. In die von uns angedeutete Lösung sind wir ebenso wenig verliebt, wie Sie in die Ihrige. Sie sollte und konnte hier nicht mehr sein als eine Art Illustration für unsere Meinung. Im übrigen und darin werden Sie mir wohl Recht geben, kann es kein Schaden sein wenn Sie, zumal aus Ihrem eigenen Lager, Einwände hören, die Ihnen Gelegenheit geben den eigenen Standpunkt nochmals zu prüfen. Wenn wir der Überzeugung wären, daß in den Theatern bis in den obersten Rang nur Hindemith's säßen und seine Freunde, wäre ja alles sehr einfach. Wir wollen ja aber gerade mindestens einen Teil der Allgemeinheit erobern und dazu gehört ein gewisses Entgegenkommen, welches beileibe nicht das Schimpfwort Kompromiß verdient.

Nun zu Freund Benn[122]. Bitte denken Sie nicht, daß uns diese Sache »verschnupft« hat, wie Sie meinen. Wir haben hier im beiderseitigen Interesse gehandelt und das Beste versucht; für mich selbst muß ich allerdings zugeben, mit einem Minimum von Hoffnung. Unsere damalige Besprechung im »Fürstenhof« hatte mir nahezu alle Illusionen genommen, aus Benn etwas brauchbar dramatisches herauszuholen. Dieser Mann liebt weder die Menschen noch die Bühne. So lange man mit sich selbst und mit Weltanschauungen ringt und Philosophie treiben will, fehlt einem jene Leichtigkeit und Überzeugungskraft, mit der man vom Theater herunter wirken kann.

Die Frage des Vorschusses wollen wir einmal vorläufig zurückstellen

---

[122] Vgl. Anm. 11.

und sie gelegentlich in einer Weise lösen, die keinem Teil weh tut. Jedenfalls rechne ich es Ihnen hoch an, daß Sie so großzügig darüber denken.
Mit herzlichen Grüßen
Ihr <Ludwig Strecker>

49 Paul Hindemith an Willy Strecker

Berlin, 26. Januar 1933

Lieber Herr Strecker,
Sie sind durchaus im Nachteil. Ihr Bruder bekam einen langen Brief, Sie nur diese paar Zeilen. Da ich fast eine Woche nicht aus dem Haus gehen konnte eines argen Hustens wegen und auch, weil ich nichts Genaues aus Plön gehört hatte, konnte ich bis jetzt nichts für die englische Sache[123] unternehmen. Am Freitag bin ich aber auf dem Auswärtigen Amt. Gelingt es mir, dort alles zu erreichen, was nötig ist, ist's gut. Ich rechne mit einem Teilerfolg und denke dann noch die anglo-germans und vielleicht die Kunstgesellschaft zu stupsen. Die Schiffsleute in Hamburg sind etwas harthörig. Am billigsten würde die Linie über Grimsby[124] fahren, sie nimmt pro Mann nur 35 Mk hin und zurück ohne Verpflegung. Das sind halt immer noch 3500 Mk. Hapag verlangt 50. Ich glaube kaum, daß man durch Holland billiger hinkommt. Ich erkundige mich jedenfalls hier auch noch. Honegger[125] war vorgestern hier; als er hörte, daß in London diese Sache geplant sei, geriet er in Eifer und wollte Paris gleich dranhängen. Ich bin neugierig, ob er's fertig bringt. Haben Sie zufällig am Montag Nachmittag die Musiktag-Kanta-

---

[123] Vgl. Anm. 82.
[124] Hafenstadt im Nordosten Englands mit Fährverbindungen nach Rotterdam und Zeebrugge.
[125] Der Schweizer Komponist Arthur Honegger (1892–1955), mit dem Hindemith seit Anfang der zwanziger Jahre befreundet war.

te im Radio gehört? Sie wurde von Plön aus übertragen und war sehr nett.

Für heute nur dies. Und schönste Grüße

Ihr

Paul Hindemith

Doch noch einiges:

– Die Chöre mache ich bald[126]. Ich habe erst mal zur Übung (weil ich so lange nichts geschrieben habe) angefangen, leichte Sopranlieder mit Klavier nach Prosatexten von Matthias Claudius[127] zu schreiben, die hauptsächlich der Nichtberufssänger daheim singen kann. Chortexte nehme ich vielleicht auch aus dem Claudius.

– Schnell noch für die Opernabteilung: Das Publikum soll natürlich alles haben, was ihm wohltut, ich will ihm nichts vorenthalten. Nur finde ich, daß mit einem richtig hingesetzten Akkord mehr getan ist und mehr und bessere Wirkung erzielt wird als mit wirklich schlechten Theatertricks wie diese Abschiedspantomime. Ich fürchte, daß diese Pantomime »kalte Zugluft« durchließe infolge ihrer Fadenscheinigkeit. Und im übrigen sind wir ja anscheinend ganz einig. Für Einwände bin ich natürlich immer dankbar, obwohl fast keine kommen können, die ich mir nicht selbst gemacht habe. Auf den Rängen sollen natürlich gar keine Hindemiths sitzen, wir wollen doch keine Inflation in diesem Artikel heraufbeschwören; aber ich bin der Ansicht, daß der Komponist halt doch besser zu wissen hat, was den Leuten vorzusetzen ist. Schließlich schmeckt eine Sache im ersten Augenblick mal nicht so ganz gut, ist

126 Der Schott-Verlag plante Anfang 1933, ein »Sing-Buch« mit einfachen dreistimmigen Chören zu publizieren, zu dem neben Hindemith auch Erwin Lendvai (vgl. Anm. 153), Armin Knab (1881–1851) und Joseph Haas (1879–1960) beitragen sollten. Ludwig Strecker glaubte Hindemith »in erster Linie lustige Soldatenlieder empfehlen zu sollen, in denen Sie ja gerade drin stecken« (Brief vom 18.1.1933). Obwohl Hindemith zusagte, komponierte er schließlich doch keine Chöre für den geplanten Band.

127 *Vier Lieder nach Matthias Claudius* (1933). Erhalten ist nur noch Nr. 2 (*Der Tod ist'n eigener Mann*), die drei anderen sind verschollen.

aber nahrhaft. Und ich bin nicht für's Nurgutschmecken. Da wir in diesem Punkt anscheinend entgegengesetzte Ansichten vertreten, werden wir uns wohl wie andere brave Männer auf halbem Wege entgegenkommen.
– Penzoldt schrieb heute, daß er an den fehlenden Szenen arbeitet.
– Noch nie in meinem Leben habe ich so viel Briefe geschrieben wie um diese Oper; Gott, muß die gut werden.
Und jetzt endgültig Schluß für heute.

50 Ernst Penzoldt an Paul Hindemith

<München>, 26. Januar 1933

Lieber Herr Hindemith! Anbei sende ich Ihnen Inhaltsangaben der noch fehlenden Szenen[128]. Es fehlt nur noch eine (Nr. 6) das sogenannte Fest. Mir ist dazu noch nichts eingefallen, was ich einigermaßen natürlich in die Handlung einfügen könnte. Bitte schreiben Sie mir, ob die übrigen Szenen im Wesentlichen sich mit Ihren Vorstellungen decken. Wenn das der Fall ist können Sie ja den ganzen Entwurf Herrn Streckern vorlegen oder vorher noch wenn es sich um wesentliche Dinge handelt den veränderten Text mir zur Einsicht schicken.
Ich hoffe, daß es Ihnen wieder gut geht. Ich habe dauernd mit meinem Magen zu tun, was meiner Arbeit nicht gerade nützlich ist. Ich habe heuer gar keine Freude am Winter und erwarte mit Ungeduld den Frühling.
Noch eines: Ich bin ganz einverstanden, wenn Frau Engel nicht die Gesangslehrerin von Susanne ist. Ich würde es für die natürlichste Motivierung halten, wenn sie mit Susannes Mutter in die Schule gegangen ist. Daß Susanne keine Mutter hat, läßt sich dann unsentimental konstatieren.
Mit den besten Grüßen von Haus zu Haus, von Stadt zu Stadt
Ihr stets ergebener <Ernst Penzoldt>

---

[128] Nicht überliefert.

51 Paul Hindemith an Ernst Penzoldt

Berlin, 6. Februar 1933 [Poststempel]

Lieber Herr Penzoldt,
sind Sie in der nächsten Woche in München? Wenn ja, würde ich gerne am 13. und 14. Sie aufsuchen[129], was sehr gut passen würde, weil ich am 15. im Radio spiele[130]. Schönsten Dank für die Restszenen[131]. Ich habe mich in der letzten Woche nicht recht darum kümmern können, weil zu viel Arbeit war und weiß deshalb noch nicht so recht damit Bescheid. Jedenfalls könnten wir ja dann ausführlich über alles einschließlich des Dialogs sprechen. Ich hoffe auch vorher noch Karl Ebert[132] zu sehen, ich will mal sehen, was er von der Sache hält. Würden Sie so lieb sein, mir kurz zu schreiben, ob Sie da sein werden? Inzwischen schönste Grüße an Sie alle von unsrer 2– und 4beinigen Familie.
Ihr Paul Hindemith
Seien Sie nicht böse, daß ich mir die Szenen bis jetzt nur oberflächlich angesehen habe. In den nächsten Tagen gehe ich dann gründlich dran und weiß bis nächste Woche Bescheid.

---

[129] Das Treffen kam zustande; Hindemith schrieb darüber am 14. Feburar 1933 seiner Ehefrau: *Gestern früh traf ich zugleich mit Ludwig Strecker den Penzoldt, dessen Schwiegermutter an plötzlicher Grippe innerhalb dreier Tage hier gestorben war und gestern mittag begraben wurde. So habe ich gestern nichts mit ihm gearbeitet, sondern nur mit dem Ludwig zusammen gegessen, bin ein bißchen spazieren gelaufen und habe dann abends ziemlich viele Nötchen geschrieben. Heute habe ich mit Penzoldt vor- und nachmittags feste gearbeitet. Wir haben zwei Szenen gemacht. Nach Frankfurt kann ich nun leider nicht fahren, ich möchte doch lieber übermorgen die fehlenden Szenen mit ihm machen, da er gerade gut im Schuß ist.* (Paul Hindemith, *»Das private Logbuch«. Briefe an seine Frau Gertrud*, Mainz, München 1995, S. 92 f.) Und am 17.2.1933 berichtete Hindemith seiner Frau aus München: *Mit Penzoldt bin ich gut vorangekommen, aber ganz fertig sind wir doch noch nicht geworden, es fehlen noch zwei allerdings nicht sehr wesentliche Szenen.* (ebd., S. 93)

[130] Hindemith spielte seine *Konzertmusik für Solobratsche und größeres Kammerorchester* op. 48 (1930), mit dem Radio-Orchester München unter der Leitung von Karl List.

[131] Vgl. Anm. 128.

[132] Vgl. Anm. 3.

52 »Münchener Entwürfe«: Fünf Szenenentwürfe und -ergänzungen[133]

Zur 1. Szene. [Hs. Penzoldt:] Oper Hindemith
Martin, Mutter.
Martin macht der Mutter Vorwürfe, daß sie gekommen ist. Es sei Herbst und das Wetter für sie gefährlich. Er meint, sie solle doch ihre Stimme schonen. Sie meint, ihre Stimme sei besser als je, nächstens wird sie {wieder öffentlich} singen. Er: es wäre ihm lieber, wenn sie nicht sänge. Sie rege sich dabei auf und sei die {den} Strapazen nicht mehr gewöhnt {gewachsen}. Sie: sie sei auf der Höhe wie immer, wie vor 20 Jahren. Das sei damals eine Zeit gewesen! Sie ist laut, Martin beschwichtigt sie, ihr Wesen ist ihm in der Öffentlichkeit etwas peinlich. Er will sie wegschicken.
Luise {Susanne} & Mutter treffen sich noch. Wenn Mutter weg ist, bittet er Luise {Susanne}, sich der Mutter anzunehmen: Sie sei krank. Sie sei freilich etwas seltsam, aber eine gute Frau und ihm die beste Mutter. Er spricht kurz über ihren damaligen Skandal, der sie zum Verlassen der Bühne zwang.

5. Szene
Hinter den Kulissen einer Varietébühne. Im Hintergrunde sieht man die Bühne und das Publikum, aus Soldaten bestehend. Ein Zauberkünstler {gibt} auf der Bühne, {Vorstellung} mit Klavierbegleitung.

---

[133] Diese Entwürfe sind zum einen als Manuskript von Hindemith überliefert, zum anderen als maschinenschriftliche Abschrift von Penzoldt mit dessen handschriftlichen Korrekturen. Bei der Textwiedergabe wurden alle Varianten berücksichtigt; die Abweichungen des Typoskripts sind in geschweiften Klammern gesetzt. Vermutlich hat Hindemith beim gemeinsamen Arbeitstreffen in München mitgeschrieben und die Entwürfe bei Penzoldt gelassen, von dem sie dann abgetippt und nach Berlin geschickt wurden. Nur so läßt sich erklären, warum Hindemiths Fassung der Szenen im Nachlaß von Penzoldt überliefert ist, die unzweifelhaft auf Penzoldts Maschine geschriebene Typoskript-Fassung dagegen im Hindemith-Nachlaß. Unklar bleibt indes, aus welchen Gründen Hindemith beim Mitschreiben noch auf den Namen Luise zurückgriff, obwohl man sich längst auf die Änderung in Susanne geeinigt hatte. Es konnte ebenfalls nicht geklärt werden, warum Penzoldt in seinem Typoskript plötzlich den Namen Ursula verwendete (so heißt eine der zentralen Figuren in Hindemiths 1933–1935 entstandener Oper *Mathis der Maler*).

Theaterdirektor mit Vorstand des Festausschusses: Direktor beklagt sich, daß er in das sonst so schöne Programm diese alte unmögliche Sängerin aufnehmen mußte. Vorstand: es ließ sich nicht anders machen. Man muß sie einmal singen lassen, damit man Ruhe vor ihr hat. Direktor: es wird ein Reinfall, wie er nie da gewesen ist. Er überzeugt den Vorstand mit Mühe, daß man ihr beibringen müßte, zu verzichten. Aber wer wird's ihr beibringen! Vorstand geht abwehrend ab, Direktor folgt ihm beschwörend. Frau Engel rauscht herein in einem uralten schrecklichen Kostüm mit den Allüren einer ganz großen Primadonna. »Wo ist meine Garderobe?« Niemand hat Zeit für sie, irgendein Beschäftigter {Bühnenarbeiter} sagt, sie solle hier ablegen. Sie ist empört, erzählt den beiden Vorhangziehern (Landsturmsoldaten) wie großartig es früher war. Blumen werden vorübergetragen, sie glaubt, sie seien für sie, auf dem Kuvert steht aber »für die Trapezkünstlerin«. Jetzt fängt sie an, ihre Stimme zu probieren, erst leise, dann immer lauter. Der Inspizient winkt ab. »Herrschaften, ich muß probieren« und singt weiter Koloraturen.

Der Zauberkünstler wird nervös, das Publikum unruhig. Ein Clown kommt gestürzt: sie solle doch still sein, das Publikum sei schon ganz aufgeregt. Sie: natürlich ist es aufgeregt, sie kommt ja auch gleich dran. Vorstand & Direktor kommen voller Verzweiflung, sie solle doch still sein. Sie ist einen Augenblick still, Direktor bietet ihr eine Abstandssumme an. Sie weist das entrüstet von sich: sie sei eine Künstlerin. Applaus, Schluß der Zaubernummer. Sie, ganz aufgeregt, macht sich zum Auftritt fertig, die beiden halten sie fest, sie reißt sich aber los und stürzt hinaus in den Applaus des Zauberkünstlers. Dieser ist böse, großes Gelächter beim Publikum. Sie will nochmals abgehen, Direktor schickt sie aber voller Verzweiflung hinaus. »Na, jetzt bleiben Sie schon draußen«. Starker ironischer Beifall und Gelächter. Theaterpersonal gruppiert sich um den verzweifelten Direktor. Sie bereitet sich ganz groß vor, fängt mit Klavierbegleitung an, große Arie zu singen auf ganz altmodische Bühnenart. Gelächter erhebt sich wieder im Publikum, das

Personal lacht. Vorstand und Direktor sind entsetzt. Direktor: »Vorhang, Vorhang!« Vorhang fällt. Sie wird stutzig, hört auf zu singen, begreift die Situation, geht von der Bühne herunter, die Noten entfallen ihr, sie geht vollkommen versteinert ab durch das Personal. Betretene Stille, eine Garderobenfrau trägt ihr ihren Mantel und ihre Tasche nach. Wie sie draußen ist, lacht alles auf, der Direktor rauft sich die Haare »so etwas ist in meinem Theater noch nicht vorgekommen. Das hat man von seiner Gutmütigkeit.« Eine Trapeznummer tritt auf, Vorhang auf.

Zur VI. Szene.
Martins Mutter kommt. Sie fällt erschöpft und gebrochen auf einen Stuhl. Die Garderobenfrau bringt ihr die Sachen nach. Luise hilft der Mutter. Diese klagt und jammert. Man habe ihr einen Streich gespielt, alles sei aus. Sie sei entsetzlich blamiert. Sie habe keinen Menschen, an den sie sich wenden könnte. Sie will bei Luise ihr Herz ausschütten. Luise tröstet sie; aber einmal käme doch der Moment, wo man aufhören muß, das müsse sie doch auch erkennen. Sie müsse nach Hause, sie habe Fieber, sie müsse ins Bett. Die Mutter wird betroffen und still. Natürlich, sie versteht alles, sie ist abgehalftert; zu nichts mehr zu gebrauchen. Sie sei ja auch hier fehl am Ort. Hier sei man lustig, man sänge. Langsam begreift sie, daß sie das Lied kennt und daß eine Männerstimme gesungen hat. Luise ist zu Tod erschrocken; steht unbeweglich, während die Mutter gebrochen abgeht. Luise schließt die Tür, stellt sich mit dem Rücken dagegen. Stepan kommt etwas zögernd aus der Nische, geht auf Luise zu, küßt sie auf den Mund, kniet vor ihr nieder und neigt den Kopf.

VIII. Szene Luise & Martin.
Klarer Winterabend. Stand eines Zeitungsverkäufers bei einer Laterne. Es ist ein Extrablatt herausgekommen: die große Offensive hat heute begonnen. Von allen Seiten kommen Leute, die das Extrablatt kaufen. Es bilden sich Gruppen, die das Ereignis besprechen. Susanne kommt auch zu dem Stand. Ein Trupp leicht verwundeter Soldaten kommt in

Feldanzügen, schmutzig, mit Verbänden, Sandsäcken, Brotbeuteln, Feldmützen. Es ist ein Lazarettzug angekommen, die Leichtverwundeten gehen zu Fuß ins Lazarett. Die Leute umringen die Soldaten, fragen sie aus, schließlich begleiten sie den Trupp. Unter den Soldaten befindet sich Martin, der den Arm in einer Binde trägt. Als er Luise erblickt und sie ihn, bleiben beide wortlos einander gegenüber stehen. Als die Leute weggegangen sind, fragt der Zeitungsverkäufer, ein alter Kriegsteilnehmer von 1870, wo Martin herkäme. Martin hört nicht hin, spricht nur schüchtern zu Luise. Der Alte erzählt in einer etwas bombastischen Weise vom Krieg 70 und vergleicht ihn mit dem jetzigen Krieg. Damals hätte doch noch persönliche Tapferkeit gegolten, heutzutage beim Grabenkrieg könnte ja nichts erreicht werden. Jeder, der einen Schuß abgegeben hat, bekommt schon das EK. Sirenen pfeifen, von weitem hört man Fliegerabwehrgeschütze und Motorsurren. Der Alte macht ängstlich sein Licht aus und flieht, fordert die beiden auf, Deckung zu nehmen. Die hören nicht auf ihn, sind ganz mit sich beschäftigt. Er berichtet wie er verwundet wurde, daß Felix gefallen ist; fragt nach seiner Mutter; erfährt, daß sie krank ist und zu Bett liegt. Die Laterne geht aus, der Fliegerangriff kommt immer näher, Scheinwerfer, großer Lärm. Leute fliehen vorüber, viel Bewegung. Dann hört alle Bewegung auf, die beiden sind ganz allein. Große stürmische Liebeserklärung Martins, die ihren Höhepunkt mit dem des Angriffes erreicht. Bombeneinschläge und viel Flak. Susanne ist fasziniert, aber plötzlich erinnert sie sich ihrer Schuld; sie vertröstet ihn, hat allerlei Ausreden. Der Angriff flaut ab. Susanne reißt sich von Martin los und läuft weg. Martin: kurze Arie über sein Verhältnis zu Susanne. Der Alte kriecht wieder hervor: es seien schwere Einschläge gewesen. Ziemlich viel zerstört, Tote und Verwundete. Martin reagiert nicht. Der Alte macht ihm Vorwürfe, daß ihm seine Erzählung gar keinen Eindruck macht. Martin nimmt seine Sachen und geht, der Alte sieht ihm kopfschüttelnd nach und richtet seine Bude wieder her.

IX. Szene

Wohnzimmer bei Martins Mutter. {Die Wände sind mit grossen Lorbeerkränzen und Photographien bedeckt. Martins Mutter} Diese liegt im Bett, sehr krank. Luise {Susanne} und ihr Vater kommen. Eine alte Zugehefrau sagt Luise {Susanne}, daß es Frau Engel sehr schlecht gehe. Sie habe hohes Fieber und phantasiere. ~~Der Sohn werde erwartet. Er sei leicht verwundet worden und soll hier in ein Lazarett kommen.~~ Unterdessen {Inzwischen} spricht der Vater mit {Frau Engel} der Mutter. Sie hat ihn rufen lassen um ihn zu bitten, Luise {Susanne} dem Martin zu geben, falls Luise {Susanne keinem andern gehöre} nicht anders versprochen sei. (Luise {Susanne hört dies und erschrickt} hört dies, ist ängstlich). Vater weiß, daß nichts ist {vorliegt, Susanne sagt ihm alles}. Mutter {Frau Engel} sagt {meint}, es sei bald zu Ende mit ihr, es sei ihr eine Beruhigung, zu wissen, daß Martin und Luise {Susanne} ein {glückliches} Paar werden. Luise {Susanne} geht auch zum Bett. Die Mutter fragt den Vater etwas betont, was eigentlich mit dem damals entsprungenen Kriegsgefangenen geschehen sei, der ihm so viel Sorgen gemacht habe. Vater weiß von nichts. Luise {Susanne} unvermittelt: erzählt die Geschichte von einem Entsprungenen, den ein Mädchen aus Mitleid aufgenommen habe. Für die Mutter wird begreiflich, daß Luise {Susanne} mit dieser Erzählung ihr ihre Schuld eingesteht. Der Vater meint, das Mädchen habe den Tod verdient. Luise {Susanne} ist vollkommen entsetzt; plötzlich erkennt sie die Größe ihrer Schuld. »Es sei aber doch aus Mitleid geschehen.« Vater: »Du hast ein gutes Herz, du ~~weißt von nichts~~ kannst dich {in so etwas} nicht hineindenken. Aber sie hat doch den Tod verdient.« Die Mutter nimmt Luisens {Susannes} Hand. »Nein, nicht den Tod.« Luise {Susanne} küßt dankbar ihre Hand. Vater & Luise ab. – Die Mutter setzt im Halbtraum die Szene weiter fort. »Nicht den Tod. Das Mädchen ist zufällig in diese Geschichte hineingekommen {hineingeraten} und ist zu beklagen, daß sie alles allein tragen muß. Wie könnte man die Schwierigkeit gut lösen?«

Martin kommt, setzt sich zu ihr ans Bett. Sie fährt in ihrem Selbstgespräch fort: »Luise {Ursula} war hier. Hast Du mit ihr gesprochen?«

Martin sagt, er liebe Luise {Ursula} mehr als je; er glaubt, daß sie ihn auch liebe. Mutter fragt, ob er dessen sicher sei. Ja, aber es sei ein großes Hindernis {vorhanden}, das er nicht kenne. Mutter sagt, sie kenne es. Er müsse die Kraft haben, Luise {Ursula} viel zu verzeihen. Er: was {immer} Luise {Ursula} auch getan habe, er würde es verstehen. Er liebt auch das, was sie tut, das gehört mit zu seiner Liebe, sonst wäre es doch keine Liebe. Mutter legt sich zurück: sie ist sicher, daß {nun} alles gut wird. »Siehst du, nun habe ich doch noch eine Rolle gut gespielt: die einer guten Mutter.« Er fragt sie besorgt, wie sie sich befinde. Sie wird immer schwächer und sagt, daß es ihr nie so gut gegangen sei. Sie fängt an zu singen: Troubadour, letzte Szene.
Er merkt, daß es mit ihr zu Ende geht, hilft ihr aber, indem er leise mitsingt. Sie fragt zwischendurch immer, ob er nicht spüre, wie gut in Form sie sei. »Wie wirkt es auf das Publikum?« Er lobt sie. Er singt weiter, {während sie stirbt} sie hört auf, sie ist gestorben. Er bricht ab, legt seinen Kopf auf ihre Hände.
Vorhang.

53 Willy und Ludwig Strecker an Paul Hindemith

Mainz, 4. März 1933

Lieber Herr Hindemith,
ich komme gerade von Antwerpen zurück, wo ich eine sehr hübsche Aufführung von »Nusch Nuschi«[134] miterlebte, die einen wirklich großen Erfolg hatte. Man hat dem »Nusch Nuschi« einige Giftzähne etwas abgefeilt, sodaß keine Gemüter mehr zu sehr chokiert wurden. Dagegen war es eine sehr hübsche Inszenierung und neuartige Darstellung, die allgemein guten Anklang und Interesse fand. Frau Korty, die die ganze Sache inszenierte und leitete, hat eine sehr glückliche Verbindung von

[134] Im März 1933 inszenierte und tanzte die russische Choreographin und Tänzerin Sonja Korty (1892–1955) in Antwerpen Hindemiths 1921 entstandene Tanzsuite *Nusch Nuschi* (nach seiner gleichnamigen Oper aus dem Jahr 1920).

Tanz und Oper zustande gebracht, indem sie die Sänger sich ebenfalls rhythmisch bewegen läßt und leicht marionettenartige persische Miniaturbilder kreierte.
Die Aufführung fand sehr großen Anklang und allgemeine Beachtung in der ganzen Gegend, sodaß ich hoffe, daß sich andere Bühnen für das sehr mit Unrecht vergessene »Nusch Nuschi« interessieren werden. In der dargebrachten Form eignet sich das »Nusch Nuschi« wirklich ausgezeichnet für Aufführungen und ich hoffe, wir werden auch in Deutschland irgendwo Interesse dafür erwecken können.
Da Sie Mitte des Monats nach Antwerpen kommen, sollten Sie doch versuchen, noch eine Aufführung dort zu erleben. Die Vlämische Oper ist allerdings, wie alle Kunstinstitute pleite und will am 15. März schließen und nur noch Operetten geben, sodaß man vorläufig in dieser Spielzeit nicht mehr wie drei Aufführungen festgesetzt hat. Ich hatte keine Zeit mehr nach der Aufführung ausführlich mit dem Direktor Bosmans[135] zu sprechen, dachte aber, daß es vielleicht diplomatisch sei, wenn Sie ihm für die erfolgreiche Aufführung danken (*Adresse: Oper Royal Flamand*), von der Sie durch mich gehört hätten, ebenso wie auch Frau Korty danken ließen, die sich eine geradezu unerhörte Mühe damit gegeben hat und zugleich nach der Möglichkeit fragten, ob eine Aufführung während Ihrer Anwesenheit möglich sei. Ich bin überzeugt, es wird Sie ebenso amüsieren, wie interessieren. Eine Kritik finden Sie einliegend.
Auch in Brüssel sprach ich mit den Leuten, die das »Lehrstück«[136] mit großer Begeisterung präparierten; Furtwängler[137] führt Ihr Philharmo-

[135] Arthur Bosmans, 1908 in Brüssel geborener Dirigent.
[136] Vgl. Anm. 102.
[137] Wilhelm Furtwängler (1886–1954) war mit Hindemith seit Anfang der zwanziger Jahre bekannt und führte als Dirigent der Berliner Philharmoniker zahlreiche seiner Werke auf. Mit seinem Zeitungsartikel *Der Fall Hindemith* griff Furtwängler im November 1934 in die monatelangen öffentlichen Diskussionen um Hindemiths *Symphonie »Mathis der Maler«* ein, die er im März 1934 selbst uraufgeführt hatte. Auf das Scheitern seines Versuchs, Hindemiths Werke vom Vorwurf des »Musikbolschewismus« zu befreien, reagierte Furtwängler mit der vorübergehenden Niederlegung seines Amtes als Dirigent der Berliner Philharmoniker.

nisches Konzert in Antwerpen auf[138], Sie selbst kommen mit Ihrem Kammermusikabend[139] – kurzum, die Hindemith-Welle in der Gegend muß gepflegt werden.
Ich selbst fahre am 13. nach London und freue mich Sie dort zu sehen.
Einstweilen herzliche Grüße <Willy Strecker>
Nachschrift des älteren Bruders:
Was ist aus München herausgekommen? Ich habe gehofft, bei meiner Rückkehr schon etwas vorzufinden. Hoffentlich sind keine neuen Schwierigkeiten aufgetaucht?
Schließlich noch die bescheidene Erinnerung an die Soldaten-Chöre[140].
Entschuldigen Sie die Eile dieses Nachsatzes.
Herzlichste Grüße
Ihr <Ludwig Strecker>

54 Paul Hindemith an Ludwig und Willy Strecker

Berlin, <circa 10. März 1933>

Verehrte Brüder,
Sie haben einige Zeit nicht von mir gehört. Hier war so ein Durcheinander, daß an Schreiben gar nicht zu denken war. Wegen der Oper schicke ich Ihnen hierbei einen Brief Penzoldts[141]. Natürlich sind für die nächsten Wochen die Aussichten schlecht, und wie weit es im Herbst möglich sein wird, neue Opern herauszubringen, weiß ich auch nicht. Nach allem, was ich hier im Musik- und Theaterbetrieb sehe, glaube ich, daß

---

[138] Anfang 1933 spielten die Berliner Philharmoniker unter der Leitung von Wilhelm Furtwängler Hindemiths *Philharmonisches Konzert* (vgl. Anm. 8) in Antwerpen und London.

[139] Am 17.3.1933 fand in Antwerpen ein Konzert des Trios Goldberg-Hindemith-Feuermann statt. Auf dem Programm standen die Uraufführung des *2. Streichtrios* (1933) von Hindemith, Ravels *Duo für Geige und Violoncello*, Mozarts *Duett für Violine und Bratsche* B-dur KV 424 und Beethovens *Trio* c-moll op. 9 Nr. 3.

[140] Vgl. Anm. 126.

[141] Nicht überliefert.

alle Theaterposten in Kürze mit stramm nationalen Jungens besetzt sein werden. Im nächsten Frühjahr, nach Überwindung der ersten Schwierigkeiten, dürften dann die Aussichten für eine Oper von Penzoldt und mir sehr gut sein. Vielleicht nicht gerade für diesen Text, obwohl man das auch nicht wissen kann. Jedenfalls ist aber Vorsicht geboten und ich bin dafür, die Arbeit an diesem Stoff einstweilen zurückzustellen und etwas anderes zu suchen. Ich habe mich schon umgetan und bin auf ein Stoffgebiet gekommen, das harmlos, interessant und im nächsten und übernächsten Jahre besonders aktuell ist: die Ereignisse bei der Inbetriebnahme der ersten Eisenbahnen. In England und in Deutschland gibt es da sehr nette Ereignisse, aus denen sich gut eine heitere Oper machen ließe. Ich will Penzoldt darauf aufmerksam machen – diese Sache liegt ihm sicher sehr gut – und auch selbst mich noch umsehen. Hoffen wir. – Die versprochenen Chöre[142] mache ich jetzt in England, in etwa 14 Tagen werden sie wohl vorliegen, – 50 % von Ihnen sehe ich ja in London, dann können wir alles besprechen. – In Antwerpen spielen wir nächsten Freitag ein neues Streichtrio[143] von mir. Hätten Sie Interesse dafür? Soll ich es schicken? Ferner könnten Sie haben ein kleines Quintettchen für Klavier, Klarinette, Trompete, Geige & Kontrabaß[144]; ich habe es vor einigen Jahren gemacht, hörte es neulich einmal und war erstaunt über das nette Stück. Ich mache noch ein Sätzchen dazu und führe das Stück am 27. in Kiel auf. Und schließlich habe ich eine ganze Reihe Lieder in Angriff genommen. 4 von Matthias Claudius[145], 4 von Rückert[146] sind schon da – es soll in Viererreihen durch die deutsche Lyrik gehen.

---

[142] Vgl. Anm. 126.

[143] Vgl. Anm. 139.

[144] Die *3 Anekdoten für Radio* (1925). Den Plan, für das Werk noch einen neuen Satz zu komponieren, realisierte Hindemith nicht; die Aufführung am 27.3.1933 in Kiel fand unter seiner Leitung statt.

[145] Vgl. Anm. 127.

[146] *Vier Lieder nach Texten von Rückert* (1933). Erhalten ist nur noch Nr. 3 (*Das Ganze, nicht das Einzelne*), die drei anderen sind verschollen.

So, das wär's wohl für heute. Auf teilweises Wiedersehen in London; ich wohne höchstwahrscheinlich im Strand Palace, weil es am praktischsten liegt.
Schönste Grüße derweil Ihr Paul Hindemith

55 Paul Hindemith an Ernst Penzoldt

<Berlin, zwischen 10. und 12. März 1933>

Lieber Herr Penzoldt,
ich habe mich gefreut, von Ihnen zu hören – umso mehr, als mir Ihr Brief[147] dasselbe sagt, was ich Ihnen schreiben wollte. Die allgemeine Dummheit, multipliziert durch die Angst der Wachsweichen übersteigt bei weitem das gottgewollte Maß. Gegen solchen Marasmus anzugehen wäre selbst Herkulessen ein lächerliches Unternehmen – uns als ausgesprochenen Nichthelden steht es gar nicht zu. Ich finde, Sie sollten die Vertagung der »Portugalesischen Schlacht« nicht tragisch nehmen[148]. Im Augenblick geht man selbstredend gegen alles an, was nicht approbierter dramatischer Parteidreck ist – aber das wird sich bald ändern und da Sie ja als einwandfreier, licht- und farbenechter Deutscher nichts zu fürchten haben, werden Sie im nächsten Winter cum gloria über die Bühnen geschleift werden. Für die Oper sehe ich um einen Schatten schwärzer. Nach allem, was ich hier höre und sehe, ist meine »Konjunktur« sehr gut und ich glaube, daß eine Oper nächstes Jahr gut gehen würde, wenn erst mal nach dem großen Intendanten- und sonstigen Schub die neuen nationalen Innocenze ihre Direktionssitze drücken gelernt haben werden. Auch wegen des Stoffes habe ich nach wie vor keine Bedenken. Weil man aber als unsicheren Faktor in unserer Rechnung die Doofheit und Verhetztheit der Menge einstellen muß und man nicht wissen kann, ob der Grat dieser Krankheiten nächstes Jahr schon erreicht sein wird, müssen wir mit die-

[147] Nicht überliefert.
[148] Vgl. Anm. 117.

sem Text abwarten. Hätten Sie denn Lust, etwas anderes mit mir zu machen? Oder hat Sie diese Sache umgeworfen? Ich wäre natürlich gerne bereit, wieder anzufangen. Wenn Sie Lust haben, möchte ich Sie auf ein Stoffgebiet aufmerksam machen, das sehr hübsch, harmlos und nächstens außerordentlich aktuell ist, und das Ihnen sicher gut liegt: Eine heitere Oper über die Eröffnung der ersten Eisenbahnen. Entweder Nürnberg-Fürth oder noch besser England (Stockton-Darlington-Trevithick-Stephenson-Rainshill-Rockett-Puffing Billy etc etc), weil dort mehr passiert ist. Wäre das nicht fein? Ich besorge mir noch genauere Literatur über diesen Fall. Wollen Sie sich nicht auch ein bißchen umtun? – Ich fahre Donnerstag nach Antwerpen und London und bin am 29. wieder hier[149]. Lassen Sie sich inzwischen durch all den Blödsinn ringsum nicht die Laune verderben. Grüßen Sie die ganze Familie von mir & meiner Frau. Und für Sie besondere Grüße Ihres Paul Hindemith

56 Ernst Penzoldt an Paul Hindemith

<München>, 13. März 1933

Lieber Herr Hindemith!
Ich freue mich aufrichtig, daß wir uns so gut verstehen. Die Idee mit der Eisenbahn (ob in England oder Nürnberg-Fürth) finde ich ausgezeichnet. Es hat sich damals ja allerlei sehr Komisches zugetragen. Ich werde auch versuchen etwas darüber aufzutreiben. Nun hat auch Ebert gehen müssen[150]. Wie sehr mich das erbittert können Sie sich denken.
Für Ihre Reise wünsche ich Ihnen alles Gute. Mit den herzlichsten Grüßen, auch an Ihre Frau
Ihr <Ernst Penzoldt>

---

[149] Am 17.3.1933 gab das Trio Goldberg-Hindemith-Feuermann in Antwerpen einen Kammermusikabend (vgl. Anm. 135); am 19.3.1933 spielte Hindemith bei der BBC in London seine *Konzertmusik für Solobratsche und größeres Kammerorchester* op. 48 (1930) unter der Leitung von Sir Henry Wood.

[150] Am 13.3.1933 stürmten SA-Trupps die Städtische Oper Berlin, ihr Intendant Carl Ebert (vgl. Anm. 3) wurde tags darauf offiziell abgesetzt.

57 Ludwig Strecker an Paul Hindemith

Mainz, 13. März 1933

Lieber Paul Hindemith,
was sind das alles für Sachen. Aber Sie haben recht und es hat keinen Sinn, unklug zu handeln. Ich treffe Mittwoch früh in Berlin ein; vielleicht kann ich Sie noch sehen.
Mit den Chören[151] eilt es nicht mehr, da wir die Sammlung abschließen mußten und ohnedies bereits zu viel Stoff hatten. Dies hindert aber nicht, daß wir die Chöre dann gelegentlich gesondert herausgeben. Aber das hat dann Zeit und wir brauchen Sie nicht zu drängen. Alle Ihre Kompositionen interessieren uns und schicken Sie sie bitte ruhig ein, damit wir sehen, was wir machen können.
Alles andere hoffentlich mündlich, evtl. mit meinem Bruder in London, der bereits dort ist.
In großer Eile
herzlichst Ihr <Ludwig Strecker>

58 Willy Strecker an Paul Hindemith

Mainz, 5. April 1933

Lieber Herr Hindemith,
hoffentlich sind auch Sie inzwischen wieder glücklich nach Berlin zurückgekehrt und haben die Verhältnisse nicht zu verändert vorgefunden.
Ich schicke Ihnen einliegend einen Brief – den ich gelegentlich zurück erbitte – des 94jährigen Eduard Speyer[152], dessen jugendfrisches, wohl-

---

[151] Vgl. Anm. 126.

[152] Es handelt sich um den in Frankfurt/Main geborenen Edward Speyer (1839–1934), der im Alter von 20 Jahren nach England auswanderte und in London ein erfolgreicher Geschäftsmann wurde. Dort veranstaltete er regelmäßig Konzerte und war einer der Gründer der Classical Concerts Society. Speyer war befreundet mit Clara Schumann und besaß eine wertvolle Sammlung von Musikautographen, Musikerbriefen und Musikdrucken.

tuendes Urteil noch immer vernünftiger ist, als das der gesamten englischen Kritik.
Ihr Trio[153] habe ich inzwischen genauer durchgesehen und finde es ein ganz prachtvolles Werk, auf das Komponist wie Verlag stolz sein können. Ich habe es bereits in Stich gegeben und wäre Ihnen für gelegentliche Übersendung der Violin- und Cellostimme dankbar.
Halten Sie es nicht für vorteilhaft, die rhythmischen Fingerzeige, die Sie selbst verschiedentlich mit Blei notiert und zum Studium für praktisch gefunden haben, in die Stimmen mitzustechen? Sie dürften zweifellos das Studium erleichtern.
Gern hörte ich auch von Ihnen Ihre streng vertrauliche Ansicht über die kunstpolitische Lage. Es ist vielleicht noch zu früh zu irgendwelchen Verhandlungen mit den maßgebenden Leuten des Kampfbundes, so lange die Gemüter sich noch nicht beruhigt haben. Aber es muß zweifellos eine gemeinsame aufklärende Aktion vorbereitet werden, damit nicht zu viel zertöpfert wird. Jede kleine Provinzstadt scheint einen Kampfbund-Diktator zu haben, der nach eigenem Ermessen Richtlinien gibt, die unbedingt von einer Zentralstelle nach vernünftigen Grundsätzen ausgestellt werden müßten. So ist in unserer Gegend z.B. Strawinsky[154] auf die Liste der bolschewistisch-russischen Juden gesetzt worden, deren Werke nicht mehr gespielt werden dürfen; Sie selbst sollen zu 50% mit Ihren früheren Werken als Kultur-Bolschewist verboten sein; Lendvai'sche Chöre (obwohl Lendvai[155] von katholischen Eltern als Katholik geboren und getauft wurde und seit einigen Jahren preußi-

---

[153] Vgl. Anm. 139.
[154] Zum »Fall Strawinsky« bemerkt Fred K. Prieberg (*Musik im NS-Staat*, Frankfurt/Main 1982, S. 53): *Hier genügte das Gerücht, er sei Jude. Es entstand natürlich, weil die engstirnigen »Säuberer« nicht begriffen, wie so viel »Entartung« – und als solche deklarierten sie sein Œuvre – bei einem Arier sich äußern konnte. Auch gelegentlich differenzierendere Betrachtungsweise änderte nichts daran.*
[155] Erwin Lendvai (1882–1949), in Budapest geborener Komponist, mußte Deutschland 1933 wegen seines politischen Engagements für die Arbeiterbewegung verlassen und emigrierte nach England.

scher Untertan ist – weiteres Ahnenstudium trieb ich allerdings nicht) vollkommen boykottiert werden etc. etc. Kurzum es scheint mir unmöglich, mit jedem einzelnen Kunstdezernenten in jeder Stadt getrennt zu verhandeln. Sie sitzen an der Quelle und wissen sicherlich über die Absichten und Möglichkeiten, in dieser Hinsicht einzugreifen, besseren Bescheid. – Unsere hiesige Musikschule, sowie das Hoch'sche Konservatorium sind durch Abgang von Sekles[156] und Gal[157] verwaist. Über die Nachfolger scheint noch nichts bestimmt zu sein. Das sind alles wichtige Fragen für die Zukunft.

An Clark[158] schrieb schrieb ich nochmals wegen umgehender Zusendung der Liste von deutschen Werken und Künstlern in England und hoffe sie im Laufe der Woche zu erhalten.

Von Ihnen selbst scheint im Ausland ausgerechnet das »Lehrstück« eben in besonderer Weise zu interessieren. Außer in Brüssel und England höre ich auch von einer geplanten Aufführung in der Schweiz[159].

Mein Bruder fuhr letzte Woche nach New York, sodaß ich Ihnen diesen Stoßseufzer als zurückgebliebener Schott Sohn mit herzlichen Grüßen übermittle.

Stets Ihr <Willy Strecker>

---

[156] Bernhard Sekles (1872–1934), dt. Komponist, von 1986 an Lehrer am Hoch'schen Konservatorium in Frankfurt/Main, 1923–1933 dessen Direktor. Hindemith war von 1913–1917 Schüler seiner Kompositionsklasse.

[157] Hans Gal (1890–1987), in Österreich geb. Komponist und Musikwissenschaftler, war 1929–1933 Direktor der Musikhochschule in Mainz. Er kehrte nach Wien zurück, von wo er 1938 nach Großbritannien floh.

[158] Vgl. Anm. 86.

[159] Aufführungen des *Lehrstücks* fanden 1933 noch am Brüsseler Konservatorium und bei der BBC in London statt, außerdem leitete Hermann Scherchen eine Aufführung am Konservatorium von Straßburg. Eine Inszenierung in der Schweiz konnte nicht nachgewiesen werden.

59 Paul Hindemith an Willy Strecker

Berlin, 15. April 1933

Lieber Herr Strecker, Sie hätten schon eher auf Ihren Brief Antwort bekommen, wenn ich nicht die ganzen Tage mit einer etwas schmerzhaften Sehnenscheidenentzündung (am Fuß) im Bett gelegen hätte. Allmählich kann ich ganz langsam wieder anfangen zu krabbeln und so sollen Sie gleich Nachricht haben. Den erfreulichen Brief des alten Knaben schicke ich Ihnen hiermit wieder. Erstaunlich ist, daß er in seinem Alter doch noch mitmacht. In England scheint tatsächlich die Zeitungskritik nur aus Schwachköpfen zu bestehen. Ich möchte mal sehen, wenn die Leute vor Antritt ihrer Laufbahn ihre Eignungsprüfung machen. Da muß es seltsam zugehen. Das Lehrstück am letzten Abend war ausgezeichnet.[160] Alles sang ohne die geringste Scheu aus vollem Halse mit. Auch dieses Stück wollten sie nächstens wiederholen. Die Triostimmen[161] kann ich Ihnen heute noch nicht schicken. Ich habe schon ein paarmal bei Goldberg[162] und Feuermann[163] angerufen, aber nie Antwort bekommen. Sobald ich sie habe, bekommen Sie sie. Die rhythmischen Merkzeichen, die sich in der Bratschenstimme finden, sind rein persönliche Hilfsmittel, die bei mir in allen Kammermusikstimmen stehen und die allerdings sehr praktisch sind. Ich weiß nicht, ob man sie gerade in dieser Form in den Druck aufnehmen kann. Wenn ja, müßte Herr Willms[164] dann noch die beiden anderen Stimmen auf dieselbe Art einrichten. – Nach allem, was hier vorgeht, glaube ich, daß wir keinerlei Grund haben, mit Sorgen in die

---

160 Vgl. Anm. 84.

161 Vgl. Anm. 139

162 Szymon Goldberg (1909–1993) war polnischer Geiger. 1931 übernahm er die Position des jung verstorbenen Geigers Joseph Wolfsthal (1899–1931) in dem Streichtrio, das Wolfsthal, Hindemith und der Cellist Emanuel Feuermann 1929 gegründet hatten.

163 Emanuel Feuermann (1902–1942), dt. Cellist, war von 1929 an Professor an der Berliner Hochschule für Musik und Gründungsmitglied des Trios Wolfsthal-Hindemith-Feuermann. Er mußte 1933 nach Wien, 1938 in die USA emigrieren und stand bis zu seinem frühen Tod in freundschaftlichem Kontakt zu Hindemith.

164 Franz Willms (1893–1946), Lektor im Schott-Verlag.

musikalische Zukunft zu sehen. Nur die nächsten Wochen muß man vorübergehen lassen. Mir ist bei den ganzen Umänderungen bis jetzt gar nichts passiert. Neulich, gleich als ich aus England kam, hatte ich mit obersten Kampfbundleuten eine große Unterredung, die sich allerdings nur auf Unterrichtsangelegenheiten bezog. Jedenfalls entnahm ich aber daraus (nachdem ich sie beruhigt hatte, daß ich kein Halb- oder sonstiger Bruchteilsjude bin), daß ich gut im Kurs dort stehe. Mittlerweile haben sie mich (allerdings nicht hochoffiziell) beauftragt, Pläne zur Änderung des ganzen Kompositions- und Theorieunterrichts einzureichen. Da ich nun weiß, wie mißtrauisch die Leute sind und da ich auch gesehen habe, daß einige, die sich anbiedern wollten, vollkommen versunken sind, möchte ich, der ich mich ja nicht einmal anbiedern will, diese von Ihnen gewünschte aufklärende Aktion nicht gerade jetzt unternehmen. Wenn Sie mir überlassen wollen, hier den günstigsten Zeitpunkt für so etwas abzupassen, können Sie versichert sein, daß ich alles versuche, was möglich ist. Eines Tages muß ich natürlich einmal den Kampfbund dazu bekommen, offiziell für meine Sachen einzutreten, aber es ist noch etwas zu früh. Im augenblicklichen Zustand der allgemeinen Unsicherheit wird nirgendwo allzu viel möglich sein; wenn Sie aber irgendwelche Sonderaktionen oder Bekehrungsversuche kleinerer Kulturbünde vorhaben, tun Sie's nur. Nur hielte ich es für richtig, keinerlei Angst oder Unsicherheit zu zeigen. Wir haben ja auch bei Gott keinen Dreck am Stecken.

Ich sehe vielleicht nächste Woche wieder irgendwelche Bonzen, ich will dann sehen, was sich tun läßt. Bei uns an der Schule ist ganz großes Durcheinander. Alle jüdischen Lehrer außer ein oder zwei ganz unersetzlichen wie Sachs[165] oder Flesch[166] müssen natürlich gehen. Auch

---

[165] Curt Sachs (1881–1959), dt. Musikwissenschaftler, war 1919–1933 Leiter der Staatlichen Instrumentensammlung und Lehrer an der Hochschule für Musik in Berlin. Nach der Entlassung aus all seinen Ämtern emigrierte er 1933 nach Paris, ab 1937 lebte er in New York, wo er bis 1957 an der New York University lehrte.

[166] Carl Flesch (1873–1944), in Ungarn geb. Violinvirtuose, unterrichtete seit 1928 an der Berliner Musikhochschule. Er wurde im Mai 1933 entlassen. 1934 floh er nach England, 1939 über Amsterdam in die Schweiz.

Schünemann[167] selbst wahrscheinlich, weil er sich durch sein Lavieren alles verdorben hat. Man spricht davon, daß Stein aus Kiel[168] Direktor werden soll (das alles unter uns!). Das wäre nicht schlecht für unsere Richtung, obwohl er auch nicht gerade ein Musterbeispiel für Mut und Standfestigkeit ist. Ich nehme an, daß man Ende Mai schon bedeutend klarer sehen wird und daß man dann auch schon sehen wird, was in der nächsten Saison ungefähr passiert. – Wir kommen nächstens nach Frankfurt hinunter. 25.–27. etwa sind wir dort. Hoffentlich sehen wir uns, entweder in Frankfurt oder irgendwo bei schönem Wetter im Taunus. – Durch meinen Drecksfuß und den großen Durcheinander in den letzten Wochen überhaupt bin ich nicht zu ernsthaften Arbeiten gekommen. Ein paar Lieder habe ich noch gemacht.[169] Ich hatte jetzt vor, eine größere Männerduosache[170] zu machen, eine Art Kantate mit Soli und vielleicht einem ganz primitiven Blechorchester, wie es in jedem Dorf zu finden ist. Nach Texten suche ich in den Nachthymnen von Novalis und im Hölderlin. Meinen Sie nicht, daß so eine Art <von> harmlosen und leichten aber doch sehr ernsten Stücken jetzt ganz angebracht wäre? Mit größeren Sachen muß man noch etwas warten.
Schluß für heute. Mein Fuß tut wieder weh, ich kann noch nicht so lange sitzen.
Schönste Grüße einstweilen
Ihr Paul Hindemith

[167] Georg Schünemann (1884–1945), dt. Musikhistoriker, war von 1920 an Professor und stellv. Direktor der Staatlichen Akademischen Hochschule für Musik in Berlin. 1933 wurde er fristlos entlassen, seine Senatsmitliedschaft der Preußischen Akademie der Künste aufgehoben.
[168] Fritz Stein (1879–1961), Dirigent, war von 1925 an Generalmusikdirektor in Kiel. Er wurde im April 1933 Nachfolger von Schünemann als Direktor der Staatlichen Akademischen Hochschule für Musik in Berlin.
[169] Vgl. Anm. 127 und Anm. 146.
[170] Dieser Plan wurde nicht realisiert.

60 Willy Strecker an Paul Hindemith

Mainz, 19. April 1933

Lieber Herr Hindemith, es tut mir leid, von Ihrer Sehnen-Entzündung zu hören, die außerordentlich schmerzhaft und langwierig ist. Hoffentlich sind Sie bald davon befreit, aber versuchen Sie nicht zu früh herumzukrabbeln, es dauert dann nur um so länger.
Ihre Ausführungen über die allgemeine Lage haben mich ebenso interessiert wie beruhigt, zumal sie sich im wesentlichen ganz mit meiner Auffassung decken. Es ist manchmal nicht ganz leicht, den gesunden Menschenverstand in der Provinz zu bewahren, wenn ihn die gesamte Umgebung verloren hat und selbst das eifrigste Ostereiersuchen ergebnislos verläuft. Ich habe festes Vertrauen, daß die Vernunft und Qualität wie überall, so auch hier entscheiden wird und freue mich, Sie auf Ihrer Durchfahrt in Frankfurt demnächst begrüßen zu können. Lassen Sie mich bitte gleich wissen, wann Sie eintreffen, damit wir etwas verabreden können, denn ich selbst muß am 28. und 29.4. zu wichtigen Verlegerversammlungen in Leipzig sein und möchte Sie auf alle Fälle gern sprechen.
Ihre Pläne mit der Männer-Chor-Kantate halte ich für sehr praktisch, Voraussetzung ist allerdings ein möglichst klarer einfacher Text, der sich dem primitiven Blechorchester anpaßt. Er braucht deshalb natürlich nicht banal zu sein, aber die Leute müssen den Text, den sie singen, verstehen können. Dies ist meiner Erfahrung nach beinahe ebenso wichtig, wie der musikalische Teil.
Von dem Trio[171] ist zunächst die Partitur im Stich. Die rhythmischen Merkzeichen wird Wilms in die Stimmen eintragen, sobald Sie sie uns zuschicken. Ich halte dieses Hilfsmittel für außerordentlich praktisch und es gefällt mir besser wie Stichnoten.
Mit herzlichen Grüßen und auf baldiges Wiedersehen
Ihr <Willy Strecker>

---

[171] Vgl. Anm. 139.

61 Paul Hindemith an Ernst Penzoldt

Berlin, 24. April 1933

Lieber Herr Penzoldt, wie geht es Ihnen denn, ich habe ja so lange nichts mehr von Ihnen gehört. Wir leben hier noch ganz unbeschädigt. Gerüchte gingen schon, ich sei in Schutzhaft (warum, weiß ich nicht), aber ich habe nichts davon gemerkt. Im Augenblick ist musikalisch gar nichts zu wollen, nach meinen Erfahrungen scheinen mir für nächstes Jahr aber gar keine schlechten Aussichten zu sein. Haben Sie einmal an die Eisenbahnpläne gedacht oder steht Ihnen der Kopf gar nicht danach? Wie weit Etienne und Luise nächsten Winter möglich ist, übersehe ich jetzt noch nicht. Schreiben Sie uns doch einmal, was Sie treiben und wie es Ihnen allen geht.
Schönste Grüße an Sie alle Ihre Paul & Gertrud Hindemith

62 Paul Hindemith an Ernst Penzoldt

Wien, 15. Mai 1933 [Poststempel]

Lieber Herr Pentzold,
ich habe die Absicht, nächsten Sonntag über München nach Berlin zu fahren und hätte gerne einiges mit Ihnen besprochen. Sind Sie um diese Zeit <in> München? Ich würde Sie dann nach meiner Ankunft anrufen[172]. Wollen Sie so lieb sein, mir noch nach hier (Wien), Hotel Imperial, Nachricht zu geben?
Mit herzlichstem Gruß an die ganze Familie
Ihr Paul Hindemith

---

[172] Am 21.5.1933 trafen sich Hindemith und Penzoldt in München; Hindemith schrieb darüber am 23.5.1933 an seine Frau: *Mit Penzoldt und seinem Schwager saß ich bis gegen 10 zusammen. Er hat natürlich noch nichts gemacht. Die Eisenbahn reizt ihn aber sehr, und er hatte sich schon die Nürnberger Zeitungen der damaligen Zeit besorgt. Wir sind so verblieben, daß er sich zum Thema in der nächsten Zeit Material besorgen will.* (Paul Hindemith, *»Das private Logbuch«*, a.a.O. [Anm. 129], S. 99).

63 Paul Hindemith an Ernst Penzoldt

Wien, 19. Mai 1933 [Poststempel]

Lieber Herr Penzoldt, Pentzold, Penzold, Penzolt, Pentzolt, Pennzold, Penntzold, Pennzolt, Penntzolt, Penntzoldt, Pentzoldt, Pennzoldt, ich komme Sonntag nach München und werde mir erlauben, Sie am späten Nachmittag anzurufen.
Schönste Grüße Ihr Paul Hindemith

64 Paul Hindemith an Ernst Penzoldt

<Sommer 1933>[173]

Lieber Herr Penzoldt,
Ihr »Herr Brummell«[174] ist vom Schleier schauriger Geheimnisse umwoben. Wahrscheinlich wird er bei mir in Berlin gelandet sein, als wir schon weg waren und da Sendungen von abnormer Größe nicht nachgeschickt werden, wird er wahrscheinlich meiner Rückkehr in Berlin harren, die am 24. September stattfinden wird. Einstweilen kann ich also weder Sie noch den mahnenden Arkadiaverlag befriedigen. Ich bin seit einigen Wochen schon aus allem Betrieb heraus, kann Ihnen also im Augenblick auch nichts über Ihre anderen Anfragen[175] sagen, ich muß erst in Berlin sehen, wie die Lage ist. Ihr Schwager wird mich wahrscheinlich in Berlin auch nicht gefunden haben. Oder doch? Wir sind Kurgäschte geworden, benehmen uns als solche stilgerecht. Alfi[176] ist auch dabei, wie denn überhaupt die ganze Reise für ihn veranstaltet

---

[173] Im Sommer 1933 hielten sich Hindemiths in den schweizerischen Alpen (17.8.–31.8. in Guarda, 31.8.–13.9. in Surlej) auf. In Hindemiths Taschenkalender findet sich unter dem 28.8. der Eintrag: *Post erledigt.*

[174] Gemeint ist Penzoldts Drama *So war Herr Brummell* über den englischen Dandy George Bryan Brummell (1778–1840), das am 7.2.1934 unter der Regie von Karl Eidlitz am Burgtheater in Wien uraufgeführt wurde. Das Stück ist 1933 im Arcadia-Verlag als Bühnenmanuskript veröffentlicht worden.

[175] Diese Anfragen sind nicht überliefert.

[176] Vgl. Anm. 55.

wurde, und er sucht schnaubend nach Murmeltieren und bellt die Ziegen an. – Für Ihren armen Dalai[177] blase ich einen speziellen Molldreiklang auf meiner wohlweislich mitgenommenen Flöte. Grüßen Sie die ganze Familie und sich selbst. Haben Sie Magneto[178] vielleicht schon mit Parkettspänen probiert? Müßte gut gehen.
Ihr Paul Hindemith nebst Frau & Hund.

65 Paul Hindemith an Ernst Penzoldt

Berlin, 13. November 1933 [Poststempel]

Lieber Herr Penzoldt,
Ihr Herr Siegel ist ist mir nach wie vor ein Brummel mit sieben Büchern. Ich werde vermutlich nie erfahren, wie er war. Trotzdem sind wir noch wohlauf und hoffen es auch zu bleiben. Wenn Sie nicht vorher einmal mit einem Musterkoffer voll Dramen nach hier kommen, hoffe ich im Laufe des Winters mit Bratschenkasten doch wieder in München zu erscheinen[179]. An bemerkenswerten Ereignissen kann ich nur mitteilen, daß wir im Besitze von zwei blauen Wellensittichen sind. In dieser braunen Welt nehmen sie sich etwas seltsam aus. Hoffentlich geht's Ihnen allen gut. In der Wüste meiner Schreibfaulheit hatte sich lediglich dieser kleine Wadi angesammelt. Jetzt ist's schon wieder aus, schade.
Ich grüße, Frau grüßt, Alfi[180] gibt Pfotchen, ich gebe Pfotchen, Frau gibt Pfotchen, Alfi grüßt.
Ihr Paul Hindemith

---

177 Name eines Wellensittichs, den Penzoldt von Ernst Heimeran (vgl. Anm. 29) geschenkt bekommen hat, der aber sehr bald gestorben ist.

178 Vgl. Anm. 115.

179 Musikpolitisch motivierte Angriffe der Nationalsozialisten gegen Hindemith erschwerten seine Konzerttätigkeit in Deutschland zunehmend und machten sie schließlich völlig unmöglich. In München trat Hindemith nie wieder als Interpret mit der Bratsche auf.

180 Vgl. Anm. 55.

Gerald Kilian

Paul Hindemiths *Symphonie »Mathis der Maler«*

Eine Deutung musikalischer Ausdruckscharaktere und formaler Strukturen als semiotische Gestaltqualitäten symbolischer Musik

In Mathis Neithardts (gen. Grünewald) »Engelkonzert« und in Paul Hindemiths sich programmatisch darauf beziehender Einleitung des ersten Satzes der *Symphonie »Mathis der Maler«* bilden formale Konstellationen, Gruppierungen und Proportionen wesentliche Strukturgrundlagen beider Kunstwerke. Darüber hinaus sind emotionale Inhalte und szenische Dramaturgien auf vergleichbare semantische Bedeutungen gegründet. Hindemiths Komposition beruht auf synästhetischen Analogien, auf der akustischen Transformation optischer Informationen; das Gemälde seinerseits nimmt u.a. als verräumlichte Zeit Bezug auf musikalische, bewegungsgeleitete und zeitliche Vorgänge. Bild und Musik können beim Betrachter bzw. beim Hörer analoge Assoziationen auslösen. Emotionale Konnotationen statten das Dargestellte bzw. die Tonfolgen mit äquivalenten sinnlichen Eigenschaften aus: im Bild werden mittels mimisch-kinästhetischer Suggestion klingende Vorgänge evoziert, in der Komposition werden musikalische Ereignisse und emotional stimulierte Bewegungsvorgänge der Bilddynamik des Grünewaldschen Altarbilds musikalisch kommentiert und zusammengeführt. Im Mittelpunkt dieser Betrachtungen sollen die den beiden Kunstwerken analogen übergreifenden ästhetischen Ideen stehen; darüber hinaus soll die Frage diskutiert werden, welche rezeptionsfunktionalen Determinanten dieser Werke beim Hörer bzw. beim Betrachter vergleichbare

Wirkungen provozieren. Mit Hilfe hermeneutischer Verknüpfungen soll die langsame Einleitung des ersten Satzes dieser Symphonie hinsichtlich ihrer Relevanz zur bildnerischen Vorlage analysiert werden. Dabei wird dem synästhetischen Impuls eine auratische Deutungsperspektive zugewiesen.
Der Mitteilungscharakter der Symphonie-Einleitung impliziert nicht nur den Verweis auf das konkrete Anschauungsobjekt, das »Engelkonzert« von Grünewald. Deshalb soll neben der Beschreibung des Ausdrucks, der atmosphärischen Charakteristik und der musikalischen Charaktere die Einordnung des funktionalen Gehalts und der symbolischen Bedeutung der *Mathis*-Einleitung vorgenommen werden. Hierfür eignet sich ein kommunikationstheoretischer semiotischer Ansatz: Die indexikalisch und ikonisch geleiteten Gestaltanalysen sind die Voraussetzung für eine semantische Interpretation.

Zur Entstehung der *Symphonie »Mathis der Maler«*

In den Jahren 1933/34 beschäftigte sich Hindemith intensiv mit der Biographie und mit dem Werk Mathis Neithardts (gen. Grünewald)[1]. Das von ihm verfaßte Libretto der Oper *Mathis der Maler* schildert das Leben Grünewalds und die Entstehung des Isenheimer Altars: Hauptperson der Oper ist der Maler Mathis Gothart Neithardt, der zur Zeit der Bauernkriege (1524/1525) infolge seiner Parteinahme für die sozialen und politischen Anliegen der Bauern und infolge seines Eintretens für die Reformation in Konfrontation mit der staatlichen und kirchlichen Obrigkeit geriet. *Von allen Höllenqualen einer zweifelnden,*

[1] Die Biographie »Grünewalds« birgt immer noch Geheimnisse: Grünewald könnte identisch sein mit Mathis Gothart, gen. Nithart, der u.a. in Seligenstadt, Würzburg, Frankfurt und Halle nachweisbar ist, der wohl Anhänger der Reformation war und in die Bauernaufstände verstrickt war; er starb 1528. Er könnte mit größerer Wahrscheinlichkeit aber auch identisch sein mit dem in Aschaffenburg gebürtigen Mathias Grünewald (Mathis Grün), der in Frankfurt und in Erbach gelebt hat und 1532 gestorben ist.

suchenden Seele geplagt, erlebte Neithardt den *Einbruch einer neuen Zeit mit ihrem unvermeidlichen Umsturz der bisher geltenden Anschauungen* [...] *Er geriet in die damals gewaltig arbeitende Maschinerie des Staates und der Kirche, hielt mit seiner Kraft dem Druck dieser Mächte wohl stand, in seinen Bildern berichtet er jedoch deutlich genug, wie die wildbewegten Zeitläufe mit all ihrem Elend, ihren Krankheiten und Kriegen ihn erschüttert haben.*[2] *An der Schwelle der Neuzeit* habe Grünewald *dem mittelalterlichen Glaubensgefühl noch einmal wie in einer allerletzten unbegreiflich entwickelten Blüte innerlichsten Ausdruck gegeben*, habe sich der lutherischen Reformation zugewendet und schließlich seine künstlerische Tätigkeit aufgegeben. Hindemith interpretierte diese Tatsache als *Resignation vor der Nichtigkeit des irdischen Werkes*, als den *Untergang eines von Verzweiflung Geschlagenen.* In Grünewalds Schicksal sah Hindemith seine eigene Situation zur Zeit des Nationalsozialismus gespiegelt: unter dem Erlebnis des zunehmenden Aufführungsboykotts und der ästhetischen Diffamierung und Ächtung durch manche nationalsozialistische Kulturfunktionäre identifizierte sich Hindemith mit dem Schicksal Grünewalds, dessen Lebensumstände ihm eine *Parallele der damaligen Zeit mit der unsrigen und vor allem mit dem einsamen Künstlerschicksal* vorführte[3].

---

[2] Paul Hindemith, *Zur Einführung*, in: Textheft zur Uraufführung der Oper *Mathis der Maler*, Stadttheater Zürich 28. Mai 1938, S. 3ff.

[3] Zit. n. Giselher Schubert, *Paul Hindemith in Selbstzeugnissen und Bilddokumenten*, Reinbek 1981, S. 80. So wie Mathis daran scheiterte, den aufständischen Bauern zu ihrem Recht zu verhelfen, so mußte Hindemith seine Ohnmacht gegenüber den politischen totalitären Verhältnissen seiner Zeit erkennen. Einige avantgardistische experimentelle Werke der zwanziger Jahre (u.a. *Mörder, Hoffnung der Frauen, Nusch-Nuschi, Sancta Susanna, Neues vom Tage*) hatten ihm früher den Ruf eines provokanten Bürgerschrecks eingebracht. In den dreißiger Jahren wurden Hetzartikel gegen ihn veröffentlicht, in denen seine Musik als »entartete Kunst« diffamiert wurde, und er sah sich zunehmend Restriktionen durch Kulturfunktionäre ausgesetzt. Furtwänglers Eintreten für Hindemith hatte keinen Erfolg: nachdem er in seinem Artikel *Der Fall Hindemith* auf das »Deutsche« in Hindemiths Symphonie hingewiesen hatte, wurde 1934 von Goebbels gegen Hindemith und Furtwängler gleichsam agitiert. Goebbels bezeichnete Hindemith als *atonalen Geräuschemacher*.

Die von Hindemith angesprochenen biographischen und historischen Parallelen finden sich in der Problematik des politischen, ethischen Engagements und des daraus resultierenden Schicksals des Künstlers in der Gesellschaft. Grünewalds politisches Engagement beruhte auf der Überzeugung, zu gesellschaftlichen Mißständen Position beziehen zu müssen; die moralische Pflicht zur aktiven politischen Stellungnahme mußte zeitweise die Kunstausübung in den Hintergrund drängen.
Für Hindemiths Standortbestimmung war die Treue zu seinen ästhetischen Idealen und zu seinem eigenen Kunstanspruch ausschlaggebend. Sein künstlerisches Bekenntnis war an die moralische Glaubwürdigkeit gebunden. Hindemith hatte nach eigenem Bekunden den *Übergang aus konservativer Schulung in eine neue Freiheit* nach dem Ersten Weltkrieg, den Bruch mit Traditionen, *gründlicher erlebt als irgendein anderer. Das Neue mußte durchschritten werden, sollte seine Erforschung gelingen; daß dies weder harmlos noch ungefährlich war, weiß jeder, der an der Eroberung beteiligt war.*[4]

Die ursprüngliche Absicht Hindemiths war es, während der Arbeit an der Oper aus deren Vor- und Zwischenspielen gleichzeitig eine viersätzige Suite zu entwickeln[5]. Die Arbeit am Libretto nahm jedoch mehr Zeit in Anspruch als erwartet, so daß die *»Symphonie »Mathis der Maler«* vor der gleichnamigen Oper vollendet war und unter Furtwänglers Leitung 1934 in Berlin uraufgeführt werden konnte. Die drei

---

Als schließlich Aufführungen seiner Werke ab 1936 unmöglich wurden, blieb ihm nur der Weg ins Exil. – Zu Artikeln, Rezensionen und Briefen zum »Fall Hindemith« sowie zur Entstehung der *Symphonie »Mathis der Maler«* s. *Mathis der Maler. Materialien für den Musikunterricht in der Sekundarstufe II*, hrsg. von Luitgard Schader, Paul-Hindemith-Institut, Frankfurt/Main 1995, S. 1ff.

4 Paul Hindemith, *Unterweisung im Tonsatz I. Theoretischer Teil*, Mainz ²1940, S. 22.

5 Der früheste Entwurf sah eine Gliederung der Oper in vier Akte vor, die jeweils im Kontext zu einem Gemälde des Isenheimer Altars standen: 1. Engelkonzert, 2. Martyrium des hl. Sebastian (in den endgültigen Fassungen der Oper mit sieben Bildern und in der dreisätzigen Symphonie entfiel diese Thematik), 3. Die Versuchung des hl. Antonius, 4. Grablegung.

Sätze (*Engelkonzert*, *Grablegung*, *Die Versuchung des heiligen Antonius*) beziehen sich auf drei Bildtafeln des Isenheimer Altars. Den ersten Satz der Symphonie (*Engelkonzert*) verwendete Hindemith auch als Vorspiel der Oper; außerdem nahm er darauf im 6. Bild seiner Oper Bezug, wenn Mathis (Grünewald) seine Vision von den musizierenden Engeln schildert. Der zweite Satz (*Grablegung*) ist mit dem instrumentalen Zwischenspiel des letzten (7.) Bildes der Oper identisch: es erklingt nach dem Tod Reginas, der Tochter des gefallenen Bauernführers Schwalb, die Mathis bei sich aufgenommen hatte; der erschöpfte Mathis hat den Isenheimer Altar vollendet und sucht Ruhe vor der Welt. Mit dem Predellabild von Grünewald hat dieser Satz die Schilderung der Trauer und Verzweiflung gemein. Der dritte Satz – *Die Versuchung des heiligen Antonius* – ist inhaltlich auf das 6. Bild der Oper bezogen: nach der Niederlage der Bauern hat sich Mathis mit Regina in den Odenwald zurückgezogen. Nachdem er Regina in den Schlaf gesungen hat (*Es sungen drei Engel*), entstehen vor seinem Auge Visionen: er sieht sich als der Einsiedler Antonius, der von Dämonen gequält wird; diese wollen ihn durch verschiedene Verlockungen dazu bringen, von seinem Glauben abzulassen. Er zeigt sich jedoch gegenüber den Verführungen standhaft. Hier spiegelt sich der Kampf im Inneren des Künstlers (Antonius = Mathis = Hindemith) gegen die Anfechtungen der Welt.

Zum Isenheimer Altar

Mathis Neithardt (gen. Grünewald) schuf den Altar 1512–1516 im Auftrag des Ordenspräzeptors des Isenheimer Antoniterklosters, Guido Guersi; die drei verschiedenen Schauseiten des Flügelaltars haben jeweils ein großes zentrales Bild, das von zwei schmaleren Außenbildern umrahmt wird. Die erste Schauseite thematisiert die Kreuzigung Christi; auf dem linken Außenflügel ist der Hl. Sebastian und auf dem rechten ist der Hl. Antonius dargestellt. Die zweite Schauseite zeigt links außen die Verkündigungsszene, in der Mitte die Menschwerdung Jesu

mit dem Engelkonzert, rechts außen die Himmelfahrt Jesu. Die dritte Schauseite stellt links den Hl. Antonius und den Hl. Paulus im Zwiegespräch dar, in der Mitte befindet sich ein Schrein mit geschnitzten Heiligenfiguren von Nikolaus Hagenauer, rechts ist die Versuchung des hl. Antonius dargestellt. Unter dem Altar befindet sich die Predella mit der Darstellung der Grablegung Christi.
Die Vorlage für den ersten Satz der *»Mathis«-Symphonie* Hindemiths bildet die Bildtafel des Isenheimer Altars mit dem Thema »Engelkonzert«: Im linken Teil des Bildes befindet sich ein kapellenartiger spätgotischer Bau mit einem Steinbaldachin. Die ornamentreiche Architektur findet eine bewegungsdynamische Entsprechung in der Schar schwebender Engel im geheimnisvoll dämmrigen Hintergrund und im vorderen heller beleuchteten Teil der Kapelle. Am Eingang und vor der Kapelle befinden sich drei große Engel; sie sind Repräsentanten der musica coelestis, die musizierend ihre Freude über die Geburt Jesu ausdrücken. Am linken Bildrand steht ein grün gefiederter Engel mit ausgebreiteten Flügeln, der eine Baßgambe streicht; sein verwunderter Blick richtet sich nach oben. Ein zweiter – rechts von ihm und Maria am nächsten stehend – spielt die viola da braccio; gegenüber dem nur schwach beleuchteten grünen Engel ist er in leuchtendes Rot und Gold getaucht. Der vorderste und am hellsten angestrahlte Engel kniet außerhalb der Kapelle; er spielt verzückt lächelnd auf seiner Tenorgambe. Die Engel scheinen ergriffen einen überirdischen Klang zu hören; ihre mystische Verklärung spiegelt sich in der Art, wie sie ihrem eigenen Spiel verinnerlicht entrückt bzw. ergriffen lauschen und in der Art, wie sie sich z.B. hinsichtlich der Bogenhaltung über eine anatomisch realistische Spielweise hinwegsetzen. Grünewald griff in dieser Darstellungsweise auf alte Szenarien zurück, wie sie seit dem Mittelalter in der Übersteigerung des realistischen Musizierens allegorisch auf eine überirdische himmlische Liturgie verwiesen.
Am Eingang zum Baldachin befindet sich Maria. Die Strahlenkrone und die helle Aureole weisen sie aus als »regina aeterna«, als die Vision der

zukünftigen und ewigen Gottesmutter, *auf der Schwelle des alten Bundes zum Neuen hin*, mit dem Blick auf die Menschwerdung Christi[6]. Auf der rechten Bildhälfte sitzt die irdische Maria. Vor dem Hintergrund einer Landschaft wiegt sie das Christuskind. Die dornenlosen Rosen, das durchsichtige Glasgefäß und der durch ein Tor verschlossene Garten hinter Maria deuten auf ihre Reinheit hin[7]. Göttlicher Glanz ergießt sich aus der Höhe über die bewölkte Erde. Im goldenen Licht der Aureole Gottes musizieren Engelschöre. Das von der Mitte des unteren Bildabschnitts nach rechts oben gerichtete metaphorische Beleuchtungsarrangement Grünewalds, das die drei musizierenden Engel aus dem Kontext herausragen läßt, transzendiert das Dargestellte ins Mystische; es gründet sich auf die topische Verwendung des Lichts als Sinnbild des Lebens, der Gottheit und der Heiligkeit im Sinne der neutestamentlichen Offenbarung. In der christlichen Mystik wurde die mystische Gotteserfahrung als Lichtschau beschrieben.
Mit den visionär bzw. entrückt in die Ferne schweifenden Physiognomien der drei musizierenden Engel, mit der Widerspiegelung des vom numinosen Geschehen Ergriffenen in ihren Gebärden und in ihren Spielhaltungen, mit der Art, wie sie sich der Wirkung der himmlischen Musik innerlich bewegt überlassen, modifizierte Grünewald tradierte Muster des himmlischen Musizierens: Seit dem frühen Christentum wurde ekstatisches Singen als Äußerung göttlich inspirierter Verzükkung gesehen[8]. In Musiktraktaten des Mittelalters – z.B. bei Jacobus von Lüttich und bei Nicolaus von Capua – wurde der Topos einer real im Himmel erklingenden Engelsmusik unter den Begriffen »musica coelestis« oder »musica angelica« behandelt. In den Visionen der Hilde-

[6] Heinrich Geissler, *Mathis Gothart Nithart Grünewald. Der Isenheimer Altar*, Stuttgart 1983, S. 104.

[7] Hierzu Ewald Maria Vetter, *Die Kreuzigungstafel des Isenheimer Altars*, in: *Sitzungsberichte der Heidelberger Akademie der Wissenschaft, philosophische historische Klasse*, 1968, 2. Abh., Heidelberg 1986, Anm. 6, S. 48.

[8] Reinhold Hammerstein, *Die Musik der Engel*, Bern ^{2}1990, S. 39f.

gard von Bingen und Heinrich Seuses wurde die himmlische Musik als wunderbare, harmonische liturgische Feier dargestellt. Die unbeschreibliche Schönheit der musica coelestis wird in der *Instituta patrum de modo psallendi sive cantandi* aus dem 11. Jahrhundert so beschrieben: *Auf daß wir* [...], *zum Himmel erhoben* [...], *die Geheimnisse schauen, mit sanftem Sinn, reiner Seele, angenehmer Würde des Geistes, einträchtiger Schwerelosigkeit, süßer Melodie, honigsüßem Jubilus, wohlklingender Stimme und unsagbarer Freude, Gott unserem Schöpfer lobsingen.*[9]

Die himmlische Engelsmusik wurde von Tinctoris in seinem Traktat *Complexus effectuum musices* (nach 1475) auch im Zusammenhang mit dem Jubilus-Singen erwähnt, das affektgeprägter Ausdruck menschlicher Frömmigkeit und mystischer Verzückung sei[10].

Zur musikalischen Deutung des *Engelkonzerts*

Die *»Mathis«-Symphonie* nimmt eine Zwischenstellung zwischen absoluter und deskriptiver Musik ein. Hindemith versuchte, in seiner *»Mathis«-Symphonie mit musikalischen Mitteln demselben Gefühlszustand nahezukommen, den die Bilder im Beschauer auslösen*[11]. Daneben finden sich deskriptive Elemente: vor allem einzelne musikalische Abschnitte des dritten Satzes lassen sich programmatisch deuten. Als symbolische Qualitäten fungieren die musikalischen Gattungen der Fuge, der Choralbearbeitung, des Hymnus und kirchentonal beeinflußte Wendungen. Es handelt sich jedoch nicht um Programmusik im strengen Sinne, da kein detaillierter Handlungsablauf geschildert wird. Besonders die polyphonen Durchführungstechniken belegen das Denken in

---

[9] Martin Gerbert, *Scriptores ecclesiastici de musica*, St. Blasien 1784, zit. n. Hammerstein, a.a.O., S. 127.

[10] Marius Schneider, *Die musikalischen Grundlagen der Sphärenharmonie*, in: *Acta musicologica*, (32) 1960, S. 202.

[11] Paul Hindemith, *Symphonie »Mathis der Maler«*, in: Programmheft der Berliner Uraufführung 1934.

den absoluten, musikimmanenten Kategorien des barocken Elaboratio-Prinzips.

Im Folgenden soll untersucht werden, auf welche Bildelemente des Grünewaldschen »Engelkonzerts« Hindemith in der Einleitung des ersten Satzes seiner *»Mathis«-Symphonie* Bezug genommen hat und mit welchen musikalischen Mitteln er Verbindungen zur bildnerischen Vorlage herstellte.
Drei G-Dur-Dreiklänge, die von den Streichern im pianissimo jeweils einen Takt ausgehalten werden, gliedern den ersten Abschnitt (A). Jeweils nach einem dieser Dreiklänge intonieren zuerst die Klarinetten und das Fagott, danach die Oboen und zuletzt die Flöten auftaktig ein steigendes Viertonmotiv; durch die Synkopierungen wirkt es schwebend, durch die breite Rhythmisierung wirkt es ruhig und abgeklärt und durch die phrygische Schlußwendung gewinnt es einen kirchenmodalen Charakter. Dieses Viertonmotiv wird zweimal eine Quint höher sequenziert (es beginnt jeweils auf *a, e, h*) und endet bei seinem dritten Erscheinen auf *fis*. Der Anfangston des im folgenden Abschnitt (B) zitierten cantus firmus (*des = cis*) schließt die harmonisch der Einleitung übergeordnete Quintenstruktur. Grundiert wird der Satz durch einen oktavierten Orgelpunkt der Hörner und Klarinetten.
Im Mittelteil der Einleitung (B) greift Hindemith auf die Technik der cantus-firmus-Bearbeitung zurück; dort zitiert er das mittelalterliche geistliche Volkslied *Es sungen drei Engel ein süßen Gesang*. Das Lied setzt mit dem Ton *des* in der Posaune ein (= enharmonisch *cis*, die Quint des Abschlußklangs *fis* des A-Teils). Es wird zweimal jeweils eine große Terz höher sequenziert; das erste Mal wird der c.f. nur von Posaunen, das zweite Mal von Holz- und Blechbläsern, das dritte Mal von Holz- und Blechbläsern sowie vom Glockenspiel gespielt. In Kombination mit der Auffächerung des cantus firmus in drei sukzessive höher ansetzenden Lagen, wodurch eine Oktave in drei gleich große Stufen geteilt wird *(des-f-a)*, vollzieht sich eine dreifache Addition der Instrumente und der Klangfarben sowie eine zunehmende Ausweitung des Klangs nach der

Höhe hin, unterstützt von dynamischen Steigerungen. Ein Kontrapunkt von drei Unisono-Streicherstimmen umspielt den cantus firmus beim ersten und beim dritten Erklingen in einem stereotyp repetierten dreizeitigen Rhythmus.
Der dritte Teil der Einleitung (A') entspricht in der Form und in der Motivik dem ersten Teil. Das neue Tonalitätszentrum *des* (Orgelpunkt der Celli) komplettiert die Teilung der Oktave in drei große Terzen (s. die cantus-firmus-Abschnitte im Mittelteil in *des-f-a*). Die Dreiklänge werden nun im Stimmtausch von den Bläsern gespielt (Des-Dur-Dreiklänge). Das Viertonmotiv erscheint sukzessiv in den Streichern in einer Terzschichtung (*des-as-f:* wenn man vom jeweiligen ersten Ton der Stimmen ausgeht), bzw. in einer Quintschichtung (*es-b-f:* wenn man den jeweils ersten Ton der Bratsche und der zweiten Violine als Verdoppelung der Orgelpunkte *des* und *as* annimmt). Der Abschnitt schließt auf dem Quintakkord *es-b-f-c-g*.
Analogien zwischen der Komposition und dem bildnerischen Kontext finden sich in einem affektiven Bereich und auf einer global gehaltenen Inhaltsebene sowie in strukturellen, formalen und symbolischen Aspekten. Ausgehend von der Beschreibung semiotischer Codes der Komposition, die ich als sinnlich-anschauliche und als expressive Bedeutungskomponenten innerstruktureller Beziehungen und ausdruckstragender Gesten der Musik verstehe, folgt meine Interpretation dem Grundgedanken, daß kraft eines durch soziokulturelle Konventionen bedingten Vorverständnisses die designativen symbolischen Bedeutungen der musikalischen Strukturen im Rahmen eines hermeneutischen Zirkels determiniert werden können. Einige der sinn- und bedeutungstragenden musikalischen Codes sind Gattungskonventionen und Stilkonventionen verpflichtet und kontextabhängig, manche der außermusikalischen funktionalen Aspekte sind einem geistesgeschichtlichen Codesystem von evidenter interpretatorischer Stringenz eingebunden. Die hermeneutische Konkretisierung des Sinns der Komposition erschließt sich letztlich aus der außermusikalisch-kultischen funktionalen Bedeutung der Symbolik.

Eine *intersensuelle Zusammenarbeit* der Sinne, die als Einheitsbildung in der Wahrnehmung definiert ist und die die intermodale, verschiedenen Sinnesgebieten zugeordnete Wahrnehmung leitet[12], ist dafür verantwortlich, daß Gemeinsamkeiten in der Rezeption musikalischer und ikonographischer Parameter zu finden sind[13].
Wenn der Sprachcharakter der vorliegenden Komposition hinsichtlich seiner semiotischen Mitteilungsqualität untersucht wird, können drei Begriffe der Semiotik die Interpretation initiierend lenken:

1. Die Indexe[14] sind stilisierte Analogien zu Affekten (*gestischen bzw. intonierten Anzeichen der seelischen Zustände*[15]). Diese ausdrucksgebundenen Komponenten schlagen sich besonders in der musikalischen Charakteristik nieder.
2. Ikone sind Nachahmungen von Naturlauten und Klängen. Sie gründen auf Bewegungsanalogien, auf Tonmalerei und auf Entsprechungen wie dünn, leicht, hell, räumlich hoch, grell, warm = hoher Ton; dick, schwer, dunkel, räumlich tief, matt, kalt = tiefer Ton[16]. So entsprechen sich z.B. Tonhöhe und Helligkeitsgrad einer Farbe, Tonstärke und Farbintensität, Tondauer und flächige Ausbreitung einer Farbe, Klangfarbe und Farbton. Ikone sind vor allem in der musikalischen Gestik aufbewahrt.

---

[12] Ivo Kohler, *Die Zusammenarbeit der Sinne und das allgemeine Adaptionsproblem*, in: *Handbuch der Psychologie*, hrsg. von Ph. Lersch, Bd. I, Göttingen 1966, S. 635ff.

[13] Diese ganzheitliche Wahrnehmungsweise ist neurophysiologisch belegt: Die Reize, die über das Auge und das Gehör wahrgenommen werden, durchlaufen zuerst stammesgeschichtlich ältere, unspezifische subkortikale Regionen, bevor sie in den spezifischen Zentren der Kortex weiterverarbeitet werden; vgl auch K.-H. Plattig, *Psychophysiologie des Gehirns*, in: Bruhn/Oerter/Rösing (Hg.): *Musikpsychologie. Ein Handbuch in Schlüsselbegriffen*, München 1985, S. 38f.

[14] C. S. Peirce unterscheidet zwischen Ikon, Index und Symbol. In verschiedenen Theorien und Systemen der Semiotik wurde die Terminologie von Peirce übernommen, wobei die Begrifflichkeit jedoch sehr unterschiedlich definiert wurde.

[15] Vladimir Karbusicky (Hrsg.), *Einleitung*, in: *Sinn und Bedeutung in der Musik. Texte zur Entwicklung des musiksemiotischen Denkens*, Darmstadt 1990, S. 11.

[16] In Abwandlung der von Albert Wellek in sechs Kategorien unterteilten »Urentsprechungen«; A. Wellek, *Der Sprachgeist als Doppelempfinder*, in: *Zeitschrift für Ästhetik und allgemeine Kunstwissenschaften* (25) 1931, S. 226–262.

3. Symbole stellen Zusammenhänge her, die nicht aus der Komposition selbst erfaßbar sind, sondern durch Konventionen, Erfahrungen oder Hinweise verständlich werden. Konstitutiv für die tonsymbolische Umsetzung ikonographischer Elemente sind in unserem Beispiel die bildnerische formale Disposition, die Raumaufteilung, die in der Musik als Zeitdimension wirkt, und die Farbmetaphorik mit ihren Beleuchtungseffekten. Diese symbolischen Bezugnahmen finden sich in der Instrumentation, in der melodischen, rhythmischen, harmonischen Disposition und in der formalen Anlage.

Die vorangegangene Bildbetrachtung lenkt die Interpretation der musikalischen Charakteristik, durch sie erfährt die musikalische Analyse Anregungen und Verknüpfungen. Synästhetisch geleitete Assoziationen lassen sich herstellen zu den musikalischen Parametern (Rhythmus, Melodik, Tempo, Dynamik, Instrumentation), der Stimmung und der Struktur der Musik. Indexikalische Assoziationen beziehen sich auf die anfangs verhaltene und dann intensivierte Dynamik, auf die über den Dreiklangsblöcken schwebenden Rhythmen der Viertonmotive als Ausdruck des mystisch Unbestimmten. Eine feierliche Wirkung geht von dem zitierten mittelalterlichen geistlichen Volkslied aus; die archaisch wirkende Melodik und Harmonik verleihen dem Mittelteil der Einleitung einen ruhigen, abgeklärten Charakter.
Vom stimmungshaften Moment geht der nächste Interpretationsschritt weiter über die sinnhafte Anschauung, zum Nachdenken über die Machart der Musik, die sich in der gestischen Qualität der Musik verwirklicht. Die aufsteigenden Tonfolgen und deren zweifache Höhertransposition sind als klangliche Aufhellung zu verstehen, sie stehen als ikonische Zeichen für einen bewegungsgeleiteten, steigenden Gestus. Mit der Aufhellung des Klanges ist ein räumlicher Effekt verbunden.
Die langsame Einleitung der *»Mathis«-Symphonie* nimmt auf die vom mystischen Erlebnis der »musica coelestis« licht- und ausdrucksmetaphorisch durchströmte Darstellung der Grünewaldschen Engel Bezug.

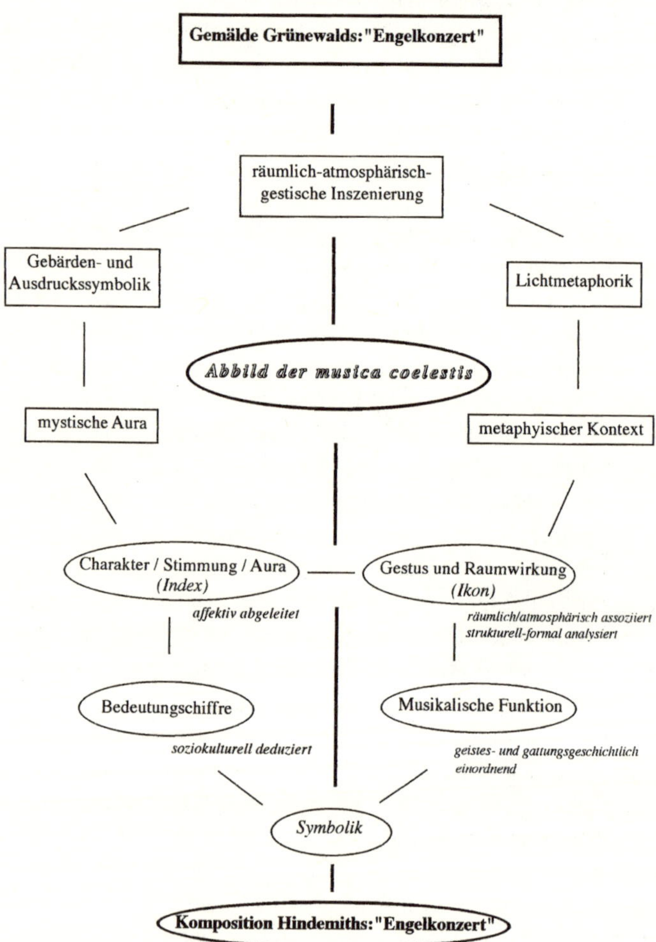

Bezüge zwischen Grünewalds "Engelkonzert"
und Hindemiths Einleitung zur Sinfonie
"Mathis der Maler"("Engelkonzert")
Gemälde Grünewalds: "Engelkonzert"
räumlich-atmosphärisch-gestische Inszenierung
Gebärden- und Ausdruckssymbolik
Lichtmetaphorik
Abbild der musica coelestis
mystische Aura
metaphyischer Kontext
Charakter / Stimmung / Aura
(Index)
Gestus und Raumwirkung
(Ikon)
affektiv abgeleitet
räumlich/atmosphärisch assoziiert
strukturell-formal analysiert
Bedeutungschiffre
Musikalische Funktion
soziokulturell deduziert
geistes- und gattungsgeschichtlich einordnend
Symbolik
Komposition Hindemiths: "Engelkonzert"

Der synkopierte, schwerelos und ruhig wirkende Rhythmus des Viertonmotivs, die zurückgehaltene Dynamik, die sich erst in den beiden letzten Takten des A-Teils crescendierend öffnet, das langsame Tempo und die langen Notenwerte, die steigende Melodik und ihre Höhersequenzierung sowie die helle Instrumentierung können räumliche und atmosphärische Assoziationen hervorrufen: es kann sich damit die Vorstellung eines sich nach der Höhe hin öffnenden, initiierenden Gestus verbinden. Die Quintsequenzierungen und der den A-Teil abschließende *Quintklang (g-d-a-e-h-fis)* erfüllen eine inszenatorische Funktion: Der dominantisch ausgerichtete Fortschreitungsimpetus hat weiterleitenden, spannungsintensivierenden Charakter, weil er die erwartete Auflösung hinauszögert; die Aufmerksamkeit wird auf das Folgende gerichtet.
Im Mittelteil der Einleitung (B) wird mittels des thematisch durch den Liedtext hergestellten Bezugs das Sujet konkretisiert: das zitierte mittelalterliche geistliche Volkslied *Es sungen drei Engel ein süßen Gesang* wird zweimal höher sequenziert und dabei zweimal dynamisch gesteigert, die Klangfarbe hellt sich durch die sukzessive Beteiligung hoher Instrumente auf, durch Oktavierungen werden die Klangkomplexe nach der Höhe hin verbreitert: diese Parameterveränderungen lassen die klanglich-atmosphärische Aufhellung im Sinne der im Bild Grünewalds Gestalt gewordenen Lichtsymbolik und der von links nach rechts heller werdenden Beleuchtung der drei Engel deuten.
Ein Interpretationsansatz, der zwischen der affektiven Assoziation und der später zu besprechenden Symboldeutung vermittelt, läßt sich aus soziokulturellen Zuordnungen und aus daraus deduzierten Reflexionen erschließen. In der Musik gibt es Ebenen normativer, durch Konventionen gebildeter Repräsentationen lebensweltlicher Sinnzusammenhänge. Daraus resultierende Begriffe fungieren als Chiffren für den Milieu- und Gattungscharakter, für die Funktion und die Bedeutung der Musik: Die atmosphärische Charakteristik, die motivische Gestik und die satztechnische Struktur wecken Assoziationen an einen feierlichen, würde-

vollen Habitus. Unter diesem Blickwinkel hat die Einleitung der Symphonie die Qualität einer stilisierten Zeremonie.

Auf dem Bild Grünewalds sind die Engel Zuhörer und ausführende Musiker zugleich. Sie lauschen einerseits ihren eigenen Klängen und sie sind andererseits Repräsentanten der musica coelestis, der im Himmel erklingenden Musik. Andachtstimmung und musikalischer Lobpreis sind auch Inhalt der langsamen Einleitung der *»Mathis«-Symphonie*: die kirchentonalen Anklänge und die oben beschriebene musikalische Charakteristik verweisen auf den religiösen und liturgischen Kontext und verleihen der Komposition die Patina des Alten, des Feierlichen. Die rezeptive Anteilnahme der Engel an der himmlischen Musik ist Gegenstand der Rahmenteile (A, A'): Von der Funktion könnte der erste Teil der Einleitung auf eine liturgische Intonation verweisen. Die Außenteile der Einleitung wären also als Präludium (A-Teil) und als Postludium (A'-Teil) zu verstehen, als Einleitung bzw. als Ausklang der himmlischen Liturgie. Die musizierende Aktivität der Engel spiegelt sich im B-Teil, wenn der Choral als Sinnbild des Engelschores erklingt.

Nach der assoziativ geleiteten Beschreibung der Stimmung, der Ausdruckscharaktere, des musikalischen Gestus und der formalen Struktur der Einleitung, nach der Zuordnung als Chiffre und nach der Deutung der Funktion folgt schließlich als letzter interpretatorischer Schritt die Verknüpfung dieser Ergebnisse mit dem außermusikalischen symbolischen Kontext. Musikalischer Ausdruck, kompositorische Faktur und symbolische Bedeutung bedingen zwar keine unmittelbar zwingende interpretatorische Konsequenz. Die außermusikalische Symbolik hat aber die Struktur der Komposition determiniert und kanalisiert letztendlich ihre Deutung. Die sukzessive bzw. reversible Bezugnahme auf ikonische, indexikalische, chiffrenhafte und symbolische Merkmale der Komposition und eine gegenseitige Beleuchtung dieser Elemente unterstützen die Interpretation.

Symbole sind willkürlich verabredete Zeichen, Sinnbilder von Ideen, Gedanken oder Gefühlen. Ein Wort, ein Bild oder ein Musikstück ist

symbolisch, wenn es über sich hinaus auf eine tiefere Bedeutungsschicht verweist. In der Einleitung der *»Mathis«-Symphonie* findet sich ein ähnlicher symbolischer Kontext wie in Hindemiths *Symphonie »Die Harmonie der Welt«* und seiner gleichnamigen Oper: Dort bezieht sich Hindemith auf die von Boethius und der Antike (vor allem durch Pythagoras) beeinflußte mittelalterliche Auffassung von der Musik als Abbild der Weltharmonie und auf dessen Einteilung der Musik in drei Klassen: Die Sätze tragen die Bezeichnungen »Musica instrumentalis«, »Musica humana«, »Musica mundana«. Boethius' Lehre von den musikalischen Zahlenproportionen (*De institutione musica*, um 500) baute auf dem Fundament orientalischer und antiker Musikanschauung auf: In der Anschauung von der »musica mundana« sind die mathematischen Gesetzlichkeiten, wie sie sich in den Intervallproportionen der klingenden Musik finden, auch Grundlage der Planetenbewegungen, diese metaphysisch aufgefaßten Zahlenverhältnisse repräsentieren kosmologische Ordnungsnormen und Naturgesetze, und sie sind damit Sinnbild des Weltprinzips.
In der mittelalterlichen Lehre von der Sphärenharmonie, der »musica mundana« – ihrerseits inspiriert vor allem durch Boethius und Martianus Capella, u. a. in verschiedenen Varianten dargelegt bei Hucbald, Remigius, Regino von Prüm, Johannes Scotus und Bernhard von Clairvaux – wurden die Gesetzmäßigkeiten der Planetenbewegungen auf übergeordnete Naturgesetze bezogen. Man stellte sich vor, der Lauf der acht Planeten vollziehe sich in konzentrischen Bahnen um die Erde: Die Abstände der einzelnen Planetensphären (die sich wie Sprossen einer Leiter zum Himmel erstrecken) entsprächen bestimmten Intervallproportionen und Tonhöhen; alles, was sich bewege, verursache Klang, darum müsse das Sternensystem, bestehend aus den Planeten und der »ultima sphaera« (»sphaera coelestis«) oder den Fixsternen, den vollkommensten Zusammenklang, nämlich die Oktave, erzeugen[17].

[17] Joseph Smits van Waesberghe, *Musikerziehung, Lehre und Theorie der Musik im Mittelalter* (= *Musikgeschichte in Bildern*, Bd. III, hrsg. von H. Besseler u. W. Bach-

Alle Schönheit beruhe auf Proportion, Maß und Zahl, so herrsche im Kosmos ewige Harmonie.
In seiner *Unterweisung im Tonsatz* wies Hindemith auf die gemeinsamen Gesetzmäßigkeiten der Proportionen hin, wie sie sich in der Obertonreihe und im Makrokosmos fänden[18]. In diesem Kontext sind in der *»Mathis«*-Einleitung die folgenden Intervalle und Symbolzahlen von Bedeutung: Oktave und Quinte sowie die Zahlen Drei und Vier. Oktave und Quinte als die einfachsten Intervallproportionen (1:2, 2:3) symbolisieren die vollkommene Harmonie[19]. Sie sind repräsentiert in den oktavierten Orgelpunkten der A-Teile, in der Aufschichtung des cantus firmus innerhalb der Oktave im B-Teil (*des-f-a-des*) und in der für die Satz- und die Formanlage konstitutiven Herausstellung der Quinte (man siehe hierzu die harmonisch der Einleitung übergeordnete Quintenstruktur, die Quintschichtung der Tetrachorde).
Seit dem Mittelalter ist besonders die Zahl Drei Symbol der göttlichen Dreieinigkeit, sie ist gleichzeitig das *Symbol alles Spirituellen*[20] und damit Abbild der göttlichen Weltordnung. In der mittelalterlichen Musiktheorie brachte man die Zahl Drei mit der himmlischen Engelshierarchie in Verbindung: Pseudo-Johannes de Muris beschrieb im 13. Jahrhundert die Engelshierarchie, die in 3x3 Engelschöre untergliedert sei. Der dreifache Kyrieruf entspreche den dreimal drei Chören der

---

mann), Leipzig o. J., S. 152. 1960 beobachtete Robert Leigthon, daß die an der Oberfläche der Sonne aufsteigenden und absinkenden Materieballen sich innerhalb von Minuten auflösen, um neuen Granulen Platz zu machen. In diesen Vorgängen hat er Regelmäßigkeiten entdeckt: Er stellte fest, daß sich in dem Auf und Ab der Granulen die Sonnenoberfläche mit 0,5 km in der Sekunde in einem fünfminütigen Zyklus hebt und senkt, d.h. schwingt; könnte man die Bewegung hörbar machen, wäre ein Ton zu hören, im Bereich von 2 bis 4,5 Hertz; s. hierzu Rudolf Kippenhahn, *Der Stern, von dem wir leben. Den Geheimnissen der Sonne auf der Spur*, Stuttgart 1990, S. 205ff.

[18] Paul Hindemith, *Unterweisung im Tonsatz I. Theoretischer Teil*, a.a.O., S. 27.

[19] Waesberghe, a.a.O.

[20] Aaron J. Gurjewitsch, *Das Weltbild des mittelalterlichen Menschen*, München 1980, S. 239f.

Engel[21]. Bernhard von Clairvaux meinte: *Ohne Zweifel bezieht sich die Zahl »Drei« wegen der heiligen Dreieinigkeit auf den Glauben und die Zahl »Vier« wegen der vier Kardinaltugenden auf die sittliche Lebensweise.*[22] Die Taktart der Einleitung (9/4) entspricht der mittelalterlichen Mensur »tempus perfectum cum prolatione maiore«, als Dreierpotenz ist sie die vollkommenste und symbolhaltigste Repräsentation einer Taktart; die Tempovorgabe (Viertel = 66), das insgesamt dreimal erklingende steigende Viertonmotiv, die jeweils dreimal erklingenden Dreiklänge in den A-Teilen, die dreifach geteilten Streicherstimmen im A-Teil, der von drei Unisono-Streicherstimmen getragene Kontrapunkt zum cantus firmus und dessen Rhythmisierung im Dreiermetrum (Ziffer 1ff.), der thematisch mit dem Engelmusizieren verbundene, dreimal intonierte Cantus firmus (Großterzraster *des-f-a-des*) sowie die gesamte Formanlage (die drei Formteile der Einleitung: ABA') stellen eindeutig die Symbolik der Zahl Drei heraus. Die Einleitung des Satzes spiegelt so den christlich-theologischen Hintergrund und den symbolischen Kontext der Trinitätslehre sowie die Hierarchie der drei Engelsebenen.

Die Zahl Vier – sie ist in den A-Teilen in der Gestalt der Tetrachorde, der Viertonmotive, präsent – spielte in der mittelalterlichen Vorstellung von der Harmonie der Welt ebenfalls eine wichtige Rolle: man unterschied u.a. vier Erdteile, vier Temperamente und vier Winde; die Harmonie der vier Elemente bildete die Grundlage für den Aufbau der Natur; die Abfolge der vier Jahreszeiten wurde in musikalischen Tonrelationen gesehen, nämlich als ein musikalischer Tetrachord, der ältesten Tongruppierung bei den Griechen; der Kosmos enthielt nach dieser Auffassung *die Weltseele in einem tetrachordalen Verhältnis*[23]. Die Multiplikation der Zahlen Drei und Vier (s. die jeweils dreifache Ver-

---

[21] *Legenda aurea*, S. 846, s. Hammerstein, a.a.O., S. 38.

[22] H. Meyer/R. Suntrup, *Lexikon der mittelalterlichen Zahlensymbolik* (= *Münstersche Mittelalterschriften* 56), München 1987, S. 529. Die Zahl Vier ist auch das Symbol der vier Evangelisten.

[23] Waesberghe, a.a.O., S. 39.

wendung der Viertonmotive in den A-Teilen) steht im mystischen Sinne für das *Eindringen des Geistes in die Materie, die Erleuchtung der Welt durch die Glaubenswahrheiten, die Errichtung der katholischen Kirche, die von den zwölf Aposteln symbolisiert wurde*[24]. Die Wesensgleichheit der trinitarischen göttlichen Personen spiegelt sich in den Viertonmotivsequenzen: die Viertonmotive sind wesensgleich, aber durch die Sequenzierungen unterschieden.

Die semantische Interpretation führte letztendlich zur geistesgeschichtlichen Einordnung der Symbolik und stellte einen dem Begriff der griechischen »musiké« (dort als Einheit von Sprache, Ton, Rhythmus und Gebärde verstanden) vergleichbaren Zusammenhang zwischen Ausdruck und Form sowie dem kulturellen Kontext der Komposition her. Aristoteles' Behauptung, Weisheit (»sophia«) setze Vollendung der »techné«, also meisterliches Können und die Summe allen Wissen voraus[25], läßt sich für Hindemiths *Engelkonzert* in dem Sinne reklamieren, daß der geistige Kontext der programmatischen Vorlage in der Summe von Natur- und Geisteswissenschaften, von Musik, Mathematik, Theologie, Philosophie und Kunst in der Komposition widergespiegelt ist.

---

[24] Gurjewitsch, a.a.O., S. 239f.

[25] Aristoteles, *Nikomachische Ethik*, 1141a12. Hierzu Thrasybulos Georgiades, *Nennen und Erklingen. Die Zeit als Logos*, Göttingen 1985, S. 234.

Gerd Sannemüller

Hindemith-Tage in Lübeck (1932)

I.

Schon im Jahre 1896 hatten in der geschichtsbewußten Hansestadt Lübeck, die auch im 20. Jahrhundert eine große musikalische Tradition vor allem der evangelischen Kirchenmusik pflegte, Bürger einen »Verein der Musikfreunde« gegründet, um die Grundlagen für ein lebendiges städtisches Musikleben verstärken und erweitern zu können. Es ist symptomatisch, daß bereits im ersten Jahr und sehr schnell die Mitgliederzahl von 840 erreicht wurde[1]. Diese Impulse sind durchaus denen vergleichbar, die einige Lübecker Musikfreunde im 18. Jahrhundert zur Einrichtung öffentlicher Konzerte veranlaßte und die auf Initiative des Organisten an St. Marien, Johann Paul Kuntzen, dort im Amt von 1733 bis 1757, etabliert wurden.

Zu Beginn des 20. Jahrhunderts entstanden künstlerische Glanzpunkte für die Stadt durch das Wirken bedeutender Dirigenten wie Hermann Abendroth (in Lübeck 1905–1911) und Wilhelm Furtwängler (in Lübeck 1911–1915). Beide begannen von hier aus große Karrieren. In den Jahren 1926–1928 leitete der Konzertpianist Edwin Fischer die Sinfoniekonzerte, dem auf seinen Vorschlag 1928–1929 Eugen Jochum von seiner Kieler Position aus folgte. Wenn auch z.B. Furtwängler neben anderen Zeitgenossen u.a. am 10. Februar 1912 *Prélude à l'après-midi d'un faune* von Claude Debussy (1894), am 9. November 1912 die *Kindertotenlieder* von Gustav Mahler (1904) und am 1. März 1913 *Der Zauberlehrling* von Paul Dukas (1897) aufführte, so bildeten doch über-

[1] Klaus Matthias, *Musikgeschichte Lübecks im letzten Halbjahrhundert*, in: *800 Jahre Musik in Lübeck*, hrsg. von Antjekathrin Graßmann und Werner Neugebauer, Lübeck 1982, S. 156–200.

wiegend Kompositionen der klassisch-romantischen Tradition die Programme; Musik der Gegenwart erklang in weit geringerem Maße.
Der allgemeine kulturelle und politische Wandel, der dem Zusammenbruch von 1918 folgte, setzte auch das Bewußtsein einer notwendigen Bewegung zum »Neuen« in der Kunst frei. »Neu« als Terminus ist kennzeichnend für einen befreienden Aufbruch, ohne nur eine Distanz zu Früherem oder eine einseitige Einordnung von gegenwärtiger Musik schlechthin zu beabsichtigen. So sind mit ihm ausdrücklich auch Forderungen nach Überwindung konventioneller und beharrender Positionen verbunden und intensive Auseinandersetzungen um ästhetische Fragestellungen, kompositorische Strömungen und gesellschaftliche Begründungen sowie die Forderung nach einem stärkeren Hervortreten von Musik der Zeit im öffentlichen Leben eingeschlossen.
Auch in Lübeck sind Bemühungen um Neue Musik festzustellen, wenngleich sie erst am Ende der zwanziger Jahre für die Öffentlichkeit manifester wurden. Es bestanden gegenüber dem Angebot an traditioneller Musik nur sporadische Aufführungen aus dem zeitgenössischen Schaffen der Nachkriegszeit, organisiert durch verschiedene private und öffentliche Einrichtungen, Gesellschaften, Vereine und dergleichen. Erst allmählich setzte sich die Auffassung durch, daß neue Musik breitere Berücksichtigung finden müsse. Wieder einmal ist es für eine Stadt in der Größe Lübecks ein bemerkenswertes Ereignis und exemplarisch für die Aufgeschlossenheit und Aktivität einiger musikinteressierter Bürger, daß sie bewußt zu einer Ausweitung des Konzert-Spektrums beitrugen und am 27. Juli 1930 die Vereinigung »Neue Musik in Lübeck e.V.« gründeten, eine Initiative, die gerade auch in der Beziehung zu Paul Hindemith besondere Akzente erfährt. Folgender Pressehinweis verdeutlicht Bestrebungen und Ziele:
In das Vereinsregister ist eine Vereinigung »Neue Musik in Lübeck e.V.« eingetragen worden. Die Vereinigung ist eine Arbeitsgemeinschaft und macht es sich zur Aufgabe, die geistigen Bewegungen der Musik der Gegenwart durch Vorträge und Aufführungen darzustellen, und will

den Hörern Gelegenheit geben, die Werke der lebenden Generation kennenzulernen und sich mit ihren Problemen auseinanderzusetzen. Für den Winter 1930/31 ist eine Folge von drei Vorträgen und fünf Konzerten in Aussicht genommen.[2]

Die Initiatoren erstrebten also, die Vielfalt der gegenwärtigen Musik bekannt zu machen, unabhängig von Richtungen und Stilen, doch kritisch in der Auswahl. Nach ihren Vorstellungen sollten Kammermusikwerke mit vertiefenden Einführungsvorträgen vorgestellt werden, die durch die gezielte Klärung von Sachverhalten Hörerfahrungen aufbauen und den Zugang erleichtern sollten.

Die Initiative zur Gründung der Vereinigung ging entscheidend von Dr. Fritz von Borries aus, der in der ganzen Zeit ihres Bestehens 1. Vorsitzender und ihr wichtigster Anreger und Organisator blieb[3]. Seinen Einsatz charakterisieren auch eine Reihe von eigenen Vorträgen, u.a. »Warum Neue Musik in Lübeck?«, »Zur Erstaufführung von Hindemiths Cardillac« und »Einführung in das Klavierwerk von Arnold Schönberg«. Konsequent, voller Idealismus und obwohl in der Breite wenig beachtet, hat der Vereinsvorstand jede Saison neue Programme vorgelegt. Unabhängig von städtischen und kommerziellen Institutionen, verfügte die Vereinigung zwar nicht über große Mitgliederzahlen, jedoch nahmen an ihren Veranstaltungen ca. 100 Zuhörer teil, deren Zahl in etwa konstant blieb.

Bei der Vereinsgründung wandte sich der Vorstand an verschiedene Persönlichkeiten mit der Bitte um Stellungnahme, u.a. auch an Paul Hindemith, dessen Antwort lautete: *Ich hoffe, daß Ihre Bemühungen zur Einführung heutiger Musik in Lübeck von dem Erfolg gekrönt sind,*

---

2 *Lübeckische Blätter* (72) 1930, S. 439.

3 Dr. Fritz von Borries (1892–1975), zuletzt Oberreichsbahnrat, war in Lübeck auch als vorzüglicher Pianist bekannt, ohne je Berufsmusiker gewesen zu sein. Wie der Sohn Kaspar von Borries mitteilte, war er mit dem in den Briefen Hindemiths an seine Frau erwähnten Fritz von Borries weder identisch noch verwandt (s. Paul Hindemith, *»Das private Logbuch«. Briefe an seine Frau Gertrud*, hrsg. von Friederike Becker und Giselher Schubert, Mainz 1995, S. 104, Anm. 322).

den sie verdienen. Da meine Stücke, sofern sie gut sind, es heute fast nirgendwo mehr schwer haben, aufgeführt und anerkannt zu werden (nur auf einigen verlorenen Posten glaubt man noch, gegen eine natürliche Entwicklung anrennen zu müssen), wird auch ein kunstinteressiertes Publikum in Lübeck nicht abseits stehen bleiben können. Ihnen und Ihren Mitarbeitern das Beste wünschend. Paul Hindemith.[4]

Bedauerlicherweise sind Veranstaltungsprogramme, eine Satzung, Protokolle, Mitgliederlisten und dergleichen nicht mehr vorhanden. Ein Archiv wurde nicht aufgebaut, persönliche Verluste lassen sich aus der zurückliegenden langen Zeit erklären. Ein großer Teil an Materialien ist vor allem durch den Bombenangriff von 1942 vernichtet worden. Die wenigen vorhandenen Dokumente hat Fritz von Borries aus seinem persönlichen Besitz zur Verfügung gestellt. Wegen zunehmender Schwierigkeiten und um erwarteten Eingriffen durch die NS-Kulturpolitik zuvorzukommen, löste sich die Vereinigung »Neue Musik in Lübeck e.V.« am 1. Mai 1933 selbst auf[5].

Durch die Uraufführung seines *3. Streichquartetts* op. 16 während der »Donaueschinger Kammermusik-Aufführungen zur Förderung zeitgenössischer Tonkunst« 1921 hatte Hindemith beträchtliches Aufsehen erregt und große Zustimmung erfahren. Doch auch Begleitskandale knüpften sich immer wieder an seinen Namen, so bei Aufführungen der Einakter *Mörder, Hoffnung der Frauen*, *Das Nusch-Nuschi* und *Sancta Susanna* (1921 und 1922), der *Kammermusik Nr. 1* op. 24a (Uraufführung Donaueschingen 1922) sowie des *Lehrstücks* (Text: Bert Brecht, Uraufführung Baden-Baden 1929). Heftige Protestaktionen diffamierten Hindemith z.B. als »Bürgerschreck«[6] und stempelten ihn noch vor den Nationalsozialisten polemisch als »Kulturbolschewisten«, als »Um-

---

[4] *Lübeckische Blätter* (72) 1930, S. 754.

[5] Mitteilung von Fritz von Borries (16. Januar 1972).

[6] Erstmals polemisch bezogen auf die Aufführung der *Kammermusik Nr. 1* op. 24a in Donaueschingen von Alfred Heuß in seinem Beitrag *Der Foxtrott im Konzertsaal*, in: *Zeitschrift für Musik* (90) 1923, S. 54f.

stürzler« und »Bilderstürmer« ab. Daß Hindemith aber auch Verständnis für seinen Stilwillen und die Vielseitigkeit seines Schaffens erfuhr, bestätigt sich nicht zuletzt durch die Berufung an die Hochschule für Musik in Berlin zum 1. Mai 1927. An dieser für die Vermittlung und vielfältige Erprobung von Musik der Gegenwart so repräsentativen Stätte übernahm er mit 32 Jahren die Aufgaben eines Kompositionslehrers.

In Lübeck findet sich der Name Hindemith erstmals auf dem Programm eines Sinfoniekonzertes vom 6. November 1922 mit einer Aufführung der Tanzsuite aus *Das Nusch-Nuschi* neben der *Feuervogel*-Suite von Igor Strawinsky, der *Musik für Orchester* von Rudi Stephan und der sinfonischen Suite *Tag und Nacht* von Ernst Ludwig Schellenberg. Geleitet wurde das Konzert von Karl Mannstaedt (1918–1925 1. Kapellmeister, 1926 Generalmusikdirektor am Stadttheater), einem Schüler Hermann Abendroths und bekannt durch sein Eintreten für zeitgenössische Musik. Die Mehrzahl der Zuhörer reagierte verständnislos und ablehnend.

Im Zeitraum bis 1932 wurden außerdem folgende Werke Hindemiths in Lübeck aufgeführt:

3. Februar 1924: *Kammermusik Nr. 1* op. 24a; Zwei Lieder aus op. 18: *Traum* und *Wie St. Franciscus schwebt ich in der Luft*

7. Januar 1929: *Konzert für Orchester* op. 38 (Städtisches Sinfoniekonzert, Leitung Eugen Jochum)

1. Oktober 1930: Kantate *Frau Musica* und die Spielmusik *Ein Jäger aus Kurpfalz* (aus Anlaß des 70jährigen Bestehens der Liedertafel des Gewerbevereins unter Mitwirkung des Städtischen Orchesters und der Lübecker Singschule)

Hindemiths *Kammermusik Nr. 4* op. 36 Nr. 3, vorgesehen für das Sinfoniekonzert am 5. und 6. Dezember 1926 unter der Leitung von

Edwin Fischer, mußte wegen Erkrankung der Solistin Alma Moodie (Violine) abgesagt werden.

In den Konzerten der Vereinigung »Neue Musik in Lübeck e.V.« erklangen – außer den Werken während der Hindemith-Tage im November 1932 – aus dessen Schaffen:
12. November 1930: Vier Stücke aus op. 37 (Klavierabend Karl Hermann Pillney)
17. November 1931: Chormusik (Titel nicht näher belegt; Leitung Fritz Jöde)
10. Februar 1932: *Das Marienleben* op. 27 (Elli Wilke, Walter Kraft)
20. Januar 1933: *Suite 1922* op. 26, *Klaviermusik* op. 37 I, *Fünftonstücke* (Klavierabend Herbert Schulze)[7]

Unter den verschiedenen Voraussetzungen lag es nahe, einen so repräsentativen Komponisten wie Hindemith für Konzerte der Vereinigung in Lübeck auch persönlich zu gewinnen. Über Vorurteile und Polemiken setzte sich der Vorstand im Bewußtsein von Hindemiths künstlerischer Bedeutung und seines Ansehens mit Entschiedenheit hinweg. Um ihn, der bis zu diesem Zeitpunkt als Interpret noch nicht in der Hansestadt aufgetreten war, einzuladen, suchte Dr. von Borries, der Vorbereitung und Durchführung der geplanten Hindemith-Veranstaltungen mit großem Elan allein realisierte, ihn in der Berliner Musikhochschule auf, wo sich beide erstmals begegneten. Das Datum ist nicht genau auszumachen; es muß zwischen Ende Juni und September 1932 angesetzt werden. Hindemith gab sofort seine Zustimmung und sagte seine Teilnahme verbindlich zu. Auch Termine und Programme wurden schon

7 Außer Hindemith wurden folgende Komponisten in den Veranstaltungen der Lübekker Vereinigung aufgeführt: Ferruccio Busoni, Arnold Schönberg (*Das Buch der hängenden Gärten*, das Klavierwerk der Jahre 1909–1928), Igor Strawinsky, Darius Milhaud, Mátyás Seiber, Hugo Distler, Walter Kraft. Bei einer Ankündigung »Musik des Ostens« (24. Februar 1933) fehlen die Komponistennamen.

bei dieser Begegnung festgelegt. Verabredet wurden drei Veranstaltungen innerhalb einer Woche, darunter ein Einführungsvortrag, den auf Vorschlag Hindemiths Dr. Heinrich Strobel übernehmen und der im Rahmen einer bestehenden Vortragsserie in der »Gemeinnützigen Gesellschaft« stattfinden sollte. Strobel, damals Musikkritiker des »Berliner Börsen-Courier«, einer der ersten Hindemith-Biographen, wählte das Thema »Hindemiths Entwicklung als Spiegel der Neuen Musik« und hielt diesen Vortrag am 22. November 1932[8]. Die möglichst vielseitige Auswahl der Kompositionen und ihre Reihenfolge im Programmablauf bestimmte Hindemith selbst. Er war sofort einverstanden mit den Vorschlägen wegen der zu beteiligenden, meist in Lübeck oder Hamburg lebenden Interpreten. Bereitwillig stellte er sein persönliches Mitwirken als Bratscher in Aussicht. Als Klavierpartner stand Walter Kraft zur Verfügung, der 1929 mit 24 Jahren in das Organistenamt an St. Marien berufen worden war, das mit Namen wie Franz Tunder und Dietrich Buxtehude eine illustre Tradition begründet hatte. Nach Orgelstudien in Hamburg war Kraft 1928 Kompositionsstudent von Hindemith auf der Musikhochschule in Berlin gewesen. Sowohl als erfahrener Pianist als auch durch Einführungsvorträge stand er der Vereinigung »Neue Musik in Lübeck e.V.« häufig zur Verfügung.

Folgende Kammermusikwerke bildeten das Programm des ersten Konzertes, das am Donnerstag, den 24. November 1932, im Saal der »Gemeinnützigen Gesellschaft« stattfand:

Kleine Sonate für Viola d'amore und Klavier op. 25 Nr. 2
Kanonische Sonatine für zwei Flöten op. 31 Nr. 3
Die Serenaden für Sopran, Oboe, Bratsche und Violoncello op. 35
Sonate für Bratsche und Klavier op. 11 Nr. 4

[8] Strobel war nach dem 2. Weltkrieg Schriftleiter der Zeitschrift *Melos* und anschließend Leiter der Musikabteilung des Südwestfunks Baden-Baden. Nach Auskunft des Senders (Dokumentation Musik) sind weder das Vortragsmanuskript noch Hinweise auf die verwendeten Schallplattenbeispiele auffindbar.

Auf Anregung Hindemiths wurde der am 20. Juni 1932 in Plön uraufgeführte *Plöner Musiktag* für Sonnabend, den 26. November 1932, ins Programm aufgenommen und bildete somit im Kolosseum den Abschluß der Veranstaltungsreihe.
Es bleibt bemerkenswert, daß Hindemith, eine der herausragenden Gestalten im deutschen Musikleben und eine äußerst beanspruchte Persönlichkeit, bereit war, für einen Aufenthalt von mehreren Tagen nach Lübeck zu kommen. In der Reihe der von der Vereinigung organisierten Konzerte blieb der Zyklus der drei Hindemith gewidmeten Abende, noch dazu innerhalb einer Woche, denn auch die Ausnahme. Zweifellos erhöhte sich die Attraktivität der Veranstaltungen durch seine persönliche Anwesenheit und seine Beteiligung als Instrumentalist. Sein Auftreten erregte beim Lübecker Publikum große Zustimmung und Bewunderung. Brachten ihm schon seine spontane Aufgeschlossenheit und Kontaktfähigkeit alle Sympathien ein, so faszinierte erst recht die Einheit des schöpferischen Musikers und des überzeugenden Interpreten, eine Einheit, deren Facetten sich bekanntlich durch den Kompositionslehrer, den Musiktheoretiker und in späterer Lebenszeit den Dirigenten noch vielseitiger rundeten.

II.

Die Kompositionen aus Hindemiths Lübecker Programm stammen aus seiner Frühphase der Jahre 1919–1924. Sein persönliches Mitwirken spiegelt unmittelbar sein begeistertes Engagement, das eigenes Musizieren stets in ihm auslöst. Darüber hinaus beleuchtet seine Werkauswahl bezeichnende Elemente seines Personalstils. *Hindemiths frühe Kammermusik ist Stoff für das Musikmachen, aber es ist zugleich Kammermusik, in der sich die Entwicklung des Komponisten mit besonderer Intensität niederschlägt.*[9]

---

[9] Ludwig Finscher, *Zur Bedeutung der Kammermusik in Hindemiths Frühwerk*, in: Hindemith-Jahrbuch 1988/XVII, S. 24.

Am Anfang der zwanziger Jahre macht sich allgemein ein stärkeres Interesse an Alter Musik bemerkbar, verbunden mit wissenschaftlichen Forschungen und Versuchen einer Wiederbelebung historischer Musikpraxis. Hindemith war seit seiner Jugend für Problemstellungen um Alte Musik sehr aufgeschlossen[10]. Schon in jungen Jahren hatte er die Kompositionen für Violine solo von Johann Sebastian Bach studiert und öffentlich gespielt. Besonders vertraut war er mit der Chaconne aus der Partita d-moll, die er bereits bei einem Konservatoriumskonzert am 7. Juni 1915 vorgetragen hatte. A. Corelli (La Folia), G. B. Vitali (Ciacona) und H.I.F. Biber (vor allem die Sonate c-moll) gehören außerdem zu seinem frühen Repertoire. Fast zufällig entdeckte er 1922 bei dem Frankfurter Geigenbauer Eugen Sprenger eine Viola d'amore, über die er im September 1922 sehr angeregt an Emmy Ronnefeldt schreibt: *Ich habe einen neuen Sport: ich spiele Viola d'amour, ein ganz herrliches Instrument, das ganz verschollen ist und für das nur eine ganz kleine Literatur besteht. Das Schönste, was Du Dir an Klang vorstellen kannst; eine nicht zu beschreibende Süße und Weichheit. Es ist heikel zu spielen, aber ich spiele es mit großer Begeisterung und zur Freude aller Zuhörer.*[11] Der warme, dunkle Klang und die spieltechnischen Besonderheiten faszinierten ihn nicht nur als praktizierenden Musiker, sondern eröffneten ihm auch weitere Perspektiven, die zu seiner Auseinandersetzung mit historischer Musik beitrugen. Die Konzerte in Italien ab 1925 mit der Cembalistin Alice Ehlers, ab 1927 im Trio mit Maurits

---

[10] *Zweifellos hat das Studium der mittelalterlichen Musik ihn* (Hindemith) *entschieden gefördert. In ihm hat er eine machtvolle Stütze gefunden, wie einer, der zu seinen Ursprüngen zurückgefunden hat.* Darius Milhaud in: Claude Rostand, *Gespräche mit Darius Milhaud*, Hamburg o.J., deutsche Ausgabe S. 649; s. ferner Paul Hindemith, *Harmonieübungen für Fortgeschrittene Teil II*, Mainz 1949, S. 21: *Gerade die Musik vor 1500 ist aber, wie sich in den letzten Jahrzehnten so oft erwiesen hat, für den heutigen Musiker eine unerschöpfliche Quelle der Anregung und Erleuchtung, die an Wichtigkeit der Musik des achtzehnten und neunzehnten Jahrhunderts mindestens gleichkommt, ja in mancher Hinsicht sie noch übertrifft.*

[11] *Jugendbriefe von Paul Hindemith aus den Jahren 1916–1919*, in: Hindemith-Jahrbuch 1972/II, S. 207.

Frank (Viola da gamba) vertieften diese Erfahrungen[12]. Ab Mitte der zwanziger Jahre bearbeitete er immer mehr für die Viola d'amore geeignete Literatur und nahm sie in sein Repertoire auf (u.a. Ariosti, Biber, Erlebach, Petzold, Rust, Stamitz, Vivaldi). Hindemiths Aufgeschlossenheit für Alte Musik dokumentieren ebenfalls die Teilnahme an der Freiburger Tagung für »Deutsche Orgelkunst« 1926 und vor allem seine vielseitige Tätigkeit in der renommierten Instrumentensammlung der Berliner Musikhochschule gemeinsam mit Curt Sachs und Georg Schünemann, die u.a. auf den praktischen Einsatz alter Blas- und Streichinstrumente und das Erreichen eines möglichst originalen Klanges abzielte[13]. Im Kompositionsunterricht bei Arnold Mendelssohn und Bernhard Sekles hatte Hindemith bereits polyphone Formen in Werken zeitgenössischer Komponisten kennengelernt und eingehend studiert. Die Violinsonaten solo von Max Reger spielten in diesem Zusammenhang eine nachhaltige Rolle; zweifellos übten sie für ihn in den Jahren 1916–1921 stilprägende Einflüsse aus. Regers Werke verstärkten Hindemiths Beziehungen zur Barockmusik, ihrer Linearität und ihrer Polyphonie, und damit seine vielseitigen Neigungen zu deren Formprinzipien Satzanlagen und kontrapunktischen Techniken. Auf das Vorbild Regers weist z.B. besonders deutlich der Schlußsatz der *Sonate für Bratsche allein* op. 11 Nr. 5 (1919) hin, eine Passacaglia und die erste, die Hindemith komponierte[14].

---

[12] Als ein Ergebnis künstlerischer und wissenschaftlicher Aktivitäten ist Hindemiths Vortrag *Über die Viola d'amore* anzusehen, den er am 20. Mai 1937 in Cremona gehalten hat, abgedruckt u.a. in: Paul Hindemith, *Aufsätze, Vorträge, Reden*, hrsg. von Giselher Schubert, Zürich/Mainz 1994, S. 125–130.

[13] S. dazu Franz Bullmann, *Hindemiths Musizieren alter Musik und die Instrumenten-Sammlung der Berliner Musikhochschule*, in: Franz Bullmann, Wolfgang Rathert, Dietmar Schenk (Hrsg.), *Paul Hindemith in Berlin*, HdK-Archiv, Band 2, Berlin 1997, S. 47–54.

[14] S. dazu Giselher Schubert, *Paul Hindemith und der Neobarock. Historische und stilistische Notizen*, in: Hindemith-Jahrbuch 1983/XII, S. 20–40, ferner Günther Metz, *Hindemith und die Alte Musik*, in: *Alte Musik im 20. Jahrhundert. Wandlun-*

Neobarocke Elemente, bei Hindemith am stärksten ausgeprägt in den Jahren 1921–1927, aber unterschiedlich integriert bis in seine letzte Lebenszeit hinein, sind in den meisten Programmpunkten des Lübecker Kammermusikabends präsent. Diese Haltung bedeutet jedoch für ihn nie eine rückwärts gewandte Anlehnung an eine Überlieferung, sondern sie ist lebendige Auseinandersetzung, die Vergangenes und Gegenwärtiges umspannt. Vor allem charakterisiert sie seinen dezidierten Willen zur stilistischen Erweiterung: *Wichtig ist immer das, was heute geschieht. Wer sich in die Historie zurückzieht, ist feige. Seine Kraft geht der heutigen Musik verloren, die darum längere Zeit benötigen wird, sich auf eine höhere Stufe zu entwickeln. Früher hat es auch Schund gegeben. Er sollte heute ebensowenig gespielt werden, wie neuzeitlicher Unfug.*[15]
Als beredtes Beispiel für Hindemiths Neigung zu Alter Musik erweist sich die dreisätzige *Kleine Sonate für Viola d'amore und Klavier* op. 25 Nr. 2 (1922), die den Lübecker Kammermusikabend eröffnete. Sie wurde im Mai 1922 komponiert, ihr erster und dritter Satz am 12. bzw. 28. Mai in Frankfurt am Main, der zweite Satz am 26. Mai in Donaueschingen. Die Uraufführung erfolgte bereits im Juni 1922 in Heidelberg durch den Komponisten und die sich intensiv für Hindemiths Schaffen einsetzende Pianistin Emma Lübbecke-Job. Zunächst ohne Opuszahl und beim Frankfurter Konzert vom 13. Mai 1925 noch als op. 25b angegeben, wird die Sonate bei der Wiesbadener Aufführung am 15. März 1928 als

---

gen und Formen ihrer Rezeption, hrsg. von Giselher Schubert (Frankfurter Studien Bd. V), S. 93–112, hier besonders S. 101, Anm. 15: *So bezweifelbar daher die Richtigkeit von Schuberts Annahme* [...] *ist, daß Hindemith »kontrapunktische Satzanlagen offenbar zunächst weniger aus Werken barocker Komponisten, sondern wohl eher und zumindest gleichzeitig aus Werken >moderner< Komponisten kennengelernt habe«, so richtig ist seine Feststellung: Kontrapunktische Techniken oder historische musikalische Ausdrucksformen hat Hindemith demnach niemals als etwas Vergangenes erfahren, von dem uns eine grundsätzliche, unaufhebbare Distanz zu trennen scheint.* – Vgl. auch Reinhold Brinkmann, *Max Reger und die neue Musik*, in: *Max Reger, 1873–1973. Ein Symposium*, hrsg. von Klaus Röhrig, Wiesbaden 1974, S. 83–111.

[15] Paul Hindemith, *Forderung an den Laien*, in: ders., *Aufsätze, Vorträge, Reden*, a.a.O., S. 43f.

op. 25 Nr. 2 eingeordnet. Kennzeichnend sind musikantische Spielfiguren barocker Prägung vor allem im ersten Satz, der – ohne eigentliche thematische Entwicklung – mit einer gelösten Musizierfreude überzeugt und durch die erweiterte Tonalität (auch Bitonales) und das spannungsreiche lineare Profil bemerkenswert ist.

Die *Kanonische Sonatine für zwei Flöten* op. 31 Nr. 3, komponiert im August und September 1923 und dem befreundeten Poul Hagemann gewidmet, ist dreisätzig. Mit ihren unterschiedlichen Ausdruckscharakteren steht auch sie einer barocken Tradition nahe. Durch ihre Übersichtlichkeit und die Besetzung erweist die Sonatine ihre Eignung als pädagogisch motivierte »Gebrauchsmusik« und ist damit eines der ersten Stücke Hindemiths für diese Zwecke[16].

Die Serenaden op. 35, eine *Kleine Kantate nach romantischen Texten für Sopran, Oboe, Bratsche und Violoncello,* wurden teils in Donaueschingen, teils in Hindemiths Schweizer Urlaubsort im Jahre 1924 komponiert. Mit der Widmung *Für meine Frau Gertrud 1924*, Tochter des Frankfurter Opernkapellmeisters Ludwig Rottenberg, war sie als Geschenk zur Hochzeit des Paares am 15. Mai 1924 geschrieben und wurde am 15. April 1925 in einem Kammermusikabend des Musik-Kollegium Winterthur uraufgeführt. Die Initiative hierzu war von dem bekannten Mäzen Werner Reinhart ausgegangen: *Ich habe seit einiger Zeit Partitur und Stimmen Ihrer »Serenaden« hier, die mir Scherchen damals schon im Manuskript gezeigt hatte und die mir einen besonders starken Eindruck machen. Ich habe nun unserm Vorstand vorgeschlagen, das Werk möglichst noch in dieser Saison in einem Kammermusikabend für die Mitglieder unseres Kollegiums aufzuführen. Ich bin nun beauftragt, Sie anzufragen, ob dies unter Mitwirkung Ihrer Frau Gemahlin (Singstimme) und mit Ihnen an der Bratsche möglich wäre.*[17]

---

[16] Die Ausführenden in Lübeck waren Gustav Scheck und Hellmuth Fick. Scheck wurde nach dem 2. Weltkrieg zum Direktor der neuerrichteten Musikhochschule in Freiburg/Br. berufen.

[17] S. Andres Briner, Paul Hindemith, Zürich 1971, S. 47. Die *Serenaden* sind die einzige

Die Serenaden bestehen aus drei Teilen, die jeweils in mehrere Stücke unterteilt sind, aber ohne Einschnitte verlaufen sollen. Die insgesamt acht vokal-instrumentalen Abschnitte erscheinen in unterschiedlichen kammermusikalischen Besetzungen, zwei von ihnen sind rein instrumental. Sie tragen folgende Titel:

I. *Barcarole* (Adolf Licht) für Sopran, Oboe und Violoncello
An Phyllis (Johann Ludwig Wilhelm Gleim)
Toccata für Violoncello
Corrente für Sopran und Violoncello
Nur Mut (Ludwig Tieck) für Sopran, Oboe und Bratsche
II. *Duett* für Bratsche und Violoncello
Der Abend (Joseph von Eichendorff) für Sopran und Oboe
Der Wurm am Meer (Johannes Wilhelm Meinhold) für Sopran, Oboe, Bratsche und Violoncello
III. *Trio* für Oboe, Bratsche und Violoncello
Gute Nacht (Siegfried August Mahlmann) für Gesang und Bratsche

Bei der kompositorischen Umsetzung der Texte suchte Hindemith keine »romantisierende« Adaption zu verwirklichen. Die Prägung durch neobarocke Merkmale charakterisiert gleich das erste Stück, die *Barcarole*, durch bewegliche 6/8-Takt-Linien, die aber keineswegs Tonmalerisches darstellen, wie es aus dem Gedichttitel abgeleitet werden könnte. Die beiden Gedichtstrophen sind durch ritornellartige Vor- und Nachspiele gebunden, deren Melodieführung möglicherweise eine Anlehnung an verschiedene Arien von J.S. Bach zeigt; am sinnfälligsten könnte sie wegen des Widmungsanlasses auf *Bereite dich Zion, mit zärtlichen Trieben, den Schönsten, den Liebsten bald bei dir zu sehn* (Weihnachtsoratorium, Kantate I, Nr. 4) zutreffen, eine Arie, die Gertrud Rotten-

Komposition Hindemiths mit einer Widmung an seine Frau, abgesehen vom *Konzert für Holzbläser, Harfe und Orchester* zur Feier der Silberhochzeit.

berg selbst gesungen hat[18]. In den folgenden Stücken sind barocke Satzbezeichnungen bemerkenswert wie Toccata[19] und Corrente; dem langsamen Instrumental-Duett folgt kontrastierend in Art einer Gigue ein sehr schneller Satz. Dieser und seine veränderte Reprise (*Der Wurm am Meer*) umrahmen die Eichendorff-Vertonung *Der Abend* und verleihen ihr durch die übergeordnete Dreiteiligkeit, die außerordentlich zurückhaltende Begleitung (Oboe) und die verhaltene Intensität des Ausdrucks eine mittelpunktartige Bedeutung. Im instrumentalen Trio (III) sind neobarocke Merkmale besonders vielfältig, so der Kanon in der unteren Oktave zwischen Oboe und Bratsche zu den klanglich reizvollen Pizzicati des Cellos, Motivbildungen mit barock-typischen Achtel- und Sechzehntel-Figuren, Imitationen und Sequenzierungen. Der eindringliche dreiteilige Schlußsatz *Gute Nacht* ist nur für Sopran und Hindemiths Lieblingsinstrument Bratsche gesetzt, ein Spiegel der Verbundenheit des Ehepaares ebenso wie die Motivgestaltung, die aus den in Töne übertragenen beiden Namensinitialen gewonnen wurde[20].

Die den Lübecker Kammermusikabend abschließende *Sonate für Bratsche und Klavier* op. 11 Nr. 4 aus dem Jahre 1919 gehört zu einem Opus mit Sonaten für Violine (Nr. 1 und 2, 1918), für Violoncello (Nr. 3, 1919) – jeweils mit Klavier – sowie für Bratsche solo (Nr. 5, 1919) und für Violine allein (Nr. 6, 1917). Sie zeigt in hohem Maße Hindemiths Auseinandersetzung mit der Form der Sonate und sein Bemühen, Herkömmliches zu überwinden. Schon während des Krieges hat sich der junge Komponist über seine Vorstellungen geäußert: *Ich möchte eine*

[18] Rudolf Stephan, *Der frühe Hindemith*, in: Hindemith-Jahrbuch 1987/XVI, S. 9–17; s. ferner Wulf Konold, *Paul Hindemiths Serenaden*, in: Hindemith-Jahrbuch 1974/IV, S. 89–96, und Günther Metz, *Hindemith und die Alte Musik*, S. 105f.

[19] Obwohl die Toccata im Barock den Tasteninstrumenten zugeordnet ist, benutzt Hindemith diese Form auch für Streicher, u.a. im ersten Satz des *Streichtrios* op. 34. Vgl. in diesem Zusammenhang auch den ersten Satz von von Igor Strawinskys *Violinkonzert* (1931).

[20] David Neumeyer, *Letter-Name Mottoes*, in: Hindemith-Jahrbuch 1977/VI, S. 29–46.

ganze Reihe solcher Sonatinen schreiben, eigentlich kleine Sonaten, da sie für Sonatinen zu ausgedehnt sind. Jede soll einen von der vorhergehenden gänzlich unterschiedlichen Charakter bekommen, auch formal. Ich will einmal sehen, ob ich in einer Reihe dieser Stücke die Ausdrucksmöglichkeiten – die bei dieser Gattung und bei dieser Besetzung keine sehr großen sind – erweitern und dem Horizont entgegen treiben kann.[21]

Die dreisätzige *Sonate für Bratsche und Klavier* op. 11 Nr. 4, komponiert zwischen dem 27. Februar und dem 9. März 1919, wurde am 2. Juni 1919 durch Hindemith und wiederum Emma Lübbecke-Job in Frankfurt am Main uraufgeführt in einem Konzert, das ausschließlich Werken von Hindemith gewidmet war[22]. Der Komponist stellt ihr folgende Anmerkung voran: *Die Sonate wird ohne Pause zwischen den Sätzen gespielt, besonders sollen der zweite und dritte Satz so gut verbunden sein, daß der Zuhörer nicht die Empfindung hat, ein Finale zu hören, sondern den letzen Satz lediglich als Fortsetzung der Variationen auffassen muß.*[23] Die dem zweiten Satz (*Thema mit Variationen*) hinzugefügte Bezeichnung *wie ein Volkslied* weist schon damals auf einen vielsagenden Zusammenhang von Lied und liedhaft gestaltetem melodischen Duktus auch im Instrumentalen hin und sollte nicht nur als eine Interpretationsanweisung gedeutet werden. Bekanntlich besaß das alte deutsche Lied, das »Volkslied«, für Hindemith einen großen Wert. Vertraut mit seinen Quellen und eingeordnet in einen bewußten Traditionszusammenhang, hat Hindemith mit ihm sein Schaffen wie auch seine

[21] Brief an Emmy Ronnefeldt vom 28. September 1918, veröffentlicht in: Hindemith-Jahrbuch 1972/II, S. 204f.

[22] Aufgeführt wurden das 2. *Streichquartett* op. 10, die Sonaten op. 11 Nr. 1 und Nr. 4 sowie das verschollene *Klavierquintett* op. 7 (1917); Programm abgedruckt in: Giselher Schubert, *Paul Hindemith in Selbstzeugnissen und Bilddokumenten*, Reinbek bei Hamburg 1981, S. 25.

[23] S. dazu Paul Hindemith, *Sämtliche Werke*, Bd. V, 6: *Streichkammermusik III*, hrsg. von Peter Cahn, Mainz 1976, S. XI.

unterrichtliche Tätigkeit komplex bereichert[24]. Als wichtiges Mittel für die Verbindung des zweiten und dritten Satzes erweist sich in dieser Sonate die Variation. Bereits die letzte unter den vier Variationen des zweiten Satzes bildet die Überleitung zum Finale. Im dritten Satz werden Elemente der Sonaten- und der Variationsform miteinander gekoppelt. Nach einem klar umrissenen ersten Thema ist das zweite Thema die 5. Variation und die Reprise, die Durchführung die 6. und die Coda die 7. Variation. Bei der 6. Variation wird ein Fugato verwandt, *mit bizarrer Plumpheit vorzutragen*, wie Hindemith angibt[25].

Die Vielfalt der farbenreichen musikalischen Sprache – z. B. freie tonale Beziehungen (neben der Grundtonart es-Moll häufig ein Es-Dur), Ganztöne, Modales, impressionistische Spuren, ostinate Figuren, geballte Zusammenklänge – ist Zeichen des frühen schöpferischen Durchbruchs. Als bevorzugtes Repertoirestück hat Hindemith seine Sonate op. 11 Nr. 4 häufig öffentlich gespielt, in Frankfurt am Main allein fünfmal. Die Resonanz auf die Uraufführung war außerordentlich positiv: *Der Erfolg des Abends war durchschlagend: Die auffällige melodische Begabung, die überraschende Sicherheit der Gestaltung und der kräftige Schwung dieses Musikers berechtigen uns doch, von einer selbständigen und den Durchschnitt weit überragenden tonschöpferischen Begabung zu reden.*[26]

Hindemith war sich um die Zeit dieser Uraufführung seiner kompositorischen Berufung immer stärker bewußt geworden. Der Vertragsabschluß mit dem Schott-Verlag ermöglichte es ihm, die Konzertmeisterposition am Frankfurter Opernhaus aufzugeben (1923). Die Entscheidung für die Bratsche als sein wesensgemäßes Instrument – motiviert durch ihre klanglichen und spieltechnischen Eigenheiten oder um beim Spielen »in

[24] S. dazu Ann-Katrin Heimer, *Paul Hindemiths Klavierlieder aus den dreißiger Jahren*, Schliengen 1998, S. 205–207.

[25] Franz Willms, *Paul Hindemith. Ein Versuch*, Köln o. J., S. 86ff. – Eine Durchführung in Form eines Fugato findet sich im zeitlichen Umkreis u. a. auch in *Lustige Sinfonietta* op. 4, erster Satz (1916) und im 2. *Streichquartett* op. 10, erster Satz (1918).

[26] Karl Holl, in: *Frankfurter Zeitung*, 10. Juni 1919, zitiert nach Dieter Rexroth (Hrsg.), *Paul Hindemith. Briefe*, Frankfurt am Main 1982, S. 86.

der Mitte des Tonsatzes« zu sein (Rudolf Stephan) – fällt in den gleichen zeitlichen Umkreis. Auch das Lübecker Programm beleuchtet die wichtige Rolle, die dieses Instrument für ihn einnimmt. Schon im Rebner-Quartett hatte Hindemith nach anfänglicher Tätigkeit als Zweiter Geiger die Stelle des Bratschers übernommen (ab 1919), in dem 1922 gegründeten Amar-Quartett, das in hohem Maße zur Verbreitung zeitgenössischer Streichquartette beitrug, spielt er ebenfalls Bratsche. Auch in Kammermusikabenden mit eigenen Werken und denen anderer Komponisten übernimmt er diesen Part. Als Solist spielt er seine Konzerte für Bratsche bzw. Viola d'amore mit Orchester in Europa und in den USA (1937–1939), die *Kammermusik Nr. 5* op. 36 Nr. 4 in europäischen Ländern allein 82mal. Die Bratschenkonzerte von Darius Milhaud und William Walton erleben durch ihn ihre Uraufführung, und in seinem eigenen *Oktett* wirkt er noch 1958 als Zweiter Bratscher mit[27]. Nach 25-jährigem Konzertieren, zunehmend selbstkritischer, gibt er als *leidvoll dressierter Podiumshengst* öffentliches Musizieren auf und schreibt nach dem Abhören seiner Sonate für Bratsche und Klavier (1939) aus den USA an seine Frau (1940): *Aber ich habe doch beschlossen, die öffentliche Spielerei endgültig an den Nagel zu hängen. Wenn sie nicht schöner ist als das, was aus dem Grammophon herauskam, ist sie nicht mehr wert, gezeigt zu werden.*[28]
Den Abschluß der Lübecker Veranstaltungsreihe bildete der *Plöner Musiktag*, eine der eigenartigsten Jugendmusik-Kompositionen Hindemiths und unter ihnen das letzte vor der Emigration aus Deutschland[29]. Geschrieben für das Internatsgymnasium in Plön/Holstein, kristallisieren sich hier viele Vorstellungen Hindemiths: das Werk ist für musizie-

---

[27] S. dazu Giselher Schubert, Hindemith als Bratscher, in: *Das Orchester* (32)1984, S. 1–4, ferner Rainer Cadenbach, *Streichquartette eines Bratschers, Musikantenmusik...*, in: Hindemith-Jahrbuch 1996/XXV, S. 84–141, ferner Dietrich Bauer, *Paul Hindemith als Bratscher*, in: Hindemith-Jahrbuch 1977/VI, S. 142–147.

[28] Paul Hindemith, *»Das private Logbuch«*, S. 419.

[29] Gerd Sannemüller, *Der Plöner Musiktag. Quellen und Studien zur Musikgeschichte Schleswig-Holsteins*, Band 4, Neumünster 1976.

rende Laien bestimmt und nicht für eine Konzertsaal-Situation, es sucht Zusammenhänge im Lebensablauf durch Musik zu akzentuieren, es ist Ausdruck einer Gemeinschaft innerhalb einer Schule und zwischen Komponist und Ausführenden und nicht zuletzt der Versuch, die Sprache einer Neuen Musik mit einer Musik für Laien ohne künstlerische Konzessionen in Verbindung zu bringen.

Hindemith, früh aufgeschlossen für vielseitige Problemstellungen des Musiklebens und voller Initiativen, die auch Fragen des Funktionalen und der Gemeinschaftsmusik umfaßten, gründete bereits 1922 gemeinsam mit Reinhold Merten, dem Korrepetitor der Frankfurter Oper, eine »Gemeinschaft für Musik« mit folgender Proklamation: *Wir sind überzeugt, daß das Konzert in seiner heutigen Form eine Einrichtung ist, die bekämpft werden muß und wollen versuchen, die fast verloren gegangene Gemeinschaft zwischen Ausführenden und Hörern wieder herzustellen.*[30] Aus Skpesis gegenüber dem bürgerlichen Konzertleben suchte Hindemith nicht nur die Kluft zwischen dem musikalischen Kunstwerk, dem Interpreten und dem Publikum zu überbrücken, sondern er wollte die Zuhörer aktivieren und ein passives Hörverhalten aufheben; zudem erstrebte er die Einordnung der Musik in Lebenszusammenhänge. Eines seiner wichtigsten Ziele war es, die Jugend zu motivieren und Verbindungen zur Musik der Gegenwart herzustellen, um deren Entfremdung und die *Gefahren eines esoterischen Isolationismus*[31] zu verringern oder sogar aufzuheben: *Was uns Alle angeht, ist dies: das alte Publikum stirbt ab; wie und was müssen wir schreiben, um ein größeres, anderes, neues Publikum zu bekommen: wo ist dieses Publikum?* [...] *Je eher das Konzert in seiner jetzigen Form abstirbt, desto schneller werden wir die Möglichkeit haben, das Musikleben zu erneuern.*[32]

---

[30] Paul Hindemith, *Gemeinschaft für Musik*, in: ders., *Aufsätze, Vorträge, Reden*, hrsg. von Giselher Schubert, Zürich/Mainz 1994, S. 8.

[31] Paul Hindemith, *Komponist in seiner Welt*, Zürich 1959, S. 10.

[32] Paul Hindemith, *Über Musikkritik* (1928), abgedruckt in: ders., *Aufsätze, Vorträge, Reden*, a.a.O., S. 37f.

Da Hindemith als Mitglied des Arbeitsausschusses der »Donaueschinger Kammermusiktage« (ab 1923) bestrebt war, möglichst viele Sparten des Musiklebens in seinem Programm zu berücksichtigen, entstanden 1926 Kontakte auch zu Fritz Jöde, dem norddeutschen Repräsentanten der Jugendmusikbewegung. Zu den Übereinstimmungen gehörten u. a. die Kritik am kommerziellen Musikbetrieb sowie die gemeinsam vertretene, von Bert Brecht formulierte These, Musikmachen sei besser als Musikhören. Nach anfänglich euphorischen Erwartungen über eine mögliche Zusammenarbeit kam es sehr bald zu unüberbrückbaren Meinungsverschiedenheiten, die schließlich zur Trennung führten; die Gründe hierfür lagen vor allem in den ideologisch fixierten Auffassungen der Vertreter der Jugendmusikbewegung über fachliche Ansprüche, eine musikalische Breitenarbeit und eine Einbindung der gegenwärtigen Musik[33]. Kurze Zeit danach verwandte Hindemith erstmals die Bezeichnung »Gebrauchsmusik« in einem öffentlichen Vortrag *Wie soll der ideale Chorsatz der Gegenwart oder besser der nächsten Zukunft beschaffen sein?* in der Berliner Musikhochschule am 18. Oktober 1927: *Ein Komponist sollte heute nur schreiben, wenn er weiß, für welchen Bedarf er schreibt. Die Zeiten des steten Für-sich-Komponierens sind vielleicht für immer vorbei. Auf der anderen Seite ist dagegen der Musikbedarf so groß, daß es dringend nötig ist, daß sich Komponist und Verbraucher endlich verständigen.*[34] Später empfindet er diesen *lächerlichen Terminus und seine an ihn gebundene leichtfertige Klassifikation* selbst als höchst unglücklich und distanziert sich mit der Bemerkung: *Musik, die über eine gewisse Zweckerfüllung nichts aufweisen kann, sollte weder geschrieben noch verbraucht werden.*[35] 1940 präzisierte Hindemith seine früheren Auffassungen: *Wenn man heute in Europa von Gebrauchsmusik reden wollte, man würde verständnislos angese-*

[33] S. Paul Hindemith, *Forderungen an den Laien* (1930), abgedruckt in: ders., *Aufsätze, Vorträge, Reden*, a.a.O., S. 42–44.
[34] Zit. nach Andres Briner, *Paul Hindemith*, Zürich 1971, S. 310.
[35] Paul Hindemith, *Komponist in seiner Welt*, Zürich 1959, S. 10–11.

hen werden, da man sich ja im allgemeinen nicht vorstellen kann, für was sonst als für den Gebrauch eine Musik geschrieben werden könnte [...] *Seitdem dient sein Name als Aushängeschild für geglückte, als Deckmantel für mißlungene Versuche* [...] *Laßt uns lieber danach trachten, eine Musik zu schreiben, die so gut ist, daß sie je nach Art, Zweck und Besetzung in allen ihr angemessenen Darstellungsformen im höchsten Maße befriedigend und damit brauchbar erscheint.*[36] Wenn Hindemith gerade in den Jahren 1926–1932 eine bemerkenswert große Zahl musikpädagogischer Kompositionen für Kinder, Jugendliche und Musikliebhaber geschrieben hat, in seiner Terminologie dem Laien gleichgestellt, so bestimmte ihn dazu sein intensives, auch in späteren Jahren wirkendes Engagement, durch das er künstlerische und erzieherische Aspekte vereinte. Seine Überzeugung von der ethischen Kraft der Musik schloß stets die bewußte Übernahme pädagogischer Verantwortung ein[37].

Das Entstehen des *Plöner Musiktag* ist einerseits aus dem dargestellten Hintergrund, andererseits aus der fast zufälligen Begegnung mit dem Plöner Musikstudienrat Edgar Rabsch zu erklären. Beide hatten sich am 19. Januar 1932 bei der Generalprobe zu einem Sinfoniekonzert in Kiel, bei dem Hindemith als Solist mitwirkte, persönlich kennengelernt. Da Hindemith über Rabschs Arbeit schon in Berlin gehört hatte und unmittelbar Einblick nehmen wollte, reiste er am Vormittag des 20. Januar nach Plön, wo er sich während einer Probe von den Qualitäten des Chores und des Orchesters der Schule sowie der Intensität Rabschs überzeugte: *Hier müssen wir einmal einen ganzen Tag Musik machen* [...] *Die Musik schreibe ich Ihnen*, äußerte er beeindruckt und entwarf in seiner impulsiven Art sofort seine Vorstellungen vom Werkaufbau, in

[36] Giselher Schubert, *Hindemiths Vorträge »Betrachtungen zur heutigen Musik« (1940). Kommentar und Erstveröffentlichung des zweiten Vortrags*, in: *Festschrift für Rudolf Stephan*, Laaber 1990, S. 519f.

[37] S. dazu Gerd Sannemüller, *Gebrauchsmusik im Schaffen von Paul Hindemith*, in: Hindemith-Jahrbuch 1992/XXI, S. 26–46; ders., *Hindemith als Musikpädagoge*, in: *Zeitschrift für Musikpädagogik* (4) 1977, S. 49–58; Stephen Hinton, *Hindemith: pedagogy and personal style*, in: Hindemith-Jahrbuch 1988/XVII, S. 54–67.

den die Räume des Internats, also das Plöner Schloß, und seine Umgebung einbezogen werden sollten. Dabei fiel bereits das Wort vom Musiktag. Hindemith beteiligte sich noch selbst an den letzten Proben. An der Aufführung am 20. Juni 1932 wirkten 250 Jungen und Mädchen im Bewußtsein eines besonderen Ereignisses mit.
Stilistisch am Ausgang der mittleren Schaffensphase stehend mit den Wandlungen, die sich durch Neue Sachlichkeit und neoklassizistische Elemente abzeichnen, bestätigt auch der *Pöner Musiktag* bei aller Gebundenheit an eine bestimmte Situation und die Notwendigkeit zur Vereinfachung die gleichen stilistischen Kriterien. Neben einer ausgeglicheneren Harmonik zeigt sich insbesondere eine eigenständigere Bildung des Melodischen und Polyphonen. Das Werk folgt dem Tagesablauf der Schulgemeinschaft in einzelnen musikalischen Stationen: *Morgenmusik – von Blechbläsern auf einem Turm aufzuführen*; *Tafelmusik – Stücke zur Unterhaltung, beim Mittagessen zu spielen*; *Kantate »Mahnung an die Jugend, sich der Musik zu befleißigen«*, nach Worten des frühprotestantischen Schulmusikers Martin Agricola; *Abendkonzert*[38]. In Lübeck wurden gegenüber der Plöner Fassung einige Umstellungen und Veränderungen erforderlich; u. a. entfiel die *Morgenmusik*. Einige Stücke mußten mit Plöner Schülern umbesetzt werden, da Harald Genzmer und Oskar Sala, Hindemiths Berliner Kompositionsstudenten, nicht wie in Plön zur Verfügung standen.
Zwischen der *Kantate* und dem *Abendkonzert* spielte Hindemith seine *Sonate für Bratsche allein* op. 25 Nr. 1, die er damals häufig öffentlich interpretierte, so auch beim Begrüßungsabend in Plön am 18. Juni 1932. Die Komposition hatte er Anfang März 1922 begonnen und bereits am

[38] Hindemith selbst hat in einem Vortrag in der Greenwich Music School in New York am 26. April 1937 über Entstehung und Ablauf des *Plöner Musiktag* berichtet; vgl. hierzu: Paul Hindemith, *Mahnung an die Jugend, sich der Musik zu befleißigen*, hrsg. und kommentiert von Gerd Sannemüller, in: *Schweizer musikpädagogische Blätter* (4) 1984, S. 157–162; ebenfalls in: Paul Hindemith, *Aufsätze, Vorträge, Reden*, a.a.O., S. 120–124.

18. März in Köln selbst uraufgeführt[39]. Die fünf Sätze sind durch eine weite Empfindungsspanne charakterisiert, sowohl melodisch ausdrucksvoll und verhalten als auch energiebetont und von unerbittlicher, mitreißender Motorik. Der dritte und fünfte Satz, beide in betontem Sarabandenrhythmus und konturierter Linearität, umrahmen den gegensätzlichen vierten, dessen auffällige Spielanweisung lautet: *Rasendes Zeitmaß. Wild. Tonschönheit ist Nebensache (♩= 600–640)*[40].
Der Erfolg dieses abschließenden Konzertes war so groß, daß Hindemith vom »südlichen« Temperament der Lübecker sprach. In der Presseberichterstattung über die drei Hindemith-Veranstaltungen wurde ausführlich und betont sachlich kommentiert, die einsatzfreudige Vorkämpferrolle der Vereinigung »Neue Musik in Lübeck« positiv hervorgehoben. Die Darstellungen aller vier Blätter der Hansestadt wirken bemerkenswert unbeeinflußt von politischen Richtungen, ganz im Gegensatz zur Stellungnahme des »Kampfbundes für deutsche Kultur« über die Uraufführung des *Musiktages* in Plön (Kieler Zeitung vom 23. Juni 1932): *Aber die Kunst Hindemiths wird als Bildungsfaktor gerade von jenem Teil des deutschen Volkes abgelehnt, der in kurzem den Charakter der Nation prägen wird.*[41]

[39] Hinweis Hindemiths in seinem autographen Werkverzeichnis: *Die zwei Sätze I und V habe ich im Speisewagen zwischen Köln und Frankfurt komponiert und bin gleich aufs Podium und habe die Sonate gespielt.* Zit. nach: Hermann Danuser, *Abschied vom Espressivo? Zu Paul Hindemiths Vortragsstil in den zwanziger Jahren*, in: Hindemith-Jahrbuch 1988/XVII, S. 34.

[40] S. dazu die Untersuchungen über die unterschiedlichen Interpretationen des vierten Satzes durch den Komponisten selbst: Giselher Schubert, *Hindemiths Bearbeitungen eigener und fremder Werke. Ein Überblick*, in: *Schweizer Jahrbuch für Musikwissenschaft*, Neue Folge (3) 1983, S. 111; Hermann Danuser, *Abschied vom Espressivo?*, a.a.O., S. 26–40, Susanne Schaal, *Interpretation als Bearbeitung*, in: Hindemith-Jahrbuch 1995/XXIV, S. 129–145; vgl. als Analogon die Anweisung Hindemiths für den *Ragtime* aus *1922. Suite für Klavier* op. 26: *Nimm keine Rücksicht auf das, was Du in der Klavierstunde gelernt hast. Überlege nicht lange, ob Du Dis mit dem vierten oder sechsten Finger anschlagen mußt. Spiele dieses Stück sehr wild, aber stets sehr stramm im Rhythmus, wie eine Maschine. Betrachte hier das Klavier als eine interessante Art Schlagzeug u. handle entsprechend.*

[41] In der konfliktreichen Auseinandersetzung mit der Kulturpolitik des NS-Regimes

Am 3. und 4. Februar 1934 ist Hindemith nochmals in Lübeck aufgetreten, diesmal als Interpret eines Konzertes für Viola d'amore von Antonio Vivaldi sowie seiner Darius und Madeleine Milhaud gewidmeten *Konzertmusik für Solobratsche und größeres Kammerorchester* op. 48, im Programm gekoppelt mit der 3. Sinfonie von Anton Bruckner. Das Konzert leitete der 1932 als Generalmusikdirektor nach Lübeck berufene Heinz Dressel, der durch dieses Engagement für den inzwischen politisch mißliebig gewordenen, bereits propagandistisch verfemten Komponisten beträchtlichen Mut bewies[42]. Für die Dauer von zwölf Jahren war das die letzte Aufführung eines Werkes von Hindemith in Lübeck bis 1946.

---

hebt Wilhelm Furtwängler Paul Hindemiths musikpädagogisches Verantwortungsbewußtsein hervor: *Ein hohes Ethos schlichter Handwerklichkeit, das Hindemith an altdeutsche Meister erinnernd kennzeichnet, scheint ihn für den Lehrberuf zu prädestinieren* [...] *So hat er seinerzeit mit dem Plöner Musiktag eine Jugendmusik geschrieben, die für das neuzeitliche schulische Musizieren richtunggebend wurde.* Zit. nach: Wilhelm Furtwängler, *Der Fall Hindemith*, in: *Deutsche Allgemeine Zeitung*, 25. November 1934.

[42] S. Klaus Matthias, *Musikgeschichte Lübecks im letzten Halbjahrhundert*, a.a.O., S. 177; Karsten Bartel, Günter Zschacke, *Variationen. 100 Jahre Orchester in der Hansestadt Lübeck (1897–1997)*, Lübeck 1997, S. 262. Die erste Komposition Hindemiths, die nach Beendigung des 2. Weltkriegs in Lübeck erklang, war 1946 die *Sinfonie »Mathis der Maler«*.

ANDRES BRINER, geboren 1923 in Zürich. Studium an Konservatorium und Universität (Germanistik und Musikwissenschaft) in Zürich. Tätigkeiten bei Radio Zürich, University of Pennsylvania, Neue Zürcher Zeitung. 1987–1998 Präsident der Paul-Hindemith-Stiftung.

ALEXANDER J. FISHER is a doctoral candidate in Historical Musicology at Harvard University. His research interests include the early German Baroque and Central European music of the early twentieth century. He is currently preparing a dissertation on German music and religion in the age of the Counter-Reformation.

WOLFGANG RATHERT, geboren 1960 in Minden/Westf. Studium der Musikwissenschaft, Philosophie und Neueren Geschichte an der Freien Universität Berlin. Promotion 1987 bei Rudolph Stephan mit *Ives-Studien* (Joachim-Tiburtius-Preis des Landes Berlin 1988, veröffentlicht München 1991 unter dem Titel *The Seen and Unseen*). Ausbildung zum Wissenschaftlichen Bibliothekar, seit 1991 Leiter der Musik- und Theaterbibliothek der Hochschule der Künste Berlin. Veröffentlichungen und Vorträge zur Musik des 19. und 20. Jahrhunderts. Mitarbeiter der Kurt-Weill-Gesamtausgabe, 1999 Habilitation.

GUNTHER NICKEL, geboren 1961. Studium der Musik und Germanistik an der Universität Oldenburg, Promotion. 1990-1994 Mitarbeiter an der achtbändigen Ausgabe sämtlicher Schriften Carl von Ossietzkys, seitdem wissenschaftlicher Angestellter in der Handschriftenabteilung des Deutschen Literaturarchivs Marbach.

SUSANNE SCHAAL, geboren 1964. Studium der Musikwissenschaft, Altphilologie, Philosophie und Italienisch an der Universität Freiburg/Br. 1991 Promotion über *Die Musica Scenica des Giovanni Battista Doni*

(Frankfurt 1993), seit 1993 wissenschaftliche Mitarbeiterin des Paul-Hindemith-Instituts, Frankfurt/Main. Veröffentlichungen zur Musik des 18. und 20. Jahrhunderts.

GERALD KILIAN, geboren 1950. Studium der Schulmusik (Lehramt an Gymnasien), Musikwissenschaft und Germanistik in Karlsruhe und Heidelberg. Promotion in Musikwissenschaft an der Universität Heidelberg (Studien zu Louis Spohr). Im Auftrag der Internationalen Louis-Spohr-Gesellschaft wissenschaftlicher Hauptherausgeber der *Neuen Auswahl der Werke von Louis Spohr*. Studiendirektor (Fachberater für Musik), Musikpädagoge, Chorleiter, weitere Arbeitsbereiche in der Lehrerfortbildung und Kommissionstätigkeiten. Veröffentlichungen u. a. zur Musik des Mittelalters, der Klassik und zur Musik des 19. Jahrhunderts.

GERD SANNEMÜLLER wirkte bis zu seiner Emeritierung (1985) als Professor an der Universität Kiel. Musikpädadogische und musikwissenschaftliche Veröffentlichungen vor allem zur Musik des 20. Jahrhunderts (u.a. Hindemith, Ravel, Lutoslawski), Herausgeber des Bandes VIII, 1 (*Sing- und Spielmusik I*) der Hindemith-Gesamtausgabe (in Vorber.).

Verzeichnis der in den bisherigen Hindemith-Jahrbüchern erschienenen Beiträge

1971/I

	Die Gründung der Hindemith-Stiftung
Ludwig Finscher	Paul Hindemith - Versuch einer Neuorientierung
Andres Briner	Hindemith und Adornos Kritik des Musikanten. Oder: Von sozialer und soziologischer Haltung
Angela Zabrsa	Hindemiths Opernprojekte
Helmut Haack	Der Finalsatz aus Hindemiths Konzert für Orchester op. 38 (1925). Kompositionsidee und Ausarbeitung
Peter Cahn	Hindemiths Kadenzen
Henri Jaton	Mon cher Maître ... une interview de Paul Hindemith
Günther Rühle	Im Angesicht der Ziele. Zum Tode von Otfried Büthe
Adolf Rebner	Mein Schüler Paul Hindemith
Max Rieple	Begegnungen mit Paul Hindemith
Heinrich Straumann	Kleine Erinnerungen an Hindemiths Züricher Zeit
Helmut Rösner	Zur Hindemith-Bibliographie und -Literatur
Marianne Reißinger	Frankfurt am Main und der 75. Geburtstag Paul Hindemiths

1972/II

Winfried Kirsch	Der späte Hindemith
Peter Cahn	Hindemiths Lehrjahre in Frankfurt
Walter Bruno Hilse	Hindemith and Debussy
Dieter Rexroth	Tradition und Reflexion beim frühen Hindemith
Bernhard Billeter	Ist Hindemiths »Unterweisung im Tonsatz« für die harmonische Analyse geeignet?
Franzpeter Goebels	Interpretationsaspekte zum »Ludus Tonalis«
Karl Laux	Skandal in Baden-Baden
	Jugendbriefe von Paul Hindemith aus den Jahren 1916-1919

1973/III

Hans Curjel	Hindemith vor Augen
Andres Briner	Paul Hindemith et l'idée d'une communauté musicale
Howard Boatwright	Hindemith's Performances of Old Music
Dieter Rexroth	Das Künstlerproblem bei Hindemith
Hellmuth Christian Wolff	Die Kammermusik Paul Hindemiths
Erwin R. Jacobi	Zu Hindemiths »Minimax«-Komposition (1923)
Dietrich Berke	Tonmaterial und Geschichte - Reflexionen über Hindemiths »Unterweisung im Tonsatz«
Glenn Gould	Hindemith: Kommt seine Zeit (wieder)?
Alfred Beaujean	Glenn Gould als Denkanstoß - Zur Neuaufnahme der drei Klaviersonaten Hindemiths
Erich F.W. Altwein	Zum Briefwechsel Paul Hindemith - Hans Kayser
Hildegard Weber	Paul Hindemiths erste namhafte Klavierinterpretin. Zum 85. Geburtstag von Emma Lübbecke-Job
Otto Zickenheiner	Hindemith-Bibliographie 1971-1973
Paul Hindemith	Hören und Verstehen ungewohnter Musik

1974/IV

	Bemühungen um Hindemith - Wozu?
Hans Heinz Stuckenschmidt	Paul Hindemiths Aufbruch und Heimkehr
Ingeborg H. Solbrig	Cultural and Political Perspectives of the Weimar Republic
Rudolf Stephan	Über Paul Hindemith
Siegfried Borris	Perspektiven zu Hindemiths kunstmoralischem Engagement
Karin v. Maur	Oskar Schlemmer und Paul Hindemith
Wulf Konold	Paul Hindemiths *Serenaden*
Geoffrey Skelton	The Teacher and his American Students
Wolfgang E. Rebner	Mein Lehrer Hindemith
Maurice Zermatten	Le couple Paul-Gertrude Hindemith
Karl Leo Gerhartz, Hermann Markard	Wer deckte für Helene den Frühstückstisch?

Alfred Beaujean	Das *Requiem* und die *Messe* auf Schallplatte
Andres Briner	Eine Schallplatten-Einspielung des *Unaufhörlichen*
Peter Cahn	Hindemith aus der Sicht statistischer Analyse
Andres Briner	Paul Hindemith und Arnold Schönberg
	Zum Briefwechsel Paul Hindemith-Hans Kayser
Paul Hindemith	Über die Viola d'amore

1976/V

Philipp Mohler	Paul Hindemith - Aus Anlaß des 80. Geburtstags
Peter Cahn	Paul Hindemith in Frankfurt
Ann Clark Fehn	*Das Unaufhörliche* - Gottfried Benns Text in der Vertonung von Paul Hindemith
James E. Paulding	*Mathis der Maler* - The Politics of Music
Janós Breuer	Die erste Bartók-Schallplatte - das II. Streichquartett op. 17 von Béla Bartók in der Einspielung des Amar-Hindemith-Quartetts
Rezensionen	Bücher und Schallplatten

1977/VI

Diether de la Motte	Hindemith neu gehört
Ludwig Finscher	Komponieren um 1915
David Neumeyer	Letter-Name-Mottoes in Hindemith's *Gute Nacht*
Dieter Rexroth	Zu den *Kammermusiken* von Paul Hindemith
Friedrich Hommel	Rückblick auf ein Experiment - Paul Hindemith und Bertolt Brecht
Gerd Sannemüller	Das *Philharmonische Konzert* von Paul Hindemith
Bernhard Billeter	Die kompositorische Entwicklung Hindemiths am Beispiel seiner Klavierwerke
Eckhart Richter	A Glimpse into the Workshop of Paul Hindemith
Dietrich Bauer	Paul Hindemith als Bratschist
Peter Cahn	Ein unbekanntes musikpädagogisches Dokument von 1927: Hindemiths Konzeption einer Musikhochschule

1978/VII

Giselher Schubert	Zur Bedeutung der Hindemith-Gesamtausgabe
Rudolf Stephan	Adorno und Hindemith. Zum Verständnis einer schwierigen Beziehung
Josef Dorfman	Hindemith's Fourth Quartet
David Neumeyer	The Genesis and Stucture of Hindemith's *Ludus Tonalis*
Winfried Kirsch	Paul Hindemiths Weinheber-Madrigale (1958)
Luther Noss	Hindemith's Concert Tours in the United States 1937, 1938, 1939
Eckhart Richter	Paul Hindemith as Director of the Yale Collegium Musicum
	Paul Hindemiths erste Reise in die USA im Jahre 1937 - Seine Briefe an Gertrud Hindemith
Annegrit Laubenthal	Hindemith-Bibliographie 1974-1978

1979/VIII

Norbert J. Schneider	Prinzipien der rhythmischen Gestaltung in Hindemiths Oper *Mathis der Maler*
Friedrich Neumann	Kadenzen, Melodieführung und Stimmführung in den *Six Chansons* und *Five Songs on Old Texts* von Hindemith
Raymond Gros	Hindemith et les Poèmes Français de Rilke
Aloys Greither	Paul Hindemith und Ladislav Černý
Wulf Konold	Hindemith, Hartmann und Zillig heute
Everett Helm	Zu Gian Francesco Malipiero
Detlef Gojowy	Arthur Lourié der Futurist
Irina Graham	Arthur Sergeevič Lourié - Biographische Notizen
Gisela Glagla	An Facettenreichtum hinzugewonnen
Sigfried Schibli	Der épatierte und der beschwichtigte Bürger

1980/IX

Dieter Rexroth	»Wohin kann sich die Musik noch entwickeln?«

Giselher Schubert	Vorgeschichte und Entstehung der *Unterweisung im Tonsatz. Theoretischer Teil*
Claudia Maurer Zenck	Zwischen Boykott und Anpassung an den Charakter der Zeit. Über die Schwierigkeiten eines deutschen Komponisten mit dem Dritten Reich
Everett Helm	Wiederaufbau des deutschen Musiklebens nach 1945 und Paul Hindemith
Detlef Gojowy	Aspekte des kompositorischen Handwerks in den 20er Jahren - Manifestationen bei russischen Komponisten
Sigfried Schibli	Zum Begriff der Neuen Sachlichkeit in der Musik
Winfried Kirsch	Die *Opera domestica*. Zur Dramaturgie des bürgerlichen Alltags im aktuellen Musiktheater der 20er Jahre
Peter Cahn	Zu einigen Aspekten des Materialdenkens in der Musik des 20. Jahrhunderts

1981/X

Hans Otte	Hindemith erinnern...
Tilo Medek	Berührungsängste und Paul Hindemith
Peter Michael Hamel	Harmonikales Denken
Günther Becker	»Verachtet mir die Meister nicht« - zu Fragen des musikalischen Handwerks
Manfred Trojahn	Die Begriffe des *Handwerks* und der *Ethik* im gegenwärtigen kompositorischen Denken
Wolfgang Rihm	Verständlichkeit und Popularität - Künstlerische Ziele?
Wulf Konold	Komponieren in der Postmoderne
	Zur Besichtigung freigegeben. Gespräche - Kritiken - Berichte zu Veranstaltungen des Hindemith-Zyklus

1982/XI

Rudolf Stephan	Neue Musik in der Bundesrepublik Deutschland 1945-1950
Theo Hirsbrunner	Le rôle de la Musique de chambre dans la première moitié du 20ème siècle
Andreas Lehmann	Hindemiths *Lehrstück*
Klaus Ebbeke	Hindemith und das Trautonium

Carl Dahlhaus	Hindemiths Theorie des Sekundgangs und das Problem der Melodielehre
Luther Noss	Hindemith's first eight months as a resident of the USA
Norbert J. Schneider	Thornton Wilder und Paul Hindemith. Zu ihrem Briefwechsel anläßlich der Entstehung von *The Long Christmas Dinner*
1983/XII	
Annegrit Laubenthal	Ausgerechnet der frühe Hindemith
Giselher Schubert	Paul Hindemith und der Neobarock. Historische und stilistische Notizen
Dieter Rexroth	Paul Hindemith und Brechts *Lehrstück*
Günther Metz	Hindemiths Lied *Stillung Mariä mit dem Auferstandenen*
Hans Vogt	Begegnungen mit Hindemith
Andres Briner	Ergänzungen und Berichtigungen zu Thornton Wilder und Paul Hindemith
Klaus Hinrich Stahmer	Der Klassik näher als dem Klassizismus. Die Streichquartettkompositionen von Strawinsky
Detlef Gojowy	Arthur Lourié der Futurist (II)
Georg Mautschka	Komponist und Pädagoge. Zu Leben und Werk von Philipp Mohler
1984/XIII	
Ludwig Finscher	Der späte Hindemith
Günther Metz	Ein Spätstil Hindemiths?
Dieter Rexroth	*Wirke mit mir!* Anmerkungen zu Hindemiths Harmonievorstellungen
Giselher Schubert	Im Geschirr des allgemeinen Narrenwagens. Aspekte des Hindemithschen Musikdenkens
Reinhold Brinkmann	Über Paul Hindemiths Rede *Sterbende Gewässer*
Kurt von Fischer	Honeggers und Hindemiths pessimistische Sicht der Musik nach 1945
Siegfried Mauser	Musikalische Poetik bei Hindemith und Strawinsky
Theo Hirsbrunner	Paul Hindemiths Traditionsverständnis dargestellt am *Gloria* der *Messe*

Hermann Danuser	»Sturmüberflaggt« - Paul Hindemiths expressionistische Moderne in den drei Orchestergesängen opus 9
Michael Zimmermann	Harmlosigkeit und Melancholie bei Christian Morgenstern und Paul Hindemith
Klaus Ebbeke	Zu Hindemiths Reger-Rezeption
Siegfried Mauser	Natur und Natürlichkeit und Hindemiths frühe Klaviermusik: Affinität und Differenzen zur Ästhetik Claude Debussys
Bernhard Billeter	Zur Wiedergewinnung von Hindemiths Klaviersonate op. 17
Annegrit Laubenthal	Skizzen, Entstehung und Formkonzept der *Sancta Susanna*
Peter Cahn	Hindemiths Klarinettenquintett op. 30 und seine beiden Fassungen
David Neumeyer	Hindemith's *hommage à Bach* in Two Early Viola Sonatas
Günther Metz	Paul Hindemiths *Kammermusik Nr. 4* op. 36 Nr. 3 für Solo-Violine und größeres Kammerorchester
Helga de la Motte-Haber	Bewegung und Stillstand
Andres Briner	Dank an einen großen Sänger. Laudatio für Dietrich Fischer-Dieskau

1988/XVII

Ludwig Finscher	Zur Bedeutung der Kammermusik in Hindemiths Frühwerk
Hermann Danuser	Abschied vom Expressivo? Zu Paul Hindemiths Vortragsstil in den zwanziger Jahren
Volker Scherliess	Musik und Technik - zu ihrem Verhältnis in den zwanziger Jahren
Stephen Hinton	Hindemith: Pedagogy and Personal Style
Albrecht Dümling	*Tun ist besser als fühlen.* Der pädagogische Aspekt bei Brecht und Hindemith
Dieter Rexroth	Dichtung und Musik - ein Entwicklungsaspekt beim frühen Hindemith
Andres Briner	Hindemiths Liedschaffen in der Umwelt des *Cardillac*

Giselher Schubert	Zur Konzeption der Musik in Hindemiths Oper *Cardillac*
Rudolf Stephan	Neue Musik in der Kroll-Oper 1927-31
Wulf Konold	Zur Theorie und Praxis der Zeitoper
Jürgen Mainka	Hindemith und die Weimarer Republik
1989/XVIII	
Friederike Becker	*Singspielhalle des Humors*. Zu den *Dramatischen Meisterwerken* Paul Hindemiths
Paul Hindemith	Notizen zu meinen *Feldzugs-Erinnerungen*
Benno Elkan	Die Unwirklichkeit der Bühne
1990/XIX	
Manfred Trojahn	Die Freiheit des Künstlers - der Künstler und die Freiheit
Rudolf Stephan	Zum Verständnis der Oper *Mathis der Maler*
Daniël G. Geldenhuys	Paul Hindemith's late sonatas: A Documentation from the Letters
Andreas Traub	Zur *Sonate für Violoncello und Klavier* (1948)
Josef Dorfman	Counterpoint - Sonata form
Lothar Prox	Anmerkungen zur Wiederentdeckung und Rekonstruktion von Film und Musik *Im Kampf mit dem Berg*
Paul Hindemith	Texte zur Filmmusik
Else Thalheimer-Lewertoff	Frühe Erinnerungen an Paul Hindemith
Hanspeter Krellmann	Zeitgenosse Paul Hindemith?
Günther Metz	Hindemith-Bibliographie 1982-1984
1991/XX	
Peter Cahn	Zum Fortwirken von Neoromantik und Neoklassizismus nach 1945
Rudolf Stephan	Aufzeichnungen zu Hindemith
Eckhart Richter	Training Prospective Composers to be *Compleat* Musicians. Hindemith's Teaching at the Berlin Musikhochschule

Jürgen Blume	Hindemiths erste und letzte Fassung der *Unterweisung im Tonsatz* im Vergleich
Dirk Wingenfeld	Hindemiths Akkordbestimmung als Grundlage für eine differenziertere Akkordklassifikation
Donald Johns	Aimez-vous Brahms?: Ein Hindemith-Schenker-Briefwechsel
Giselher Schubert	Ludwig Rottenberg über Schenker. Zwei Dokumente
Tomi Mäkelä	Ambivalenz und gezielte Mißverständlichkeit
Michael Kube	Am Quartettpult. Paul Hindemith im Rebner- und Amar-Quartett. Teil 1
1992/XXI	
Rudolf Stephan	Komponieren um 1920
Gerd Sannemüller	Gebrauchsmusik im Schaffen von Paul Hindemith
Hermann Danuser	Hindemith als Kammermusiker. Zu einigen historischen Aufnahmen des Amar-Quartetts
Julius Berger	Irritationskraft. Hindemiths Sonate op. 25,3 für Violoncello solo aus dem Blickwinkel eines Interpreten
Gerhard Sauder	Hindemith und die Literatur der zwanziger Jahre
Klaus Velten	Paul Hindemiths frühes Liedschaffen
Elisabeth Schmierer	Monumentalität und Pathos. Zu den Orchestergesängen op. 9
Kurt von Fischer	Musikalische Annäherungen an Georg Trakl
Andreas Traub	Eine Ehrenrettung Kirchers
Michael Kube	Am Quartettpult. Paul Hindemith im Rebner- und Amar-Quartett. Teil 2
1993/XXII	
Friedbert Streller	Expressionismus - Nach-Expressionismus - oder Neue Sachlichkeit? Paul Hindemith in den Strömungen und Tendenzen der 20er Jahre
Michael Kube	Die Faktur der Ekstase. Zu Kontext, From und Harmonik von Hindemiths *Sancta Susanna*
Stephen Hinton	*Lehrstück:* An Aesthetics of Performance
Elisabeth Schwind	Die Künstlerproblematik in Hindemiths *Cardillac.* Zur zweiten Fassung von 1952

Thomas Seedorf	Des Goldschmieds neue Kleider. Zur Zweitfassung des *Cardillac*
Andres Briner	Paul und Gertrud Hindemiths literarische Interessen. Eine Studie aufgrund der Bibliothek in Blonay und einiger Materialien im Hindemith-Institut
Michael Kube	Am Quartettpult. Paul Hindemith im Rebner- und Amar-Quartett. Teil 3
1994/XXIII	
Andres Briner	Maß und Seele. Dem Paul-Hindemith-Institut zu seinem 20jährigen Bestehen
Andreas Traub	Eine Perotin-Bearbeitung Hindemiths
Peter Ackermann	Musikgeschichte und Aufführungspraxis. Paul Hindemiths *Versuch einer Rekonstruktion der ersten Aufführung* von Monteverdis *Orfeo*
Wolfgang Rathert	Zu Paul Hindemiths Bearbeitung des 100. Psalms von Max Reger
Susanne Schaal	Wahn und Wille. Hindemiths Bearbeitung des Duetts Nr. 16 aus *Cardillac* (1952)
Theo Hirsbrunner	Paul Hindemith und Darius Milhaud. Gemeinsamkeiten und Kontraste
	Die Widmungsträger von Paul Hindemiths *Konzert für Orchester* op. 38
1995/XXIV	
Luitgard Schader	Werk und Werke bei Paul Hindemith
Rudolf Stephan	Paul Hindemiths Streichquartett op. 32
Ann-Katrin Heimer	Eine unbekannte Quelle für Hindemiths Englischhorn-Sonate
Mark Delaere	Analysing Contrapuntal Music. Some Remarks on the Fugues in C and F from Hindemith's *Ludus Tonalis*
Otto Bruckner	Betrachtungen zu Paul Hindemiths Orgelsonaten
Susanne Schaal	Interpretation als Bearbeitung
Klaus-Dieter Krabiel	Das *Lehrstück* von Brecht und Hindemith

1996/XXV

Wolfgang Rathert	Was wird mit Hindemith geschehen? Stand und Perspektiven des Hindemith-Bildes
Rudolf Stephan	Über Hindemiths »Klang«
Michael Kube	Zum Stilwandel in Hindemiths frühen Streichquartetten (1915–23)
Rainer Cadenbach	»Streichquartette eines Bratschers, Musikantenmusik...«. Zur Rolle der Bratsche in Hindemiths Kammermusik für Streicher
Mathias Hansen	»Neues von heute und morgen«. Zeitoper – Hindemith – Schönberg: Ein revisionsbedürftiges Thema
Giselher Schubert	Hindemith und Weill. Zu einer Musikgeschichte der zwanziger Jahre
Dietmar Schenk	Paul Hindemith und die Rundfunkversuchsstelle der Berliner Musikhochschule
Martin Elste	Hindemiths Versuche »grammophonplatteneigener Stücke« im Kontext einer Ideengeschichte der Mechanischen Musik im 20. Jahrhundert
Reiner Nägele	Götterdämmerung im Reich der Töne. Zu einem neuentdeckten Autograph zweier Chorlieder von 1927
Viktor Beljaev	Paul Hindemith. Eine Skizze

1997/XXVI

Harald Genzmer	Der Unterricht bei Paul Hindemith
Albrecht Riethmüller	Versuch über Hindemith
Ludwig Finscher	Paul Hindemiths geschichtlicher Ort
Hans Zender	Freiheit und Systeme. Paul Hindemith und das kompositorische Denken unseres Jahrhunderts
	Veranstaltungen zum Hindemith-Jahr 1995
	Mathis der Maler in London. Rezensionen
Michael Fuller	Hindemith's *Mathis der Maler*. A Parable for our Times
	Diskographie
Giselher Schubert	Hindemiths Briefe an Hans Boettcher

1998/XXVII